Nobles and Nobility in Medieval Europe

CONCEPTS, ORIGINS, TRANSFORMATIONS

Plate 1. The memorial plaque for Count Geoffrey of Anjou (father of King Henry II of England). Multicoloured enamel plate, 63 x 32 cm, Musée de Tessé, Le Mans. The inscription reads: ENSI TVO PRINCEPS PREDORUM TURBA FVGARUNT: ECCLESIISQUE QVIES PACE VIGENTE DATVR ('From thy sword, O Prince, hordes of plunderers have fled: and, with the blossoming of peace, tranquillity is bestowed upon the churches'). Conservation: Le Mans (France), Musée de Tessé; cliché: Musées du Mans (France).

Nobles and Nobility in Medieval Europe

CONCEPTS, ORIGINS, TRANSFORMATIONS

EDITED BY

Anne J. Duggan

THE BOYDELL PRESS

First published 2000
The Boydell Press, Woodbridge
Reprinted in paperback 2002
Transferred to digital printing 2007

ISBN 0 85115 769 6 hardback
ISBN 0 85115 882 X paperback

The Boydell Press is an imprint of Boydell & Brewer Ltd
PO Box 9, Woodbridge, Suffolk IP12 3DF, UK
and of Boydell & Brewer Inc.
668 Mt. Hope Avenue
Rochester, NY 14620, USA
www.boydellandbrewer.com

A catalogue record for this book is available
from the British Library

Library of Congress Catalog Card Number: 99–087553

This publication is printed on acid-free paper

Contents

I. Early Middle Ages

II. Central Middle Ages

III. Late Middle Ages

Illustrations

Publication of this volume was aided by a grant from The Isobel Thornley Bequest Fund of the University of London

Contributors

Dr Stuart Airlie, Department of Medieval History, University of Glasgow

Professor Martin Aurell, C.E.S.C.M., University of Poitiers

Professor T. N. Bisson, Department of History, Harvard University

Dr Maria João Violante Branco, Universidade Aberta de Lisboa, Portugal

Dr D. A. Carpenter, Department of History, King's College London

Dr Anne J. Duggan, Department of History, King's College London

Dr Paul Fouracre, Department of Historical and Cultural Studies, Goldsmiths, University of London

Professor Piotr Górecki, Department of History, University of California, Riverside

Professor Steinar Imsen, Historisk Institutt, University of Trondheim, Norway

Mr Martin Jones, Department of German, King's College London

Professor Régine Le Jan, Centre de Recherche sur l'Histoire de l'Europe du Nord-Ouest, Université Charles-de-Gaulle, Lille 3

Professor Janet L. Nelson, Department of History, King's College London

Professor Timothy Reuter, Department of History, University of Southampton

Professor Jane Roberts, Department of English, King's College London

Dr Jennifer Ward, Department of Historical and Cultural Studies, Goldsmiths, University of London

Abbreviations

a.	anno
Berger	Adolf Berger. *Encyclopedic Dictionary of Roman Law*, Transactions of the American Philosophical Society, New Series, 43 pt 2 (Philadelphia, 1953; repr. 1991)
c.; cc.	capitulum; capitula
c.	*circa*
CCCM	Corpus Christianorum, Continuatio Mediaevalis (Turnhout, 1953–)
ch.; chs	chapter, chapters
EHR	*English Historical Review*
ep.	epistola
JL	P. Jaffé, *Regesta Pontificum Romanorum ad annum 1198*, ed. W. Wattenbach, S. Loewenfeld, F. Kaltenbrunner, and P. Ewald, 2 vols (Leipzig, 1885–88)
MGH	*Monumenta Germaniae Historica:*
Capitularia	*Capitularia regum francorum*, ed. A. Boretius and V. Krause, 2 vols (Hanover, 1883–97; repr. 1957)
Poet. Lat.	*Poetae Latini aevi Carolini*, i–ii, ed. E. Dümmler, iii, ed. V. Traube (Berlin, 1881–86) = *Poetae latini medii aevi*, i–iii
SRG	*Scriptores rerum Germanicarum in usum scholarum ex Monumentis Germaniae historica separatim editi*, 61 vols (Hanover, et alibi, 1839–1935; variously re-edited and reprinted)
SRG, NS	*Scriptores rerum Germanicarum*, New Series (Berlin, 1922–)
SS	*Scriptores* (in folio), 32 vols in 34 (Hanover, 1826–1934)
MPH	*Monumenta Poloniae Historica. Pomniki dziejowe Polski* (Lwów/Kraków, 1864–93, repr. Warsaw, 1960–61)
MPH n.s.	*Monumenta Poloniae Historica – Series Nova. Pomniki Dziejowe Polski – Seria II* (Kraków and Warsaw [alternately], 1952–)
MTB	*Materials for the History of Thomas Becket, Archbishop of Canterbury*, ed. J. C. Robertson and J. B. Sheppard, RS 67, 7 vols (London, 1875–85)
NglL	*Norges gamle Love*, iii (Christiania/Oslo, 1849)
PBA	*Proceedings of the British Academy*
pd	printed
PL	*Patrologiae cursus completus, series latina*, ed. J. P. Migne, 234 vols (Paris, 1844–1955)

RHES	*Revista de História Económica e Social*
RPH	*Revista Portuguesa de História*
RS	Rolls Series: *Rerum Britannicarum medii ævi scriptores: Chronicles and Memorials of Great Britain and Ireland during the Middle Ages, published under the direction of the Master of the Rolls* (London, etc., 1858–1911)
repr.	reprint
SCH	*Studies in Church History*
s.a.	*sub anno*
s.v.; *s.vv.*	*sub verbo*; *sub verbis*
TRHS	*Transactions of the Royal Historical Society*

Preface

With the exception of David Carpenter's chapter, all the papers in this volume were presented at the Third International Conference held under the auspices of the Centre for Late Antique and Medieval Studies at King's College London in the Great Hall of the College in April 1998. The theme was 'Nobles and Nobility in the Middle Ages', and the conference was planned to enable comparisons to be made across time, from the fifth to the late fifteenth century, and between very different areas and phases of political development, embracing regions as diverse as England (before and after the Norman Conquest), France, Poland, the Romano-German empire, Norway, and Portugal. One of the highlights of the conference was a performance of courtly music presented in the College Chapel by members of the College Choir, under the direction of Mr David Trendell.

Our grateful thanks are due to the British Academy, the Royal Historical Society, and the Humanties Research Committee of King's College London, all of whom provided financial assistance for various aspects of the Conference; to the Isobel Thornley Bequest, whose generous grant made possible the publication of this volume; to the Music faculty of King's for use of the Viscount St David's Room; to the Dean of King's, who allowed the College Chapel to be used for the concert; and to Janet L. Nelson, who translated the papers presented by Martin Aurell and Régine Le Jan.

In addition, the editor wishes to thank the Musées du Mans and the Radio Times Hutton Picture Library for permission to reproduce the illustrations in Plates 1 and 2.

AJD
King's College London
3 June 1999

In Memoriam

CHARLES DUGGAN

Introduction

Anne J. Duggan

'Indeed, I am not "sprung from an ancient line of kings" ',[1] wrote Thomas Becket in 1166, rising to the taunt that he had been raised from poverty through the king's favour, 'nevertheless, I prefer to be a man in whom nobility of mind creates nobility than one in whom nobility of birth degenerates.'[2] This response neatly encapsulates the two principal elements in the construction of nobility in the Middle Ages: distinction based on birth, blood, and lineage and distinction of character and intellect – and expresses the recurrent theme that the one could and often did exist without the other. By the time that Thomas Becket (himself very much a *parvenu*, born of mercantile parents with some knightly affiliations, but not knightly status) was embroiled in his great dispute with Henry II (who was affronted when Herbert of Bosham pointed out that he was not the son of a king!), the broad shape of the European nobility had come into being and was poised to consolidate itself even further. Evidence of its self-consciousness, wealth, and status is everywhere to be seen: celebrated in vernacular *chansons*, reflected in the newly created and hugely popular Arthurian literature, emblazoned on tombs and personal seals, and its members commemorated as founders and patrons of churches, monasteries, and hospitals. They were notable and noted in chronicles and annals; they divided the lordship of lands and peoples among themselves and shared the government of realms with kings and emperors. But who were they, these 'nobiles', where did they come from, how did they acquire the precise power and status which they enjoyed, and how did they then manage to hold on to that power and transfer it, sometimes through many generations, to later descendants who would bear their names? How, indeed, was the concept of 'noble' and 'nobility' constructed? – for what we see is not merely the acquisition and maintenance of landed wealth, but the creation of an ideology which justified their superior status and attributed to them a dynastic right to rule based on descent from noble ancestors.

To begin with the terminology. The English nouns 'nobles' and 'nobility'

---

[1]   Horace, *Carmina*, i. 1, 1:

        Maecenas atavis edite regibus,
        O et praesidium, et dulce decus meum.

[2]   *MTB*, v, ep. 223 at p. 499: 'Non sum reuera "attauis editus regibus"; malo tamen is esse in quo faciat sibi genus animi nobilitas, quam in quo nobilitas generis degeneret.'

derive not from Old English but from French and ultimately from Latin; and it was the *lingua franca* of late Latin that provided the semantic basis for the terminology of 'nobility' in the Latin-derived languages adopted by many of the Germanic peoples that established their rule in the Western Roman empire in the fifth and sixth centuries; and even where Latin did not become the language of the people, progressive Christianization brought the language of the Vulgate, the Latin Fathers, and the liturgy, and with it much of the Roman vocabulary of nobility. Underlying the Germanic actualities lay the inheritance of Roman constructions of a civil aristocracy, based on birth and civic/imperial service. Roman law principally distinguished between free and unfree and between citizen and non-citizen, but the Roman world distinguished also between 'patricians' and 'plebeians', and the distinction between 'nobiles' and 'ignobiles' established itself in the realities of legal, social, and political life. The term *nobilis* (noble) meant both well-known, distinguished, famous (and infamous) and well-born – *nobili genere nati*. Cicero, a *novus homo* himself, was sensitive to the gradations of Roman society. His description of the lady Clodia as 'a woman not only noble but notorious' ('Cum Clodia muliere *non solum nobili, sed etiam nota*') played on the contradiction between her high status (*nobilis*) and her alleged lack of reputation (*nota*).[3] The legal texts do not supply a definitive list of those enjoying privileged status, but there was a dual penalty system in operation which distinguished not only between the legal categories of free and unfree but between those of higher and those of lower social status. Capital punishment, for example, in all its forms, was generally imposed only on the *humiliores*, those below the rank of decurion;[4] and the *honestiores* were generally spared degrading penalties like condemnation 'to the mines or to public labour, nor are they exposed to the beasts, nor beaten with rods', or subjected to torture.[5] As in Anglo-Saxon England (and much of the Germanic world), this differentiation extended also to the categorization of offences: 'An injury is judged to be grave . . . because of the person to whom it is done, when the victim is a senator, or equestrian or decurion, or someone else of conspicuous prestige . . .'[6] What these *honestiores* enjoyed was *honor* (esteem, respect) and *dignitas* (an honourable prestige which merits respect and reverence).[7]

The Roman world also constructed a language of privilege. Its official docu-

---

3 *Pro Caelio*, 13, 31. Cf. Neal Wood, *Cicero's Social and Political Thought* (Berkeley, 1988), esp. pp. 90–104.

4 Except for particularly heinous crimes like treason, parricide, and, from the late third century, participation in magic and armed burglary of a temple at night.

5 Peter Garnsey, *Social Status snd Legal Privilege in the Roman Empire* (Oxford, 1970), pp. 105–78, esp. p. 135, quoting an opinion of Marcianus from *Dig.* 49. 18. 3. Although the general pattern of exemption for the *honestiores* and veterans (who were legally assimilated to the decurions) is clear, there were exceptions: see *ibid.*, pp. 142–5.

6 Garnsey, *Social Status*, pp. 199–201, esp. 201–2, quoting a late third-century commentary. For a discussion of privileged groups (senators, equestrians, decurions, veterans, soldiers, and magistrates), see *ibid.*, pp. 234–59; and for the proposition that the social and legal ordering emerged in late Republican times, see *ibid.*, p. 279.

7 Garnsey, *Social Status*, pp. 221–33, 'The vocabulary of privilege', esp. pp. 223–5.

ments used a hierarchy of honorific styles of title and address which settled into a three-fold ranking of *illustres* (highest officials: Prefects of the city of Rome, *magistri militum, quaestores sacri palatii*, but could also be conferred by the emperor, by *codicilli honorariae dignitatis*);[8] *spectabiles* (second rank of officials),[9] and *clarissimi* (senators and those of senatorial rank).[10] Visible marks of distinction emerged at the same time. The broad purple stripe (*laticlavus/clavus latus*) on tunic or toga marked senators and their sons, and later the higher dignitaries of the empire; the narrow purple stripe on the toga (*clavus augustus*) marked those of equestrian rank.[11] Familiarity with this world of social and political gradations surely underlies the well-known distinctions in St Paul's First Letter to the Corinthians, where, in Jerome's Latin Vulgate, the 'potentes' and 'nobiles' of the world are compared with the 'infirma' and 'ignobilia'/'contemptibilia', whom God has chosen to confound the strong, and 'ea quae non sunt (those who are nothing)', whom He has chosen to bring to nought 'ea quae sunt (those who are something)'.[12] Paul was, famously, a free-born Roman citizen ('. . . hic enim homo civis Romanus est') of the first century AD,[13] and his letters resonate with echoes of that world of rank and privilege which the Christian Gospel was set to dissolve into a new community of believers, where there is neither slave nor free.

How far the Roman construct was transmitted to the 'barbarians' who assumed the rulership of Roman or formerly Roman territories in the fifth and sixth centuries is a matter of some debate;[14] but the emergence of an élite – a nobility – and a language to describe it can be readily discerned. Writing in a Northumbrian monastery in the early eighth century, Bede tells of a captive who was recognized as not 'of common stock' (*de paupere uulgo*) but 'of noble family' (*de nobilibus*) from 'his appearance, his bearing, and his speech' (*ex uultu et habitu et sermonibus eius*).[15] The context is the late seventh-century wars between Anglo-Saxon kingdoms; the language of the record, the refined

---

8   Berger, pp. 491b–492a, *s.v.* Illustris.
9   Berger, p. 712a–b, *s.v.* Spectabilis.
10 Berger, p. 390a–b, *s.vv.* Clara persona, Clarissimatus, Clarissimus.
11 Originally the cavalry in the Roman army, the *equites* became a distinct social category – a 'nobility' of rich men who obtained their wealth from commerce (forbidden to senators) and tax farming (*publicani*). Reorganized under Augustus, they monopolized the highest administrative positions in the empire, with the right to wear a gold ring (*ius annuli aurei*): Berger, p. 455a–b, *s.v.* Equites.
12 1 Cor. 1: 26–8, '. . . non multi potentes, non multi nobiles . . . et infirma mundi elegit Deus, ut confundat fortia. Et ignobilia mundi, et contemptibilia elegit Deus, et ea quae non sunt, ut ea quae sunt destrueret.' (AV: 'not many mighty, not many noble are called . . . and God hath chosen the weak things of the world to confound the things that are mighty; and the base things of the world, and things which are despised, hath God chosen, yea, and things which are not, to bring to nought things that are.')
13 Acts, 22: 26
14 Fouracre, p. 19; Le Jan, pp. 61–4.
15 *Bede's Ecclesiastical History of the English People*, ed. Bertram Colgrave and R. A. B. Mynors (Oxford, 1969), p. 402, lines 29–30, cited by Jane Roberts, p. 72.

Latin of an Anglo-Saxon monk; but it tells of visible distinctions between 'nobles' and 'the common people' which were recognizable in a seventh-century prisoner-of-war, and no doubt visible also in the Northumbrian society from which Bede sprang. Monks, as Janet Nelson says, citing a Carolingian capitulary of 817,[16] knew the difference between 'nobles' and others; but the lexicological evidence presented by Jane Roberts shows that vernacular writers were equally sensitive to the nuances of status. The surviving monuments of early English composition provide many clusters of words to describe status, esteem, and rank: *ænlic, eorlic, hlāfordlic, þegnlic* (lordly, noble), compounds including *æþel-* (noble condition, based on birth) and *weorþ-* (honour-), and nouns *aldorþegn* (senior noble), *þegn* (noble); while the Old English epic *Beowulf* provides two outstanding examples of 'nobility' in Beowulf himself and the heroic Æschere.[17] This latter character tells us much about the early English concept of nobility: he is a generous, brave, shield-bearing companion of the king. These are the qualities of an aristocracy of war – an aristocracy which earned its reputation on the battlefield; but underlying the conceptualization is recognition of birthright, or perhaps, more properly, of the obligations that attach to 'noble' birth. Æschere's depiction as a 'shield-bearing companion of the king' is also highly significant, since association with the circle of the ruler was to remain a pervasive mark of nobility throughout the medieval period: in larger kingdoms, a mark of the higher nobility; in smaller kingdoms and non-royal lordships, a mark of nobility in general. So, 'noble' birth, military prowess, and royal service (especially military) seem to be characteristics of the post-Roman nobility.

What can be discovered of early Frankish society in sub-Roman Gaul reveals a clear recognition of rank and its inheritance. Such concepts are readily discernible in the writings of Gregory of Tours and in the saints' lives discussed by Paul Fouracre, but it is not entirely clear how far the Franks had assimilated to Roman ways. Theirs was a warrior élite – not so dissimilar from that of the Old English world described in *Beowulf* – and in the case of the ruling family, the Merovingians, also one of descent. That élite assumed control of a late Roman world whose system of privilege accommodated both nobility of birth and office and nobility by wealth, and conferred special rights and exemptions on soldiers, and where status, power, and office were monopolized by a relatively small number of distinguished families. The fact that a Gallo-Roman 'nobility' can be traced through the period of Frankish conquest and settlement down to the seventh or even eighth century in some regions of Francia is evidence of the endurance and adaptability of that class; it is evidence also of

---

[16] *MGH Capitularia*, i, no. 170 (817), c. 27, p. 345: Nelson, App. 1, no. 14.

[17] The range of such terms and variants is very wide and their meanings richly nuanced: see below, pp. 71–3. Old English law codes, equally, display recognition of and concern with the gradations of status, as they lay down monetary penalties assessed according to the rank of the injured party in descending order from king, archbishop, bishop, or ealdorman, to the 'common man' (*ceorl*).

the survival at least in formal terms of late Roman patterns of government. Based more on economic capacity (land and its rents and produce) than on office, but forming the class from whom office-holders were usually drawn, their position depended on birth (inheritance of family estates and the honour that went with them) and the offices which they expected to fill (episcopal, abbatial, civil). Carried from the Roman world were not only the civil and ecclesiastical structures of government (the *civitas* and the diocese) but a population and an élite accustomed to working in and through them. How far the Frankish leaders grafted the Roman model onto their own traditions of dominion remains problematic, but the survival in some regions of the late Roman aristocracy alongside the Frankish made for some degree of assimilation. Not surprisingly, therefore, the picture that Paul Fouracre finds among the Franks in Merovingian Gaul is one of complexity and contradiction: 'even as some people were entering the nobility, others were sinking to a social level below it. In this sense élite formation was an unending process, with movement throughout the social spectrum as wealth was continuously accumulated and dispersed.'[18] This conclusion might profitably be applied to the whole of Latin Europe, throughout the Middle Ages and beyond. There is always an 'old élite' – or one claiming ancient descent – and upwardly mobile aspirants seeking entry to the charmed circle; but the problem is to discern the process of creation.

Two studies on contrasting regions from the northern and eastern peripheries of Latin Christendom throw interesting light on the question of élite formation. Steinar Imsen's analysis of the *Hirdskrá*, the customs governing the Norwegian king's liegemen and household, demonstrates the existence of tiered élites among the king's supporters and servants and of concentric circles of status arranged around them. Although all *hirdsmen* were bound by oath to the king, there were differentials of rank, privilege, and status, from dukes and earls, through to 'lendmen', who received royal land, acted as advisers, and were allowed armed retinues, and 'skutilsveins', who were not. Though technically not hereditary, the tendency was for the status of lendman and skutilsvein to circulate within a small number of leading families. Moreover, in what was evidently a deliberate assimilation of forms and concepts prevalent elsewhere in Europe, lendmen and skutilsveins were given titles of honour as 'barons' and 'ridder' (knights), respectively, and addressed as 'herra' from 1277 onwards. Compared with the nobilities of other regions, however, their social origins were modest. They were drawn from the 'better', that is, the wealthier farming families of the kingdom. What in fact distinguished them from their free neighbours was 'their exclusive relationship to the king, which gave them what we might call noble status'.[19]

By contrast, Piotr Górecki illuminates what one may call the self-creation of nobility in twelfth- and thirteenth-century Poland. Although he is reluctant to

---

18 Fouracre, p. 23.
19 See below, pp. 205–10.

use the term 'nobility', preferring the phrase 'patterns of social privilege', he shows that land ownership and military ability were the basis of a status which could be transmitted to one's heirs. His analysis of the witness-lists of charters issued to monasteries in the late twelfth and thirteenth centuries reveals an already established terminological hierarchy of 'counts' (*comites*), 'lords' (*domini*), and 'knights' (*milites*), although he is hesitant about precise definitions. Instead, he emphasizes the fluidity of social status in a border region where central authority was weak and the opportunities for successful depredation (and therefore improvement in one's position) were correspondingly large, and cites the career of one Peter Stoszowic in Silesia, who seems to have progressed 'from banditry to lordship' in a period of thirty years, so that he emerged with the title of *comes*.[20] Equally interesting is the way in which this emerging 'nobility' identified itself by family names, inheritance of family lordship, the use of signs and symbols, and the enjoyment of privileged status. What began as successful brigandage could become the foundation of an honourable name. Membership of that nobility seems to have been rather widely drawn, however. Like the equestrian order in imperial Rome, the Polish knighthood attached itself to the *honestior* rank and shared its privileges, being distinguished by birthright, military service to the king/duke, and the possession of the *ius militare*: specific rights of jurisdiction and lordship over neighbours, tenants, and peasants.[21] How far the better-documented Polish phenomenon offers significant parallels with the establishment of the early Frankish 'nobility' is an interesting question which might be pursued.

Similar but more developed patterns are found in Iberia, in the context of another border society, where the expansionist wars against the Moors provided perfect conditions both for the formation of a military élite and for its consolidation. In Portugal, for example, the movement south in the twelfth century occasioned not only the creation of a specific military nobility, but the elevation of the count of Portugal to kingship, and the creation of a new Christian kingdom. These conditions also provided the context for noble self-admiration. By the late thirteenth century, the Portuguese nobility was busy constructing an image of itself as heirs of the warrior crusaders who had, with the king, pushed back the borders of Islam and created the kingdom. The Lineage Books compiled between 1280 and 1340 propagated a highly developed sense of dynastic nobility, identified by family name and family lordships, and self-consciously aware of its family identity.[22]

Such increasing emphasis on dynastic lordship advantaged noble women who were honoured and endowed as the transmitters of noble lineage, and increasingly educated to take their places in a self-consciously noble world. Airlie, Le Jan, and Nelson see evidence of this tendency in the Carolingian

[20] See below, pp. 136–7.
[21] Casimir the Great (mid-fourteenth century) did not distinguish between the 'privileges' of 'knighthood' and 'nobility'.
[22] Maria João Violante Branco, below, pp. 223–8.

world and Ward stresses the self-consciousness of rank and lineage evinced by noblewomen themselves in the later Middle Ages. For, the more the nobility stressed the legitimacy and distinction of its descent, the more it emphasized and protected the high status of its mothers, wives, sisters, and daughters. Maria João Violante Branco highlights the elevated status of noble women in Portugal: their sharing in family inheritance and their ability to control their inherited land, even after entering religious houses. Teresa Sanches, for example, daughter of King Sancho I and former wife of Alfonso IX of León, created a Cistercian nunnery for herself at Lorvão (following the expulsion of the male Benedictines), but nevertheless inherited a large domain from her father and continued to govern her inheritance in her own name. She issued privileges using her royal style as queen, and participated fully in the political affairs of the kingdom for half a century, until her death (1250) in the odour of sanctity.[23] And Thomas Bisson's discussion of princely nobility shows that more than a century earlier Countess Matilda of Tuscany could be treated as one of the very noble rulers of her day. Equally, since rank and inheritance could be transmitted by women, marriage to an elevated heiress, or to a member of a royal family, could be a source of elevation for the man. Airlie and Le Jan both stress how attachment to the Carolingian family through female members was an important element in the consolidation of noble lineages in the ninth and tenth centuries. The elevation of Boso of Vienne and Arnulf 'the Bad' of Bavaria, the one as king, the other as an all-but king, owed a great deal to their Carolingian descent.[24] And it was through women, principally, that Henry II of England acquired his extensive territories: the kingdom of England and the duchy of Normandy through his mother, the Empress Matilda, daughter and heiress of Henry I; the great duchy of Aquitaine (equivalent to a quarter of France) by marriage (1152) to its heiress Eleanor. Equally, David Carpenter draws attention to the importance of heiresses in the turbulent world of the Welsh Marches in the thirteenth century – and to their strenuous defence of their rights. Maud de Braose's defence of Painscastle in the 1190s was so celebrated that the castle was re-named Castle Maud in her honour; and it is likely that her great-granddaughter Maud Mortimer played a similar role in respect of the great fortresses of Radnor and Wigmore in the mid-1260s.[25] Just as many medieval queens were able to play active rôles in the power-politics of their day,[26] so noble women expected (and were expected) to be more than biological agents in dynastic transmission. They were as aware as their male siblings of their rank, status, and rights; and many showed themselves as determined as their husbands and sons to defend and advance the family honour.

Marriage to an aristocratic heiress, or to a princess of the royal family, was a

---

[23] See below, pp. 242–3.
[24] See below, pp. 30–3.
[25] See below, p. 201.
[26] *Queens and Queenship in Medieval Europe*, ed. Anne J. Duggan (Woodbridge, 1997), pp. xix–xxii.

means of upward mobility for a successful soldier or bureaucrat, or for an upwardly mobile noble. Yet there was a countervailing tendency also, especially in the later Middle Ages, when the growing use of primogeniture and male entail and the establishment of what Ward calls 'a Europe-wide concept of the noble family as a dynastic lineage, with a male head, heroic ancestry, coat of arms, and chivalrous reputation'.[27] In regions where these tendencies became prevalent, even distant male cousins were preferred to daughters as inheritors of the family name and title. But no single pattern prevailed. Dynastic accident, political miscalculation, or economic mismanagement – or combinations of all three – created fundamental instabilities which caused some families to thrive and prosper and others to decline, and careful management of marriage and inheritance policies was required to ensure the survival of wealth and status from generation to generation. Such preoccupations lay at the heart of the transformations that Régine Le Jan finds in the otherwise remarkably stable nobility that emerged from the Carolingian empire in the tenth century, where the descendants of Charlemagne's *proceres* exploited the disintegration of Carolingian power after 888 to consolidate their hold on counties and duchies which they transformed into dynastic lordships for transmission to their descendants. And it was dynastic lordship, underpinned by a strong sense of inherited territorial rights, which in David Carpenter's view finally dictated Roger Mortimer's abandonment of Simon de Montfort in the barons' war.[28]

Although nobility tended increasingly to clothe itself in extravagant dress and trumpet its claims to a superior code of ethics, Górecki and Reuter emphasize that its origins and maintenance were often much less virtuous than the later legends portrayed. The Peter Stoszowic who made himself into some sort of count did so by aggression; and the problem of the *raubritter* (robber knight) was certainly not confined to thirteenth-century Poland. Le Jan comments on the phenomenon in tenth-century Francia.[29] An effective fighter of modest means, either on the way up or on the way down the social scale, had ample opportunity to make a name and fortune for himself in areas where the local nobility was weak or not yet itself established. Moreover, he could make himself useful – possibly even distinguish himself and earn honour – in wars of expansion or defence. A considerable element of the lordship which became established in the early Middle Ages was based on conquest or aggression and was maintained by what Reuter calls 'direct and unmediated coercive force'.[30] Such considerations led Pope Gregory VII, echoing the even earlier Augustine of Hippo,[31] to challenge the authority of the princes of his day in a letter to Bishop Hermann of

---

[27] Ward, pp. 249–54.
[28] See below, p. 203.
[29] See below, pp. 68, 136–7.
[30] Reuter, p. 87.
[31] *De doctrina Christiana*, i. 23 (*PL*, xxxiv, 27).

Metz in 1081 (although castigating 'kings and dukes', its criticism could have been applied to much of the lesser nobility as well):

> Who does not know that kings and dukes derived their origin from men, ignorant of God, who with intolerable presumption and blind greed established their power over other men who were their equals by pride, perfidy, rapine, murder, and every sort of crime, under the stimulus of the devil, the prince of this world?[32]

Dominion of man over man is here described as satanic! How then could the wielders of such power justify their claims? A little wash of Aristotelianism could be applied, but to the simple question of why the nobility were 'better' and therefore better suited to rule, there was no single answer. One strategy was to construct an image of warrior nobility, formed at the beginning of the region's history, which had earned its rank and status by fighting for the land against common enemies. For the Iberians, the Reconquest provided fertile ground for such conceptualization (and, indeed, for the actual acquisition of lands and lordships), later celebrated in the Lineage Books compiled in Portugal and Navarre.[33] A similar pattern can be discerned in the way in which the princely nobles, clerical and lay, male and female, discussed by Thomas Bisson were described by their biographers. Where nobility of parentage could be claimed, it was stressed; but greater emphasis was placed on effective and notable action. Heroic struggle against the enemies of one's race or religion or land was a powerful claim to the renown that was a constituent of nobility.[34] Such emphasis was to be enduring. When, in the early nineteenth century, King Louis-Philippe proposed to celebrate the ancient and honourable nobility of France in the Salles des Croisades in Versailles, such was the competition to be included in the grand array of the noble descendants of the crusaders that a veritable industry of faked or doctored genealogies, supported by forged charters, sprang up to substantiate aristocratic claims not just to ancient but to heroic lineage.[35] Justification by (legitimate) conquest underlay the claims of the Anglo-Norman baronage in post-Conquest England. Like their Iberian counterparts they could point to a specific historical event to justify their position and status. In their case it was the share-out of the spoils of victory which followed William the Conqueror's triumph at Senlac (Hastings) in 1066. When King Edward I's judges demanded to see the warrant by which the earl of Surrey (John de Warenne) exercised exempt jurisdiction in his estate, he allegedly drew

---

32 *Das Register Gregors VII*, ed. E. Caspar, *MGH, Epistolae Selectae*, ii (2 fascs, Berlin, 1920–23), viii. 21, pp. 547–63, at. p. 552: 'Quis nesciat reges et duces ab iis habuisse principium, qui Deum ignorantes superbia rapinis perfidia homicidiis postremo universis pene sceleribus mundi principe diabolo videlicet agitante super pares, scilicet homines, dominari ceca cupidine et intollerabili presumptione affectaverunt?'

33 See below, pp. 223–8.

34 See below, ch. 7.

35 J. Riley-Smith, 'Past and Present', in *The Past and the Present: Problems of Understanding* (Oxford, 1993), pp. 75–92 at pp. 77–8.

Anne J. Duggan

Plate 2. A Carolingian count, ninth-century. Detail of fresco, oratory of St Benedict, Malles Venosta (Trentino-Alto Adige, Italy). Radio Times Hutton Picture Library.

his rusty sword and declared, 'Here's my warrant . . . For the king did not by himself conquer and subject the land: our progenitors were his partners and supporters.'[36] It was an answer which would not have come all that amiss from the mouth of the anonymous Carolingian count who is depicted holding his great sword with both hands in a 'presentation of arms' gesture in the famous ninth-century fresco in the church of St Benedict in Malles Venosta (Trentino-Alto Adige, Italy).[37] For the thirteenth-century English earl and the ninth-century Carolingian count, as well as for the nobility throughout Europe, the sword was both a symbol of noble status and the means of its creation and defence.

Another strategy was to legitimize the nobility's possession of coercive force. Ecclesiastical writers of the Carolingian period constructed a theory of aristocratic and royal government which both accepted and transformed the conceptualization of military power by emphasizing the public and Christian duties of those who exercised it. The emperor Louis the Pious became a *miles Christi*, and the *militia saecularis* of the lay aristocracy, whose function was seen as the defence of the weak, paralleled the *militia Christi* of the monastic order.[38] Three centuries later, a similar justification was emblazoned on the plaque made to commemorate Count Geoffrey of Anjou, who died in 1151 (see Frontispiece). Arrayed in the heraldic symbols that set him apart from his vassals and fellow nobles, his unsheathed sword is raised aggressively against the enemies of public order, while the inscription proclaims, 'From thy sword, O Prince, hordes of plunderers have fled: and, with the blossoming of peace, tranquillity is bestowed upon the churches.' Those 'plunderers', of course, were men not very different from himself, and his own protection of churches was sometimes a mixed blessing, but the image of lawful force protecting the weak against lawless force is dramatically conveyed.

Corresponding concepts of the altruistic use of military power underpinned the chivalry described in the *chansons de geste* and celebrated in the Arthurian literature composed in the twelfth and early thirteenth centuries. Such works created a literary glorification of the ideals and mores of a nobility and knighthood increasingly informed by Christian values. Written for this now self-conscious 'aristocracy', they both described and helped shape their self-consciousness and the mores expected of an élite defined by birth, dominion, wealth, and the profession of 'knightly' arms. The works of Hartmann von Aue reflect this world very nicely. Here the Arthurian myth creates an imagined world in which the ideals of this élite are celebrated and propagated.[39] Indeed,

---

36 Walter of Hemingburgh, *Chronicon*, ed. H. C. Hamilton, 2 vols (London, 1849), ii, 6: 'Ecce, domini mei, ecce warrentum meum . . . Non enim rex per se terram devicit et subjecit, sed progenitores nostri fuerunt cum eo participes et coadjutores.' Although probably apocryphal (Sir Maurice Powicke, *The Thirteenth Century 1216–1307* [Oxford, 1953], p. 521 and n. 2), the account conveys historical truth.
37 Cited by Le Jan, p. 64.
38 Le Jan, pp. 64–6.
39 See below, ch. 9.

such literature shaped as much as it reflected; and Martin Aurell rightly emphasizes the role of royal and other courts in civilizing regional nobilities, and in
creating a common ethos of manners and mores across Europe in the later
Middle Ages (although the pace of that development varied from region to
region).[40]

Parallel with what we may call the literary construction of a chivalric code,
one can see the emergence of political and ethical paradigms applied to the
upper nobility. By the end of the twelfth century, Thomas Becket could describe
the 'noble' Count Philip of Flanders as one who

> combines nobility of birth with the gift of discretion in the government of
> the state [and] is certainly worthy of the greatest honour: he restrains
> wrongdoers with firm justice, governs his law-abiding subjects with mod-
> eration and gentleness, respects and protects the Church, receives Christ in
> His ministers, calls forth the esteem of everyone with his kindness, and
> binds their affection by indulgence and favours. He does not vent his rage
> on his subjects, nor seek opportunities under the pretext of justice whereby
> he may torment the poor and exhaust and despoil the rich. More than is
> usual among his neighbours and contemporaries, he knows how 'to spare
> the submissive and subdue the proud'[41] – once the distinguishing quality of
> the noble Caesars.[42]

No doubt devised to flatter the great count, this little eulogy combines two
themes in medieval nobility: distinguished birth – born from noble stock, from
titled parents – and the attributions of 'nobility': justice, moderation, respect for
God and the Church, and restraint in the exercise of power. In much the same
way that the Carolingian nobles were assimilated to the divinely appointed royal
office of the *domus carolingica*,[43] one of their descendants is here compared
with the even earlier archetype of Roman imperial government. A similar combination of 'nobility of birth' and 'nobility of action' is found in a letter to
Queen Margaret of Sicily: 'Although we have never seen your face, we cannot
be ignorant of your renown, made illustrious by the distinction of noble blood
and adorned by the reputation of many outstanding virtues.'[44] Again, the

---

40 See below, pp. 269–71.
41 Virgil, *Aen.* vi. 853.
42 *MTB*, vii, ep. 558, at pp. 67–8 (with medieval spellings restored): 'Honore siquidem
    maximo dignissimus est cui ad gubernandum imperium adest nobilitas generis, prudentia
    suffragatur: delinquentes cohercet rigore iustitie, subditos obtemperantes iuri mansuetudi-
    nis moderatione gubernat, ecclesiam ueneratur et protegit, in ministris suis suscipit Chris-
    tum, et uniuersorum gratiam benignitate prouocat, et obsequiis et beneficiis obligat
    affectiones, non seuit in subditos, nec occasiones iustitie pretextu querit quibus cruciet
    pauperes, exhauriat et spoliet copiosos. Hec fuit quondam nobilium generositas Augusto-
    rum, quam iste preter conterminalium et coetaneorum morem exercet, qui saluberrime et
    honestissime nouit et consueuit "parcere subiectis, et debellare superbos." ' Note the use
    of *imperium* in its sense of 'state'.
43 Le Jan, p. 55.
44 *MTB*, vii, ep. 595 at p. 142: 'Licet faciem uestram non nouerimus, gloriam tamen non pos-

approach is adulatory – but the underlying assumptions are significant. The deep roots of the modern adage 'noble is as noble does' can be found here. Equally telling are the string of nouns, verbs, and adjectives used to construct the image of nobility: *gloria, claritas generosi sanguinis, illustrare, insignis.* For the Latin reader, these words were redolent with echoes of the late antique world. Indeed, Queen Margaret was addressed with titles of honour once reserved for the Roman emperors and their highest officials: 'Serenissime domine . . . Margarete . . . illustri regine Siculorum [To the most serene lady . . . Margaret . . . illustrious queen of the people of Sicily]'.[45] *Serenissimus* was used of the later emperors; *illustris* of the highest rank of imperial officials.[46] The words scintillate! In similar vein, Becket wrote to the princely bishop, Henry of Winchester, brother of King Stephen and cousin of Henry II: 'Thus, father, should a man of noble blood and the distinguished descendant of ancient kings[47] . . . adorn the nobility of his birth',[48] and he emphasized the immunity which 'nobility, prudence, wealth of goods and friends'[49] conferred on him. Here again, the run of Latin nouns in the conclusion conjures up the essential components of the Roman construction of the dignity which confers privilege and exemption: 'nobilitas, prudentia, copia rerum et amicorum'.

The Romanizing tinge of these examples was no mere echo of a lost age, however, for they derive from letters written in the name of an archbishop of Canterbury by a learned entourage that included John of Salisbury (author of *Policraticus*, one of the most important medieval treatises on royal government) among its members. For John and many of his colleagues, the literary and legal remains of the classical period provided not just useful exempla, but valid models for the government of their own world. The eulogy addressed to Count Philip of Flanders should not therefore be dismissed as classicizing rhetoric. It expressed an ideal in which concepts of Christian duty and Roman public service were combined into a philosophy of good government, applicable to all rulers, king and noble alike. The routine application of the adjective 'noble' to counts and earls[50] (as well as kings), combined with the creation of chivalrous codes of courtly conduct, carried with it an expectation that their rule should be

---

sumus ignorare, quam et generosi sanguinis illustrat claritas, et multarum magnarumque uirtutum decorat titulus, et fame celebritas numerosis preconiis reddit insignem.'

45 *MTB*, vii, ep. 595 at p. 142.

46 Berger, p. 702a, *s.v.* Serenissimus; pp. 491b–492a, *s.v.* Illustris.

47 An echo of Horace, *Carmina*, i. 1, 1: see n. 1 above.

48 *MTB*, vii, ep. 549 at p. 45: 'Sic, pater, decet uirum sanguine generosum, et clarum atauis regibus . . . generis exornare nobilitatem.'

49 *Ibid.*, at p. 46 'nobilitas, prudentia, copia rerum et amicorum'. As brother of King Stephen, Bishop Henry (of Blois) shared with Henry II descent from William I himself, the progenitor of the Norman line of kings.

50 E.g. Rotrou II of Perche, 'maiorum sanguine generosus et propria uirtute nobilis (noble through the blood of his forefathers, noble too in his own virtue)': *MTB*, v. ep. 138 at p. 247. For the illustrious genealogy of the Perche family see *The Ecclesiastical History of Orderic Vitalis*, ed. M. Chibnall, 6 vols. [1969–80], i, 212.

legitimized not only by their descent from 'noble' progenitors but also by their conduct, and by their commitment to just and lawful government. Thus the nobility came increasingly to conform to norms of behaviour created not simply by their own self-regarding reflections but by the demands of the political rôles which the emergence of nation-states imposed on them.

I

Early Middle Ages

1

The Origins of the Nobility in Francia

Paul Fouracre

Any review of work on the early medieval nobility quickly reveals that historians use the term 'nobility' to refer to an élite which was open, imperfectly defined, and subject to regional variation. With regard to the Frankish nobility, one can apply a series of normative statements about its origins and nature, but any general observations must always be qualified, or even contradicted, in the light of particular case studies. We can, for instance, observe that Frankish sources laid great emphasis on birth as the basis of nobility. That a person was 'born noble' was a standard way of indicating high social status at the beginning of Saints Lives, at least from the early seventh century onwards. Yet the Frankish nobility was by no means a closed élite. One can detect sentiments of exclusiveness, a horror, almost, of people who had risen from below to occupy the highest positions. This was contempt based on real, not just imagined, cases of dramatic upward social mobility: that of Leudast, for instance, Gregory of Tours's *bête noir*, who became count of Tours, or that of Ebbo, allegedly a serf, who became Archbishop of Reims and was said to have betrayed his lord and benefactor, the Emperor Louis the Pious, in a predictably base manner.[1] It is often said that this was an élite which channelled property through sons, but we can find cases in which daughters received equal shares of a given inheritance. Female inheritance rights were supposedly postponed behind males, except that sometimes they were not. Unforgettable here is an extraordinary passage in the (probably) late seventh-century *Formulary of Marculf* which gives a model for a charter in which a father states that the custom of preferring sons to daughters as heirs is 'impious'. Since all his children are God-given and he loves them all equally, he wishes to divide his property among them equally, thus making his daughter the equal and legitimate co-heir of her brothers.[2]

The Frankish élite was also one which apparently united family wealth with political and ecclesiastical high office, and expected to pass on wealth and office to the next generation. These expectations were, however, often disappointed. It was an élite which paid attention to distant kindred when it suited, say in times

---

1 On Leudast, see Gregory of Tours, *The History of the Franks*, trans. L. Thorpe (London, 1974), v, cc. 48–50, pp. 314–23. On Ebbo, J. Martindale, 'The French Aristocracy in the Early Middle Ages: A Reappraisal', *Past and Present*, lxxv (1977), 3–22.
2 *Marculfi Formularum Libri Duo*, ed. A. Uddholm (Uppsala, 1962), ii. 12, p. 218.

of feud when it was necessary to mobilize all available support, but which at other times, and especially at moments of inheritance, ignored all but the closest relatives. The family might thus sometimes appear to have a rather exotic cognatic structure, or it might look much more like the modern two-generational family. As for marriage, both endogamous and exogamous practices can be observed. No wonder the nature and structure of the early medieval noble family is topic of lively debate. As Régine Le Jan argues in her recent and most impressive survey of this whole subject, the Frankish nobility was sufficiently pliable to allow the Carolingian rulers to attempt to shape it into a supportive body. This they tried to do by restricting the range of people entitled to have their own armed following, and by encouraging links between the most privileged people over a wide area. They favoured exogamous marriages by insisting on the forbidden degrees of marriage, and they also encouraged families across the different areas of their empire to build up bonds of friendship and spiritual ties. This linkage, and the dispersal of key families throughout the widespread territories ruled by the Carolingians, was, she argues, a basic means of government.[3] As Stuart Airlie has put it, the concept of an 'imperial aristocracy' deliberately dispersed across continental Europe, the so-called *Reichsaristokratie*, may need to be qualified in all sorts of ways, but nevertheless, 'it is worth preserving as a useful tool as it offers insights into the structure of the empire and the social history of the aristocracy'[4] – that is, the Carolingian Empire, and its aristocracy, which is usually taken to mean the couple of hundred or so families which provided the counts, bishops, and abbots who effectively ran it. It is this group which Régine Le Jan characterizes as pliable, and it is this group which provides those case histories which allow us to see how normative ideas of custom actually worked out in practice. Janet Nelson's recent investigation into how one noble lady, Erkanfrida, tried to exercise her power and responsibility is a model of how the particular case can be used to demonstrate the social reality within which the customary norms should be understood.[5] It has long been accepted that the origins of these aristocratic families was mixed. In a seminal piece of work which focused on Burgundy, K.-F. Werner traced important Carolingian families back from the ninth into the early seventh century and demonstrated that they had Gallo-Roman, Burgundian, and Frankish ancestors. Intermarriage reflected the history of the area, with successive newcomers marrying into the native élite.[6]

No one takes issue with Werner's findings for what is a very select group of

3 R. Le Jan, *Famille et pouvoir dans le monde Franc (VIIe–Xe siècle)* (Paris, 1995). These themes recur throughout this magisterial work, but the basic thesis is succinctly stated on p. 98.
4 S. Airlie, 'The Aristocracy', *The New Cambridge Medieval History*, ii, ed. R. McKitterick (Cambridge, 1995), ch. 16, pp. 431–50, at p. 434.
5 J. L. Nelson, 'The Wary Widow', *Property and Power in the Early Middle Ages*, ed. W. Davies and P. Fouracre (Cambridge, 1995), pp. 82–113.
6 K.-F. Werner, 'Bedeutende Adelsfamilien im Reich Karls der Grossen. Ein per-

families in Burgundy. On the other hand, the origins, culture, and standing of the Frankish nobility in general has been subject to fierce debate.[7] It is a debate which got caught up in the wheels of the even bigger question of whether the development of early medieval Europe owed more to 'Germanic' or 'Roman' influences. Was the nobility of Francia (as opposed to the Frankish nobility) descended from Gallo-Roman natives or from Germanic invaders? Werner's answer, 'both', is clear for the élite, but what about the lesser nobility? Or, was the aristocracy one of blood or one of service? If it was one of blood, and that blood was not Roman blood, did it introduce new and non-Roman customs, culture, and institutions into society? Or if it were one of service, do we see the nobility preserving Roman institutions through the tenure of positions derived from the offices of late Roman provincial government? At issue here is the ultimate question about the affective nature of power: was society built around the private power of chieftains whose ascendancy was based on blood, following, and loyalty? Or was the political structure based on public power mediated through a hierarchy of offices and services?

Recent scholarship tends to dissolve these global questions, not least because we no longer think in terms of a kind of basic opposition between concepts of 'Germanic' and 'Roman' culture and institutions, or between notions of 'public' and 'private' power. At the same time we recognize that there is no decisive answer to the question of how the nobility in Francia came into being. For not only was that nobility so broadly constituted and so much subject to regional variation that it becomes impossible to argue a single origin for all nobles, we also understand that our perception of what the nobility was like is warped by the vagaries of our source materials. The amount of source material has, as it were, to reach a critical mass before one can identify family structures or behaviour. That is to say, we have to be able to track families across several generations before we can identify patterns of behaviour, and this tracking only becomes possible when we have a sufficient number of charters from which we can build up a picture of property relations in a given locality. This we can usually do only from the eighth century onwards. For the later sixth and seventh centuries we must rely more heavily on narrative sources which concentrate on that élite which was involved in high politics centred on the royal court, and which mention particular people only when they took part in dramatic events. This is as true of hagiography as it is of chronicles. These sources give us a little information about individuals, but rather less about families. In lieu of any

sonengeschichtlicher Beitrag zum Verhältnis von Königtum und Adel im frühen Mittelalter', in *Karl der Grosse*, i, ed. W. Braunfels (Dusseldorf, 1965), pp. 83–142, trans. as 'Important Families in the Kingdom of Charlemagne' in *The Medieval Nobility*, ed. and trans. T. Reuter (Amsterdam, 1978), pp. 137–202.

7   For the outlines of this debate, see F. Irsigler, *Untersuchungen zur Geschichte des frühfränkischen Adels*, Rheinisches Archiv, 69 (Bonn, 1969) and H. Gahn-Hoek, *Die fränkische Oberschicht im 6. Jahrhundert. Studien zu ihrer rechtlichen und politischen Stellung*, Vorträge und Forschungen, 21 (Sigmaringen, 1976).

firmer information to go on, attempts have often been made to identify families from the names of individuals on the basis that common or similar name elements are likely to indicate membership of the same family. This method of identification (Namenforschung) from narrative sources tends to give a picture of huge loosely knit families which were spread right across the Frankish realm. For the later period, charters tend to show smaller families, close knit and concentrated in a much smaller region. And for a period even earlier than that covered by the narrative sources, archaeology gives us yet another impression, namely, of an élite which was only just beginning to differentiate itself from the rest of the community. Different types of source material therefore reveal different aspects of the nobility. It would, however, be a mistake to privilege one aspect over the others, or to assume that they should be placed in a chrono-logical sequence of development. Taken together these different characteristics serve, rather, to emphasize the variety of the Frankish nobility, and suggest that the single term 'nobility' should comprehend a spectrum of people which stretched from the leaders of small communities of several hundred people, through to an élite group of families which dominated a single county, to that supra-regional élite which would later make up the *Reichsaristokratie*.

Unlike 'nobility', the term 'aristocracy' was not used by the Franks. We use it, often vaguely, to refer to one end of the spectrum, the 'more important fami-lies', that is to an élite within an élite. Some people we place in this super élite because we judge that they were very important, simply because they were mentioned in narrative sources. Otherwise we assume that certain jobs or offices were so important that their holders must have been top people. This would be true of bishops, abbots, dukes, counts, or a few other high officials. Finally, we can identify a few terms, such as *optimates, proceres*, or *illustres*, which desig-nate high status without reference to office. Often we would refer to any or all of these important people as 'magnates', a term we can use as a safer alternative to 'aristocracy', in that it appears to leave more open questions about how the élite was formed. For two reasons we assume that the magnate group was an open élite which recruited members from the layer of people directly below it. First, the inclusion of office-holders in the group suggests that it was possible to climb the social hierarchy as one's career progressed. This is certainly demonstrable for churchmen. Second, good evidence for strong social competition suggests a real prospect of advancement at all levels. The kind of people who might have had hopes of advancement through service, reward, marriage, or luck we may see in those who appear in the magnates' followings as locally important people who regularly witnessed their charters. Lastly, can detect a large group of lesser nobles in those who appear in the circles of smaller churches and monasteries, and who often became privileged tenants of the church. It is not possible to draw a clear line between these people and the non-nobles, for there were other community leaders, such as *boni homines, rachymburgi*, or (in Brit-tany) *machtierns*, whose status was never clearly associated with nobility, but who nevertheless exercised considerable influence in law courts and in commu-nity affairs generally. The point in describing the social spectrum of nobility in this way is firstly to re-emphasize its width, and secondly to demonstrate that its stratification is one which we have deduced, not one which they ever expressed.

As Werner showed, it is possible to detect the origins of some of those at the top end of the spectrum. The results of his name-research are consistent with the occasional references to ethnic identity in our narrative sources. Together they speak of an ethnic diversity which we must add to observations on the social complexity of the nobility. In different regions we can see different origins. In the source-rich Auvergne, for instance, we can see a Gallo-Roman élite conserving its wealth and privilege from the fifth through into the eighth centuries.[8] In the unlikely case that the Franks and others who invaded this area were naive of a nobility, one must assume that the more ambitious among them would have wished to acquire comparable status to these successful landowners, counts, and bishops. In the Meuse-Moselle-Rhine region to the north, archaeology gives a quite different picture of élite formation, with, as we have seen, an élite which still at the end of the sixth century was not quite separate from the rest of the community.[9] Yet within this region was Trier, where people with Roman names and the high-status title *senator* are visible into the mid-seventh century. No doubt this pattern of new and old was repeated in other areas. Nor is it unlikely that in some places at least three processes might have been at work: élite formation at community level, the raising of status through association with, or service to, newly created religious and political institutions in the locality, and the establishment, forcible or otherwise, of magnate groups in the region.

The diverse origins of the nobility and regional variations in the assessment of social status are reflected both in the variety of law codes in operation in Francia and in the way in which law and custom were hard to distinguish from each other. A legal system which could comprehend a variety of local laws and customs was one tailored towards mediation between nobles from different regions and of different origins. But at the same time as it facilitated communication between those of different traditions, the judicial process helped to preserve the differences. The preservation of different legal traditions in fact became something of a political principle, for it was a way of representing Francia as an empire made up of many peoples. But by 'peoples' we should understand the leaders, the nobles. Law thus provided a common means by which nobles of different origins could protect their property, and this was because of, not in spite of, the variety of laws in operation. Particular law codes,

---

8 See I. Wood, 'The Ecclesiastical Politics of Merovingian Clermont', *Ideal and Reality in Frankish and Anglo-Saxon Society: Studies Presented to J. M. Wallace-Hadrill*, ed. P. Wormald (Oxford, 1983), pp. 34–57.

9 See the compelling studies of two different parts of this region: F. Theuws, 'Landed property and Manorial Organisation in Northern Austrasia: Some Considerations and a Case Study', *Images of the Past: Studies on Ancient Societies in Northwestern Europe*, ed. N. Roymans and F. Theuws (Amsterdam, 1991), pp. 299–407; G. Halsall, *Settlement and Social Organization: The Merovingian Region of Metz* (Cambridge, 1995).

famously, did not distinguish nobles from other people, although they did assign higher levels of compensation to those in royal service. This fact has been a key element in the 'origins debate', for if the nobility did not figure in the earliest law codes, it has been argued, then perhaps they did not exist when the codes were first drawn up. If so, it would follow that the only way to achieve higher status was through service to the king. But inasmuch as law's principal aim was to protect property, and nobility was associated with wealth, then law effectively protected noble status. Custom more obviously protected status and privilege by allowing for redress against those slights to honour and reputation which could not be given a tariff in terms of injury or easily proved in a law court. Service was indeed an important element in the formation of a nobility, but it was one element among many. Rulers certainly aided the formation by providing opportunities for service. From sixth-century legislation we see what was possibly a numerous group of people given a special status as armed servants of the king. These were the *antrustiones*. In addition there were the *centenarii* who functioned as royal agents at local level and who were in one instance treated as *antrustiones*. Were these people made noble through royal service? At a higher social level, it was by and large only those who were already powerful who were given high office, and the holders of high office must have had a distinct advantage in competition with other nobles. But at the same time as they stimulated the formation, and stratification, of a nobility, rulers also helped to preserve its diversity, not only by recognizing the high status of people of different backgrounds, but also by adding to the means through which people's status could be raised.

We cannot discuss the origins and development of the Frankish nobility without thinking about the resources at its disposal. As ever, we cannot see the details of this until numbers of surviving charters greatly increase in the eighth century. These documents tend to show us nobles holding fractions of estates and struggling to rationalize dispersed lands, or even to stay afloat in the face of divided inheritances. It has therefore often been supposed that the nobility 'originally' held compact estates which were then divided in each generation for purposes of inheritance, causing something of a crisis of resources for those noble families whose original holding had been on the small side to begin with. This idea of diminution through partible inheritance may be true of lands which had been acquired from the king, but there is no reason to believe that there was ever an age in which most nobles held undivided estates. Why should there have been such an age? Or, more to the point, if there was one, when was it?

With the exception of grants of large blocs of former royal land to the church, the earliest charters show family or 'allodial' land held in fractions or *portiones*. People can be seen buying, swapping and shuffling land holdings in order to build up larger and more efficient units. Charters certainly recorded this activity and no doubt facilitated it, but there is no reason to believe that they called it into being. Many families were indeed so short of resources that further division of their lands would have deprived some or all members of the wealth needed to maintain noble status. It is, however, illogical to imagine that this happened only in the eighth century as the culmination of a process which had been going on for generations, for it was a continuous process. The important point here is that we must assume that even as some people were entering the nobility, others were sinking to a social level below it. In this sense élite formation was an unending process, with movement throughout the social spectrum as wealth was continuously accumulated and dispersed. The basic factor here was that there was not enough wealth to maintain relative social status across generations, and the result was that there was fierce competition for wealth at all social levels, and at all times. It was competition which made the Frankish nobility essentially biddable and ready to serve those of higher status, be they counts, dukes, bishops, abbots, or kings. The essential precondition both for the formation of an élite, and for competition within that élite, was the existence of a stable work-force made up a tied peasantry. It was this labour resource which made it possible to take control of portions of land through inheritance, exchange, purchase, or through reward for service, and to profit from that land immediate-ly. Social mobility among the nobility was thus predicated upon a degree of social immobility at peasant level, and it is of course true that a dependent peas-antry was formed at different times in different places. This observation hugely undermines any notion that the Frankish nobility came into being at roughly the same time, everywhere.

What muddies the question of origins even more, is the fact that in Francia élite formation took place against a background of cultural homogenization. A written culture which was latinate and Christian and very much the same every-where masks diversity of origins. For example, an area such as Central Germany which had been outside the zone of late Roman bureaucratic tradition until the mid-eighth century, then suddenly began to produce large numbers of charters, as if the nobility there was as familiar with this way of recording transactions as, say, their counterparts in the Auvergne who had been doing it for centuries. As Régine Le Jan has explained, in this culture the very terms used to describe family relationships were Roman and archaic.[10] It is the conformity of this written culture which allows us to draw up normative statements about the nature of the Frankish nobility, but which also makes it essential to qualify those statements with the evidence of case studies. The complexity which these studies reveal is not in the least surprising given the diverse origins of the Frankish nobility and the difficult competitive conditions in which it operated. If we accept that the formation of the Frankish nobility was a slow, variable, and possibly endless process, this conclusion leads us to a final set of questions. Given that new peoples were recruited to the Frankish empire in the eighth and ninth centuries, when, if ever, did the process of formation come to an end? If we say that the formation of the élite was both bottom up (from the organization of a dependant peasantry) and top down (through service to rulers), what provoked subsequent change within it? Did this happen (top down) when the

---

[10] R. Le Jan, *Famille et pouvoir*, pp. 162–75.

Frankish rulers lost power and nobles exercised more authority in their own right? Or was it provoked from below as more wealth was produced in the countryside, thus taking the edge off that competitive need which drove magnates into royal service and into supra-regional politics? And lastly, and most awkwardly, we must ask whether we really do see change across the Frankish period, for example in inheritance patterns or in the status of noble women, or whether it is the case that as we have more detailed sources we can understand older patterns in a more nuanced and subtle fashion.

2

The Nearly Men: Boso of Vienne and Arnulf of Bavaria*

Stuart Airlie

The motto of this paper is taken from the writings of a man who was made noble, rather than born such: Alfred, Lord Tennyson. In his version of the story of King Arthur, *The Idylls of the King*, Tennyson describes a world of petty rulers struggling among themselves and reluctant to yield to Arthur's authority: '. . . for most of these,/ colleaguing with a host of petty kings,/ Made head against him, crying, ''Who is he/ That he should rule us ?'' ' This sort of question was asked with some urgency in the Carolingian world of the late ninth century as the descendants of Charlemagne lost their monopoly of the kingship to 'petty kings', *reguli*. These petty kings came from the ranks of the aristocracy. How did they make the leap from nobility to royalty? What sort of power and authority did they have to acquire before they could make this leap and how, and how well, did they convince their peers of their special status? One well-known answer to the question is Karl Ferdinand Werner's argument that the component parts of the Carolingian empire, the *regna* within the *regnum*, emerged as territorial principalities. Such a view has much to commend it, but its sheer loftiness, its view of long-term processes across the whole empire, means that it pays insufficient attention to the crisis of legitimacy that was a real concern for contemporaries as this new world emerged. At the political level, and probably at the structural level too, Jean Dunbabin's characterization of the new kingdoms and principalities as 'a series of brilliant improvisations' is, I think, more helpful for us in our attempt to reconstruct the realities of political upheaval.[1]

I will explore these upheavals through considering the careers of two men,

* I am grateful to Tim Reuter and Herbert Schneider for advice on points of detail.

1 J. Dunbabin, *France in the Making 843–1180* (Oxford, 1985), pp. 91–2; a similar point is made in D. Bates, 'West Francia: The Northern Principalities', *The New Cambridge Medieval History, III, c. 900–1024*, ed. T. Reuter (Cambridge, forthcoming); I am grateful to David Bates for letting me read this in advance of publication. K. F. Werner's views are accessible in his two volumes of essay collections: *Structures politique du monde franque (VI–XII siècles)* (London, 1979) and *Vom Frankenreich zur Entfaltung Deutschlands und Frankreichs* (Sigmaringen, 1984); see also his 'Völker und Regna', *Beiträge zur Nationsbildung in Deutschland und Frankreich*, ed. C. Brühl and B. Schneidmüller, *Historische Zeitschrift*, xxiv (1997), 15–43. A welcome fresh perspective on the east Frankish

great magnates of the late ninth and tenth centuries: Boso of Vienne and Arnulf 'the Bad' of Bavaria. Both men established formidable power bases: Boso a kingdom based in Provence and Burgundy, and Arnulf in Bavaria, a duchy understood by contemporaries to be a *regnum*. Yet the achievement of both men was ephemeral. Boso was hounded by the Carolingian kings and Arnulf remained duke, not king. Separated in time and space – Boso proclaimed himself king in 879 and was associated with centres such as Vienne, Arnulf's 'royalty' dates from 919 and was rooted in centres such as Regensburg – their political achievements' transience has led to them both appearing in Patrick Geary's outstanding recent study of historical memory, as political actors who fell into oblivion.[2]

It is precisely this problematic nature of their achievement and identity that makes them such useful figures for anyone considering the nature of aristocratic and royal authority in a period of storm and stress. Their separateness in space and time is also important as it underlines the point that we are dealing from 879 onwards with a crisis (a term perhaps best understood here as an 'acceleration of the historical process') that dominated the high politics of the late Carolingian and early Ottonian world and that lasted for some considerable time.[3] Indeed one point that emerges from contemplation of Boso's career is one about time, about chronology. Boso made his bid for a crown in 879, that is, almost a decade before the deposition of Charles the Fat triggered the emergence of non-Carolingian kings in 888. In other words, the tenth century – if we see it as a century of rival monarchies and principalities responding to a legitimation deficit – started early. Boso's kingship in 879 is therefore perhaps the start of a long tenth century.

That contemporaries did perceive that there was a legitimation deficit, a crisis of authority (using 'crisis' here in its general sense of 'emergency'), is the first main point that I wish to establish. Carolingian rulers and their aristocratic followings had a variety of problems to contend with in the late ninth century, such as the military threat posed by Vikings, Hungarians, and Saracens and the instability generated by a series of youthful and short-lived kings after the deaths of Louis the German (876) and of Charles the Bald (877). Combined with all this was a key dynastic problem. The Carolingians were running out of legitimate adult male heirs. For all that Carolingians were kings by the grace of God and that kingship was an office, a *ministerium*, it was, in the words of Michael

duchies is offered in M. Becher, *Rex, Dux und Gens: Untersuchungen zur Entstehung des sächsischen Herzogtums im 9. und 10. Jahrhundert* (Husum, 1996). Tennyson's lines are from first poem in the Idylls of the King cycle, 'The Coming of Arthur', *The Poems of Tennyson*, ed. C. Ricks (London, 1969), p. 1472.

2 P. Geary, *Phantoms of Remembrance: Memory and Oblivion at the End of the First Millennium* (Princeton, 1994), pp. 34, 153–7.

3 K. Leyser, 'The Crisis of Medieval Germany', *Proceedings of the British Academy*, lxix (1983), 409–43, repr. in K. Leyser, *Communications and Power in Medieval Europe. The Gregorian Revolution and Beyond* (London and Rio Grande, 1994), pp. 21–49, at p. 23.

Wallace-Hadrill, 'a *ministerium* that started at birth'.[4] The *stirps regia* was special. Frankish kingship was hereditary, as Charles the Bald, following Gregory I, had proclaimed.[5] Yet Boso's coronation showed that the claim of the *stirps regia* to exclusivity could be challenged. The shadow of that challenge, the shadow of the actual Boso and the *reguli* in waiting, hangs over the writing of a loyalist such as Notker of St Gall, who wrote before 888. We can be sure that such anxious broodings were not confined to Notker in his far-flung monastery.[6] The banding together of three Carolingian rulers (with troops supplied by a fourth) to crush Boso shows how seriously Boso's move was taken.[7]

The most eloquent statement of the problem can be found in the testimony of Regino of Prüm, who wrote after the appearance of the non-Carolingian rulers: 'On his [Charles the Fat's] death the kingdoms over which he had ruled, deprived of a legitimate heir, separated out from the body of his empire and each, instead of waiting for its natural lord, chose a king from its own bowels. This was the cause of great wars. Not that the Franks lacked princes with the nobility, courage, and wisdom to rule over kingdoms; rather their equality of ancestry, dignity, and power enhanced the discord, for none was so outstanding that the others could submit to him without losing face.'[8] The lucidity of Regino's analysis makes it very attractive to historians.[9] For all his perceptiveness, however, Regino was a relatively detached observer of the scene. (The fact that his abbacy was disturbed by aristocratic violence is not necessarily a symptom of the crisis of royal authority.) For our immediate purposes the testimony of the king-makers, the great archbishops of the empire, is more enlightening.

Suspicion of the status of new rulers as well as the rehearsing of the virtues of Carolingian blood against the *ad hoc* claims of the 'kinglets' can be found in the

4 J. M. Wallace-Hadrill, 'A Carolingian Renaissance Prince: The Emperor Charles the Bald', *PBA*, lxiv (1978), p. 184.
5 *MGH, Capitularia*, ii, no. 300, c. 1, p. 450. The relevant older scholarship on hereditary and elective kingship is available in two collections edited by E. Hlawitschka: *Königswahl und Thronfolge in fränkisch-karolingischer Zeit*, Wege der Forschung, 247 (Darmstadt, 1975) and *Königswahl und Thronfolge in ottonisch-frühdeutscher Zeit*, Wege der Forschung, 178 (Darmstadt, 1971).
6 Notker, *Gesta Karoli Magni Imperatoris*, ii.12, ed. H. F. Haefele, *MGH SRG*, NS, xii (Berlin, 1959), 70–1; S. Airlie, '*Semper fideles*? Loyauté envers les Carolingiens comme constituant de l'identité aristocratique', *La royauté et les élites dans l'Europe carolingienne*, ed. R. Le Jan (Lille, 1998), pp. 129–43, at p. 141.
7 *Annales Vedastini, a.* 880, *Annales Xantenses et Annales Vedastini*, ed. B. von Simson, *MGH SRG* (Hanover/Leipzig, 1909), p. 47; R.-H. Bautier, 'Aux origines du royaume de Provence: de la sédition avortée de Boson à la royauté légitime de Louis', *Provence Historique*, xxiii (1973), 41–68, at pp. 54–61.
8 Regino, *Chronicon, a.* 888, ed. F. Kurze, *MGH SRG* (Hanover, 1890), p. 121; translation based on that in T. Reuter, *Germany in the Early Middle Ages 800–1056* (London and New York, 1991), p. 121. There is an extensive commentary on this passage in my forthcoming book on Carolingian politics.
9 See, for example, F. Staab, 'Jugement moral et propagande: Boson de Provence vu par les élites du royaume de l'Est', *La royauté et les élites dans l'Europe carolingienne*, pp. 365–82, at pp. 365–6.

writings of Archbishops Fulk of Reims and Hatto of Mainz. Fulk had come to maturity in the service of Charles the Bald and the events of 888 had made him think hard about the nature of royal dynastic legitimacy. He was not simply a Carolingian legitimist – he had not wanted Odo as west Frankish king in 888 and had only accepted him under pressure of events. By 893, Fulk was backing the Carolingian Charles the Simple and in a letter sent to the eastern Carolingian, Arnulf, he contrasted Charles' sound Carolingian origins with Odo's power which was only the power of a tyrant who was not part of the legitimate royal house.[10] Fulk's views were echoed in a letter of another great prelate, Hatto archbishop of Mainz (891–913), who very probably knew Fulk's text through his contacts with Arnulf's court. Hatto was writing to justify the elevating of Louis the Child (900–911) to the east Frankish throne on the grounds of his hereditary claims. He had to assert the primacy of these claims in the face of the fact that Louis was a child: 'although he is very youthful . . . we prefer to follow old custom rather than novelties . . . lest the kingdom fall into pieces'.[11] Both Hatto and Fulk knew that non-Carolingians could be kings and both knew that, in times of crisis, claims based on birth could be made to yield to those based on suitability. Their views on heredity vis-à-vis suitability were neither new nor consistent, but they were being generated by crisis, in Burckhardt's sense. Such texts form part of a group that stretches well into the tenth century, a group of texts in which various claims to royal power and authority are critically examined. It is in this group that we can place, for example, the prophecy proclaiming the fragility of Ottonian rule placed in the mouth of Bishop Radbod of Utrecht (899–917) in a text written some decades after his death.[12]

---

[10] Flodoard, *Historia Remensis Ecclesiae*, iv. 5, ed. M. Stratmann, *MGH SS*, xxxvi (Hanover, 1998), pp. 380–3; T. Kölzer, 'Das Königtum Minderjähriger im fränkisch-deutschen Mittelalter', *Historische Zeitschrift*, ccli (1990), 291–323, especially pp. 300–1. There is a deft sketch of Fulk's career and ideas in J. L. Nelson, ' ". . . sicut olim gens Francorum . . . nunc gens Anglorum": Fulk's Letter to Alfred Revisited', *Alfred the Wise: Studies in Honour of Janet Bately*, ed. J. Roberts, J. L. Nelson, and M. Godden (Cambridge, 1997), pp. 135–44.

[11] H. Bresslau, 'Der angebliche Brief des Erzbishofs Hatto von Mainz an Papst Johann IX', *Historische Aufsätze Karl Zeumer zum 60. Geburtstag als Festgabe dargebracht* (Weimar, 1910), pp. 9–30, at p. 27; H. Beumann, 'Die Einheit des ostfränkischen Reichs und der Kaisergedanke bei der Königserhebung Ludwigs des Kindes', *Archiv für Diplomatik*, xxiii (1977), 142–63, repr. in H. Beumann, *Ausgewählte Aufsätze aus den Jahren 1966–1986* (Sigmaringen, 1987), pp. 44–65, at pp. 57–8.

[12] *Vita Radbodi Episcopi Traiectensis*, c. 6, ed. O. Holder-Egger, *MGH SS*, xv (Hanover, 1887), 571 with comment and context in K. Leyser, *Rule and Conflict in an Early Medieval Society: Ottonian Saxony* (London, 1979), p. 96. Radbod's own writings echo the prophecy attributed to him: see his *Libellus de Miraculo S. Martini*, ed. O. Holder-Egger, *MGH SS*, xv, 1244; U. Penndorf, *Das Problem der Reichseinheitsidee nach der Teilung von Verdun (843)* (Munich, 1974), pp. 28ff; see also n. 17 below. The writings of Hucbald of Saint-Amand also fit into this context; see J. Smith, 'The Hagiography of Hucbald of Saint-Amand', *Studi Medievali*, xxxv (1994), 517–42, at p. 540.

It is apparent that contemporaries were very much aware of the fact that the challenges to the Carolingian dynasty made authority shaky. The point that I wish to stress here is that such perceptions should not be imagined as confined to the 'academic' speculations of a cloistered élite. The letters of Fulk and Hatto did not merely reflect events; they were intended to shape them. The world of these texts was connected to the world of politics. We can see this in the political liturgy of our two regions. Thus we find that a sacramentary from late ninth-century Provence differs from its model, the Sacramentary of Angoulême, by offering prayers for the success in battle, not of the king, but of 'thy servants', that is the counts or bishops. This shift is seen by Michael McCormick as revealing how the 'local authorities of a moribund Carolingian empire . . . assumed the liturgical trappings of royal power'.[13] Something similar can be seen in Bavaria where, in a Regensburg sacramentary, Duke Arnulf featured by name in the prayers for the Christian people.[14]

In this world traditional rivalries and jockeying for power and status among the aristocracy were made more complicated by the fact that the Carolingians were no longer the exclusive royal house. A glance at our two archbishops will make this clear. As members of the political élite, high churchmen had always been involved in the political events of the day; one thinks of Hincmar, Fulk's predecessor at Reims. But Hincmar had not crossed the watershed of 887/888. Hatto of Mainz may appear from one angle as a defender of Carolingian claims to royal status, but he had close links of association with one of the great aristocratic families of east Francia, the 'Conrads'. Such links were not in themselves a new phenomenon. What was new, after 887/888, was that such a family could itself become royal and indeed Conrad I did become king of east Francia in 911, an event that Archbishop Hatto was instrumental in bringing about.[15]

Fulk's case is even more instructive. Among the would-be kings of 888 was Fulk's own relative Wido, margrave of Spoleto; the great princes of the church now found that their own family could bid for royal status; episcopal meditation on royal office acquired a new urgency.[16] In fact, Fulk was to find that the political upheavals of the period brought dangers as well as opportunities. He perished in 900 at the hands of a vassal of Count Baldwin II of Flanders. It is of course very difficult to establish that there was an escalation of violence in the

---

13 M. McCormick, *Eternal Victory* (Cambridge, 1986), pp. 386–7; the text is edited in M. McCormick, 'A new ninth-century witness to the Carolingian mass against the pagans (Paris, B.N., lat. 2812)', *Revue Bénédictine*, xcvii (1987), 68–86, at p. 79 and note McCormick's sketch on p. 77 of the local historical context.

14 The prayer is contemporary with Duke Arnulf and is in Brussels, Bibl. Royale, MS. 1814–16, fol. 241v and fol. 242r, discussed in H. Schneider, 'Eine Freisinger Synodalpredigt aus der Zeit der Ungarneinfälle (Clm 6245)', *Papstum, Kirche und Recht im Mittelalter: Festschrift für Horst Fuhrmann zum 65. Geburtstag*, ed. H. Mordek (Tübingen, 1991), pp. 95–115, at pp. 98–9; cf. Geary, *Phantoms of Remembrance*, p. 155.

15 G. Althoff, *Amicitiae und Pacta, MGH Schriften*, xxxvii (Hanover, 1997), 63–6 and 240–63.

16 C. Brühl, *Deutschland-Frankreich: die Geburt zweier Völker* (Cologne, 1990), p. 374.

post-888 period, let alone establish a connection between such violence and the problems of royal authority, and one might therefore hesitate to draw general conclusions from Fulk's death. None the less, it is worth noting that Radbod, bishop of Utrecht, and like Fulk a man who grew up at the court of a powerful Carolingian ruler, bracketed Fulk's untimely death with that of Zwentibold of Lotharingia as part of the general upheavals of the cosmic order.[17] Old hands such as Notker, Regino, Fulk, Hatto, and Radbod knew that their world was changing. Fulk shows us this in his texts, his actions, and his death.

We must balance any sense we may detect of a nostalgia for Carolingian legitimacy with the fact that it existed in specific historical contexts to which it might have to yield. In the years following the great divisions of the Carolingian empire in the ninth century such as those of Verdun (843) and Meersen (870), members of the aristocratic élite may have wanted a Carolingian king for their particular kingdom, but that élite was attached to its kingdom as well as to Carolingian rulers. Thus in 911 the east Franks did not turn to the west Frankish Carolingian ruler Charles the Simple, but chose Conrad I because he was a member of their political community.[18] Thus there were sharp limits to nostalgia or feelings of dynastic legitimism; new polities had evolved. But there were also limits to such evolutions. New polities were fragile and old claims of legitimacy could still be potent. In 911 the Lotharingians did opt for Charles the Simple, not Conrad, and while this was partly an expression of the Lotharingian aristocracy's hostility to Conrad rather than straightforward expression of allegiance to a bearer of the potent name of Charles, the latter factor played a part. Charles the Simple certainly thought in 'frontierless' terms as *rex Francorum*.[19] All this means that at the political level, identities and boundaries could be fragile. The new kingdoms and principalities continued to be haunted by the broad horizons of the old world. Such tensions between the old world and the new are clearly visible in the careers of Boso and Arnulf. These careers reveal a form of frantic political creativity as a response to the tensions we have been examining.

If the *stirps regia*, the royal line, was in trouble, could figures such as Boso and Arnulf act as substitutes for it? Was there any way in which they could be classified as belonging to that royal line? Could Carolingian blood, or a Carolingian connection, make a magnate a king in waiting? The brief answer to this question seems to be that royal blood was sometimes, but not always, necessary

[17] Radbod, *Carmina*, I.i, ed. P. von Winterfeld, *MGH*, *Poet. Lat.*, iv (Berlin, 1909), pp. 161–2; for further textual ripples stemming from the death of Fulk, see K. Ugé, 'Creating a Usable Past in the Tenth Century: Folcuin's "Gesta" and the Crises at Saint-Bertin', *Studi Medievali*, xxxvii (1996), 887–903.

[18] Brühl, *Deutschland-Frankreich*, p. 403.

[19] Once Charles the Simple was recognized by Lotharingia, the following formula appeared in his charters from 20 December 911 onwards: 'largiore vero hereditate indepta'; for its first appearance, see *Recueil des Actes de Charles III le Simple, roi de France (893–923)*, ed. P. Lauer (Paris, 1949), no. 67. On the significance of this, see B. Schneidmüller, 'Regnum und Ducatus: Identität und Integration in der lothringischen Geschichte des 9. bis 11. Jahrhunderts', *Rheinische Vierteljahrsblätter*, li (1987), 81–114, at pp. 104–5.

for that leap from magnate to king or 'prince', but it was not, on its own, sufficient. As Sherlock Holmes remarked, watch-dogs that do not bark are significant. The counts of Vermandois, descendants of Bernard the Carolingian king of Italy, did not bark in 888, that is they made no bid for a crown. Similarly, the young Charles the Simple was passed over as a candidate.[20] Royal blood alone was not sufficient. On the other hand, while Duke Conrad of Franconia must have found his family connection to the Carolingians helpful in becoming king of east Francia in 911, what really counted was the closeness to the centre of royal government that he had assiduously built up in the previous reign. Among the 'kinglets' of 888, neither Odo nor Wido had royal blood.[21]

None the less, royal blood, or a claim to belong to the Carolingian house, mattered to contemporaries and matter to us as such claims reveal something of the categories according to which political actors operated. Many of the claims to belong to the royal house are now hard to establish and seem to have been traced by contemporaries through marital connections. In this period such identity was flexible and hence there was room for manoeuvre. Arnulf of Bavaria was connected to the Carolingian family though the nature of that connection remains elusive. The connection was important enough for a contemporary observer to link it with the fall of Engildeo, margrave of Bavaria, in 895 and the subsequent promotion of Liutpold, Arnulf's father, in his place.[22] It is generally assumed that Liutpold's relationship to King Arnulf was through the latter's mother Liutswinde; the gaps in our evidence mean that this cannot be proven; what cannot be denied, however, is that contemporaries perceived Liutpold as a kinsman of the Carolingians.[23]

This Carolingian connection mattered for Duke Arnulf. He held power in Bavaria because he was the son of his father yet he possessed a Carolingian aura. He bore the name of Arnulf, the seventh-century bishop of Metz who was

20 K. F. Werner, 'Die Nachkommen Karls des Grossen bis um das Jahre 1000 (I.–8. Generation)', *Karl der Grosse. Lebenswerk und Nachleben*, ed. H. Beumann and W. Braunfels, 4 vols (Düsseldorf, 1965–67), iv, 403–79, at p. 436; Brühl, *Deutschland-Frankreich*, p. 371.

21 On the kinglets of 888, see Werner, 'Die Nachkommen', p. 417 and Brühl, *Deutschland-Frankreich*, pp. 370–2. We cannot be certain that Conrad was related to the Carolingians; compare H.-W. Goetz, 'Der letzte "Karolinger"? Die Regierung Konrads I. im Spiegel seiner Urkunden', *Archiv für Diplomatik*, xxvi (1980), 56–125, at p. 60 with the scepticism of D. Jackmann, *The Konradiner: A Study in Genealogical Methodology* (Frankfurt, 1990), pp. 78–9.

22 *Annales Fuldenses*, a. 895, ed. F. Kurze, *MGH SRG* (Hanover, 1891), p. 125. See E. Dümmler, *Geschichte des Ostfränkischen Reiches*, 3 vols (Leipzig, 1887–8), iii, 395 and K. Reindel, *Die Bayerischen Luitpoldinger 893–989. Sammlung und Erläuterung der Quellen* (hereafter *Luitpoldinger*) (Munich, 1953), no. 2, pp. 2–4.

23 As previous note; see also Reindel, *Luitpoldinger*, no. 34, pp. 49–50 and R. Hiestand, 'Pressburg 907. Eine Wende in der Geschichte des ostfränkischen Reiches?', *Zeitschrift für bayerische Landesgeschichte*, lvii (1994), 1–20, at pp. 9–11. C. Bowlus has recently stressed the uncertain nature of the assumptions concerning Liutswinde but his attempts to link Liutpold to the Carolingians via a Welf connection remain speculative: C. Bowlus, *Franks, Moravians and Magyars: The Struggle for the Middle Danube, 788–907* (Philadelphia, 1995), pp. 314–16.

the ancestral holy man of the dynasty. This holy ancestor of the Carolingians was present in contemporaries' minds as the dynasty came under challenge. We find him associated in east Francia with his imperial namesake Arnulf of Carinthia, the one Carolingian king among the new rulers of 888.[24] It was this Arnulf who had appointed Liutpold, his kinsman, to Bavaria and who himself spent much time there. Our Arnulf, the duke of Bavaria, bore the name of the Carolingian ruler who favoured his father and was thus also associated with Arnulf of Metz. The date of birth of Arnulf of Bavaria is unknown but he must have been born in the reign of his namesake.[25] Liutpold was pushing his Carolingian connections up a notch or two. His son bore the name of the reigning Carolingian; this name was not traditionally a kingly name and had been mainly reserved in the ninth century for illegitimate royal sons.[26] King Arnulf himself was illegitimate in that his mother Liutswinde was not married to Carloman. This had not prevented him becoming king, but he himself recognized the power of names to mark out their bearers. His two sons by concubines bore non-royal names while his son by Queen Uota was given the immensely resonant royal name of Louis. In calling his son Arnulf, Liutpold reveals to us not only an awareness of the existence of the contemporary system of name-giving but also how that system could be manipulated. Liutpold was being cannily ambitious. He shrank from giving his son a full-blooded royal name such as Louis, but the name of Arnulf was sufficiently highly charged to mark out the Liutpoldinger of Bavaria as special. Liutpold was nominating his son for great things. Arnulf was to be described, in a text stemming from Regensburg in his own time as duke, as 'stemming from the line of emperors and kings'.[27]

With Boso the situation is more complex. Boso's name is not a Carolingian one, but his relations through marriage with the royal house were intense: his aunt married King Lothar II; his sister married King Charles the Bald; he himself married Ermengard, daughter of the emperor Louis II; finally, in 878 he betrothed his daughter to the son of King Louis the Stammerer.[28] We have here a remarkable tally of four 'direct hits' in three generations. What is particularly striking is the fact that Boso himself married a Carolingian woman. In the mid-

[24] Regino, *Chronicon*, a. 880, p. 116; Poeta Saxo, v, lines 123–48 and 415–20, ed. P. von Winterfeld, *MGH, Poet. Lat.*, iv, 58–9 and 65; O. G. Oexle, 'Die Karolinger und die Stadt des heiligen Arnulf', *Frühmittelalterliche Studien*, i (1967), 250–364, at pp. 361–2; Leyser, *Rule and Conflict in an Early Medieval Society*, p. 6.

[25] K. Reindel, 'Herzog Arnulf und das Regnum Bavariae', *Zeitschrift für bayerische Landesgeschichte*, xvii (1954), 187–252, repr. in *Die Entstehung des deutschen Reiches (Deutschland um 900)*, Wege der Forschung, 1 (Darmstadt, 1956), 213–88, there at p. 235.

[26] R. Le Jan, *Famille et pouvoir dans le monde franc (VIIe–Xe siècle)* (Paris, 1995), p. 204.

[27] 'de progenie imperatorum et regum est ortus', *Fragmentum de Arnulfo duce*, ed. P. Jaffé, *MGH SS*, xvii, 570; K. Schmid, 'Das Problem der Unteilbarkeit des Reiches', *Reich und Kirche vor dem Investiturstreit*, ed. K. Schmid (Sigmaringen, 1985), p. 13.

[28] See the family tree in Le Jan, *Famille et Pouvoir*, p. 455 and *Annales de Saint-Bertin*, a. 878, ed. F. Grat, J. Vieillard, and S. Clemencet (Paris, 1964), p. 229; I find F. Staab's attempt to telescope mid-ninth-century Bosos into one person thought-provoking but unconvincing, Staab, 'Jugement moral et propagande'.

ninth century Carolingian kings had been sparing indeed in giving their daughters in marriage to members of the aristocracy.[29] Boso needed Carolingian permission to marry Ermengard; the death of her father in 875 opened the way for Charles the Bald to grant her to Boso in furtherance of his Italian schemes and of his plans to advance Boso to a very high status indeed.[30] The significance of Ermengard's Carolingian blood for contemporaries is spelled out in Hincmar's waspish account of how Ermengard nagged Boso into claiming a crown: 'She kept on goading him into action. She declared that, as the daughter of the emperor of Italy and the one-time fiancée of the emperor of Greece, she had no wish to go on living unless she could make her husband a king.'[31] Stripped to its essence, this is a description of marriage into the Carolingian house as dynamic motor driving its beneficary upwards to exalted heights.

A variety of evidence survives to testify just how exalted Boso was. According to Regino of Prüm, writing after the whole episode of Boso's kingship had unfolded, Boso was a connoisseur of degrees of legitimacy within the Carolingian family. Regino tells us that Boso despised the sons of Louis the Stammerer as being of inferior birth (*degeneres*). Further, we know that Boso named his son Louis, a resonant full royal name; the message was clear: Boso's son was to be perceived as Carolingian.[32] Boso's wife and son were Carolingian and thus reflected back a form of Carolingian identity on Boso. The roots of this identity lay in the patronage of Boso's master, Charles the Bald. He had not only showered offices upon Boso, he had turned him into what we might call an honorary Carolingian. He had granted him a Carolingian woman as his wife; further, Charles had him stand as godfather to his son by Richildis, Boso's sister.[33] Boso was woven into the great web of ritual and commemoration that Charles spun as representation of his kingship before his own followers and before God. In 875 Charles issued a charter for St Denis when he visited the great abbey to celebrate Easter. Charles charged the monks to keep seven lamps burning before the altar of the Trinity, the space behind which he had chosen to be the location of his tomb; these lamps were for his father and mother, himself, his first wife, his second wife (Richildis, sister of Boso), his children, and for Boso together with his late follower Wido and other unnamed followers.[34] As so

---

29 Le Jan, *Famille et pouvoir*, p. 300.
30 Despite Hincmar's hostile account in *Annales de Saint-Bertin, a.* 876, p. 201, it is impossible to imagine the marriage taking place without Charles the Bald's consent; see Regino, *Chronicon, a.* 877, p. 113.
31 *Annales de Saint-Bertin, a.* 879, p. 239; translation from *The Annals of St-Bertin*, ed. and trans. J. L. Nelson (Manchester, 1991), p. 219.
32 Regino, *Chronicon, a.* 879, p. 114; this had not, however, prevented Boso from earlier betrothing his daughter to one of them, see n. 28 above. On Boso's name for his son see Le Jan, *Famille et pouvoir*, p. 205.
33 *Annales de Saint-Bertin, a.* 877, p. 211; on Boso's offices and ducal crown, *ibid., a.* 876, p. 200.
34 *Recueil des actes de Charles II le Chauve, roi de France*, ed. G. Tessier, 3 vols (Paris, 1940–55), ii, no. 379 and cf. no. 471; E. Ewig, 'Remarques sur la stipulation de la prière dans les chartes de Charles le Chauve', *Mélanges J. Stiennon* (Paris, 1982), pp. 221–33.

often in representations of Carolingian royalty, the aristocracy shares in the special status of the kings by being enfolded in the prayers and commemoration in this sacred site.[35] But the site was a royal abbey; Charles' thinking, as revealed in the charter, was essentially dynastic; he spent the Easter season at Saint Denis with his pregnant queen.[36] Only two followers were singled out by name in the commemoration arrangements: Wido and Boso. Wido was dead; Charles had already taken steps to have him commemorated in 869. Boso, however, was very much alive and was to be closely associated with Charles and his family in other royal charters.[37]

Charles' determination to marginalize his son by his first marriage by confining him to Italy together with the fact that Richildis was bearing sickly sons meant that Boso's closeness to the royal house was of potentially enormous significance.[38] Could Charles have been contemplating naming Boso as successor? Charles had forged bonds of kinship to bring Boso into the royal family. What this shows us is that while contemporaries believed in categories of ancestry and blood they were not prisoners of them; they knew that kinship could be artificial as well as natural; categories of ancestry and blood could be skilfully manipulated. The fact that Boso, like Liutpold, gave his son a Carolingian name shows that this system was understood by contemporaries.

Whatever claims to quasi-royal authority Boso and Arnulf may have possessed, such claims had to be activated. Neither man could rely on some inevitable historical process to carry him from the ranks of the nobility to the heights of royalty. What triggered their claims? Their bids for promotion were not in fact inevitable; they were not the product of securely based territorial powers and fixed identities. Both men faced being driven from a privileged position at the political centre to a peripheral status and their response was to proclaim a new centre.[39] These men were driven by pressure.

Boso's great patron had been Charles the Bald. After Charles' death in 877, he retained close links with Charles' son and successor Louis the Stammerer but he was not able to reproduce the same uniquely privileged relationship, though he tried hard to do so.[40] Even as his charters proclaimed that they were issued at the request of Boso, Louis did not single out Boso as someone to be prayed for. Instead, the spiritual beneficiaries of a charter for abbot Geilo, issued at the request of Boso, were Louis's father Charles the Bald and his mother Ermen-

[35] J. L. Nelson, *Charles the Bald* (London and New York, 1992), pp. 246–7; J. L. Nelson, *The Frankish World, 750–900* (London and Rio Grande, 1996), pp. 99–131.

[36] *Annales de Saint-Bertin, a.* 875, p. 197.

[37] *Recueil des actes de Charles II le Chauve*, ii, no. 325, no. 378, no. 444; see Ewig, 'Remarques sur la stipulation de la prière dans les chartes de Charles le Chauve', p. 225.

[38] On Charles' plans for Louis and the open succession, Nelson, *Charles the Bald*, p. 250.

[39] For a classic account of centre–periphery relations, see C. Geertz, 'Centers, Kings and Charisma: Reflections on the Symbolics of Power', in C. Geertz, *Local Knowledge. Further Essays in Interpretive Anthropology* (New York, 1983), pp. 121–46.

[40] *Annales de Saint-Bertin, a.* 878, pp. 229–30.

trude as well as his own wife and offspring.[41] Boso's sister had been Charles' second wife; Louis' mother was Charles' first wife, and so his dynastic focus necessarily shifted away from Boso. The political landscape was shifting. On Louis' accession in 877 Archbishop Hincmar of Reims had identified six great magnates with whom Louis had to come to terms, but by the time of Louis' death in early 879 only three of that sextet were still enjoying royal favour.[42] Boso was one of the three survivors, but how long could he maintain his position? The death of Louis the Stammerer triggered a succession crisis that posed the twin threats of division of the kingdom and intervention by the kings of east Francia.[43] Such threats were dangerous for great magnates such as Boso because their high position was founded on a delicate network of patronage and favour. K. F. Werner has characterized Boso's energetic cultivation of Charles the Bald, Louis the Stammerer, and the papacy as 'completely opportunistic', but Boso had to run like this in order to keep still.[44] It was only through enjoying exalted patronage that magnates could rise above their peers and their own competitive kinsfolk.[45] Boso had risen spectacularly high. He had nowhere to go but down.

As the spring and summer of 879 wore on, the political situation grew more complex with a very real prospect looming up of those parts of the kingdom where Boso held *honores* being auctioned off to Louis the Younger, the east Frankish king.[46] Amidst uncertainty and complicated manoeuvring Boso prepared to transform himself. In a charter of July 879, his *intitulatio* reads 'I Boso, by the grace of God that which I am (Ego Boso, Dei gratia id quod sum).' Copious reference is also made here to his wife's Carolingian status: she is referred to as 'proles imperialis'.[47] Boso was here deploying language of transformation, transformation through grace and through a good marriage. He was taking out political insurance and he cashed in the policy in October 879. In

---

41 See the charters of Louis the Stammerer in *Recueil des actes de Louis II le Bègue, Louis III et Carloman II, rois de France*, ed. R.-H. Bautier *et al.* (Paris, 1978), no. 27 and cf. no. 20.
42 Contrast the roll-call of magnates in Hincmar's *Ad Hludowicum Balbum regem*, c. 7, *PL*, cxxv, cols 986–7, written in 877, with that in *Annales de Saint-Bertin, a.* 879, p. 234.
43 *Annales de Saint-Bertin, a.* 879, pp. 234–9; K. F. Werner, 'Abt Gauzlin und die westfränkische Reichsteilung von Amiens (Mórz 880)', *Deutsches Archiv für Erforschung des Mittelalters*, xxxv (1979), 395–462.
44 Werner, 'Abt Gauzlin und die westfränkische Reichsteilung', p. 425.
45 S. Airlie, 'The Aristocracy', *New Cambridge Medieval History II c.700–c.900*, ed. R. McKitterick (Cambridge, 1995), pp. 431–50, at pp. 443–8.
46 *Annales de Saint-Bertin, a.* 879, pp. 235–8; *Annales Vedastini, a.* 879, pp. 44–5; detailed analysis in Werner, 'Abt Gauzlin'.
47 *Recueil des actes de Rois de Provence (855–928)*, ed. R. Poupardin (Paris, 1920), no. 16; for comment on the language of this charter, see K. Brunner, 'Der fränkische Fürstentitel im neunten und zehnten Jahrhundert', *Intitulatio II. Lateinisch Herrscher- und Fürstentitel im neunten und zehnten Jahrhundert*, ed. H. Wolfram, Mitteilungen des Instituts für österreichische Geschichtsforschung, Ergänzungsband, 24 (1973), pp. 179–340, at pp. 246–54 and Airlie, '*Semper fideles*?', p. 140.

September, Louis the Stammerer's two sons had been crowned and the west Frankish kingdom was divided. Also in that month a new Carolingian prince was born, Charles the Simple, posthumous son of Louis the Stammerer. Boso's king-making ceremonies at Mantaille and Lyons in October were his response: he was the true ruler, and he was as nearly a Carolingian as was possible. It is in this light that we should interpret Regino's remark that Boso despised the sons of Louis the Stammerer as being of inferior, or illegitimate, status.[48] Boso's attitude to them was not consistently this straightforward, but when the chips were down, the expressing of doubts over their status could serve only to enhance Boso's own. Boso was a connoisseur of Carolingian royalty but political upheaval forced him to cease serving it and instead to assume it.

A similar pattern can be detected in the career of Arnulf of Bavaria. To some extent, his situation is more difficult to understand as we do not have a detailed account of his king-making ceremony on which to focus as we do for Boso's 'election' at Mantaille. As we shall see below, the nature of Arnulf's kingship has divided historians. What is perfectly clear, however, is that Arnulf, like Boso, saw a position of high status come under threat; it was under pressure that he reached for grace. If the key event from which Boso's enforced rise stemmed was the death of his patron Charles the Bald, for Arnulf it was the battle of Pressburg (Bratislava) in July 907. Here, a major expedition against the Magyars met catastrophic defeat and a host of Bavarian leaders fell, including the archbishop of Salzburg, the bishops of Freising and Säben, and Arnulf's father, Duke Liutpold.[49] Despite the heaviness of the defeat, Bavaria proved resilient, as witnessed by the fact that Arnulf seems to have inherited his father's power and to have gone on to establish impressive military credentials by inflicting defeats on the Magyars in 909, 910, and 913. This indicates that Bavaria remained a formidable military force and was in no danger of disintegrating under Magyar pressure.[50]

What Pressburg did mark, however, was a change, essentially a decline, in Bavaria's access to the centres of power and patronage in the east Frankish kingdom. Up until his death on the battlefield in 907, Liutpold had appeared frequently in the charters of the east Frankish kings, particularly as 'intervening'

---

[48] '. . . pro nihilo ducens adulescentes filios Ludowici et velut degeneres despiciens . . .', Regino, *Chronicon, a.* 879, p. 114; on the ceremonies at Mantaille and Lyons, see P. E. Schramm, *Kaiser, Könige und Päpste*, 4 vols (Stuttgart, 1968–1971), iv, 249–66.

[49] Sources are conveniently gathered in Reindel, *Luitpoldinger*, no. 45, pp. 62–70; there is some disagreement among modern commentators on the nature and location of the Bavarian military action but all agree on the great scale of the defeat: H. Wolfram, *Grenzen und Räume. Geschichte Österreichs vor seiner Entstehung* (Vienna, 1995), pp. 272–3; K. Brunner, *Herzogtümer und Marken* (Vienna, 1994), p. 53 and Bowlus, *Franks, Moravians and Magyars*, pp. 258–66.

[50] Reindel, *Luitpoldinger*, nos 50, 51 and 54, pp. 93–4, 94–8 and 103–6; Reindel, 'Herzog Arnulf und das Regnum Bavariae', pp. 247–9; Brunner, *Herzogtümer und Marken*, p. 54; the Magyar threat should not, however, be underestimated, see Reuter, *Germany in the Early Middle Ages*, pp. 127–30 for a balanced account.

on behalf of a variety of recipients of royal favour. After Pressburg, Bavarians still benefited from royal charters, but Duke Conrad of Franconia (the future King Conrad I) 'intervened' for them and became the dominant figure at the royal court. Liutpold's son Arnulf is glaringly absent from the charters of Louis the Child.[51] This change in the nature of Bavarian access to the centre, and in the case of Arnulf a probable blocking of such access, was paralleled by a dwindling of visits by the centre to Bavaria. Under the Carolingian rulers Arnulf and Louis the Child, the great power centre of Regensburg was frequently visited, but after 906 Louis the Child turned to the north and west of his kingdom and King Conrad I (911–918) seems to have visited it only once.[52] This is not to say that Conrad was not interested in Bavaria, or indeed in the Liutpoldinger; he married Liutpold's widow and Arnulf probably attended on him in 912.[53] But by 914 Conrad and Arnulf clashed and when Conrad did come to Bavaria he came as an enemy. Three months after ravaging Regensburg, Conrad was at the synod of Hohenaltheim which condemned Arnulf as a rebel. Losing status at the centre of the east Frankish kingdom, Arnulf was driven from his duchy while Conrad sought to woo the churchmen of Bavaria by compensating them for damages sustained in the campaign while deploying ecclesiastical sanctions against Arnulf. Arnulf did not 'rise' to power; he lashed himself to the mast in a storm.[54] Conrad failed to tame Arnulf militarily but his own death in 918 was followed by the bid of Duke Henry of Saxony to become king of the east Frankish realm. This represented a threat of further marginalization for Arnulf.[55]

Neither Boso nor Arnulf should be seen as inevitably rising to royal or quasi-royal status. They were driven to act before they were toppled from Fortune's wheel. We can also find instability, or at least fluidity, at the level of structure. The territorial and familial power-bases of Boso and Arnulf were not as solid or as well-established as one might imagine. Modern historians' labels for Boso, Boso of Provence or of Vienne, obscure the fact that his kingdom was centred round Vienne only by accident. Charles the Bald had installed Boso in Vienne in 871, but Boso's horizons remained those of a member of the

---

51 Arnulf is referred to only once in the charters of Louis the Child, Reindel, *Luitpoldinger*, no. 47, pp. 76–7; on the relative prominence of Liutpold and Conrad in royal charters, see Reindel, 'Herzog Arnulf und das Regnum Bavariae', pp. 237–9 and above all Hiestand, 'Pressburg 907', pp. 5–11.
52 A. Schmid, 'Die Herrschergräber in St Emmeram zu Regensburg', *Deutsches Archiv für Erforschung des Mittelaters*, xxxii (1976), 333–69, at 353–6; Goetz, 'Der letzte "Karolinger"?', pp. 72–90; C. Brühl, *Palatium und Civitas*, 2 vols (Cologne, 1975, 1990), ii, 225.
53 Reindel, *Luitpoldinger*, no. 53, pp. 101–2.
54 *Ibid.*, nos 55, 56 and 57, pp. 107–15; Reindel, 'Herzog Arnulf und das Regnum Bavariae', pp. 257–60; Hiestand, 'Pressburg 907', pp. 15–18; Becher, *Rex, Dux und Gens*, pp. 199–201. Conrad was probably present at the synod of Hohenaltheim which thundered against Arnulf; its proceedings are edited by H. Fuhrmann, *Die Konzilien Deutschlands und Reichsitaliens 916–1001. Teil I, 916–960*, ed. E.-D. Kiehl, *MGH, Concilia*, vi (Hanover, 1987), no. 1, pp.1–40; see especially c. 35, pp. 37–8; commentary in G. Bührer-Thierry, *Évêques et pouvoir dans le royaume de Germanie* (Paris, 1997), 92–104.
55 Hiestand, 'Pressburg 907', p. 4.

Reichsaristokratie.[56] He did not confine himself to Vienne. Instead he pursued interests over the whole of the west Frankish kingdom. He was abbot of St Gaugericus at Cambrai; he assisted Louis the Stammerer in Aquitaine in 872 and became count of Berry; in 875 we find him with Charles the Bald at Saint Denis and then he spent much of 876 in Italy; in 878 he entertained Louis the Stammerer at Troyes.[57] Boso seems in fact to have spent little time in Provence. What counted for him were connections at court and in this he was typical of the high aristocracy of his time. Further, the territories which he controlled at the time of his bid for a crown in 879 did not form a coherent bloc. Territories of Burgundy (including Vienne and Lyon) had undergone a bewildering series of divisions, actual and projected, through the course of the ninth century and were to be subjected to disputed claims in the tenth. There was no fixed region over which Boso could be king.[58] He did not receive complete backing from the area in which his kingship came to be centred. He could not count on family support.[59] Nor did he want to be king of a region. He proclaimed himself to be king, not king of Burgundy-Provence. Boso did not rise on the basis of a prefabricated *regnum.*[60]

Boso, like others among the new rulers, had his roots in the wide Carolingian world, a world that remained frontierless for such great men, though below them deep-rooted regional nobles can be observed.[61] The case of Arnulf and Bavaria may appear different. After all, he was active some decades after the watershed years of 879 and 888. Furthermore, Bavaria was a much more coherent territory than what became Boso's kingdom. Originally a duchy under the rule of the Agilolfings, it had passed into Carolingian hands at the end of the eighth century, but had retained a strong sense of identity in the century that followed. This identity was not merely the residue of older traditions but was actively built up in the ninth century as Bavaria acted as a kingdom or sub-kingdom within the Carolingian empire. The existence of a centre such as Regensburg and the frequent presence after *c.* 850 of Carolingian kings there and elsewhere in Bavaria not only helped focus such identity, but meant that what might seem to

---

[56] *Annales de Saint-Bertin, a.* 871, p. 179.

[57] Bautier, 'Aux origines du royaume de Provence', pp. 44–8.

[58] G. Castelnuovo, 'Les Élites du royaumes de Bourgogne (milieu IXe–milieu Xe siècle)', *La royauté et les élites dans L'Europe carolingienne,* ed. Le Jan, pp. 383–408.

[59] On the 'gaps' in Boso's kingdom, see Bautier, 'Aux origines du royaume de Provence', pp. 50–4. Boso's own brother Richard formed part of his entourage in the summer of 879 while he was preparing his leap from magnate to king, *Recueil des actes des rois de Provence,* no. 16; by 880, however, he had defected back to the Carolingians and was actively campaigning against Boso, *Annales de Saint-Bertin, a.* 880, p. 247. Another brother remained in safe obscurity in Lotharingia and took no part in the high-profile careers of Boso or Richard, Airlie, 'The Aristocracy', p. 447.

[60] Bautier, 'Aux origines du royaume de Provence', pp. 49–50; Castelnuovo, 'Les élites du royaume de Bourgogne', pp. 383–92.

[61] Airlie, 'The Aristocracy', p. 448; Castelnuovo, 'Les élites du royaume de Bourgogne', pp. 392–5, 401; much of Becher, *Rex, Dux und Gens,* makes the same point, e.g. at pp. 19–20, 66–108.

be a peripheral part of the Carolingian world actually enjoyed the benefits of an open frontier to the east as well as access to the key political centre that was the royal court. Bavaria was stable in a way that other duchies in east Francia were not.[62]

Bavaria may have been relatively stable but it was not fixed or static and the Liutpoldinger did not hold power there in unchallenged serenity. The blinding of Engelschalk by members of the Bavarian aristocracy at Regensburg in 893 and the fall of Engildeo in 895 highlight the existence of feuds and resentments in the political landscape.[63] Nor need we assume that all members of the Liutpoldinger family were on the same side. When Otto I struck at Eberhard, Arnulf's son and successor in Bavaria, he granted the duchy to Arnulf's brother Berthold. The parallel with Boso's brother Richard is striking.[64] Bavaria was dynamic and was part of a wider world. This can be observed on various levels. The Miracle-book of St Waldburga, written at the close of the ninth century, reveals that the convent of Monheim in the diocese of Eichstätt attracted high-ranking pilgrims from Bavaria, Alemannia, Franconia, and Swabia; Monheim retained the interest of the Carolingians themselves, including the west Frankish king Charles the Simple. Cultural–religious links remained active and the pilgrimages of the great were not purely religious activities.[65] Other links also remained operative; among the troops gathered at the palace of Altötting in 892 to support King Arnulf's military thrust eastwards were Saxons; the dynamic history of the palace of Altötting itself in this period shows how the re-allocation of fiscal lands meant that royal patronage could still effect shifts in the Bavarian landscape in the late ninth and early tenth century.[66] The bonds of empire functioned.

---

62 A classic statement of this view is Reindel, 'Herzog Arnulf und das Regnum Bavariae', especially at pp. 215–42; lucid summary in Reuter, *Germany in the Early Middle Ages*, pp. 13–14; see also Hiestand, 'Pressburg 907', pp. 3–4. Becher notes that Bavaria was a relatively stable territorial–political entity, *Rex, Dux und Gens*, p. 153, but his book's demonstration of the fragility of Saxon identity surely has implications for our understanding of the other duchies. On the role of Regensburg in this region see P. Schmid, *Regensburg. Stadt der Könige und bayerischen Herzöge im Mittelalter* (Kallmunz, 1977) and Brühl, *Palatium und Civitas*, ii, 219–55 and on the relations between centres and peripheries in the Carolingian empire, see J. Smith, 'Fines Imperii: the Marches', *New Cambridge Medieval Medieval History II c.700– c.900*, ed. McKitterick, pp. 169–89.

63 *Annales Fuldenses*, a. 893, a. 895, pp. 122, 125; cf. Reindel, 'Herzog Arnulf und das Regnum Bavariae', pp. 239–41 and Bowlus, *Franks, Moravians and Magyars*, pp. 268–318.

64 J. Fried, *Der Weg in die Geschichte. Die Ursprünge Deutschlands bis 1024*(Frankfurt, 1994), p. 492; on Berthold's connections among the aristocracy, Althoff, *Amicitiae und Pacta*, pp. 342–4.

65 A. Bauch, *Ein bayerisches Mirakelbuch aus der Karolingerzeit. Die Monheimer Walpurgis-Wunder des Priesters Wolfhard* (Regensburg, 1979), pp. 124–35; see also the perceptive review of this by J. L. Nelson, *Journal of Ecclesiastical History*, xxxiii (1982), 117–19.

66 Becher, *Rex, Dux und Gens*, p. 152; Bowlus, *Franks, Moravians and Magyars*, pp. 226–7; on Altötting, W. Störmer, 'Die Anfänge des karolingischen Pfalzstifts Altötting', *Ecclesia*

Arnulf and the Liutpoldinger fit into this dynamic and not entirely stable world. We should not think of Bavaria as a closed, solid base that was ready to give Arnulf power and which gave that power a neat definition. Liutpold should certainly be seen as belonging to, or as aspiring to belong to, the *Reichsaristokratie* and Arnulf should probably be seen in this light too. Liutpold acted as patron for men outside Bavaria and Arnulf's *intitulatio* in a remarkable charter describes him as 'duke of the Bavarians and adjacent regions'. Arnulf certainly had ambitions in Italy.[67] Most important, the nature of Arnulf's rule in Bavaria remains more obscure or ambiguous than one might think. His father Liutpold certainly bestrode Bavaria with the power of a duke but he may not officially have held such a title.[68] Like his father, Arnulf was a dominant figure in Bavaria, but it is possible that he did not become duke until some years after the battle of Pressburg. His view of his status appears to have been lofty; we have already seen that his title in one charter reads 'Arnulf by the divine ordaining of providence duke (*dux*) of the Bavarians and of the adjacent regions' and he addresses 'bishops, counts, and leaders of this kingdom'. Much of this charter smacks of royalty, though Arnulf's title is firmly non-royal. It is, however, a difficult charter to date and may not reveal Arnulf's fully fledged ducal status in 908 (its nominal date) but may reflect the status he won through military prowess up to 913.[69] If the charter reveals that Arnulf's view of his status was nearly royal, that makes it easier to believe that he and his supporters might well have seen in the uncertainty following the death of King Conrad I an opportunity for Arnulf to have become king in east Francia. That is to say, he did not aim merely at regal status in Bavaria, but to become king of the Reich. The prospect of Conrad being succeeded by the Saxon duke Henry did not bode well for Arnulf's relations with the royal centre; making his own bid for the crown himself would resolve that problem. The sources do not permit us to give a definite ruling on the events of 918–919, but the care Henry took both to subdue Arnulf militarily and to accommodate him politically points to Arnulf's kingship being seen as a definite possibility in contemporary eyes.[70]

et Regnum: Beiträge zur Geschichte von Kirche, Recht und Staat im Mittelalter. Festschrift für Franz-Josef Schmale zu seinem 65. Geburtstag, ed. D. Berg and H.-W. Goetz (Bochum, 1989), pp. 61–71 and cf. Wolfram, *Grenzen und Räume*, p. 197.

67 Reindel, *Luitpoldinger*, no. 10 (Liutpold), no. 48 (Arnulf), p. 15, pp. 77–80; Reindel, 'Herzog Arnulf und das Regnum Bavariae', pp. 256, 272, 278.

68 Reindel, *Luitpoldinger*, no. 45, p.70; Reindel, 'Herzog Arnulf und das Regnum Bavariae', p. 242; Brunner, *Herzogtümer und Marken*, p. 50.

69 *Reindel, Luitpoldinger*, no. 48, pp. 77–80; Reindel, 'Herzog Arnulf und das Regnum Bavariae', pp. 242–6. Reuter offers lucid commentary on the charter but is perhaps too confident of its dating from 908, *Germany in the Early Middle Ages*, p. 130; for a wider discussion of this document and its context, see Brunner, 'Der fränkische Fürstentitel im neunten und zehnten Jahrhundert', pp. 243–6, Hiestand, 'Pressburg 907', pp. 14–15 and Becher, *Rex, Dux und Gens*, pp. 199–200.

70 The key source here is the entry at the year 920 (for 919) in the Salzburg annals: 'Bawarii sponte se reddiderunt Arnolfo duci et regnare eum fecerunt in regno Teutonicorum',

More could be said about the careers of both Arnulf and Boso. They both took care, for example, to ensure that churchmen played a key role in the legitimation of the special status of their rule.[71] Arnulf and Boso experienced different fates and acted in rather different landscapes. One might argue that Boso's career made Arnulf's possible and that constitutes a gap between them that makes comparison difficult. Despite all this, we have seen that comparison can be fruitful. Both men, like the other new rulers of the era, faced problems as well as opportunities. In responding to these problems, they found that they had to create themselves as a new type of ruler. If the principalities that emerged in the wake of the crisis of Carolingian legitimacy were indeed improvisations, they were so not in the sense of being the cadenzas of a classical concerto, but were perhaps closer to the uncomfortable sounds of bebop in jazz, the frantic product of driven men.[72]

Annales ex Annalibus Iuvavensibus antiquis excerpti, ed. H. Bresslau, *MGH SS*, xxx (Leipzig, 1934), p. 742; these annals are brought together with other relevant sources in Reindel, *Luitpoldinger*, no. 61, pp. 119–31. The Salzburg entry is, however, particularly problematic, not least because the phrase 'in regno Teutonicorum' seems anachronistic and may stem from the twelfth-century copyist rather than faithfully reflect tenth-century terminology; among the vast literature the most helpful commentary can be found in Reindel, 'Herzog Arnulf und das Regnum Bavariae', pp. 260–74; H. Beumann, 'Die Bedeutung des Kaisertums für die Entstehung der deutschen Nation im Spiegel der Bezeichnungen von Reich und Herrscher', *Aspekte der Nationenbildung im Mittelalter*, edd. H. Beumann and W. Schröder, *Nationes* i (Sigmaringen, 1978), pp. 317–65 and reprinted in Beumann, *Ausgewählte Aufsätze aus den Jahren 1966–1986*, pp. 66–114, there at pp. 94–8; Hiestand, 'Pressburg 907', 19–20; Becher, *Rex, Dux und Gens*, 213–21. There is a clear account of the source-problem and of Arnulf's status in Reuter, *Germany in the Early Middle Ages*, pp. 137–46. The *Fragmentum de Arnulfo duce* (as above n. 27) confines Arnulf to a ducal title but surrounds him with kingly attributes (including royal descent) while systematically denigrating Conrad I and Henry I as unkingly kings; on the importance of this Regensburg text, see Leyser, *Rule and Conflict*, p. 96 and Geary, *Phantoms of Remembrance*, p. 153.

71 On Boso, see Schramm, *Kaiser, Könige und Päpste*, ii, 249–66; on Arnulf, Bührer-Thierry, *Evêques et pouvoir*, pp. 29–31, 47–8, 81–2, 157–60.

72 On contemporary response to bebop as a form of fast and dissonant improvization, see D. Stowe, *Swing Changes: Big Band Jazz in New Deal America* (Cambridge, Mass. and London, 1994), pp. 202–20.

3

Nobility in the Ninth Century

Janet L. Nelson

My aim in this paper is a modest one. By way of a very brief survey of the pre-medieval history of the idea of nobility, and an only slightly less brief account of the appearances of the term *nobilis* and its cognates in capitularies, I want to see something of what the idea of nobility meant to ninth-century lay people by looking through the eyes of three writers working in the generation just after Charlemagne.

1. Late antiquity

It is always as well to start with the Fathers, for it was they who already got under way that synthesis of classical with Christian moral ideas which underlies so much of what was thought and written in the Middle Ages. This is very evidently true in the case of nobility. One form of entrée, or foray, into a large field is to consider the appearances of *nobilis* and related terms in the works of St Jerome, and then in Jerome's Vulgate Bible (the latter not a hard task with the lovely new concordance to hand).[1] In Jerome's works, the terms *nobilis, nobilitas, nobilitare* occur no fewer than 474 times: more even than in Ambrose or Augustine.[2] In Jerome's letters are a number of appearances of a theme that would become a topos: 'noble by birth, but in Christ nobler still'.[3] In a letter to his friend Pammachius, Jerome exclaimed: 'In our times Rome possesses what the world did not know before: then few of the wise or powerful or noble were Christians, now many wise and powerful and noble men are monks – and among them all, my Pammachius is wisest, most powerful, and most noble!' Further ennobling those already noble, Christianity comfortably incorporated traditional Roman notions of family, rank, and office in its own hierarchy of values, while

---

1   B. Fischer, *Novae Concordantiae Bibliorum Sacrorum iuxta Vulgatam versionem critice editam*, 5 vols (Stuttgart-Bad Canstatt, 1977), iii, cols 3334–5 ('nobilis', 'nobiliter').
2   The statistic comes from an unpublished paper by M. R. Salzman, which I gratefully acknowledge here.
3   Jerome, ep. 118.5. Cf. epp. 66.6; 57.12. Jerome employs the theme even more emphatically in writing to women: e.g. epp. 22.11, 39.4, 107.13, 108.1, 123. 1, 130.1. See K. Torjesen, 'In praise of noble women: asceticism, patronage and honor', *Semeia*, lvii (1992), pp. 41–64.

emphasizing the noble virtues of self-discipline and (if in a new sense) public-spiritedness.[4]

In Jerome's Vulgate Bible, there are eighteen occurrences of *nobilis* and its cognates in the Old Testament, seven in the New Testament, and eleven in the two apocryphal but firmly Vulgate books of Maccabees. Briefly, Jerome used the terms *nobilis*, etc in ways that would be thoroughly familiar and intelligible for his late-Roman audience, ways, that is, that blended the moral with the sociological. *Nobilis* meant 'high-minded', but also meant 'of high birth' and 'of high status': someone who was, literally, *well known* amongst his fellows, a notable.[5]

Some examples: in Deuteronomy 1: 15, Moses declares, 'Tulique de tribubus vestris viros sapientes et nobiles et constitui eos principes, tribunos et centuriones' (Authorized Version: 'So I took the chiefs of your tribes, wise men and known, and made them heads over you, captains over thousands and captains over hundreds'). In the final chapter of Proverbs, chapter 31, entitled in the Vulgate, 'Carmen de muliere forti', verse 23 reads: 'Nobilis in portis vir ejus quando sederit cum senatoribus terrae' (AV: 'Her husband is known in the gates when he sitteth among the elders of the land'). Ecclesiastes 10: 16–17 embodies a whole ideology of kingship: 'Vae tibi terra cujus rex puer est et cujus principes mane comedunt. Beata terra cujus rex nobilis est, et cujus principes vescuntur in tempore suo ad reficiendum, et non ad luxuriam' (AV: 'Woe to thee, O land, when thy king is a child, and thy princes eat in the morning. Blessed art thou, O land, when thy king is the son of nobles, and thy princes eat in due season, for strength and not for drunkenness'; New English Bible: 'Woe betide the land when a slave has become its king and its princes feast in the morning. Happy the land when its king is nobly born, and its princes feast at the right time of day, with self-control, and not as drunkards'). The message here is about control and self-control. The advantages of royal adulthood are reinforced by a strength of character that goes with high birth. The king's nobility is inseparably linked with aristocratic discipline.

The New Testament references are fewer, but assume a similar understanding of nobility as denoting high social status. Acts 17: 4, for instance, tells how, after Paul and Silas preached at Thessalonica, 'quidem ex eis crediderunt . . . et mulieres nobiles non paucae' (AV: 'And some of them believed . . . and of the chief women not a few').

Finally, in Maccabees, which, it is worth noting, were among the favourite biblical books of earlier medieval readers and commentators, nobility denotes varying combinations of status, high birth, and moral excellence. 1 Maccabees 1: 7 tells how the dying Alexander the Great 'vocavit pueros suos nobiles qui secum erant nutriti a juventute et divisit illis regnum suum' (New English Bible: 'He summoned his generals, nobles who had been brought up with him from

---

4 Cf. P. Brown, *The Body and Society* (New York, 1988), pp. 341–65.
5 Etymologically, *nobilis*, *nobilitas*, etc., are derived from *noscere*: to know. See *Oxford Classical Dictionary*, *s.v.*

childhood, and divided his empire among them'). The absence of any moral connotation in the term noble here contrasts strikingly with 2 Maccabees 14: 42, describing the death of the Jewish patriot Razis, who committed suicide rather than be arrested by the wicked agent of the Hellenistic ruler Ptolemy: 'gladio se petiit, eligens nobiliter mori potius quam subditus fieri peccatoribus et contra natales suos indignis injuriis agi' (NEB: 'He preferred to die nobly rather than fall into the hands of criminals and be subjected to gross humiliation'). Here Jerome's Latin injects powerful moral force into the original.

Before leaving late antiquity, I shall draw attention to the sole appearance of the term 'noble' in the Rule of St Benedict: 'Si quis forte de nobilibus offerit filium suum Deo in monasterio, si ipse puer minor aetate est, parentes eius faciant petitionem . . . et cum oblatione ipsam petitionem et manum pueri involant in palla altaris, et sic eum offerant.'[6] There was a clear connexion between the practice of child oblation and high social rank.

2. The Capitularies

Appearances of *nobilis* and its cognates in Carolingian capitularies are not numerous.[7] This is not surprising: after all, it is well-known that *Lex Salica* contains no mention of a nobility, and that may be linked, in turn, with the fact that noble vocabulary appears extremely seldom in the Theodosian Code.[8] In Roman as in Frankish law, the only recognized legal categories were free and unfree.[9] *Nobilis*, in other words, was not a Roman-legal term. This makes it the more interesting that among the references which do occur in capitularies, a disproportionate number are in those from east of the Rhine,[10] including some pertaining to the Saxons.[11]

Technically, then, Thegan was right when he said of Louis the Pious to Ebbo of Reims, 'Fecit te liberum, non nobilem, quod impossibile est [He made you free, but not noble because that is impossible].'[12] But this was a legalistic, and highly personalized, remark. Few made the ascent, as Ebbo had, from serf to *potens*. Relevant again is the distinction between social and legal status. For, by

---

6 *Regula Benedicti* , c. 59, ed. A. de Vogüé and J. Neufville, 3 vols, Sources chrétiennes, 182 (Paris, 1972), ii, 632; trans. in *The Rule of St Benedict*, ed. and trans. J. McCann (London, 1952), p. 135.

7 See Appendix 1. This list is indicative rather than fully comprehensive.

8 D. Schlinkert, *Ordo Senatoriu: und nobilitas. Die Konstitution des Senatsadels in der Spätantike*, Hermes Einzelschriften, 72 (Stuttgart, 1996), p. 72.

9 Gaius, *Institutiones*, I, 9, which must slightly qualify the argument of T. Reuter, 'The End of Carolingian Military Expansion', in *Charlemagne's Heir: New Perspectives on the Reign of Louis the Pious*, ed. P. Godman and R. Collins (Oxford, 1991), pp. 301–495, at p. 401.

10 Appendix 1, nos. 5, 6, 12.

11 Appendix 1, nos. 3, 4.

12 Thegan, *Vita Hludowici imperatoris*, c. 44, ed. E. Tremp, *MGH SRG*, NS lxiv (Hanover, 1995), 232. The fundamental studies remain J. Martindale, 'The French Aristocracy in the Early Middle Ages: A Reappraisal', *Past and Present*, lxxv (1977), 5–45, repr. in Martin-

the eighth century at any rate, _nobilis_ appears in Frankish narrative sources with a clear sense of acknowledged social rank. The Continuator of Fredegar, for instance, adds the term to the _Liber Historiae Francorum_'s descriptions of 'the Frank' Bodilo whom King Childebert II flogged _contra legem_, and of Ansegisel, father of Pippin of Herstal.[13] Thegan wrote as a noble for nobles: the parvenu Ebbo, the fall-guy of 834, was an easy target – and the exception that proved the rule. Thegan's audience of noble _potentes_ could take the character-assassination of Ebbo on board, and nod smugly.

The capitulary references make sense in this context. Monks knew the difference between nobles and others;[14] and everyone knew what it meant to say that noble men should learn their law in full.[15] _Nobilis_ occurs in reference to child oblates, following c. 59 of the Rule of St Benedict,[16] suggesting a link between oblation and noble rank which was notably explicit in the famous, contested case of the Saxon noble Gottschalk.[17] It occurs in references to women and marriage.[18] With this may be linked the association of nobility with women in narrative sources: in the _Liber Historiae Francorum_, for instance, it is the married-in women of the Pippinids that attract the label _nobilis_, or even _nobilissima_, while Thegan stresses the nobility of Louis the Pious's mother, Hildegard.[19] This reflects the huge contribution of these women as heiresses and power-brokers to the Carolingians' rise and the maintenance of their regime. Greater emphasis on Christian marriage is a further corollary. You will not get a

dale's collected papers, _Status, Authority and Regional Power_ (Aldershot, 1995), esp. pp. 5, 16–17, and H.-W. Goetz, ' "Nobilis". Der Adel im Selbstverständnis der Karolingerzeit', _Vierteljahrschrift für Sozial- und Wirtschaftsgeschichte_, lxx (1983), 153–91. Cf. R. Le Jan, _Famille et pouvoir dans le monde franc_ (Paris, 1995), pp. 31–4; and the chapters by S. Airlie, 'The Aristocracy', and H.-W. Goetz, 'Social and Military Institutions', in _The New Cambridge Medieval History_, ed. R. McKitterick, ii (Cambridge, 1995), 431–50, 451–80, both with excellent bibliographies. For incisive comments on the semantic range of _nobilis_, whether as adjective or noun, in various literary, epigraphic, and diplomatic contexts, D. Bullough, 'Charlemagne and his Achievement in the Light of Recent Research', _EHR_, lxxxv (1970), 59–105, at pp. 76–84, is still invaluable.

13 Continuator of Fredegar, c. 2, ed. J. M. Wallace-Hadrill, _The Fourth Book of the Chronicle of Fredegar with its Continuations_ (London, 1960), p. 81; cf. _Liber Historiae Francorum_, c. 45, ed. B. Brusch, _MGH, Scriptores rerum Merovingicarum_, ii (Hanover, 1888), 318; Continuator of Fredegar, c. 3, p. 83; cf. _Liber Historiae Francorum_, c. 46, p. 320.

14 Appendix 1, no. 11.

15 Appendix 1, no. 9; cf. nos. 7 and 10.

16 Appendix 1, nos. 2, 8.

17 See M. de Jong, _In Samuel's Image: Child Oblation in the Early Medieval West_ (Leiden, 1996), pp. 77–91. In the Saxon context, _libertas_ meant noble status. Cf. below, p. 47.

18 Appendix 1, nos. 1, 13, 16. Cf. _MGH, Capitularia_, ii, no. 252, c. 4, p. 207, for the case of a noble Frank trying to repudiate his Saxon wife, on the grounds that they do not use the same laws. As pointed out by M. Becher, _Rex, Dux und Gens: Untersuchungen zur Entstehung des sächsischen Herzogtums im 9. und 10. Jahrhundert_ (Husum, 1996), p. 96, this husband may have 'instrumentalized' gentile difference in order to get rid of his wife.

19 _Liber Historiae Francorum_, c. 48, p. 323; cf. Continuator of Fredegar, c. 5, pp. 84–5; Thegan, _Vita Hludowici imperatoris_, c. 2, in _MGH SRG_, NS lxiv, 176: '. . . nobilissimi generis Suauorum puella'.

nobility reckoned by the social rank of *both* parents, still less will you get hypergamy working (that is where men can enhance their nobility by marrying up), unless you bother about monogamy and about women living up to their rank. Finally, nobility appears occasionally in ninth-century capitularies as the identifying trait of the Frankish élite.[20]

3. Three ninth-century writers

I have chosen Einhard, Dhuoda, and Nithard, all of them lay persons, writing primarily for lay audiences, though as both the Capitulary of Coulaines and Nithard explicitly say, *nobiles* included men of both clerical and lay *ordines*. In Einhard's *Vita Karoli*, there are just four occurrences of *nobilis* and its cognates. In Dhuoda's *Manual for William*, there are seven. In Nithard's *Histories*, there are eleven.[21]

In these three authors, the vocabulary of nobility is used alongside other terms that denote élite groups: *Franci, fideles, proceres, primates, comilitones*, and so on. The term noble in some contexts keeps its classical sense, in Einhard, who quotes Charlemagne's epitaph with its praise of his 'nobly amplifying his empire' (Appendix 2, A4) and in Dhuoda, who reminds her son to 'hide your nobility in lowliness of mind' (Appendix 2, B3). Further, both Einhard and especially Nithard are strikingly conscious of the Saxons' nobility, both as a legal category, and as a sociological phenomenon (Appendix 2, A2; C6, 7, 8). The Saxons thus paradoxically become for Nithard a veritable model of nobility (C6). Despite all this, all three lay writers inhabit a Frankish world of thought and language in which the terms noble and nobility denoted traits of moral character and social standing assumed to have a fundamental significance. This is clear in Einhard's references to the *nobiles ex Francia* who troubled Carloman's peace and quiet in Italy, and to Queen Hildegard's 'outstanding nobility' (Appendix 2, A1 and 3). It is clearer still in Dhuoda's reference to King Charles the Bald's 'double nobility', and in her dismissal of the utility of 'noble blood' if the blood is tainted by immoral conduct: bad blood corrupts the body itself (Appendix 2, B1, 4). Tellingly, she addresses her son as 'noble boy' at moments of particularly heartfelt concern for his moral well-being: 'oratrix tibi, nobilis

---

20 Appendix 1, nos. 14, 15. Cf. the Ansegis preface, in some manuscripts headed, 'In Christi nomine incipiunt capitula episcoporum regum maximeque omnium nobilium Francorum . . .', ed. G. Schmitz, *Die Kapitulariensammlung des Ansegis, MGH, Capitularia regum Francorum*, NS, i (Hanover, 1996), 431.

21 Appendix 2, using Einhard, *Vita Karoli*, ed. O. Holder-Egger, *MGH SRG* (Hanover, 1911), English translation, P. E. Dutton, *Charlemagne's Courtier. The Complete Einhard* (Peterborough, Ontario, Canada, 1997); Dhuoda, *Liber Manualis*, ed. with French translation by P. Riché, Sources chrétiennes 225 (Paris, 1975), English translation C. Neel, *Handbook for William: A Carolingian Woman's Counsel for her Son* (Lincoln, Nebr., 1991); Nithard, *Historiarum Libri IV*, ed. with French translation by P. Lauer, *Nithard: Histoire des fils de Louis le Pieux* (Paris, 1926), English translation B. Scholz, *Carolingian Chronicles* (Ann Arbor, Mich., 1970).

puer, adsisto in cunctis'; and the final sentence of the book: 'Vale et vige, nobilis puer, semper in Christo' (Appendix 2, B6, 7).

But it is Nithard who reveals in most striking fashion the currency of the idea of nobility as a social rank, and as a collective manifestation of that rank, nowhere clearer than in the controlled discipline (*moderatio*) of the war-game (Appendix 2, C5). The collective sociological sense of nobility is clear in the notion of a regional élite: *tanta nobilitas ex his regionibus* (Appendix 2, C3). The old moral sense of nobility comes across clearly in the description of the brother-kings' *qualitas* and *unanimitas*, their *prudentia* and *eloquentia*, and their *concordia* (Appendix 2, C2): all, says Nithard, *iocunda ac merito notanda*, 'joyful things and well worth noting' – 'noting' both as 'recording' and as 'remarking', the latter recalling the original etymology of 'noble' as 'well-known'. Most significant of all, perhaps, is the political context in which nobility is manifest: in Einhard, by the noble Frankish visitors to Rome who cannot pass up the chance to salute their former lord (Appendix 2, A1); in Nithard, by the king's concern for his nobility, his fear that their lives might be put at risk, and his explicit statement of his own dependence on them (Appendix 2, C2, 3, 10, 11). Nowhere is this clearer than in the passage (C1) where Nithard first introduces Charles's men, and says that their nobility consisted in preferring death to dishonour.[22] Nithard borrowed that idea, partly from the classical notion of dying for one's *patria*, more directly, though, from the Second Book of Maccabees 14: 42.[23] But look how he reinflected it. Charles' men were prepared, not to commit suicide, but to die in battle; and they were willing to die, not to spare themselves subjection to the wicked or torture that derogates from their birth (*contra natales suos*), but to avoid betraying their king.[24] This new nobility, for all its classical and biblical traits, was intimately bound to a political virtue that was both un-classical and un-Maccabaean. What other ninth-century Frankish layfolk thought about nobility we cannot directly know, but for Einhard and Dhuoda, and, especially, Nithard, nobility was never nobler than when displaying its faithfulness to Carolingian kingship.[25]

---

[22] Cf. also C9, on King Louis the German 'nobly . . . yet with lawful slaughter, repressing the rebellious people in Saxony'.

[23] Cf. p. 45, above. The fine paper of Hagen Keller, '*Machabaeorum pugnae*. Zum Stellenwert eines biblischen Vorbilds in Widukinds Deutung der ottonischen Königsherrschaft', in *Iconologia Sacra: Mythos, Bildkunst und Dichtung in der Religions- und Sozialgeschichte Alteuropas. Festschrift für Karl Hauck zum 75. Geburtstag*, ed. H. Keller and N. Staubach (Berlin, N.Y., 1994), pp. 417–37, at 424, n. 47, notes the influence of 2 Macc. 14: 42 on Widukind, *Rerum gestarum Saxonicarum Libri Tres*, iii, 46, ed. P. Hirsch and H. E. Lohmann, *MGH SRG*, 5th edn (Hanover, 1935), p. 127. As far as I know, Nithard's echo of the passage has not previously been noticed.

[24] Interestingly, Hrabanus Maurus in his Commentary on Maccabees, dedicated to Louis the German, did not take the chance to discuss nobility in reference to either 1 Macc. 1: 7 (cf. above, p. 44), or 2 Macc. 14: 42, *PL*, cix, cols 1132, 1254–5, though he did use the latter passage as a springboard for reflections on the permissibility of suicide.

[25] Since completing this paper, I have read K. F. Werner, *La naissance de la noblesse* (Paris, 1998): the conclusions of the above paper accord fairly well with Werner's basic argument.

Appendix

1. Nobility in Carolingian Capitularies

1. *MGH Capitularia*, i, no. 14 (755), c. 15, p. 36: 'ut omnes laici publicas nuptias faciant tam nobiles quam ignobiles'.

2. no. 23 (789), c. 12, p. 63: 'de filiis nobilium qui offeruntur'.

3. no. 27 (797), c. 3, p. 71: 'item placuit omnibus Saxonibus ut ubicumque Franci secundum legem solidos XV solvere debent, ibi nobiliores Saxones solidos XII, ingenui V, liti IIII componant.'

4. no. 27 (797), c. 5, p. 72: 'Si quis de nobilioribus ad placitum mannitus venire contempserit, solidos quatuor componat, ingenui duos, liti unum.'

5. no. 112 (799/800), c. 11, p. 227: 'ut nullus episcopus vel abbas atrahere audeat res nobilium [MS: 'mobilium'!] causa ambitionis, sicut in canone Cartaginense continetur cap. V.'

6. no. 112 (799/800), c. 44, p. 230: 'nullus de nobilibus neque abbas neque presbiter tondeatur antequam examinentur.'

7. no. 36 (802), 17, p. 107: '[in case of applying the 30-year rule relating to the ownership of a church, let the possessor] adhibitis veracibus et nobilibus testibus . . . vindicat.'

8. no. 37 (802), c. 23, p. 108: 'de filiis nobilium vel pauperum qui offeruntur'.

9. no. 60 (802/813), c. 3, p. 147: 'comites quoque et centenarii et ceteri nobiles viri legem suam pleniter discant.'

10. no. 87 (787/813?), c. 2, p. 186: [about church property] 'Ut de rebus earum inquisitio a nobilioribus homines [*sic*] circummanentibus fiat.'

11. no. 170 (817), c. 27, p. 345: 'ut abbas . . . ad portam monasterii cum hospitibus non reficiat; in refectorio autem omnem eis humanitatem manducandi et bibendi exhibeat. Et ipse cum episcopis, abbatibus, canonicis, nobilibus unde reficiuntur causa caritatis sumat.'

12. no. 154 (826/7), c. 9, p. 313: 'Quia ergo constat in aecclesia diversarum conditionum homines esse, ut nobiles et ignobiles, servi, coloni, inquilini et cetera huiuscemodi nomina, oportet ut quicumque eis praelati sunt clerici vel laici, clementer erga eos agant.'

13. no. 196 (829), c. (51), p. 42: 'De nobilibus feminis quae amissis viris repente velantur . . . '.

14. *MGH Capitularia*, ii, no. 254 (Coulaines, 843), p. 254: 'fideles nostri, tam in venerabili ordine clericali quam et inlustres viri in nobili laicali habitu constituti . . . '.

15. no. 272 (Pîtres, 862), p. 305: [on effects of Viking incursions]: 'nobiles nostri et de episcopali ordine et de aliis ordinibus interierunt et capti . . . sunt aut redempti aut interempti.'

16. no. 252 (Tribur, 895), c. 38, p. 235: 'quisquis liber libertam . . . legitime

in matrimonium duxerit, ulterius habere debebit tamquam unam ex nobili genere progenitam.'

2. Nobility in Einhard, Dhuoda, and Nithard

a. Nobility in Einhard's *Vita Karoli*

1. c. 2: [On Carloman after his monastic retirement in 747 to Monte Soracte]: 'Sed cum ex Francia multi nobilium . . . Romam . . . commearent et eum [Karlomannum] velut dominum quondam suum praeterire nollent, otium . . . crebra salutatione interrumpentes locum mutare conpellunt.'

2. c. 8: 'plures tam ex nobilitate Francorum quam Saxonum et functi summis honoribus viri consumpti sunt'.

3. c. 18: [Hildegard] 'praecipue nobilitatis femina'.

4. c. 31: [Charlemagne's epitaph] 'qui regnum Francorum nobiliter ampliavit'.

b. Nobility in Dhuoda's *Liber Manualis*

1. III, 4, p. 148: 'adhuc tene quod est [Karolus] generis ex magno utrumque nobilitatis orto progenie'.

[cf. III, 8, p. 166: 'Inclitos atque praeclaros seniori tuo regiae potestatis eximios parentes atque propinquos, tam ex paternitatis illustrem quam ex matrimonii dignitatum ascendente originem, . . . time, ama, venera et dilige eos . . . .']

2. IV, 7, p. 230: [after talking about rancour and wrath] 'Quod absit a te, nobilis puer!'

3. IV, 8, p. 244: 'in paupertate etenim mentis tuam nobilitatem supplici corde latitare semper'.

4. IV, 8, p. 248: 'Quae utilitas, fili, in sanguine nobili, si propter iniustitias corpus corrumpatur suum, descendens ad corruptionem ut lugeat semper?'

5. V, 1, p. 268: 'Arbor pulcher nobilisque folia gignit nobilia et fructus afert aptos.'

6. IX, 5, p. 334: 'Oratrix tibi, nobilis puer, adsisto in cunctis.'

7. XI, 2, p. 368: 'Vale et vige, nobilis puer, semper in Christo.'

c. Nobility in Nithard's *Histories*

1. II, 4: '[Charles' men] elegerunt potius nobiliter mori quam regem proditum derelinquere.'

2. II, 9: '[Charles and Louis] tam ex sacrosancto ordine episcoporum quam et laicorum viros nobiles, prudentes, benivoles deligant [as envoys].'

3. III, 3: '[Charles said] ut a Mosa usque Sequanam regnum, quod illi dederat, nequaquam congruum videretur, ut illi [i.e. Lodhario] obmitteret, praesertim cum tanta nobilitas illum secuta de his regionibus esset . . . '.

4. III, 6: 'omnemque nobilitatem excedebat fratrum [Charles and Louis] sancta . . . concordia'.

5. *Ibid.*: 'Eratque res [the war-game] digna pro tanta nobilitate nec non et moderatione spectando.'

6. IV, 2: '[Saxones] ab initio tam nobiles quam et ad bella promptissimi multis inditiis persaepe claruerunt.'

7. *Ibid.*: 'Que gens omnis in tribus ordinibus divisa consistit: sunt etenim inter illos qui edhilingui sunt, qui frilingi sunt, qui lazzi illorum lingua dicuntur; Latina vero lingua, hoc sunt: nobiles, ingenuiles atque serviles.'

8. *Ibid.*: 'Sed pars illorum quae nobilis inter illos habetur in duabus partibus in dissensione Lodharii ac fratrum suorum divisa . . . est.'

9. IV, 4: 'Lodhuvicus etenim in Saxonia seditiosos . . . nobiliter, legali tamen cede, compescuit.'

10. *Ibid.*: 'Karolus mandat . . . in meditullio, qua vellet, missi illorum convenissent: non enim se tot nobilium virorum salutem neglegere debere dicebat.'

11. *Ibid.*: 'Erant quidem octoginta electi ex omni multitudine omni nobilitate praestantes, quorum interitus ni praecaveretur, maximam sibi fratrique suo posse inferre iacturam aiebat.'

4

Continuity and Change
in the Tenth-Century Nobility*

Régine Le Jan

'As far back as the memory of man can go, the ancestors of his ancestors were all most noble. There was not one who was unknown as far as his family went, there was not one who could easily be found unworthy of his line. But he surpassed all the rest, apart from the excellence of emperors and kings, in the glory of his talents and in all kinds of intellectual qualities.'[1] Thus Ruotger described the lofty nobility of Bruno, brother of Otto I. That nobility was rooted in the past, but expressed itself in the present through the radiance of the imperial family and the personal qualities of the archbishop. There was no change, then, in the way the tenth-century nobility represented itself. Illustrious ancestors, a noble family, kin, and friends, social recognition, and personal freedom: these were what made a noble in the seventh century as in the tenth. Those were the constants. Yet the political and social context changed in the tenth century. The weakening of royal power, the growth of the principalities, the establishment of a world of castles, all transformed the ways in which power was exercised, and had profound effects on the ruling class. An attempt to assess factors of continuity and factors of change is therefore timely. This is no easy task; however, for the tenth century continues to pose serious problems for modern historians. I shall not go into the debates over the mutation of the year 1000. Instead, I shall address three urgent questions concerning the political and social changes of the tenth century: first, that of the relations between kingship and nobility, second, the transformation of kinship networks, and third, the emergence of the *militia*.

1. Kingship and nobility

Continuities are especially strong in the realm of representation, that is, in ideology. The social order instituted by God at the beginning of time was founded on

---

* I am grateful to Jinty Nelson for translating this paper.

1 Ruotger, *Vita Brunonis*, 1. 2, ed. R. Rau, *Ausgewählte Quellen*, 22, p. 182: 'Attavorum eius attavi usque ad hominem memoriam omnes nobilissimi, nullus in eorum stirpe ignotus, nullus degener facile reperitur, hic tamen omnes, salva augustorum et regum excellentia . . . artium gloria et omnigena animi superabat industria.'

respect for hierarchy, status, and social distinction. It implied and justified the domination of the noblest over the mass of the population. As in earlier times, nobles continued to base their social, political, and economic pre-eminence on birth, illustrious ancestry, and public service.[2] These nobles constituted the Frankish *populus* exalted by the legislators of Pippin III as a Chosen People in the new Prologue to the *Lex Salica*, composed *c*. 763–764. The nobility were thus closely linked to the royal *ministerium* defined by Carolingian bishops at the beginning of the ninth century. The ideology of the eighth and ninth centuries was one of consensus, which bound nobility and royalty together in the same exercise of power.[3] It was this same ideology of consensus that Flodoard and Richer developed in their historical writing. Richer carefully noted that King Ralph 'took counsel with the great men on affairs of state'.[4] But the case of Hagano, which led to the downfall of Charles the Simple in 922, revealed changes that had affected the balance of powers in the preceding decades: by the king's favour, Hagano, a Lotharingian, had entered the royal council, become a *potens*, despite being, so the great men said, 'of obscure birth'.[5] The magnates finally revolted, and chose Robert as king. He was the brother of Odo, the first non-Carolingian king to reign in Francia, from 888 to 898. In fact, what the magnates objected to in 920–922 was the king's claim to choose his counsellors from outside the narrow circle of the high aristocracy of West Francia. Richer also reports how in 939 the magnates of Lotharingia met King Louis IV and bitterly reproached him with having taken all his decisions without seeking counsel. If he listened to their advice, they told him, things would go well for him. That was why they had assembled together to find out what he wanted and take account of his wishes. They were ready, if the king wanted, to help him against his enemies with their counsel and their weapons, on land and on sea.[6] The ideology of consensus was recalled once more; and this would happen over and over again up until the twelfth century. Yet there was a difference of scale compared with the discourse that developed in the ninth century: the magnates were no longer bound to offer aid and counsel by virtue of their fidelity to the king, by the imperative of the *communis utilitas*, or by the application of the law, but

---

2   R. Le Jan, *Famille et pouvoir dans le monde franc (VIIe–Xe siècle). Essai d'anthropologie sociale* (Paris, 1995); and K. F. Werner, *Naissance de la noblesse* (Paris, 1998).

3   J. Hannig, *Consensus fidelium. Frühfeudale Interpretationen des Verhältnisses von Königtum und Adel am Beispiel des Frankenreich und in Italien* (Paderborn, 1989); R. McKitterick, 'L'idéologie politique dans l'historiographie carolingienne', in *La royauté et les élites dans l'Europe carolingienne du début du IXe aux environs de 920*, ed. R. Le Jan (Lille, 1998), pp. 59–70.

4   Richer, *Historiarum Libri IIII*, i, 49, ed. G. Waitz, *MGH SRG* (Hannover, 1877), p. 31: '. . . cum apud principes rem publicam consuleret . . .'

5   Richer, *Historiae*, i. 15, p. 12. Cf. Le Jan, *Famille et pouvoir*, pp. 137–8.

6   Richer, *Historiae*, ii. 16, p. 47: 'Quo tempore Belgicorum principes ad regem conveniunt ac Lauduni apud eum conquerentur, eo quod inconsultus omnia appetat. Si eorum quoque consiliis adquiescat, in bonum exitum res suas deventuras memorant. Ad hoc etiam sese convenisse, ut quid velit eis iniungat, quod cupit ingerat. Si velit, consilio et armis, terra marique, contra hostes sese congressuros.'

rather as the counterpart of their effective participation in royal decision-making. Here we have clearly reached a system of personalized political relationships.

The Carolingians wanted to organize society hierarchically, by relying, at the top, on a few great families from which they chose their brides and whom they associated with them in the exercise of power. In the ninth century, social ascent was achieved through closeness to the king, and through alliances with the royal family.[7] The *domus carolingica*, that is, the lineage organized around the transmission of the *regnum*, thus dominated a vast cognatic *stirps regia*. These great families in their turn commanded extensive networks of kinship and fidelity in a such a way that the whole Carolingian nobility could be thought of, in the end, as a vast *familia*, arranged around the *stirps regia* and the *domus carolingica*. The failure of the Carolingian enterprise was sealed, first in 879, then, definitively, in 888, when the princes elected kings who did not belong to the Carolingian family. As Stuart Airlie has shown,[8] the Carolingians had continued to impose the idea that their power was 'natural', even though they themselves had emerged from the aristocracy and seized that power in a *coup d'état* which swept aside four centuries of Merovingian legitimacy. Thanks to the Church and the magnates of the kingdom, this noble family had become the royal family. It had then sought its legitimacy in God, and it adopted a new royal title, *gratia Dei rex*, which invoked the divine grace attached to this king's power. The Carolingians had also developed the ideology and the practice of consensus. In 879 first of all, then in 888, consensus was broken. The magnates reckoned that the Carolingian family no longer had a monopoly of royal power, even if no one challenged its legitimacy. Gradually and inexorably, all the princely families came to assert a power similar to that of the king, a power founded in God.

Of course, the events of 888 can also be explained in terms of the rise of the princes and the progressive weakening of royal power. The Carolingian social and political system rested on the king's ability to control the distribution of *honores*, and to impose spatial mobility on the magnates. It also depended on the stability of large aristocratic groupings which saw to the advancement of their members through the acquisition of wealth and *honores*. Aristocrats needed to exercise public offices, whether secular or ecclesiastical, and to accumulate these, in order to protect themselves against the dangers posed by partible inheritance. The Carolingians allowed the development of a good deal of heritable succession to *honores*, together with much spatial mobility for the élite: thanks to these features, all the sons of nobles could aspire to the exercise of high office in the king's service.

In the second half of the ninth century, the direct inheritance of office became established. The accumulation of hereditary offices, the rooting of great families

---

7   Le Jan, *Famille et pouvoir*, pp. 293–4; S. Airlie, ' *"Semper fideles"*? Loyauté envers les Carolingiens comme constituant de l'identité aristocratique', in *La royauté*, ed. Le Jan, p. 133.

8   ' *"Semper fideles"*?', *ibid.*, pp. 129–43.

in specific regions and their bonding with the local nobility, along with the development of vassalage, combined to bring about the appearance of principalities in France, and of duchies in Germany and Italy. The great magnates now had enough political weight to make their choice of ruler, and to impose the idea that from now on, should they so wish, they could elect as king one of their own number. At the same time, they came to think of their heritable offices as constituting a family *honor* which the individual magnate held, as it were, in trust. They claimed, within their principalities, a power similar in nature to the king's: a power no longer delegated by the king, but deriving from God and from the virtues of the noble family. When Bernard 'Hairy-Paws' dared to call himself *gratia Dei comes*, first in 864, then in 886, a decisive frontier had been crossed.[9] Other princes more or less quickly followed his example;[10] parallel with this, the count's wife came to be entitled 'countess' (*comitissa*). These titles expressed a claim to power based on divine approval and familial legitimacy: a dynastic power.[11]

A century and a half later, around 1025, Adalbero, the aged bishop of Laon, who is often seen as a product of Carolingian tradition and who was himself descended from an illustrious family related to the Carolingians,[12] identified himself with the spirit of 888: 'What ancestry confers, no act of will can break. Noble lineages descend from royal blood. For kings and princes [alike], praise of their high qualities is fitting.'[13] Here we can see the development of an idea, in part, but only in part, derived from ninth-century ideology: the idea of a high nobility allied to the royal family, closely linked with the king, and justifying its superiority in terms of birth. Yet Adalbero was also a man of his own time: it was no longer the age of a single royal family but an age of princes. The Carolingian dynasty had been replaced by a number of royal families. Tenth-century kings all attached themselves to the Carolingians through women,[14] nor did they fail to exploit their distinguished origins when necessary. According to Wipo, Conrad II was descended from the Merovingians through his mother, and Wipo

---

9   C. Lauranson-Rosaz, 'Le roi et les grands dans l'Aquitaine carolingienne', in *La royauté*, ed. Le Jan, p. 428.

10 Le Jan, *Famille et pouvoir*, p. 139; cf. Airlie, 'Semper fideles?', p. 140.

11 Le Jan, 'L'épouse du comte: évolution d'un modèle et idéologie du pouvoir', in *Femmes et pouvoirs des femmes*, ed. S. Lebecq, R. Le Jan, A. Dierkens, and J.-M. Sansterre (Lille, 1999), pp. 70–1.

12 C. Carozzi, Introduction to his edition of Adalbero of Laon, *Carmen ad Rotbertum regem: poème au roi Robert* (Paris, 1979), pp. xv–xvi.

13 Adalbero, *Carmen*, Carozzi, ed., p. 2: 'Quod genus attribuit, dirimit non ulla voluntas./ Stemmata nobilium descendunt sanguine regum./ Regibus et ducibus bona est de virtute locutum.'

14 Robert the Pious claimed descent from the Carolingians through his great-grandmother Beatrice of Vermandois, daughter of Count Herbert I and mother of Duke Hugh the Great. Rudolf of Burgundy was the son of the Carolingian princess Mathilda, daughter of Louis IV 'd'Outremer'. Wipo claimed Merovingian descent for the Salians, and Carolingian descent for Conrad's wife Gisela. Conrad's mother was certainly an Ottonian princess.

also stressed the Carolingian descent of Conrad's wife.[15] The princes were not far behind. Witger, a monk of St-Bertin, wrote a genealogy of the counts of Flanders, in which he grafted the descent-line of the Marquis Arnulf onto that of the Carolingians in order to underline the royal origin of the Flemish comital dynasty.[16] In a cognatic kinship system, marital alliances were essential: it was through these that all the princely and ducal dynasties of the eleventh century could boast of belonging to one of the *stirpes regiae*.

2. From mobility to putting down roots

The hallmark of the Carolingian aristocracy was its spatial mobility. Obviously, the princes who were elected kings in 879 and 888 had been, until then, representatives of the regional aristocracies, Provençal, Burgundian, and Italian respectively, who had chosen them.[17] Before being elected, they had held high office in what were to become their kingdoms: Boso had been duke in Provence, the Rudolfians had been counts and marquises in Transjuran Burgundy, while Berengar's family had held the marquisate of Friuli. Their kindreds were, nonetheless, of Frankish origin, and Austrasian–Frankish in particular. They enjoyed closeness to the Carolingian family – the famous *Königsnähe* identified by German historians – and moreover, as Guido Castelnuovo has shown for the Bosonids and Rudolfians, they constituted 'an imperial élite' that originally lacked any firm anchorage in a particular territory.[18] All of them had shared in those organized migrations of Frankish élites towards the regions that Carolingian kings wanted to control more firmly. Berengar's father, Eberhard, had been among those members of the Frankish–Alamannic élite who had been drawn into Italy in successive waves after the conquest of the Lombard kingdom.[19] Eberhard arrived in Friuli in 828, and died there sometime after 865.[20] His brother Adalard was abbot of St-Bertin in north-western Francia, while another brother, Berengar, had been marquis of Gothia. Eberhard's son, Berengar,

---

15 Wipo, *Gesta Chuonradi II imperatoris*, ed. H. Bresslau, *MGH SRG*, 61 (Hannover 1915), pp. 24–5.
16 E. Freise, 'Die *Genealogia Arnulfi comitis* des Priesters Witgers', *Frühmittelalterliche Studien*, xxiii (1989), 203–43.
17 For Burgundy, see G. Castelnuovo, 'Les élites des royaumes de Bourgogne (milieu IXe–milieu Xe siècle)', in *La royauté*, ed. Le Jan, pp. 383–408.
18 *Ibid.*, p. 391.
19 See G. Tellenbach, 'Der großfränkischer Adel und die Regierung Italiens in der Blütezeit des Karolingerreichs', *Studien und Vorarbeiten zur Geschichte des großfränkischen und frühdeutschen Adels* (Freiburg im Breisgau, 1957), pp. 40–70; E. Hlawitschka, *Franken, Alemanen und Burgunder in Oberitalien (774–962)* (Freiburg im Breisgau, 1960). One member of the Widonid family became duke of Spoleto in 842, another, king of Italy in 889: Hlawitschka, 'Die Widonen im Dukat von Spoleto', in *idem, Stirps regia. Forschungen zu Königtum und Führungsschichten im früheren Mittelalter. Ausgewählte Aufsätze, Festgabe zu seinem 60. Geburtstag*, ed. G. Thomas and W. Giese (Frankfurt, 1988), pp. 125–58.
20 C. La Rocca and L. Provero, 'The Dead and their Gifts: The Will of Eberhard, Count of

succeeded his father in charge of the march of Friuli, while his brothers' careers
unfolded in northern Francia. It was in northern Francia, too, that Eberhard and
his wife Gisela founded the abbey of Cysoing, where both were to be buried.[21]
At the same time, in the mid-ninth century, Charles the Bald's kingdom
attracted members of the Frankish–Alamannic élite.[22] The Bosonids and
Rudolfians came from further east, to be installed by King Charles during the
860s and 870s in Burgundy and Provence where they were to control extensive
territories. Yet they did not forget their Lotharingian and Alemannic links.[23] In
Aquitaine, the descendants of Count William, founder of the monastery of Gel-
lone, were to found a principality: they too were scions of an illustrious Frankish
family. Bernard of Septimania, son of Count William, became a marquis in the
Midi, but his shifts of political allegiance, which finally led to his execution by
Charles the Bald in 844, were those of a member of the imperial aristocracy, not
of a southern prince.[24] Élite mobility was maintained by the system of the distribution of *honores*: that system remained in the king's hands, so long as he
respected, broadly speaking, aristocratic expectations of inheriting high office.
The quest for *honores*, associated with succession that was partly heritable and
with élite mobility, thus sustained large, dispersed, aristocratic groups while
safeguarding royal pre-eminence. In the second half of the ninth century, these
groups were destabilized by the break-up of the empire and the firm establishment of inherited office. These led to the formation and taking root of lineages
established in a particular territory, and anchored in *honores* that had become
patrimonies. French scholars have coined the apt term topolineages (*topo-
lignages*).

Between the ninth century and the eleventh, the ruling class was remarkably
stable. The princes and dukes of the tenth and eleventh centuries were the
descendants of families that had belonged to the ninth-century imperial aristocracy, just as the castellan families of the eleventh century were often descended
from the families of ninth-century royal vassals.[25] But the ruling class's
biological continuity with the Carolingian past should not disguise a transformation in the ways in which power was transmitted, and the effects of that transformation on the organization of aristocratic groups. Princely families became

Friuli, and his Wife Gisela, Daughter of Louis the Pious', in *Rituals of Power in Late
Antiquity and the Early Middle Ages*, ed. F. Theuws and J. L. Nelson (Leiden, 2000) forthcoming. See also H. Krahwinkler, *Friaul im Frühmittelalter. Geschichte einer Region
vom Ende des fünften bis zum Ende des zehnten Jahrhunderts* (Vienna, Cologne, Weimar,
1992).

[21] *Cartulaire de l'abbaye de Cysoing*, ed. I. de Coussemaker (Lille, 1886). Cf. Le Jan,
Famille et pouvoir, p. 443.

[22] J. L. Nelson, 'The Frankish Kingdoms, 814–898: The West', in *The New Cambridge
Medieval History*, ii, ed. R. McKitterick (Cambridge, 1995), pp. 110–41, esp. 134.

[23] G. Castelnuovo, 'Les élites', p. 389.

[24] On Bernard's Frankish and empire-wide concerns, see M. Aurell, 'Pouvoir et parenté dans
la marche hispanique', in *La royauté*, ed. Le Jan, pp. 471–2.

[25] K. F. Werner, 'Untersuchungen zur Frühzeit des französischen Fürstentums I–VI', *Die*

increasingly organized in lineages around an *honor* that was now a patrimony, handed on to the next in line. Some families began by continuing to partition their lands between heirs, as the comital family of Flanders did on the death of Count Baldwin II in 918: the heart of the principality went to the eldest son, Arnulf, while the more recently acquired southern part went to the younger son, Adalulf. The Vermandois family did something similar in 945.[26] Other families, in Catalonia, for instance, experimented with joint succession.[27] In the end, the princely *honor* ceased to be divided, passing instead to one son, usually the eldest. The topolineage system thus led to the exclusion from the inheritance of younger sons and also of daughters. The unity of the descent-group emerged strengthened, however, because all the children played essential roles in the stability of the lineage's power: the younger sons were endowed with strategic offices, often in the Church, which provided a source of power and prestige but at the same time gave the man concerned a stake in the *honor*, inside as well as outside it. Thus Liudolf, the third son of Adalbert of Vermandois was consecrated bishop of Noyon in 979, while Robert, brother of Duke Richard II of Normandy, became archbishop of Rouen. Guy, brother of Count Geoffrey 'Greymantle' of Anjou, became abbot of Cormery, Villeloin, Ferrières, and St-Aubin, Angers: in other words, of the main abbeys in the *honor* of Anjou. The marriages of the daughters also served to strengthen the lineage's influence, both outside the *honor* through the creation of homogamic alliances, and within it, through hypergamy, with selected vassals marrying 'up' into the comital family, their fidelity to that family being thus guaranteed. Daughters' marriages were arranged more systematically than before, to multiply allies and strengthen the lineage's security. The progressive establishment of direct inheritance, and a growing emphasis on an ecclesiastically approved model of conjugal marriage and family, brought about a redefinition of the way in which rights were transmitted, of marriage strategies, and, last but not least, of woman's place in the family. The role of the noble wife in the bosom of the household was redefined.[28] She shared more directly in the household's management, and, above all, she became the chief vector of nobility, the mirror in which the family saw itself reflected. This occurred within a matrimonial system that sons experienced as increasingly rigid, constrained as each one was to find himself a wife at least as noble as himself, in order to reinforce his family's nobility.[29]

Kinship structures remained, nevertheless, fundamentally cognatic. On the one hand, the transmission of the aristocratic *honor* was not patrilineal but

Welt als Geschichte, 18 (1958), pp. 256–89, 19 (1959), pp. 146–93, and 20 (1960), pp. 87–119; *idem*, 'Bedeutende Adelsfamilien im Reich Karls des Grossen', in *Karl der Grosse*, ed. W. Braunfels, 5 vols (Düsseldorf, 1965–67), i, 83–142; *idem*, 'Die Nachkommen Karls des Grossen (1–8 Generation), *Karl der Grosse*, iv, 403–82.

26 Le Jan, *Famille et pouvoir*, pp. 420–1.

27 M. Aurell, *Les noces du comte: mariage et pouvoir en Catalogne (785–1213)* (Paris, 1995), pp. 44–51.

28 Le Jan, 'L'épouse du comte', p. 72.

29 Le Jan, *Famille et pouvoir*, pp. 302–5; Aurell, *Les noces*, pp. 69–78.

direct: that is to say, in the absence of sons, daughters could inherit, even if male domination meant that their rights were exercised by their husbands. Further, the new descent system implied a more intensive use of kin ties. The lineage had to concentrate its forces in order to strengthen itself, and guarantee its internal and external security. Counts often entrusted kinsmen with offices which they themselves could not take on, especially ecclesiastical ones. To this end, they drew on cousinly ties. The most dynamic lineages were precisely those that managed to bring together a cognatic kindred in a single, hierarchical, group. Thus Wichman of Hamaland and Thierry of West Frisia, Count Arnulf I of Flanders' sons-in-law, became in succession counts of Ghent. Topolineages became integral parts of extended family networks that remained centred on alliance and hypergamy, and on a large cognatic kindred. They exploited cousinly links which contributed to their strength and offered security.

The closing down of the market in *honores*, and the turning of public offices into patrimonies, thus brought about the formation of topolineages using bonds of fidelity and kinship to consolidate their positions and to compete with each other. The system favoured the mobility of younger sons: Otto and Odo-Henry, younger sons of Hugh the Great, made their careers in Burgundy, while Otto of Warcq, younger son of Adalbert of Vermandois, set off for the Meuse valley where his descendants founded the line of the counts of Chiny.[30] At the same time, each lineage group was constantly liable to suffer tensions that inexorably led to the formation of secondary lineages, formed, in their turn, out of family power based on patrimonial lands, with a resultant tendency to become independent. In northern France, for instance, advocacies played an important role as local anchorage-points: this happened in the case of the family of Everard of Arques, sprung from the line of Eberhard and Gisela, and linked with the family of the counts of Flanders, who held the advocacy of St-Bertin at Arques.

Further south, kindreds clustered around castles. Such was the case with the Harduin-Corbo family, who can be traced from the ninth century in the Loire valley region, and who held the castle of Rochecorbon from the end of the tenth century on.[31] The process of power-fragmentation characteristic of the tenth and eleventh centuries was therefore intimately linked to lineage organization. From the 960s and 970s onwards, this process speeded up at every level. At the top, the emergence of second-generation principalities went along with the emancipation of viscounties, some of which turned into counties while others kept their old titles. Once having turned their *honor* into a patrimony, some viscounts benefited from favourable circumstances (minorities, wars) to extend their own domination, to reject princely tutelage, and to found principalities of their own. This trend reached the level of the castellany which had meanwhile become the underpinning of comital power. Thus the feudal system pushed to the extreme the principle of fidelity on which the Carolingians had tried to base their regime.

---

[30] M. Bur, *Chronique ou livre de fondation du monastère de Mouzon* (Paris, 1989), pp. 120–6; Le Jan, *Famille et pouvoir*, p. 424.
[31] Le Jan, *Famille et pouvoir*, p. 423.

Feudalism led to the development of centrifugal forces, to the fragmentation of powers, and to the segmentation of society. Some lineages resisted more successfully than others. With favourable conditions, the most dynamic lineages developed a sense of dynasty, and relied on kin ties and fidelity to control wider territories and power-centres. The Arnulfian counts of Flanders expressed their dynastic self-consciousness in their choice of the abbeys of St-Peter, Ghent, and St-Bertin as family mausolea, in their choices of names for their children, and in a genealogy. Operating with hierarchical bonds of fidelity and with real or artificial kinship ties, they entrenched their power.

3. Nobility and *militia*

In the 920s, Abbot Odo of Cluny wrote the Life of Gerald of Aurillac, a count of the later ninth century. Gerald had succeeded in living a holy life without quitting the *militia saecularis*. 'God', wrote Odo, 'allowed the layman who belonged to the *ordo pugnatorum* to bear the sword in order to defend the unarmed people, just as, so it is written, every evening the innocent flock is defended from the wolves. For he who fights for God in driving out the mad throughout the whole land does not obscure his glory.'[32] Odo defined the mission of the *armata militia*: to protect the Church, to bear the sword against its enemies, to rein in the pride of violent men, to fight against those who unjustly oppress the peasantry and the *inermes*, to look after orphans and widows.[33] The Life of Gerald of Aurillac quickly became a veritable mirror of knighthood. The *ordo pugnatorum* takes us back to the tripartite Indo-European scheme that had emerged at Auxerre with the monk Haimo in the 860s.[34] In his Commentary on the Book of Revelation, Haimo put forward the idea of a society of three orders, the *sacerdotes*, the *milites*, and the *agricultores*.[35] Before 875, Heric of Auxerre in his Miracles of St Germain had reworked this into three functions: the *milites* became the *belligerantes*, the *agricultores* the *agricolantes*, and the *sacerdotes* the *oratores*.[36] It was Dominique Iogna-Prat's achievement to reveal the importance of the school of Auxerre for the emergence of the threefold scheme at the level of learned discourse in the 860s. Iogna-Prat has also shown how this

---

32 *Vita sancti Geraldi Auriliacensis comitis*, PL 133, col. 647C: 'Licuit igitur laico homini in ordine pugnatorum posito gladium portare, ut inerme vulgus velut innocuum pecus a lupis, ut scriptum est, vespertinis defensaret . . . Non igitur obscurat ejus gloriam, quod pro causa Dei pugnavit . . . .' The essential study of the Life of Gerald is S. Airlie, 'The Anxiety of Sanctity: St Gerald of Aurillac and his Maker', *Journal of Ecclesiastical History*, xliii (1992), pp. 372–95; cf. also J. L. Nelson, 'Monks, Secular Men and Masculinity c. 900', in *Masculinity in Medieval Europe*, ed. D. Hadley (London, 1999), pp. 121–42.

33 *PL* 133, col. 616.

34 D. Iogna-Prat, 'L'école d'Auxerre et le schéma des trois ordres', *Annales E.S.C.*, 1986/1, 101–26.

35 *Idem*, 'L'école', p. 108.

36 *Miracula sancti Germani*: ' . . . aliis belligerantibus, agricolantis aliis, terius ordo estis'; cited in Iogna-Prat, 'L'école', p. 113.

scheme was derived from classical Roman tradition by way of the learned com-
mentaries of Isidore of Seville and Hrabanus Maurus.[37] In our present context, it
is worth asking how far the appearance and diffusion of a scheme known to
ninth-century scholars corresponded to actual social change: in other words, did
the militarization of the nobility come about as a consequence of transformations in the way power was exercised, or was the tripartite scheme a response to
the appearance of a new *militia* which then developed further in the tenth
century?

The magnates of the Carolingian period wore the *cingulum militiae* which
had symbolized the exercise of high public office since Roman times.[38] Like
Roman nobles, they bore an *honor*, they wielded a public responsibility, or if
they themselves did not, then their ancestors had done so before them. They
carried the title *illuster vir*, or sometimes *nobilissimus*, titles of Roman origin.[39]
Yet it is difficult to agree entirely with K. F. Werner when he claims that the
medieval nobility was nothing but the heir to the senatorial nobility of Rome,[40] a
militia defined by high-level service to the state.[41] True, all nobles did share, in
some sense, in the wielding of public authority. Yet, even taking account of the
fact that the status derived from holding *honores* could be inherited, the concept
of *militia* hardly seems to have operated before the 820s, precisely, perhaps,
because it was bound up with service, whereas nobility entailed social liberty.
Carolingian nobility was closely linked to Carolingian rulership, but it was not
created by kings, as Stuart Airlie has rightly observed.[42] Even if nobility served
the king, it was not merely 'post-Roman'. Certain institutions seem to have been
directly inherited from Rome, and the written word played an important role in
the ninth century.[43]

Social practice, and the way in which power was exercised, had nevertheless
changed profoundly since Roman times. If we define early medieval society
following Max Weber's model,[44] it combined institutional forms inherited from

---

[37] Iogna-Prat, 'L'école', pp. 101–26.

[38] J. M. Van Winter, '*Cingulum militiae*', *Revue d'histoire du droit*, xliv (1976), 1–92; J.
Flori, *L'essor de la chevalerie XIe–XIIe siècle* (Paris, 1986), p. 216; K. F. Werner, 'Du
nouveau sur un vieux thème. Les origines de la "noblesse" et de la "chevalerie" ',
Comptes rendus de l'Académie des Inscriptions et Belles-Lettres 1985, pp. 186–200, and
idem, *Naissance de la noblesse* (Paris, 1998).

[39] See R. Le Jan, '*Domnus, illuster, nobilissimus*: les mutations du pouvoir au Xe siècle', in
Haut Moyen Age: culture, éducation et société, études offertes à Pierre Riché , ed. M. Sot
(Paris, 1990), pp. 439–49.

[40] Note, in this context, that the nobility of Rome was not limited to senators but also
included *curiales* who served the state at their level, that is, the city: cf. J. Durliat, 'Les
fonctions publiques de la noblesse gallo-franque (481–561)', in *Nobilitas*, ed. O. G. Oexle
and W. Paravicini (Göttingen, 1997), pp. 194–201.

[41] Werner, 'Du nouveau sur un vieux thème', pp. 186–200.

[42] Airlie, ' "*Semper fideles*"?', p. 139.

[43] R. McKitterick, *The Carolingians and the Written Word* (Cambridge, 1989).

[44] M. Weber, *Economy and Society: An Outline of Interpretive Sociology*, ed. G. Roth and C.
Wittich (Berkeley, 1978), pp. 212–301.

Rome with a personalized social practice based on exchange.[45] The weakening
of the state since Antiquity had caused political relationships to be reconstructed, in a crucially significant way, on a logic of personalized bonds that
entailed reciprocity: an exchange of services between groups and individuals.[46]
The medieval nobility thus did not have the same hierarchy of values as the
Roman nobility: it sought not *otium* but battle. It was fundamentally a warrior-
nobility which justified its supremacy through its capacity to give protection, a
capacity transmitted by birth, and symbolized by the bearing of arms.[47] The
wielding of weapons was a social marker, and having armed force at one's
disposal conferred an instrument of fierce competition for power and prestige:
the military obligations owed by free men to the king were linked with the
nobles' right to have their own military retinues. The keystone of social organization was the power to protect, intrinsically linked with the right to a warrior-
retinue and to the personal obligations that united the leader to his companions.[48] King and nobles shared this capacity to protect – the very essence of
their honour in a system where public and private were profoundly intermeshed.
The symbolic force of richly decorated weapons, carriers of social superiority,
and the ceremonial investiture with weapons that marked young men's entry
into the adult world and their access to power,[49] together with the ritual of the
gift of weapons to the strongest: all this typified a society in which personalized
relationships assured social reproduction. Forms of ritual and gestural communication made it possible to reaffirm differences of social status.[50] By holding

45 On gifts, see M. Mauss, 'Essai sur le don', *Sociologie et anthropologie* (Paris, 1950),
English translation by I. Cunnison, *The Gift: Forms and Functions of Exchange in
Archaic Societies* (New York, 1967); also A. Weiner, *Inalienable Possessions. The
Paradox of Keeping-While-Giving* (Berkeley, 1992); recently M. Godelier, *L'énigme du
don* (Paris, 1996); and forthcoming papers in *Rituals of Power*, ed. Theuws and Nelson.
46 G. Althoff, *Spielregeln der Politik im Mittelalter. Kommunikation in Friede und Fehde*
(Darmstadt, 1997), p. 2.
47 J. Durliat, 'Les fonctions publiques', p. 203, has also stressed that the *Franci* of the early
Merovingian period included all those men who received a salary from army funds. But he
puts too much emphasis on the institutional side; that is only one aspect of the early medieval system of social and political relationships. On the importance of weapons, see Le
Jan, 'The Conferring of Weapons and Frankish Rituals of Power: Continuity and Change
in the Carolingian Period', in *Rituals of Power*, ed. Theuws and Nelson.
48 Le Jan, 'Satellites et bandes armées dans le monde franc (VIIe–Xe siècle)', *Le combattant
au Moyen Age* (Nantes, 1991), pp. 97–107.
49 K. Leyser, 'Early Medieval Canon Law and the Beginnings of Knighthood', in *Institu-
tionen, Kultur und Gesellschaft im Mittelalter: Festschrift für J. Fleckenstein*, ed. L.
Fenske, W. Rösener, and T. Zotz (Sigmaringen, 1984), pp. 553–60, repr. in Leyser, *Communications and Power in Medieval Europe*, i, *The Carolingian and Ottonian Centuries*,
ed. T. Reuter (London, 1994), 51–72; J. L. Nelson, 'Ninth-Century Knighthood: The Evidence of Nithard', repr. in Nelson, *The Frankish World* (London, 1996), pp. 84–5; R. Le
Jan, 'The Conferring of Weapons' forthcoming.
50 Leyser, 'Ritual, Ceremony and Gesture: Ottonian Germany', in *idem, Communications
and Power*, i, 89–213; G. Althoff, 'Demonstration und Inszenierung', *Spielregeln der
Politik*, pp. 229–57.

high office, the magnates of the Carolingian period enrolled themselves in a continuation of the Roman nobility. In a system of representation characteristic of élites, the nobles participated in the common weal,[51] that is, in a form of public service. But the Carolingian nobility defined itself first and foremost by the bearing of weapons: it offered protection, and it issued orders. This is well illustrated by the portrait of a Carolingian count painted on the wall of the church of St Benedict at Malles, in the Tyrol (Plate 2). This man carries a sword, symbol of his noble status and function. From the end of the eighth century onwards, the noble who voluntarily abandoned the world to offer himself to Christ's service laid his weapons on the altar. The laying down of the *cingulum militiae* meant the renunciation of all public functions.[52] In the ninth century, men subjected to public penance likewise had to divest themselves of their sword-belt, and lay their arms on the altar.[53] The Church thus kept for itself the right to make nobles renounce their public functions the moment they infringed the rules of their rank.

There is no mistaking the importance of the reign of Louis the Pious in the evolution of thought about the social orders (*ordines*). A threefold social ranking appeared as early as 828, in the work of the monk Ermold the Black.[54] At least twice in his poem on Louis the Pious, Ermold classed society in three orders, even though he did not quite use that noun. The first time was in the context of Louis's coronation by his father at Aachen in 813, the second was in the context of the pope's arrival at Reims in 816. In both cases, the emperor went ahead of, and 'ordered' (*ordinat*) the clergy (*clerus*), the people (*plebs/populus*), and the nobility (*proceres/senatus*).[55] The emperor was the *pater*, as Ermold stresses, and so was placed in a special *ordo* of his own. Tripartition is certainly here: the nobility is clearly distinguished from the *populus*. This offers a contrast to eighth-century historiography which had been careful to shelter behind the single term *populus*, even when that meant, in reality, nothing other than the nobility.

During these same years, Carolingian churchmen took account of the nobility's military calling, and integrated that into the ideology they were constructing. To this end, they took up the old concept of *militia*, well-known to all learned persons in the early Middle Ages. At the same time, though, they transformed it in a double sense: they centred it on the notion of warfare, and they christianized it. Isidore of Seville had provided them with some help, for in his *Etymologies* he had assembled a mass of ancient learning, and, in ix. 3, he

---

[51] J. L. Nelson, 'Kingship and Royal Government', in *The New Cambridge Medieval History*, ii, ed. R. McKitterick, 383–430, at p. 427.
[52] *Concilium Triburiense* (895), ed. A. Boretius, *MGH Capitularia*, ii, no. 252, c. 55, p. 242.
[53] Le Jan, 'The Conferring of Weapons'.
[54] I am grateful to Bruno Judic for drawing my attention to these passages.
[55] Ermold, *In Honorem Hludowici. Poème sur Louis le Pieux*, ed. E. Faral (Paris, 1964), line 703, p. 56: 'Gaudet Aquis clerus, plebs, proceresque pater; line 858, p. 68: 'Tunc Hludowicus agens clerum populumque senatum . . .'

dealt with the meanings of the vocabulary of *militia*.[56] He had retained a purely military significance for the term, which anyway fitted its etymology. Likewise, in ix, 4, describing the three tribes of Rome that Romulus had created, Isidore defined these as *senatores, milites,* and *plebes*.[57] Hrabanus Maurus in his *De universo*, dedicated to King Louis the German in 844, repeated this same three-fold division, together with all Isidore had had to say about *militia*. But Hrabanus left out the prohibition against slaves taking up arms.[58] In fact, slaves were sometimes enrolled in armies in the Carolingian period, when the father-land was in danger. In his *De procinctu romanae militiae*, Hrabanus quoted Vegetius' *The Art of War*, one of the ancient works most often made use of in the ninth century. Hrabanus went into detail on the training of a Roman soldier and on the various types of military service. He added, in Carolingian vein, that the *miles* was a warrior who fought 'for his liberty, for the life of his king, for the defence of the fatherland, and for the maintenance of fidelity to the prince'.[59] Here too Hrabanus amplified his chapter on the Roman *militia* with a Christian interpretation. He asserted that *milites Christi* were those who fought against the Devil and struggled bravely against the vices. Eternal life, not earthly reward, was promised to those who fought the good fight. Hrabanus cited 2 Corinthians 10: 4, in which St Paul contrasted carnal weapons with spiritual ones.[60] The whole of Christian society was thus defined as a *militia*. The two *militiae* joined in the same warfare, each with its own distinct kinds of weapons. Dhuoda meant something similar when she told her son William 'to make every effort, in the midst of his fellow-warriors serving in this life, to conduct himself in such a way that he might in the end deserve, along with the servants and soldiers of Christ, through service not separately but collectively performed, to rejoin as a free man with free men that kingdom which has no end.'[61] Shortly before Dhuoda wrote, Hrabanus, in his *De laudibus sanctae crucis*, had depicted Louis the Pious as a *miles Christi*.[62] The emperor was a warrior of Christ, fighting for justice and peace, and for the realization of the *imperium christianum*, by the weapons of faith. Sedulius Scottus, in his *Liber de rectoribus christianis*, written in the 860s, insists on the fact that the just and good ruler who wishes to conquer triumphantly and to evade spiritual and carnal enemies, must be equipped and

---

56 Isidore, *Etymologiae*, ix. 3, 'De regnis militiaeque vocabulis', ed. M. Reydellet (Paris, 1984), pp. 118–55.

57 *Ibid.*, ix. 4, p. 161.

58 Hrabanus, *De Universo*, xvi, c. 3, *PL* 111, col. 452D.

59 Hrabanus, *De procinctu romanae militiae*, ed. E. Dümmler, *Zeitschrift für deutschen Altertum*, xii (1879), 443–51.

60 Hrabanus, *De Universo*, xvi, c. 3, *PL* 111, col. 451C.

61 Dhuoda, *Liber Manualis. Manuel pour mon fils*, iv. 4, ed. and trans. P. Riché, pp. 28–32: 'Volo ut talem te inter comilitones temporaliter servientium satagere studeas, qualiter in finem, cum famulis et militibus Christi, non sequestrate sed pluraliter militando, liber cum liberis merearis iungi in regnum sine fine mansurum.'

62 E. Sears, 'Louis the Pious as *Miles Christi*. The dedicatory image in Hrabanus Maurus's *De laudibus sanctae crucis*', in *Charlemagne's Heir: New Perspectives on the Reign of Louis the Pious*, ed. P. Godman and R. Collins (Oxford 1990), pp. 605–28.

protected by spiritual weapons, that he must win, clad in the breastplate of justice, the helmet of hope, and protected by the shield of faith, and must gleam with the sword of the divine word.[63]

After Louis the Pious's reign, the ideology of consensus which had characterized the Carolingian period since at least the 720s found its complement in a christological ideology in which Carolingian royal power derived from Christ's. In his *Poem in Honour of Louis*, Ermold has Charlemagne say: 'Francia gave me birth, Christ granted me honour, and gave me the kingdom of my forefathers to hold.'[64] A little later, Louis declares: 'I know that it is not through my merits but through His grace that Christ has made me heir to the throne.'[65] The representations of the king in the great bibles of Charles the Bald's reign belong in the same ideological context. Warriors carry the weapons given to the king by Christ so that he can defend the Church, and protect the poor and oppressed. The king who bears the weapons of the Spirit as well as those of the flesh is positioned immediately beneath Christ the King. Under the orders of the emperor, as *miles Christi*, the *militia saecularis* also has its part in the divine plan, alongside the *militia Christi* comprising clergy and monks.[66] In the clergy's ideological construct, the *militia* is associated with the royal *ministerium* and with the bringing into existence of the *imperium christianum*. The definition of a *militia* in the service of the *imperium christianum* was thus the idealized version of that hierarchy of protections and services on which Carolingian social order rested. The Carolingian nobility became a christian *militia*, which with its weapons served the order willed by God.

Ermold's threefold division of society was not really a functional one. The monks Haymo and Heiric of Auxerre wanted to take account of the social realities of their times. They defined true functions. In their presentation, compared with Ermold's, the clergy had not changed; but the magnates had become the warriors while the *populus/plebs* were the cultivators of the soil. Under Louis the Pious, too, Jonas of Orléans wrote that 'the lay order must serve justice, and defend by arms the peace of Holy Church'.[67] He maintained the fiction of the *populus* in arms. Yet in the troubled political conditions of the late ninth century, simple free men more and more often gave up joining the army, and warfare increasingly became the exclusive business of the nobles and their warrior-retinues, Heiric's *belligerantes*, or Odo of Cluny's *ordo pugnatorum*. We should consider whether the ninth- and tenth-century clergy's use of the

63 Sedulius Scottus, *De rectoribus christianis*, c. xvi, ed. S. Hellmann (Munich, 1906), p. 76.

64 Ermold, *In Honorem Hludowici*, p. 56: 'Francia me genuit, Christus concessit honorem,/ Regna paterna mihi Christus habere dedit.'

65 *Ibid.*, lines 946–7, p. 74: 'Non meritis, ut credo, meis, sed patris honorem/ Hunc miserans Christus cessit habere mihi.'

66 On the two *militiae*, see D. Barthélemy, 'La chevalerie carolingienne', in *La royauté*, ed. Le Jan, pp. 171–5, repr. in Barthélemy, *La mutation féodale a-t-elle eu lieu?* (Paris, 1998), pp. 210–14.

67 Jonas, *Historia Translationis Sancti Huberti*, PL 106, col. 389: '[ut] laicus ordo justitiae deserviret, atque armis pacem sanctae ecclesiae defenderet.'

concept of *militia* was not a way of grasping the idea of a group of powerful men rather than the idea of a nobility, for Carolingian nobles were not called *milites* any more than were their tenth-century counterparts.

The diffusion of the term *miles/milites* in tenth-century narrative sources and charters was linked with a change in the way power was exercised. To control the countryside and impose their 'protection' upon it, the powerful relied increasingly on castles. Castle-building increased rapidly after *c.* 930 and still more so after *c.* 960. Their lords had them guarded by companies of warriors, *milites*, defined, therefore, by their military function. The *milites* formed part of the *armata militia*. But were they noble? Scholars for some time now have been able to show that the Carolingian nobility was split into two distinct levels, that of the magnates (*proceres*) and that of the 'other nobles'. It is also clear that there was biological continuity between that upper level and the *domini* of the eleventh century, that is, the counts, advocates, and greater lords.[68] On that basis, Dominique Barthélemy has pushed the continuity argument just as far as it will go, claiming that the appearance of the word *milites* means no more than a change in the terminology used for the lower level of the nobility, that *miles* essentially denotes an honourable status, a kind of nobility, rather than any 'professional' function.[69] True, there was much continuity in the ruling class between the ninth century and the eleventh, and it is quite likely that tenth-century *milites* were recruited from the descendants of the (lower-level) Carolingian nobility. Yet that does not mean that all nobles became *milies*, nor that peasants too could not be involved, still, in military service.

At the level of representation, moreover, the *milites*, even if they were noble, were not defined either by birth or by their membership of a noble family. They were defined by their military profession, in the service of magnates. It was that which gave them the chance to rise in the social scale, and made the group open to those who were not noble. The late ninth and tenth centuries were certainly a period of social mobility. Magnate pressure no longer spared the lower-level nobles, many of whom signed up as *milites* to escape falling into ignoble dependance. Conversely, peasants might try to get involved in military service in order to rise in the social scale, but this did not ennoble them. At this social level, both 'descending' nobles and 'rising' peasants were subjected to the same demands of service as vassals. Since noble status entailed arms-bearing and power-wielding, military service could hardly be synonymous with nobility. In the ninth century, not everyone who served a magnate in a military capacity was himself noble. Despite royal legislation, the magnates' armed retinues continued to be largely composed of warriors without land-holdings of their own. Hence these men lived off the *stipendia* their lay or ecclesiastical masters granted them. They received bed and board, and, above all, the indispensable equipment of the

---

[68] Cf. above, n. 25.

[69] D. Barthélemy, 'Chevalerie et noblesse autour de l'an mil', *La mutation de l'an mil a-t-elle eu lieu?* (Paris, 1998), pp. 219–91, esp. 272–5.

professional warrior, namely weapons and a horse.[70] Likewise, many tenth-century *milites* were nothing but mercenaries or unbeneficed warriors: they could not be recognized as nobles if they were not born noble and did not enjoy social freedom.

Social freedom was certainly linked with possession of public land, 'noble' land, and allowed a man to exercise rights conferred by his birth. Jean-Pierre Poly has suggested that at the beginning of the sixth century, the *terra salica* mentioned in *Lex Salica*, which passed only to the males of the family, was a kind of tax-exempt military holding, which each soldier–farmer received from the Roman state as the price of his military service. This is an interesting hypothesis, even though it looks more likely that it was the *gens* which received lands, on condition that the leading men distributed it among the warriors and family-heads. Nobles, for their part, also received benefices carved out of public lands.[71] All this might confirm the essentially military calling of the entire Frankish people, and especially its nobility. The possession of noble land would thus be the lowest common denominator – common, that is, to all nobles great and small. It also symbolized the social freedom that allowed such men to develop the characteristic traits passed down to them by their ancestors, the power to give protection and to maintain order and peace. Nobility and knighthood are not antithetical concepts, but neither do they wholly coincide.

It is equally clear that there is a sharp contradiction between the ideological scheme which assigned to knights the classical peace-making virtues possessed by kings and nobles, and the actual conduct of these knights which was ceaselessly denounced by monks. The system in fact generated violence, for the castles that were the sources of power and profits were also the stakes for which men engaged in *werrae*, private wars. The weakness of all central authority allowed all kinds of physical assaults and acts of brigandage to be perpetrated. Monks fervently denounced disorders that seemed to presage the end of the world. While bishops receded into the background, monks assumed the right to control the internal functioning of aristocratic society, increasingly imposing on the world their own penitential and monastic vision. Hugh of Fleury's portrait of King Robert the Pious recalls Odo's portrait of Count Gerald: these knights of the *saeculum* were soldiers of Christ. Without quitting the world, they put their swords at the Church's service and agreed to submit to the harsh demands of monastic penance. There, perhaps, lies the biggest change of all.

---

[70] T. Reuter, 'Plunder and Tribute in the Carolingian Empire', *TRHS*, xxxv (1985), 75–94.
[71] J.-P. Poly, *Les féodalités* (Paris, 1998), p. 80.

5

The Old English Vocabulary of Nobility

Jane Roberts

1. Using a notional classification

Any attempt to take the concept of nobility back beyond the Norman Conquest immediately comes up against an obvious problem of recognition. What words did the Anglo-Saxons use for nobles and nobility? When Dr Duggan asked me to write on the Old English vocabulary for nobles and nobility, she had it in mind that I should look at the evidence to be found in the recent *Thesaurus of Old English* (*TOE*),[1] a pilot study for the forthcoming 'Historical Thesaurus of English'.[2] It is therefore necessary, at the outset of this article, to indicate briefly the relevance of this research tool to my topic.

The *TOE* presents a conceptual classification of the extant English vocabulary of the Anglo-Saxons, arranged in 18 main categories:

Table i

01 The Physical World	06 Mental Faculties	12 Social Interaction
02 Life and Death	07 Opinion	13 Peace and War
03 Matter and Measurement	08 Emotion	14 Law and Order
04 Material Needs	09 Language & Communication	15 Property
05 Existence	10 Possession	16 Religion
	11 Action and Utility	17 Work
		18 Leisure

These eighteen categories fall into three discernible groups: categories 1 to 5 relate to the external world; categories 6 to 11 to the mind and to aspects of behaviour on an abstract level; and categories 12 to 18 to society and its adaptation of the physical world. The metalanguage of the *TOE* makes it possible to

---

1 J. Roberts and C. Kay with L. Grundy, *A Thesaurus of Old English*, 2 vols, King's College London Medieval Studies, 11 (London, 1995).

2 For details of the 'Historical Thesaurus' project see C. Kay, '*Historical Thesaurus of English*: Progress and Plans', in *Corpora across the Centuries*, ed. M. Kytö, M. Rissanen, and S. Wright (Amsterdam and Atlanta, Ga., 1994), pp. 110–20, and C. Kay and I. Wotherspoon, '*Historical Thesaurus of English*', in *Dictionaries of Medieval Germanic Languages: A Survey of Current Lexicographical Projects*, ed. K. H. van Dalen-Oskam, K. A. C. Depuydt, W. J. J. Pijnenburg, and T. H. Schoonheim, International Medieval Research, 2 (Turnhout, 1997), pp. 47–54.

identify those places where the words *noble* and *nobility* cluster. Its definitions, based on the information to be found in the standard Anglo-Saxon dictionaries, reflect the considered views of generations of scholars.[3] The thesaurus allows us to see their judgments, rearranged according to meaning.[4] To gather together the central words for the notions 'noble' and 'nobility' we need to consult two of these eighteen categories: category 7 'Opinion' in the second block for more abstract vocabulary; and category 12 'Social Interaction' for words more specific to people and their positions in society. Yet a thesaurus, by its very nature, is only one arrangement of its contents, and once its contents are arrayed, other arrangements inevitably spring to the mind of its user. Inevitably, therefore, some word senses appropriate to the discussion of Old English vocabulary for nobles and nobility will appear in other places, but these two categories should present the principal forms. To check up on examples of these words in context there are the invaluable resources now available to us all in the materials provided by the Toronto *Dictionary of Old English* project.[5]

2. A 'real' context

Any attempt to take the concept of nobility back beyond the Norman Conquest immediately comes up against an obvious problem of recognition. What words did the Anglo-Saxons use for nobles and nobility? Whereas the umbrella terms used for the two earlier international conferences organized by the Centre for Late Antique and Medieval Studies have a comfortingly English ring to them (*king, queen,* and even such abstract words as *kingship* are native words, after

---

3   The principal dictionaries used were *An Anglo-Saxon Dictionary*, ed. J. Bosworth and T. N. Toller (London, 1898); *An Anglo-Saxon Dictionary: Supplement*, ed. T. N. Toller (London, 1921); *An Anglo-Saxon Dictionary: Enlarged Addenda and Corrigenda*, ed. A. Campbell (Oxford, 1972); J. R. Clark Hall and H. D. Meritt, *A Concise Anglo-Saxon Dictionary*, 4th edn (Cambridge, 1960). The materials edited for the *TOE* did not draw on the resources of the *Oxford English Dictionary* (*OED*), ed. J. A. H. Murray and W. Craigie (Oxford, 1933), which provide the working archive of the parent 'Historical Thesaurus of English' project.

4   This overview of the vocabulary for nobles and nobility, it must be stressed, reflects the meanings given words within Old English contexts. For historical interpretation of some of the terms used for noblemen, see the important articles by: H. R. Loyn, 'The Term *Ealdorman* in the Translations Prepared at the Time of King Alfred', *EHR*, lxviii (1953), 513–25; idem, 'Gesiths and Thegns from the Seventh to the Tenth Century', *EHR*, lxx (1955), 529–49; A. T. Thacker, 'Some Terms for Noblemen in Anglo-Saxon England, *c.* 650–900', *Anglo-Saxon Studies in Archaeology and History*, BAR British Series, xcii (1981), 201–36; J. Gillingham, 'Thegns and Knights in Eleventh-Century England: Who Was Then the Gentleman?', *TRHS*, 6th series, v (1995), 129–53.

5   *A Microfiche Concordance to Old English*, ed. A. DiPaolo Healey and R. L. Venezky (Toronto, 1980); *A Microfiche Concordance to Old English: The High Frequency Words*, ed. R. L. Venezky and S. Butler (Toronto, 1985). The five letters then edited by the Dictionary of Old English team were also consulted: Fasc. D, 1986; Fasc. C, 1988; Fasc. B, 1991; Fasc. Æ, 1992; Fasc. Bēon, 1992; Fasc. A, 1994.

all),[6] with nobles and nobility we must attempt to find corresponding terms from pre-Norman English, without the comforting sense of recognition of known words still in use. However, etymology is often a false friend, as reflection on even the Old English form *cyning* should remind us (*cyning* could then, as most recently in the ballads, be used of leaders we would now regard as subordinate to a king; and the consecration of Alfred as a boy in Rome might therefore have been appropriate for any of the sons of his father). The word senses of the *TOE* derive from contexts in which they are recorded, and they are presented alongside modern English explanations. By way of proem to an examination of the evidence to be found in the *TOE*, I should like to look at some of these terms in context.

Two literary figures provide a valuable glimpse of the Anglo-Saxon view of nobility. In the first, a hero of the future is recognized; and in the second a leader grieves for a dead follower. Both my examples are taken, inevitably, from *Beowulf*, and they appear in the early part of the poem, long ago among the legendary Spear-Danes, in an age when men were famed for their courageous deeds, when 'ða æþelingas ellen fremedon'.[7] Yet it takes a man from another people, Beowulf, to deal with the great ogre, Grendel, who had ravaged King Hrothgar's hall for twelve years. Beowulf is the first of my two examples of a noble. He is introduced as 'Higelaces þegn' (line 194), that is one of the aristocratic warriors in King Hygelac's service. From his arrival in Danish territory to take on the Grendel affair, Beowulf is recognized as a man of unusual qualities by the guardian of the shore:

> Næfre ic maran geseah
> eorla ofer eorþan   ðonne is eower sum,
> secg on searwum;   nis þæt seldguma,
> wæpnum geweorðad,   næfne him his wlite leoge,
> ænlic ansyn.[8]

> (I have never seen in the world a greater noble than one of you, a man in splendid armour, is: that is no mere retainer tricked out with weaponry, unless his splendour, his noble appearance, belie him.)

Beowulf is an unusually impressive nobleman (the speaker has not seen anyone 'maran . . . eorla'), singularly striking because of his noble ('ænlic')

6   On consulting the *OED*, it may come as a surprise to learn that the noun *queenship* is first recorded for 1536 with the meaning 'dignity or office of a queen', twice thereafter for the seventeenth century, and twice for the nineteenth century; with its alternative meaning 'personality of a queen; (her) majesty' the *OED* gives examples of usage for 1603, 1694, and 1767. Even *kingship*, apart from an unusual occurrence early in the first half of the fourteenth century, is recorded as in continuous use only from the seventeenth century onwards, although it can be compared with the more general Old English *cynescipe*.

7   *Beowulf and Judith*, ed. E. van Kirk Dobbie, Anglo-Saxon Poetic Records, 4 (New York, 1953), line 3.

8   *Ibid.*, lines 247–51

appearance.[9] A comparison with Imma springs to mind: a prisoner taken in the wars of Ethelred of Mercia, Bede tells us that he was identified as not 'of common stock' (*de paupere uulgo*) but 'of noble family' (*de nobilibus*) from 'his appearance, his bearing, and his speech' (*ex uultu et habitu et sermonibus eius*).[10] When Beowulf has done what he came to Denmark to do, made Hrothgar's hall habitable again at night, he is recognized as one marked out for kingship. He therefore falls into two other categories: not just noble, he is a hero; and he is to become a king. Here in this early passage within the poem Beowulf is marked out already as not just a mere retainer ('seldguma').[11]

For an archetypal noble in *Beowulf* we must look further in that Danish section of the poem where time is given to establishing the sense of a court and its protocols. Beowulf, as is well known, struggled mightily with Grendel, holding him so firmly in his grip that the dying monster fled to the marshland, one arm missing. When the monstrous mother of Grendel comes out from the fens to wreak vengeance for the death of her son, she seizes Æschere, my second example. Hrothgar, king of the Danes laments his lost companion in these words:

> Dead is Æschere,
> Yrmenlafes   yldra broþor,
> mine runwita   ond min rædbora,
> eaxlgestealla,   ðonne we on orlege
> hafelan weredon,   þonne hniton feþan,
> eaferas cnysedan.   Swy[lc] scolde eorl wesan,
> æþeling ærgod,   swylc Æschere wæs![12]

(Æschere, Yrmenlaf's elder brother, is dead – my privy counsellor and adviser, my shoulder-to-shoulder companion. When in battle we shielded our heads, then foot-combatants engaged [and] heroes [lit. men wearing boar-crested helmets] clashed. As a man should be, a pre-eminent [nobleman], so was Æschere.)

A man who served his lord both as privy counsellor and shoulder-to-shoulder companion in battle was undoubtedly important. If we backtrack a little in the

---

9   See Table iv, where *ænlic* is listed. It is noteworthy that the extant corpus of Old English yields so many adjectives to describe Nobility.

10 See *Bede's Ecclesiastical History of the English People*, ed. B. Colgrave and R. A. B. Mynors (Oxford, 1969), p. 402, lines 29–30. The Old English Bede translates *de nobilibus* by 'æðele strynde' (*The Old English Version of Bede's Ecclesiastical History of the English People*, ed. T. Miller, 4 vols, Early English Text Society, Original Series, 95–6, 110–11 [1890–98], i, 328, line 17).

11 As Hygelac's nephew Beowulf was, like the captured young man Imma, of noble birth. It is interesting to note that Imma in the Old English Bede is termed 'cyninges þegn' (Miller, *The Old English Version*, p. 326, line 15 (translating *minister . . . regis*, and compare p. 328, line 22).

12 *Beowulf and Judith*, ed. E. van Kirk Dobbie, lines 1323–9. It is unfortunate that *æþeling*, one of the key-terms, is emended into the text here, but the grounds for this emendation are long-accepted as well-based.

poem, Æschere is described as one of the nobles ('æþelinga anne', line 1294) when seized by Grendel's mother, and we are told instantly that he was Hrothgar's 'hæleþa leofost/on gesiðes had be sæm tweonum,/ rīce randwiga' ('the most beloved of men in the rank of the companion throughout the world, a mighty shield-warrior', lines 1296–8) and 'aldorþegn . . . þone deorestan' ('the bravest senior nobleman', lines 1308–9). This man was a treasure-giver (men mourn for their giver of treasure: 'æfter sincgyfan', line 1342), whose hand had dealt out almost every desire ('welhwylcra wilna', line 1344). Æschere, it has always seemed to me, is, in the poem *Beowulf*, the noblest man who does not become a king. Apart from Æschere, all who are described as treasure-givers are kings or the wives of kings. It is, however, difficult to convey the full force of words like *eorl* or *hæleð*. Sometimes they seem bleached of all heroic connotations and are best rendered 'man'; equivalences such as hero, nobleman, warrior, and even earl, which the Victorians were happy to use, no longer seem suitable. Equally, the adjectives *rīce* and *dēor(e)* could as easily be translated by 'noble' as by 'brave' or 'mighty'. Here, as so often in heroic narrative, we find the paradigm of a noble in a death eulogy. So, in the fourteenth century, the index to Arthur's heroic nature is expressed in the outpouring of grief for Gawain in the alliterative *Morte Arthure* and in the fifteenth century in Sir Hector's lament for Launcelot in Malory's *Morte Darthur*. The *Beowulf*-poet's depiction of Æschere epitomizes the heroic ideal of Anglo-Saxon times. It is hardly surprising therefore that it should bring together some of the keywords for nobles and nobility in Old English.

3. The lexical field for nobility

The general terms for Nobility appear in category 7 'Opinion' of the *TOE*. In the succession of major sub-categories, each given its separate number, the two sub-categories where Nobility words cluster are highlighted:

Table ii

7. Opinion
   07 Judgement, forming of opinion
   07.01 Appraisal, appraising
   07.02 Goodness
   07.03 Evil
   07.04 Consideration, esteem
   07.05 Disrespect, irreverence
   07.06 Pride
   07.07 Humility
   07.08 Reputation, fame
   07.09 Shame, disgrace
   07.10 Beauty, fairness

The first of the relevant sub-categories, 07.02 'Goodness', is itself arrayed in four sub-divisions, the last of which, 07.02.04 'Excellence', contains two groups of words concerned with the abstraction nobility:

Table iii

07.02 Goodness
07.02.01 Right, virtue
07.02.02 Good, what is beneficial, advantageous, etc.
07.02.03 Perfection
07.02.04 Excellence
07.02.04.01 Excellence, virtue, goodness
07.02.04.02 Nobleness, nobility, dignity
07.02.04.03 Nobleness, excellence, nobility, magnificence
07.04.02.03.01 Peculiar excellence

Here the succession of entries indicates that category 07.02.04.02 'Nobleness, nobility, dignity' is a particular realization of excellence, distinct in having some components of nobility and/or dignity, and that the next parallel entry, category 07.02.04.03 'Nobleness, excellence, nobility, magnificence', differs again in having a component of magnificence. The actual word groups are:

Table iv

07.02.04.02 Nobleness, nobility, dignity: æþelborennes, (ge)þungennes
. **Noble, distinguished:** æþelboren
. **High in worth, dignity, etc.:** hēalic
. **Excellent, distinguished:** ǣmyrce[og], geþungen
. **(Of a tribune) noble, commanding:** duguþlic[g]
                        See 12.08.01 Magnanimity; 12.08.02.03.01 Honourable

07.02.04.03 Nobleness, excellence, nobility, magnificence: æþelcundnes[o], æþelu,
       (ge)micelnes, mōd, þrymm, weorþfulnes, weorþnes, weorþscipe
. **Excellent, choice, fair, noble:** ācoren, æltǣwe, ǣnlic, æþele, æþellic, ānlic,
       gecoren, dēore, dēorwierþe, dryhtlic, ēacen, fæger, frēolic, fūslic, hēalic,
       micel, rōt, til, weorþfullic, wlitig, wrǣst
. **Noble, excellent, splendid:** betlic[p], clǣnlic, hrēþēadig[p], mǣre, mǣrlic, micellic,
       regallic, þrymful[p], þrymlic, þrȳþful, unwāclic[p], weorþful, weorþlic
. **Lofty, noble:** ūphēah

At every level of the *TOE*, the defining phrases reflect the evidence for meaning drawn from the major dictionaries of Old English, the dots indicating subordination. Each form was assigned its position on the evidence of meaning. It is interesting therefore to see where the resulting networks are dominated by particular roots. In Table iv the central terms clearly draw on the roots *æþel-* and *weorþ-* for the expression of nobility. Six word senses contain the element *æþel-* (*æþelborennes, æþelboren, æþelcundnes[o], æþelu, æþele, æþellic*), and six contain *weorþ-* (*weorþfulnes, weorþnes, weorþscipe, weorþfullic, weorþful, weorþlic*; compare also the mutated form in *deorwierþe*). It is perhaps no accident that the *weorþ-* forms all occur at a greater level of specificity, for a component of appraisal separates these closely related groups. The superscript letters after forms serve to inform the reader that a word is restricted in distribution. Thus, the **o** flag after *æþelcundnes*[o] alerts us to an otherwise unattested word in Alfred's version of Boethius.[13] Forms restricted to glossing use can be very odd, as for example the singleton *æmyrce*, flagged **og**: the elements of this nonce-word, which stands against *egregius*, add together as 'not murky', the **g** indicating that it is not in a running text but in glossing materials. Similarly, a superscript **p** draws attention to a word found only in poetic texts (e.g. *betlic*, *hrēþēadig* and *unwāclic* among the adjectives), and very occasionally a **q** queries the actual existence of a form. The flags provide a filter, allowing the reader to sift out some of the least well-supported extant forms. Thus, *duguþlic*, which is found only glossing *tribunic(e)*and is flagged **g**, may have been coined in an attempt to explain a Latin phrase rather than to translate it. These four flags reflect the information to be found in the major Anglo-Saxon dictionaries. Obviously it is impossible to be certain of their accuracy until the work of the Toronto *Dictionary of Old English* project is complete, but their presence affords a preliminary categorization of those words which are either infrequent or restricted in use. Checking under the cross-reference to 12.08.01 'Magnanimity' for entries that contain the adjective 'noble' picks up a few more terms: the compound *rihtæþelo* for 'true nobility of mind': and four adjectives meaning 'of noble spirit': *hēahmōd*[p], *mōdig*, *swīþmōd*[p], *wlanc*.

The second relevant sub-category of abstract words in category 07 'Opinion' is to be found in 07.08 'Reputation, fame'. Here the words that touch on the notion of nobility come near the top of the sub-category, at 07.08.01 'Nobility (of character, rank, etc.)':

Table v

7.08 Reputation, fame
07.08.01 Nobility (of character, rank, etc.)
07.08.02 Honour, glory
07.08.03 Honour, veneration
07.08.04 An ornament, honour, glory
07.08.05 Glorifying, making great, glorification
07.08.06 Exaltation
07.08.07 Glory, splendour, magnificence
07.08.08 Nobleness, honour, glory
07.08.09 Renown, fame, glory

Interestingly, category 07.08 'Reputation, fame', altogether lacks the *æþel-*

---

13 The word is used to convey a sense of great magnificence. See *King Alfred's Old English version of Boethius: De Consolatione Philosophiae*, ed. W. J. Sedgefield (Oxford, 1899), p. 46, lines 12–14: *7 þeah hwa wexe mid micelre æþelcundnesse his gebyrda, 7 þeo on eallu(m) welu(m) 7 eallu(m) wlencu(m) . . .*' (and even should anyone thrive with great nobility of birth and prosper in full prosperity and pomp . . .).

root, possibly because the focus is not on nobility but rather on the achievement of fame as an aspect of nobility:

Table vi

07.08.01 Nobility (of character, rank, etc.): hēanes, weorþnes
. **A man of mark:** esne
.. **A great man:** woruldfruma[o]
.. **Flower of a people:** duguþ
.**Excellent, distinguished, high-ranking:** hēah, hēahheald[q]
    hēah(ge)þungen, welweorþe[o]
.. **Eminent, pre-eminent:** foremǣrlic[o], frēamicel[og]
.. **Of great excellence:** wel(ge)þungen
.. **Old and distinguished:** ealdgeþungen[o]
.. **Desirous of honour, excellent:** weorþgeorn
.. **Eager for glory:** ārhwæt[p], dōmgeorn[p], gielpgeorn, lofgeorn
                     See 12.01.01.06.05 ff. Nobility

The general words at the head of the group, abstract nouns ending in '-ness', are built on root elements *hēah-* and *weorþ-* that appear frequently in the groups of words for nobles and nobility in Old English. The first of these word senses is still used today in much the same meaning, fossilized in terms used of the monarch. The second, *weorþnes*, seems to have disappeared quickly in the post-Conquest period: 'worthness' is attested twice only in the *OED*;[14] and a new formation, the ancestor of 'worthiness', built on the adjective *weorþig-*, is by far more limited in its range of meanings than was the Old English *weorþnes*. In the Anglo-Saxon period both these words, *hēa(h)nes* and *weorþnes*, covered a wide range of senses throughout the lexicon. A glance at their addresses in the *TOE*, listed in the Index volume, indicates both their polysemous nature and their differing meanings. Whereas *hēa(h)nes* is found in five categories, *weorþnes* appears in two only. The underlying spatial sense of 'high', like 'up', favours metaphoric extension, and the senses of *hēa(h)nes* spread widely through the lexicon: at 05.10.05.03.03 'Height, loftiness, sublimity'; 05.10.05.03.04 'Depth, deepness'; 07.08.01 'Nobility (of character, rank, etc.)'; 11.07.04 'Superiority, pre-eminence, primacy'; 12.01.01.06.05 'Nobility, noble condition'; and 16.01.02 'The heavens, sky'. By contrast the senses of *weorþnes* are all to be found in categories 07 'Opinion' and 12 'Social interaction': at 07.02.04.03 'Nobleness, excellence, nobility, magnificence'; 07.06.05 'Pomp, splendour, magnificence'; 07.08.01 'Nobility (of character, rank, etc.)'; 07.08.02 'Honour, glory'; 12.01.01.06.05 'Nobility, noble condition'; and 12.02 'A public office'. Quite a few of the other words in 07.08.01 (Table vi) may have been restricted in use: two adjectives, *ārhwæt* and *dōmgeorn* in the last line, occur only in

---

[14] The first *OED* citation is from the 1258 proclamation of Henry III, and it is descended from the Old English *weorþnes*; the second, from 1486, looks like a by-form of the later word *worthiness*. Thus, new forms may have been quick to colonize the wide range of meanings covered by the Old English *weorþnes*.

poetry; and some others are recorded once only. By comparison with 07.02.04.02 and 07.02.04.03 (Table iv) finer levels of subordination are shown here. Reading upwards through the levels we see that *esne* 'a man of mark' has 'nobility (of character, rank, etc.)'; and that *woruldfruma*[o] 'a great man' is 'a man of mark' who has 'nobility (of character, rank, etc.)'. Were we to read on into sub-category 07.08.02 'Honour, glory', we should find the element *weorþ* dominant there, alongside the word *ār*. Any examination of the history of the concept 'honour' for the whole history of the English language would have to take account of both *ār* and *weorþscipe* as central terms for the Anglo-Saxon period.

The italicized cross-reference at the foot of Table vi points forward to word senses gathered into the third section of the *TOE*, to category 12 'Social Interaction', where matters of power and control are presented. Here the words for nobles are to be found, together with the terms of rank by which their pecking order in society is measured:

Table vii

12.01.01.06 Condition, rank, standing
12.01.01.06.01 Rank, position due to birth
12.01.01.06.02 Superior
12.01.01.06.02.01 (High) rank, status, degree
12.01.01.06.03 Of middle rank
12.01.01.06.04 Inferiority of status, lowest place
12.01.01.06.05 Nobility, noble condition
12.01.01.06.06 Gentle birth, nobility
12.01.01.06.07 Royal/princely status/dignity
12.01.01.06.07.01 A royal race
12.01.01.06.08 A person of rank, elder, great man

The first of the highlighted sections deals with nobility or the noble condition:

Table viii

12.01.01.06.05 Nobility, noble condition: æþelnes, æþelu,
    hēahnes, weorþnes
. **Noble, of noble rank:** æþele, dryhtlic, eorlcund, eorlisc[o]
.. **Equally noble:** full æþele
.. **Very noble:** efenæþele
. **Possessed of honours, noble, honourable:** weorþ
. **Noble, illustrious:** frēo, hēalic, weorþful, wīdcūþ
. **Lordly, noble:** eorlic, hlāfordlic[g], þegnlic
. **With high quality:** hēalīce
.. **In the manner of a lord:** dryhtlīce
See 07.08.01 Nobility

As with Table iv, the central terms again draw heavily on the root *æþel-*, which appears five times in this group, for the recognition of nobility, and on *weorþ-*

for its appraisal, a root behind three word senses here. Four other roots represented in this group are also to be found underlying quite a few Anglo-Saxon
words for men of rank: *dryht-*, *eorl-*, *hlāford-* and *þegn-* (see Table x). They
appear more or less interchangeable, which cannot surprise, given the lack of
any precision of differentiation among the related nouns in heroic narrative.
From this group the reader of the *TOE* is referred back to the more general terms
in Section II, which were presented in Table vi. When the complementary
Tables vi and viii are read together it is clear that *æþelu*, if not the central term
for the concept of nobility in Old English, is one of a leading group of cognate
words. Both *hēah-* and *weorþ-* forms again play a significant part in the lexical
field. One adjective, *eorlisc*, is marked **o** as found once only, although for us it
has acquired a sense of frequency through its use by historians in such phrases
as '*eorlisc* families'.[15] The flags, it should be remembered, relate to Anglo-
Saxon usage only, as must be plain from the **g** (i.e. restricted to glosses) flag on
hlāfordlic (lordly).

The abstract noun *æþelu* appears also among the leading sense forms for the
noble condition secured by noble birth:

Table ix

12.01.01.06.06 Gentle birth, nobility: æþelborennes, æþelu, eorlgebyrd[P]
. **Of gentle birth:** æþelboren, æþelcund, dēorboren, forþboren
. **More highly born:** betboren[o], borenra
. **Well born, noble:** betstboren, cynegod[P], cynnig[g], þegnboren[o], welboren
. **Noble, gentle:** frēolic, gesīþcund
. **Noble, kingly:** cynewyrþe

12.01.01.06.07 Royal/princely status/dignity: æþelinghād[o], cynedōm,
   cynehād, cynescipe
. **Kingliness, distinction, royal excellence:** cynelicnes[o]
. **Kingly, royal:** cynelic
. **Queenly:** cwēnlic[op]

12.01.01.06.07.01 A royal race: cynecynn
. **A rightful royal line:** ealdhlāfordcynn[o]
. **Royally born:** cyneboren

Here we need glance only for a moment at the specifically royal words in the
lower part of Table ix to see the dominance there of the *cyne-* element. Such is
the cohesiveness of 12.01.01.06.07 that the singleton *æþelinghād* looks mis-
placed. The passage in which it occurs tells how King Edgar, once he had come
to his 'cynedome', remembered promises he had made God 'on his

---

15 See, for example, H. R. Loyn, *Anglo-Saxon England and the Norman Conquest*, 2nd edn
   (Harlow, 1991), p. 222, in relation to Godwin's family. The form is not given an entry in
   the *OED*, although its existence is noted under *earlishness*, which has one citation for
   1876 ('The Earl had no particular earlishness about him').

æþelincghade'[16] – hence its interpretation 'princely state' in the standard dictionaries. Because the terms contrast with one another, perhaps 'cynedome' is to be understood as referring to royal dignity rather than the kingdom. Apparently in the everyday world of tenth-century England the compound *æþelinghād* was used of Edgar's state before he became king, and, from what we have seen above, the root *æþel-* more typically supplied word senses that contain a 'noble' component. By contrast, the message of 12.01.01.06.07 is that to be *cyne-* was typically to be 'royal'. The word might be better placed in 12.01.02.06.06 as denoting the noble status to which Edgar belonged by birth. It was, of course, a rank retained but improved upon; and a placing in the wider earlier group might therefore, as for *cynewyrþe*, seem more appropriate.

4. Problems of register

We have identified the words that Anglo-Saxons might have used when discussing aspects of the abstraction nobility. Before examining the more specific words used to designate nobles it is necessary to consider the problems presented by register. We find in the poem *Beowulf* the aims and values of an aristocratic society. As we saw, its opening is set among the Danes long ago and its focus is on men who quintessentially did deeds of bravery. But how are we to translate 'ða æþelingas' of line 3? Wrenn's list suggests the reader should select from '*noble retainer; prince; hero; man; warrior:* according to context', a well chosen set of possibilities that indicate the width of reference of *æþeling*.[17] The heroic register does not supply us with words that point to the delimitation of greater and lesser nobles. In part, this is because the poet changes the terms used according to context. So, near the end of the poem *Beowulf*, Ongentheow, a great king of the Swedes, is introduced as 'se froda fæder Ohtheres,/eald ond egesfull' ('the aged father of Ohtere, old and terrible', lines 2928–29), and while in control of a savage battle is described as 'se goda' ('that good man', line 2949), 'frod, felageomor' ('wise and old, very sad', line 2950), 'eorl' ('hero'? 'noble'? 'man'? 2951). As the brothers who cut him down close in, Ongentheow is unafraid, but 'gomela' ('aged', line 2968) and he diminishes into an 'ealdum ceorle' ('old man', line 2972). At death he is given his full rank as 'cyning,/folces hyrde' ('king, guardian of the people', lines 2980–1) – and the achievement of his slayer is thereby enhanced. Stylistic variation brings together in reference to one man the terms king, noble, and common man – or *cyning, eorl,* and *ceorl.*[18] Were we looking at a legal code, we should think of these terms as mutually exclusive. For example, in a law concerned with breaking and entry

---

[16] *Leechdoms, wortcunning, and starcraft of Early England: being a collection of documents, for the most part never before printed, illustrating the history of science in this ccuntry before the Norman conquest,* ed. T. O. Cockayne, RS, 35 (1864–66), iii, 438, line 5.

[17] *Beowulf,* ed. C. L. Wrenn (London, 1953).

[18] Contrast N. J. Higham, *An English Empire: Bede and the Early Anglo-Saxon Kings* (Manchester and New York, 1995), p. 239, who sees in the use of these three terms of Ongen-

into property, we find careful distinctions made for fines according to the rank of the property holder:

> Cyninges burgbryce bið CXX scill., ærcebiscepes hundnigontig scill., oðres biscepes 7 ealdormonnes LX scill., twelfhyndes monnes XXX scill., syxhyndes monnes XV scillinga; ceorles edorbryce V scill.[19]

> (Breaking and entry into the king's dwelling shall be 120 shillings, the archbishop's 90 shillings, of another bishop or of an ealdorman 60 shillings, of a man of 1200–shilling wergild 30 shillings, of a man of 600–shilling wergild 15 shillings; breaking and entry into a common man's enclosure 5 shillings.)

In the aristocratic world created for us by the *Beowulf* poet there are no such legalistic distinctions. Some great men are older and wiser or have achieved recognition as being of the flower or *duguþ*, some are younger and still among the promising *geoguþ*.

Tangentially, it is worth remembering that when Alfred ruminated on the state of learning in his letter to his bishops, he was, I think, fairly specific in the target group to be educated: the 'gioguð' (youngsters) of 'friora monna' (of noble men):

> . . . mē ðyncð betre, gif īow swǣ ðyncð, ðæt wē ēac sumæ bēc, ðā ðe nīedbeðearfosta sīen eallum monnum tō wiotonne, ðæt wē ðā on ðæt geðīode wenden ðe wē ealle gecnāwan mægen, ond gedōn, swǣ wē swīðe ēaðe magon mid Godes fultume, gif wē ðā stilnesse habbað, ðætte eal sīo gioguð ðe nū is on Angelcynne friora monna, ðāra ðe ðā spēda hæbben ðæt hīe ðǣm befēolan mægen, sīen tō liornunga oðfǣste, ðā hwīle ðe hīe tō nānre ōðerre note ne mægen, oð ðone first ðe hīe wel cunnen Englisc gewrit ārǣdan.[20]

> (. . . it seems better to me, if it seems so to you, that we should translate some books, those which it is most necessary for all men to know, into the language that we can all understand, and that we should bring it about, as with God's help we very easily can, that all the young nobles who are now among the English, those who have sufficient wealth that they may be so deployed, be set to school for as long as they can be put to no other useful purpose until the point at which they are able to read written English well.)

Because for English speakers today 'free', the descendant of Old English *frēo*, essentially means without restraint, we have lost the habit of mind that links the adjective free with notions of nobility – although such a meaning was to remain

---

theow evidence in support of the view that *ceorl* may 'have been at a comparatively early date a term redolent with qualities which were considered appropriate to the naming of children of noble or even royal rank, both in fact and fiction.'

[19] *The Laws of the Earliest English Kings*, ed. F. L. Attenborough (Cambridge, 1922), Alfred 40 §1.

[20] *Sweet's Anglo-Saxon Reader in Prose and Verse*, ed. D. Whitelock (Oxford, 1967), pp. 6–7, lines 56–64.

in use through into Chaucer's day and beyond. The adjectives *frēolic* and *frēo* (see Tables iv, viii, and ix) were among the commonest words with the meaning 'noble' in Anglo-Saxon times, but across time their connotations of nobility have dropped away. As a result, when we meet them in Old English, they are false friends. We recognize and acknowledge words that look more poetic or more unusual; the words we think we still know are those we are often least likely to understand.

5. Persons of rank

When the *TOE* was complete, it came as a shock to see how very small part of the vocabulary was specific to matters of noble rank or standing (a mere four pages out of the 716 pages of the classification). The extant Anglo-Saxon vocabulary contains many terms for kings, rulers, and leaders. By contrast, there are rather fewer word senses that are sufficiently specific to appear under 12.01.01.06.08 'A person of rank, elder, great man', the final section of category 12.01.01.06 'Condition, rank, standing':

Table x

12.01.01.06.08 A person of rank, elder, great man: eald,
ealdormann, ieldest, ieldra, geræswa[p], (ge)rēfa, gesīþ,
gesīþmann, þegn, þeningmann, wita
. **Who is a Dane, a jarl:** eorl
. **Holder of land below a jarl:** hold
. **A person of rank, noble:** æþeling, beorn[p], domne, eorl,
forþman[o], gummann[op], hlāford, hlāfording, ord, rād(e)cniht,
sibæþeling[op]
.. **Chief noble:** forþþegn
.. **Nobles collectively, nobility:** duguþ, ealdorduguþ[p],
gōdsǣd[op], ord, rihtcynecynn, rihtcynn
.. **A noble lady:** cwēn, forþwīf[og], hlǣfdige, (ge)sīþwīf
... **Queen dowager:** sēo ealde hlǣfdige
.. **A noble child:** cynebearn
.. **A youth of gentle birth:** cild
. **A thane:** þegn
.. **Status of thane:** þegnscipe
.. **Thane in a burgh:** burhþegn
.. **Thane of a shire:** scīrþegn
.. **A secular thane:** woruldþegn
.. **Fit to rank as a thane:** gesīþcund
. **Man of 600–shilling wergild:** sixhynde man
.. **Having 600–shilling wergild:** sixhynde
.. **Man of 1200–shilling wergild:** twelfhynde mann
... **Having 1200–shilling wergild:** twelfhynde
. **A title of rank or dignity:** nama
.. **Majesty:** cynescipe
.. **Lord:** domne, eorl, hlāford
.. **Lady:** domne, hlǣfdige

Here, in category 12.01.01.06.08 'A person of rank, elder, great man', we recognize terms familiar from histories of Anglo-Saxon England. These, I would suggest, are the bulk of the Old English words for persons of rank; and once they are identified it becomes possible both to examine them as a group and to seek any other words of like meaning at other places in the *TOE* classification. It is a small crop of forms; and I hope that as you have moved down to this level of specificity you have gained a sense of the wider lexical fields within which they operate. Very few of the forms in this box appear only in this group. For the most part, words such as 'lord' and 'lady' are polysemous, appearing in different senses at other places within the *TOE*.

Table x presents the relevant evidence from the whole vocabulary of Anglo-Saxon England as recorded in the standard dictionaries. If we leave aside both the words that are infrequent (**o**: *forþman*, **p**: *(ge)ræswa*; *ealdorduguþ*; **op**: *gummann, sibæþeling, gōdsæd*; and **og**: *forþwīf*) and the phrases because they do not carry distributional evidence (*sēo ealde hlæfdige, sixhynde mann, twelfhynde mann*), there remain words which are likely to have been in general use. Of those words that remain, a few occur only in this section of the *TOE* and may therefore have been restricted to this domain: *þeningmann, hold, rād(e)cniht* (a Middle English rather than Old English word),[21] *forþþegn, rihtcynecynn, rihtcynn, (ge)sīþwīf, burhþegn, scirþegn, woruldþegn, sixhynde, twelfhynde*. I could wish that the section included *eorlscipe*, a noun restricted to poetry, with the meaning of 'status of nobleman', but only after the final editing of the *TOE* did I come across an article in which the case for this meaning is convincingly argued.[22] It is to be found in the *TOE* only in 06.02.07.06, meaning 'courage, boldness, valour'. The Anglo-Saxons did not, it seems, have anything much by way of a specialized vocabulary for the stratification of their nobility, but that would change under the Normans. New ideas of knighthood and chivalry were to spread throughout Europe, and with newly elaborated notions of nobility came new words.

Eventually, in England, most of the old terms of rank fell out of use, as did much of the more general vocabulary for nobles and nobility. Of the polysemous words in Table x, some word senses (*cwēn* 'a noble lady' > *queen*; *cild* 'a youth of gentle birth' > *child*; *þegn* 'a thane' > *thane*) lingered in romance and heightened narrative, and were even reinvigorated in the romantic revival. Obviously *lord* < *hlāford* and *lady* < *hlæfdige* remain in use. Today's form *earl* in part reflects the Old English *eorl*, although its prototypical meaning derives rather from its cognate Scandinavian competitor *jarl*.[23] The word *æþeling* or

---

21 This word, which is not to be found in either the *OED* or the *Middle English Dictionary*, should be flagged q for Old English. It is cited from the *Textus Roffensis* in the Bosworth–Toller dictionary (I, under 'rād-cniht') as '*A title equivalent to that of sixhynde man*').

22 R. C. Sutherland, 'The Meaning of *eorlscipe* in *Beowulf*', *Publications of the Modern Languages Association of America*, lxx (1955), 1133–42

23 See Loyn, 'Gesiths and Thegns', p. 533; J. McKinnell, 'On the Date of The Battle of

atheling was, according to the *OED* description, 'in later writers restricted as a historical term to a prince of the royal blood, or even to the heir-apparent to the throne'. Gradually the nobility groups were eroded. Symptomatic is the disappearance of the commonest Old English adjectives, as consultation of the drafting files for the 'Historical Thesaurus' shows.[24] More specific forms, for example *eorlcund* and *gesīþcund*, appear not to have outlasted the Anglo-Saxon period. Even *æþele* became infrequent, persisting longest in alliterative poetry, although *frēo* continued with the meaning 'noble' to 1554, and *frēolic* to about 1500. New terms, built on *nobl-* and *gent-*, are recorded as coming into use as early as the thirteenth century, for example: *gentle* (*a.* 1225), *gentrice* (*a.* 1225), *noble* (*a.* 1225), *noblesse* (*a.* 1225), *gentlewoman* (*c.* 1230).[25]

The words and phrases of Hrothgar's lament for Æschere are for the most part poetic, lacking the specificity of terms of rank in other registers. Hrothgar speaks of Æschere with affection, as the noblest/dearest of men, a close companion in battle, a counsellor admitted to his privy thoughts. One phrase only, 'on gesīðas had' ('in the rank of companion', line 1297), has about it the clear ring of status, because *hād* so often points to rank in Old English. Was Æschere *gesīþcund*?[26] The word has, according to the dictionaries, two meanings: 'noble, gentle' (at 12.01.01.06.01 in the *TOE*: see Table ix); and 'fit to rank as a thane' (at 12.01.01.06.08: see Table x). The first of these is certainly appropriate to the poem *Beowulf*. The second, more specific, sense is not inappropriate to Æschere, especially as the poet does not categorize any other noble with the phrase type *on ~es hād*. Æschere was, as we have seen, singled out as the noblest of Hrothgar's companions. He was not just a *þegn*, but an 'aldorþegn' – a '*princeps*' rather than a prince. The limiting element *ealdor-* adds a significant component of meaning, making it clear that he was one of the senior followers of Hrothgar. The word appears not with persons of rank in Table x but in Table ix at 12.01.01 07 ('A follower', as 'a principal retainer'). It appears in six texts only in Old English and may always have had a literary flavour.[27] Unferth, also

---

Maldon', *Medium Ævum*, xliv (1975), 121–36; *The Battle of Maldon*, ed. D. G. Scragg (Manchester, 1981), pp. 26–7; D. Crouch, *The Image of Aristocracy in Britain 1000–1300* (London, 1992), pp. 46–50.

24 Few of the adjective word senses of Table iv continue into the Middle English period.
25 These are the first dates of usage for each in the *OED*.
26 Loyn, 'Gesiths and Thegns', pp. 530–8, points to the possession of property as marking out this rank.
27 Outside *Beowulf* the word *ealdorþegn* is used five times: of the senior officers of Holofernes's army (*Judith*, 241); of Satan as the leader of the fallen angels (*Christ and Satan*, 65); of Peter as Christ's '(e)aldorþegn' (Vercelli homilies, 5.110 and 15.162); and of Peter and Paul as 'ealdorþegnas' of Christ (*Menologium*, 130). For *Judith*, see *Beowulf and Judith*, ed. E. van Kirk Dobbie. For *Christ and Satan*, see *The Junius Manuscript*, ed. G. P. Krapp, The Anglo-Saxon Poetic Records, 1 (New York, 1931). For *Menologium*, see *The Anglo-Saxon Minor Poems*, ed. E. van Kirk Dobbie, The Anglo-Saxon Poetic Records, 6 (New York, 1942). For the two prose instances, from a manuscript that also contains poetry, see *The Vercelli Homilies and Related Texts*, ed. D. G. Scragg, Early English Text Society, Original Series, 300 (Oxford, 1992).

one of those close to Hrothgar, behaves ignobly for much of Beowulf's visit to the Danes, and nobility words are conspicuously absent in the descriptions of him. We see little of Wulfgar, who knew 'duguðe þeaw' ('the mode of behaviour expected of one of the company of senior men', line 359 – or courtly custom). No other men of Hrothgar's court are named. In the heroic poetry of Anglo-Saxon England Æschere alone is singled out as an 'aldorþegn', and he is a nobleman to be ranked with Gawain or Launcelot. The *Beowulf* poet created nobles whom he placed in a heroic past, men who were *æþelingas* known for deeds that demonstrated their *eorlscipe*, but to us translations that make use of old words like *atheling* and *earlship* have at best a Victorian ring. We no longer recognize the width of reference such words once held.

6

Nobles and Others:
The Social and Cultural Expression of
Power Relations in the Middle Ages

Timothy Reuter

This contribution was conceived as an exploration of some of the ways in which the evident power of the medieval *ceti dirigenti* was created and maintained,[1] as a good opportunity to do some hard thinking about what seemed and still seems to me to be one of the most important issues facing medievalists. The return on investment has turned out lower than expected, and I am now certain that better scholars have been here and returned, if not empty-handed, then at any rate not bearing the armfuls they had initially hoped for. Although the source and nature of political, social, and cultural power is a subject which historians in general and medievalists in particular have instinctively tended to shy away from, there is an extensive and highly sophisticated literature on the subject in the related disciplines of sociology and political science. I shall draw, tentatively, on some of this, without claiming anything like expert or comprehensive knowledge of the literature. The topic requires not an article but a large book; what is offered here is a series of possible entry points to the understanding of a complex of problems, and such answers as may appear are in the main highly provisional.

One reason for the difficulties lies, as it so often does, in the development of historiographical tradition. We are all familiar with the medievalists' division of labour in this area, though we may not have articulated that familiarity to ourselves. Power relations amongst the upper classes, for which we have from most periods a good deal of evidence, have been the object of subtle analyses, using a range of methodologies. Together, these constitute a modern approach to medieval political history, which includes not only traditional political narrative and constitutional history but also what Johannes Fried has called *neue Verfassungsgeschichte*, 'new institutional history'.[2] With this, we know where

---

1 The version published here retains much of the initial lecture form; the footnoting is light and bibliographically eclectic. Fuller bibliography may be found in the other papers in this volume, and in T. Reuter, 'The Medieval Nobility in Twentieth-Century Historiography', in M. Bentley, ed., *Companion to Historiography* (London, 1997), pp. 177–201.
2 T. Reuter, 'Pre-Gregorian Mentalities', *Journal of Ecclesiastical History*, xlv (1994), 465–74, at p. 466.

we are and where we are going, even if the journey is not so certain as to become dull.

The history of the exercise of aristocratic power over virtually everybody else is quite different. We have more evidence of the results of that exercise than of the exercise itself. Its investigation has often enough been left to economic historians, who have tended to treat it as a given in the short run and as determined by economic trends in the long run – as no doubt, amongst other things and taking the long run as the one in which we are all dead, it was. Relations *between* nobles, however defined, and peasants, however defined, are not only differently documented; historians (and usually different kinds of historian) have perceived and conceptualized them differently from relations *amongst* members of the *ceti dirigenti*. The same goes for relations between nobles and other town-dwellers, a separate subject about which little will be said here for reasons of space. Even Marxist and Marxisant historians, who have been governed by what still seems to me to be the essentially correct perception that the economics of exploitation in pre-capitalist modes of production depended on extra-economic coercion, have had relatively little to say about how that coercion actually functioned, and about whether to coneptualize it as a coercion which was always present and felt or as an 'in-the-last-instance' coercion which underlay other, subtler forms of domination, social control, and interaction.

A final difficulty to be mentioned at the outset is the sheer range of the subject, and the relative shortage of useful source-materials. It is the 'long *ancien régime*', from around 1300 to around 1800, which starts to have material of real substance to offer, and historians of the early and high middle ages working on this topic can only envy their late medieval and early-modern colleagues, who have material at their disposal which is simply not available to medievalists. Answers to many of the questions posed here are likely to be best provided by microhistory, but though we may admire the work of historians like Carlo Ginzberg, Emmanuel Le Roy Ladurie, David Sabean, or Alan MacFarlane we cannot easily emulate it, though we can draw on some of it for suggestive analogy and analysis.[3] However, it is not only a matter of sources but of temporal and regional variation. We are here considering social relationships which might be described as 'classed' or 'casted' (by analogy with 'gendered'); but these relationships found articulations which were undoubtedly 'gendered', and were also 'aged' and 'regioned' and differentiated in other ways as well. Which may be no more than a rather neologistic way of saying that things varied a lot. In these circumstances, impressionistic generalizations cannot be the end-product, only a set of opening hypotheses, to be tested on the ground against specific power relations in specific contexts.

The basic question to be posed is 'how did they get away with it'? The members of the élite strata of the societies we study as medievalists, at most times and in most places, were mainly concerned with competition amongst

---

[3] D. Sabean, *Power in the Blood* (Cambridge, 1984), is particularly suggestive for the issues raised here.

themselves to increase or maintain their share in the fruits of domination. It was in this competition that they appear to us and seem to have appeared to themselves to have invested the bulk of their time, energy, and resources: the global domination of these strata over the rest of society was, so it seems, something which largely took care of itself. The Middle Ages are not unique in this, of course: it is characteristic of all human societies beyond the hunter–gatherer stage of development. What we have to do now is to move from banal generalization to investigation of the specific forms taken by this automatic and largely unchallenged domination in medieval western Europe.

We should not, of course, ignore the contribution of direct and unmediated coercive force, in particular of bullying and brutality, to such dominance.[4] To acknowledge that the medieval world was not run using permanent coercion, unlike, say, a slave-plantation or a gulag or a chain-gang, is not to rule out the possibility of the use of force altogether.[5] In the early Middle Ages at least it was definitely on the agenda. Gregory of Tours offers a truly horrific story of a low-status couple who married against the will of their lord and took refuge in a church. The priest mediated a settlement by which the lord promised never to part them in life; but after they had emerged from the church he fulfilled his promise by having them buried alive in the same pit.[6] Of course there are folktale overtones in this story, as in other anecdotes which turn on the oath which is observed to the letter whilst being broken in spirit (Isolde's oath to Mark, for example, echoed in the close of *Grettissaga*, or the treachery practised by Hatto of Mainz against the Babenberger Adalbert). But here we are closer to reality. Nothing we know about the behaviour of Merovingian rulers and aristocrats towards each other suggests that they would have been incapable of such actions, and such behaviour was not confined to the barbarian era. Professor Bisson, I, and others have recently been engaged in debating the nature of the Feudal Revolution, and while we have disagreed on many things, we are agreed that much tenth- and eleventh-century domination was established by methods confined in our own era to mafiosi and terrorists, whether state or otherwise.[7]

The inherent possibility of physical brutality lay behind much verbal and gestural brutality. Marc Bloch has a nice discussion of the case of a twelfth-

---

4 This is especially worth noting given a recurrent tendency amongst social and economic historians to stress the cooperative and communitarian elements in early medieval lord–peasant relationships; for a classic example see the debate between H. Vollrath, 'Herrschaft und Genossenschaft im Kontext frühmittelalterlicher Rechtsberatungen', *Historisches Jahrbuch*, ci (1981), 33–71, and H.-W. Goetz, 'Herrschaft und Recht in der frühmittelalterlichen Grundherrschaft', *Historisches Jahrbuch*, civ (1984), 392–410.

5 Even in these examples, we still have to distinguish between the permanent and visible reminder of the possibility of coercion and its permanent exercise. Not even chained galley-slaves were whipped continuously.

6 Gregory of Tours, *Historiarum libri decem*, v. 3, ed. B. Krusch and W. Levison, 2nd edn, *MGH, Scriptores Rerum Merovingicarum*, i/1 (Hanover, 1951), pp. 197–8.

7 T. N. Bisson, 'The "Feudal Revolution"', *Past and Present*, cxlii (1994), 5–42; D. Barthélemy, 'Debate: the "Feudal Revolution" I', *Past and Present*, clii (1996), 196–205;

century aristocrat, Joel, who was reclaiming possession of a serf, Warin, who had allegedly been freed by his father, because he was refusing to cooperate with Joel's pious patronage of the monastery of Marmoutier. The Marmoutier *notitia* which records this gives Joel's words as follows: 'Greatly irritated against him, I told him that he was my *collibertus*, that I could sell him or burn him and give his land to whomever I wished, as being my *collibertus*' land.' Bloch commented, quite rightly, that there was no legally acknowledged right to burn servile dependents in twelfth-century France, and noted that 'no fire was lit and no confiscation took place'.[8] The dispute ended with a settlement which was quite favourable to Warin. But to see Joel's threats as mere idle bluster, designed to cover up his weakness when faced with a situation which he could not and in fact did not control, is to miss some of the point.[9] He may not actually have been able to burn Warin (or even have intended to do so); but he lived in a world where he could *make* such threats with complete impunity and where perhaps not much could have stopped him from carrying them out had he chosen to do so, even if he might have suffered some mild penalty thereafter.

Moreover, we should not underestimate the functional effect of collective aristocratic behaviour. Notoriously, the three orders model of society which emerged in the course of the ninth and tenth centuries implied mutual obligations of support and protection between lords and dependents. Though Georges Duby saw it as losing its charms and also its abilities to reflect social reality by the early thirteenth century, this may reflect more its fossilization as an idea than its loss of power over minds. It can be found well articulated in a fifteenth-century Lollard tract, for example,[10] and it is the implicit theoretical underpinning of the relationship of mutual support and protection explored by Otto Brunner in his study of late medieval German seigneurialism, *Land und Herrschaft*.[11] It is a construct to which we shall have to return when considering the

S. D. White, 'Debate: the "Feudal Revolution" II', *Past and Present*, clii (1996), 205–23; T. Reuter, 'Debate: the "Feudal Revolution" III', *Past and Present*, clv (1997), pp. 177–95; C. J. Wickham, "Feudal Revolution" IV', *Past and Present*, clv (1997), pp. 195–208; T. N. Bisson, 'Reply', *Past and Present*, clv (1997), pp. 208–25.

8   M. Bloch, 'The "Colliberti": A Study in the Formation of the Servile Class', in M. Bloch, *Slavery and Serfdom in the Middle Ages*, ed. W. R. Beer (Berkeley, 1975), pp. 93–149 at pp. 99–103.

9   For a more nuanced reading of this episode and the role of anger within it see R. E. Barton, ' "Zealous Anger" and the Renegotiation of Aristocratic Relationships in Eleventh- and Twelfth-Century France', in *Anger's Past: The Social Uses of an Emotion in the Middle Ages*, ed. B. H. Rosenwein (Ithaca, 1998), pp. 153–70, at pp. 153–4, 161–3.

10 *Jack Upland, Friar Daw's Reply and Upland's Rejoinder*, ed. P. L. Heyworth (Oxford, 1968), ii, 11–17: 'Preestis office to preche þe gospel truli and to preze in hertei deoutli, to mynistre þe sacramentis freli, to studie in Goddis lawe oonli, and to be trewe ensuampleris of holi mennes lijf continuli, in doyinge and in suffringe. Lordis office to iustifie mysdoersin ward & to defende Goddis seruauntis from letters of her office. Comouns office to truli labour for þe sustinaunce of hem silf, & for prestis and for lordis doynge wel her office.' Cited in an anonymous final-year Glasgow dissertation in 1998.

11 Most conveniently consulted in O. Brunner, *Land and Lordship: Structures of Govern-*

ideological arm of noble domination. Here we may follow the recent study by Gadi Algazi and stand the notion on its head.[12] For against whom did the labouring classes need those who fought to protect them? Against those who fought. Algazi gives a very plausible functional explanation of the collective effects of a culture of aristocratic feuding: since such feuding was primarily directed against other aristocrats' infrastructure, against the crops, utensils, houses, and animals on which their rural dependents relied to keep themselves alive and produce surplus value for their superiors, it reproduced the need for protection from lords as a collective, even though individual lords might be the economic and political losers in such feuding.

Less extreme forms of bullying and coercion were also important. Michael Toch has drawn attention in an important article to the ritual use of force and of brutally undeferential language in establishing domination: 'He gave him a strong slap in the face, saying, you shall be my servant.' Lords demanded without social graces: 'They forced the peasants to show them the way.' The bad-tempered unpredictability of lords reflected the lack of social restraint they felt in their dealings with inferiors, for whom social and physical humiliation were constantly present as a possible outcome.[13] Even saints, who as we know were by and large noble, readily used force when they appeared in visions to members of the lower orders. Often they *had* to do so. Saints who wished to approach the great in this world behaved like courteous aristocrats: rather than burst directly into the dreams of the great, they let them know that they required attention, just as a noble calling on another noble would have himself announced. Such was the fear inspired in the serving orders by their masters that saints frequently needed to appear more than once in visions and with escalating terror, using force in order to persuade the messengers to take the message.

Yet at no point are we dealing *solely* with the direct application of arbitrary coercive force. One aspect of the way in which élites maintain their dominance is today quite well understood and theorized: they equip themselves with a whole series of social markers which express and actualize that dominance. In particular, they use the social markers of appearance, speech, dress, food, and rituals of social interaction. Let us examine these in turn.

Nobles were immediately recognizable as such. First of all, they were better fed, and therefore larger. Horst Fuhrmann has pointed out that whereas average heights in the rest of the population were considerably lower than they are today, the skeletal evidence for identifiable members of royal and high aristocratic families suggests that many of them were of much the same height as

ance in Medieval Austria, trans. H. Kaminsky and J. van Horn Melton (Philadelphia, 1992), with a valuable historiographical introduction; the discussion of *Schutz und Schirm* can be found at pp. 218–22.

12 G. Algazi, *Herrengewalt und Gewalt der Herren im späten Mittelalter: Herrschaft, Gegenseitigkeit und Sprachgebrauch* (Frankfurt, 1996).

13 M. Toch, 'Asking the Way and Telling the Law: Speech in Medieval Germany', *Journal of Interdisciplinary History*, xvi (1986), 667–82.

middle-class males in the OECD countries today.[14] He was drawing specifically on evidence from eleventh- and twelfth-century Germany, but his conclusions clearly have much wider validity. Moreover, aristocratic families took some pains to preserve this physical differentiation. It is a commonplace in discussions of monastic life to say that monasteries were used, amongst other things, as a dumping ground for old and physically and mentally disabled members of aristocratic families. A frequently cited comment by a twelfth-century abbot is that 'some are lame, others are one-eyed, blind even, others are one-armed, but on the other hand, all are noble', and it is not difficult to collect other examples of the blind, lame, and simple-minded in monasteries.[15] Generally this behaviour-pattern has been considered in terms of the social role of monasteries – it gives a fresh gloss on the phrase 'care in the community', and aristocratic investment in closed communities can be seen as welfare provision as well as piety – but it clearly had an important functional explanation as well. By literally shutting 'imperfect' members of their families away from view, aristocrats collectively preserved a social image of themselves as different from others. In a world where mental and physical disabilities were common and visible, aristocrats appeared collectively exempt from such scourges.[16]

The fact that aristocrats were well fed was in itself a social marker, quite apart from any physiological effects this may have had. To be noble was to eat meat rather than vegetables and to drink wine rather than water or ale.[17] Charlemagne's irritation with his doctors at being put on a diet of stews rather than roast (Einhard implies that this was low-cholesterol food, but it may simply have been a matter of poor teeth in old age) was, I think, not just the grumpiness of the senior citizen forced to change his dietary habits, but also annoyance, perhaps even concern, at losing grip on a social marker.[18] Karl Leyser suggested that there was a practical reason for the notoriously excessive meat-

14 H. Fuhrmann, *Germany in the High Middle Ages, c. 1050–1200* (Cambridge, 1986), pp. 9–10.

15 P. Johnson, *Equal in Monastic Profession* (Chicago, 1991), p. 46: in the twelfth century Bondeville contained 'two simple-minded girls' and Obazine had a child blind from birth. See also M. de Jong, *In Samuel's Image: Child Oblation in the Early Medieval West* (Leiden, 1996), pp. 168–9, and the well-known observations of Peter, abbot of Andernes on taking office in 1161 about the drunk, the lame, and the blind in his monastery 'but almost all are noble', cited by P. Delehaye, 'L'organisation scolaire au XIIe siècle', *Traditio*, v (1947), 230.

16 For a suggestive analogy, consider the way the East India Company dealt with Europeans who went mad: W. Ernst, *Mad Tales from the Raj* (London, 1991), pp. 23–4, 37. The company also insisted that the European widowed and destitute be forcibly repatriated if their inability to command European status markers threatened the dominant classes' image; *ibid.*, pp. 11–16.

17 A. Guerreau-Jalabert, 'Aliments symboliques et symbolique de la table dans les romans arthuriens (XIIe–XIIIe siècles)', *Annales E.S.C.*, xlvii (1992), 561–94. My colleague Chris Wickham refers me to M. Montenari, *Alimentazione contadina nell'alto medioevo* (Naples, 1979), which I have not yet been able to see.

18 Einhard, *Vita Karoli Magni*, c. 22, ed. O. Holder-Egger, *MGH SRG* (Hanover, 1911), p. 27.

consumption of Frankish and post-Frankish aristocratic warriors: it was a high-protein diet needed to sustain stamina in battle.[19] But it also set dominant élites apart from those they dominated: to eat meat, and often in large quantities and daily except for the church's feast-days, was quite literally conspicuous consumption. Even where dietary patterns intersected, as they clearly did with bread, social markers were maintained, white bread being for the toffs and coarse brown bread for the plebs, whether we look at the *imaginaire* of Arthurian romance or at the provisions for pensions in kind found in twelfth-century Westfalian charters.[20]

The most obvious social marker of our own society, dress, clearly served as one in medieval societies also. I shall pass over the details here, not because they were unimportant, but because here especially, as a historian with a pronounced lack of visual sense and a lack of grounding in *Realienkunde*, I am aware of my own shortcomings. We may note one or two aspects of dress as a social marker which appear to have been crucial. First, there is the importance of particular kinds of clothing as defining the aristocratic self-image, most notably furs: remember Adam of Bremen's remark that we – meaning us aristocrats – were willing to risk our immortal souls for the sake of a sable coat.[21] Remember also that church councils took repeated pains to ensure that even high-ranking clerics did not appropriate these symbols of secular aristocratic domination: no fur coats, no brightly coloured, because expensively dyed, clothing.[22] Second, there is the importance which dress played in the sumptuary codes which were drawn up with increasing frequency in most parts of Europe from the twelfth century onwards.[23] Partly this was a question of increasing ease of acquisition. Even today, the simple investment of economic resources is enough to acquire high-status clothing and other external social markers (at least in the forms offered by well-known brand-names like Armani and Boss – *really* exclusive tailors are said, in the UK at least, to require introductions and proof

---

[19] K. Leyser, 'Money and Supplies on the First Crusade', in *Communications and Power in Medieval Europe: The Gregorian Revolution and Beyond*, ed. T. Reuter (London, 1994), pp. 77–95, at p. 86.

[20] Guerreau-Jalabert, 'Aliments symboliques'; F. Irsigler, '*Divites* und *pauperes* in der Vita Meinwerci: Untersuchungen zur wirtschaftlichen und sozialen Differenzierung der Bevölkerung Westfalens im Hochmittelalter', *Vierteljahrschrift für Sozial- und Wirtschaftsgeschichte*, lvii (1970), 449–99.

[21] Adam of Bremen, *Gesta Hammaburgensis Ecclesiae Pontificum*, iv. 18, ed. B. Schmeidler, *MGH SRG* (Hanover, 1917), pp. 245–6.

[22] Cf. John of Salisbury's account of the protests against such a prohibition at the council of Reims (1148): *Historia Pontificalis*, ed. M. Chibnall (London, 1956), p. 8. The prohibition was a long-standing one; cf. the authorities cited in Gratian, Causa xxi, questio iv.

[23] A subject in itself; for an introduction see A. Hunt, *Governance of the Consuming Passions* (Basingstoke, 1996); C. K. Killerby, 'Practical problems in the Enforcement of Italian Sumptuary Law, 1200–1500', in *Crime, Society and the Law in Renaissance Italy*, ed. T. Dean and K. J. P. Lowe (Cambridge, 1994), pp. 99–120; D. O. Hughes, 'Sumptuary Legislation and Social Recognition in Renaissance Italy', in *Disputes and Settlements*, ed. J. Bossy (Cambridge, 1983), pp. 69–99.

of status before offering their services). This was evidently already becoming true in the later middle ages; but it was also a question of what was most immediately obvious as a social marker. To place restrictions on the acquisition of the obvious front-rank marker was to put a trip-wire well in front of the citadel, though we shall have to consider later how successful such efforts were.

Another very obvious social marker was the organization of space. This could be the subject of a paper in itself, and I can only make a few points here. The first is that we are easily inclined to forget the *cultural* aspects of such phenomena as *incastellamento* or the nucleated village of the high and late middle ages with its tenements grouped around a church (usually the lord's church) and a lordly dwelling which was on a quite different scale from other houses. These are not simply the incidental spatial by-product of an intensification or reorganization of lordship; they are its continuing social and cultural expression. More generally, we have to recognize that the rhythms of most medieval landscapes were punctuated by visible signs of aristocratic dominance in the form of fortifications, dwelling-houses, churches, and, not least important, monasteries and other religious houses, where for much of our period the memory of those who were important and had names was preserved and that of those who were not important was not. Ecclesiastical and urban historians have long acknowledged the significance of spatial shaping in towns for religious and secular purposes, but it was also present in the countryside.

Perhaps most important of all the markers was speech. Even in our own society, the acquisition of dominant speech-patterns and other forms of what Pierre Bourdieu calls 'cultural capital' remains more difficult than appropriating other social markers,[24] and in medieval western Europe it was very difficult indeed. The defining characteristic of those who did not belong was their 'rustic speech'. It was the inability of the free peasants of Wolen to make themselves understood at the royal court 'because of their rustic speech' which lost them their lawsuit against their lord in the mid-eleventh century: in effect, they were frozen out and ignored.[25] This is also a specific example of the more general phenomenon that the possessors of Bourdieuesque 'social capital', those who 'know how things are done', exercise control over any games which are being played – this is not just a matter of speech, but of manners. It is a commonplace of vernacular literature that even the aristocrat as completely unknown stranger is recognizable as someone who must be treated as an aristocrat by his 'courteous speech'.[26] But it is not only a matter of how you speak, but also of how you exchange speech. Michael Toch has reminded us how pronouns expressed

---

[24] P. Bourdieu, *Outline of a Theory of Practice* (Cambridge, 1977), pp. 171–87.

[25] T. Reuter, *Germany in the Early Middle Ages, c. 800–1056* (London, 1991), p. 215.

[26] Thus the hero of *Ruodlieb* is instantly recognized as noble by the huntsmen he meets on entry into the Great King's kingdom: *The Ruodlieb*, i. 72–94, ed. C. W. Grocock (Warminster, 1985), p. 32. Dr Stuart Airlie has reminded me that Bede's account of the captured noble Imma also implies that it was difficult if not impossible for a noble to conceal his nobility: *Bede's Ecclesiastical History of the English People*, iv. 22, ed. B. Colgrave and R. A. B. Mynors (Oxford, 1969), pp. 400–4.

differentiation: second person singular for the lower orders, second person plural for the higher ones (the use of third person singular and third person plural, which create a linguistic space in which high and low are prevented from addressing one another directly at all, appears to be post-medieval). He has also stressed the expectational shaping of speech exchanges:

> the lord does most of the speaking, while the peasant takes the part of the silent listener. . . . This verbalized taciturnity reflects the experience that talking to and being talked to by a lord are dangerous. By waiting for his superior to speak, the peasant conforms to the pattern of deference.[27]

There are, of course, some difficulties in apprehending past reality here. Though we can read the imaginative literature of the medieval past with sensitivity in order to recreate some aspects of past reality, we are in the last resort dealing with an *imaginaire*: there is no one-to-one correspondence. Even types of source which might at first sight appear to provide a more direct representation turn out to be problematic; as Patrick Geary has recently pointed out, the inscribing of direct speech in records and narratives does not somehow magically fix and preserve orality like a tape-recorder or video-recorder, but instead creates a 'fictive character' within the written record, one which is disjoint from actual past utterances.[28] Toch, for example, cites a late-medieval court record as an example of deferential speech:[29]

> Questioned . . . as to the lord's right to collect deceased tenants' cattle and belongings, this man admits that such has indeed been unchallenged practice. 'But whether this is the monastery's right or not, he does not know'. Despite this disavowal, he continues: 'He also says that the lords have this declared as their right, and he has never heard that anyone has taken them to court on this.'

But although this might seem an example of 'acquiescence plus reticence', it is clearly also a lawyer's translation of whatever the peasant might actually have said into 'evidence' that the claim has not been challenged (and therefore has the status of prescriptive right). It is a rewriting of what was actually said in terms which make it useful to those for whom the rewriting was being done.

The collective effect of all these social markers was to create a world in which aristocrats were unmistakably different, immediately recognizable. For themselves, at least, the dominant classes reinforced these perceptions by constructing a classed world. The evident differences were legitimated and explained by representations and myths of origin. The legal and social status of Catalonian peasants and their lords' legal right to mistreat them (the wonder-

---

27 Toch, 'Asking the Way', p. 670.
28 Orally at a seminar in Southampton, March 1998; see his forthcoming contribution to the proceedings of the Royal Historical Society's conference on Oral History, held in March 1998.
29 Toch, 'Asking the Way', p. 675.

fully named *ius maletractandi*) were accounted for by their alleged descent from those who had failed to remain faithful at the time of the Islamic conquest: their past cowardice legitimized their present subordination.[30] In Hungary, their alleged descent from those who had failed to respond to a military summons by Attila had a similar effect.[31] Elsewhere, the dominant classes equipped themselves with origin myths which legitimated their difference: Trojan descent and the like made them outsiders within by right of past conquest. Noah's curse of Ham and his descendants was also pressed into service. The emergence of the rhetorical question 'Who was then the gentleman?' across late-medieval Europe was not a spontaneous appeal to the classless state of nature in the Garden of Eden; it was a ju-jitsu attempt to wrest control of historical legitimation away from those who possessed it. Such myths were reinforced by constructions of the rural population which dehumanized them. In imaginative literature and in visual representations they were presented as semi-monsters, brutish, wild, inhuman (depictions which they shared with Jews, Saracens, and other outsiders). Even those voices which urged their treatment as defenceless fellow-humans and as Christians did so within the context of an 'in spite': in spite of their bestiality.[32]

The collective effect of the appropriation of exclusive social markers and the construction of legitimatory myths was to create a sense of confidence – even if this overlay unease and fear – amongst the dominant. One way in which this found expression was in a whole series of stories about aristocrats who had to disguise themselves but were unable to do so, or at least to do so completely effectively.[33] A few examples from the high middle ages may illustrate this. Becket, fleeing from the council of Northampton to France disguised as a lay brother, was nearly recognized from the way in which he looked at a hawk which a nobleman was carrying: I imagine that it was not only the connoisseurship with which he viewed the bird, as has generally been surmised, but also the fact that he was, by looking closely at a nobleman's hunting-animal, failing to maintain the social distance which would have been appropriate for someone of

30 P. Freedman, 'Catalan Lawyers and the Origins of Serfdom', *Mediaeval Studies*, xlviii (1986), 288–314; 'Cowardice, Heroism and the Legendary Origins of Catalonia', *Past and Present*, cxxi (1988), 3–28.
31 R. C. Hoffmann, 'Outsiders by Birth and Blood: Racist Ideologies and Realities Around the Periphery of Medieval Culture', *Studies in Medieval and Renaissance History*, vi (1983), 14–27. See also K. Schreiner, 'Religiöse, historische und rechtliche Legitimation spätmittelalterlicher Adelsherrschaft', in *Nobilitas: Funktion und Repräsentation des Adels in Alteuropa*, ed. O. G. Oexle and W. Paravicini, Veröffentlichungen des Max-Planck-Instituts für Geschichte, 133 (Göttingen, 1997), pp. 376–430.
32 P. Freedman, 'Sainteté et sauvagerie: deux images du paysan au moyen âge', *Annales E.S.C.*, xlvii (1992), 539–60.
33 For a fuller discussion of the anecdotes discussed in this paragraph, see T. Reuter, 'Die Unsicherheit auf den Straßen im europäischen Früh- und Hochmittelalter: Täter, Opfer und ihre mittelalterlichen und modernen Betrachter', in *Träger und Instrumentarien des Friedens im hohen und späten Mittelalter*, ed. J. Fried, Vorträge und Forschungen, 43 (Sigmaringen, 1996), pp. 169–201, at pp. 196–7.

his assumed rank, which threatened to give him away. Hugh Capet was also suspected of being not what he claimed to be when returning from Rome in disguised after visiting Otto II in 980, and of course Richard Lionheart's disguise failed him altogether when returning from the Third Crusade. William Longchamps, attempting to flee from Dover in disguise in 1191, was exposed to the crowd by his lack of knowledge of English: this too I would gloss not as an absolute ignorance of the language, though that is conceivable, but as an inability to command the appropriate socio-linguistic register. These anecdotes and others like them may reflect past reality, but they also reflect the élite's own self-image: our nobility shines through unmistakably even when we try to disguise ourselves.

So far I have tried to suggest ways in which the dominant classes saved themselves the trouble of constantly having to apply a Leninist 'who whom?' by the exercise of a Gramscian social and cultural hegemony. But this is open to at least two objections. The first is that it is still, by and large, history from above. It explains how the dominant classes constructed the world and expected it to function, but assumes too readily that those for whom it was constructed accepted the construction. The second, even more fundamental, is that, even if we do assume that it functioned more or less as I have suggested, that does not in itself explain dominance, because the appropriation of social markers and the ability to define the world are not the cause of dominance but belong to its products.

As to the first point, that we cannot assume that the social and cultural hegemony which I have just sketched to you was actually received in the way which theories of hegemony assume, I largely agree. The work of the contemporary anthropologist and sociologist, James Scott, is particularly helpful in this respect. His work on *Weapons of the Weak* shows how dominance is in fact most often resisted not through open defiance, which would today be dangerous, just as it would have been in our period, but through acts of sabotage, pilfering, going slow, and so forth: all of these are easily enough documented from our period.[34] Note also that most, though not all, openly articulated movements of resistance in our period, from the *Stellinga* uprising in the ninth century through the Patarini movement in the eleventh to the Jacquerie in the fourteenth century,[35] were shaped vertically as much as horizontally: there are at the least elements of conflict within the dominant classes visible, in the course of which a minority group has recourse to the manipulation of popular discontent.

[34] J. C. Scott, *Weapons of the Weak: Everyday Forms of Peasant Resistance* (New Haven, 1985).

[35] E. J. Goldberg, 'Popular Revolt, Dynastic Politics and Aristocratic Factionalism in the Early Middle Ages: the Saxon *Stellinga* Reconsidered', *Speculum*, lxx (1995), 467–501; H. Keller, 'Pataria und Stadtverfassung, Stadtgemeinde und Reform: Mailand im "Investiturstreit" ', in *Investiturstreit und Reichsverfassung*, ed. J. Fleckenstein, Vorträge und Forschungen, 17 (Sigmaringen, 1973), pp. 321–50, at pp. 324–35; D. M. Bessen, 'The Jacquerie: Class War or Co-opted Rebellion?', *Journal of Medieval History*, xi (1985), 43–59.

Scott also has important things to say about the way in which cultural and social hegemony can be publicly affirmed while being privately denied or rejected: there is a public transcript, to which the hegemonial group can – generally – command or compel assent, but this does not necessarily extend inside people's heads.[36] The siphoning off of physically or mentally 'imperfect' members of the aristocracy into religious houses is an example of this: it may indeed, as I have suggested, have helped to create and sustain a public transcript of aristocratic perfection, but that does not necessarily mean that no one was aware of the existence of a 'hidden transcript' in which this perfection was known to be mythical: monastic servants and dependents would have had such knowledge, and been able to think accordingly, even if they could not challenge the public transcript openly.

There is an important further point about dominance, which is that it was (and is) not in practice exercised in such a way as to emphasize the *group* us/them distinctions, but on the contrary in such a way as to play these down. Kipling's Indian short stories give quite a good steer on the kind of differentiation with which we must reckon. His Anglo-Indians have, amongst themselves, a collective view of 'the natives' and a whole range of social markers which distinguish them from those over whom they rule. But they are careful, in dealing with *individual* 'natives', to observe social distinctions within the dominated group. There are those who must be treated with respect (and who presumably gain in status within their own social segment from the fact that they *are* treated with respect), and there are those who need not be so treated. This has to be borne in mind when we look at relationships between the lordly class and rural non-nobles. True, we find lords dealing with rural communes and village collectives, but we should not assume that these non-noble groupings were internally structured on an egalitarian basis. It is not hard to find the equivalents of village elders in our period, if we begin to look. Just as nobles, as we noted at the outset, invested the bulk of their time, energy, and resources in competition amongst themselves, so too did those whom they dominated, though such competition is much less clearly visible to us in our surviving source materials.

Such competition in practice had the effect of diverting attention from the real 'who whom' of medieval societies. So also did the fact that much dominance was exercised through intermediaries. Peasants and others not only did not find it easy to deal with nobles because of the latter's cultural dominance; they had, much more often, to deal with representatives of various kinds: reeves, bailiffs, mayors, overseers. These intermediaries often themselves became the primary focus of resentment. There is a whole set of anecdotes which play on what might be called the Haroun al-Raschid theme, where the ruler or lord goes unknown amongst his people, or meets them directly in unexpected circumstances, and hears their plaints: the well-known tale of Geoffrey of Anjou meeting a forester

---

[36] J. C. Scott, *Domination and the Arts of Resistance* (New Haven, 1990), especially chapter IV, pp. 70–107: 'False Consciousness or Laying it on Thick?'

and learning from him how his agents deceived him and oppressed his people is one example.[37] We know that lords mistrusted their agents – think of the provisions in the *Capitulare de villis*, or Meinwerk of Paderborn, arriving at one of his *curtes* and, finding weeds in the fields, ordering the wife of the *villicus* to be deprived of her 'ambitious clothing'.[38] The triangulation of lords, their agents, and their dependents helped to create a veiling solidarity between lords and dependents: it is significant, I think, that many of the hostile stories about social climbers who appropriated the social markers of the dominant classes, concern precisely such intermediate figures, from the reeves of Ekkehard of St Gall onwards. This is not only true of historical and hagiographical sources, but also of imaginative literature: the criticism of social climbing implicit in *Meier Helmbrecht* is a good example.[39]

But perhaps the most fundamental objection to explanations of aristocratic dominance in terms of Gramscian cultural hegemony is that even to the extent that this actually functioned as posited, this functioning was the effect of a dominance which was logically and structurally prior to it, not the other way round. Partly, of course, this is a matter of how we see the world. We can and do and should avoid the aporia of cause and effect, chicken and egg, by considering past societies as functioning systems. In E. P. Thompson's memorable formulation: 'class is not this or that part of the machine but *the way the machine works* once it is set in motion – not this and that interest, but the *friction* of interests – the movement itself, the heat, the thundering noise'.[40] But a systemic approach carries its own dangers; in particular, it makes it more difficult to account for substantial change across time, and this is a serious difficulty here. Although I have so far presented the kind of undifferentiated middle ages of which we are all professionally socialized to be deeply suspicious, we must be aware of the fact that the aristocratic dominations of the eighth and of the fifteenth centuries, though they shared common elements of substance, were not identical. I want to conclude by sketching the trajectory of aristocratic domination in our period.

I have already by implication argued that there was a shift of emphasis as time progressed from direct dominance to indirect dominance by means of the social and cultural markers I have listed. This is not one of those simple developments beloved of historians by which everything becomes more complex and

---

37 Discussed, along with other examples, by T. N. Bisson, '*Feudal Revolution*', pp. 35–9.

38 *Capitulare de Villis*, ed. V. Boretius and A. Krause, *MGH Capitularia, i* (Hanover, 1893), no. 32, pp. 83–90; the suspicion is summed up in c. 60, p. 88: 'Nequaquam de potentioribus hominibus maiores fiant, sed de mediocribus qui fideles sint'. For Meinwerk's difficulties with his *villici*, see *Vita Meinwerci episcopi Patherbrunnensis*, cc. 147–51, ed. F. Tenckhoff, *MGH SRG* (Hanover, 1921), pp. 78–80; the story of the ambitious reeve's wife is told in c. 148.

39 See *Peasant Life in Old German Epics: Meier Helmbrecht and Der arme Heinrich*, trans. C. H. Bell, Records of civilization: Sources and studies, 13 (New York, 1931).

40 E. P. Thompson, *The Making of the English Working Class*, 2nd edn (Harmondsworth, 1968), p. 939.

sophisticated until we arrive at the unimaginable complexity and sophistication of our own societies; it reflects the *diffusion* of aristocratic domination between the early and the late middle ages. The transformation of nobility to incorporate (at least in some respects) previously non-noble groups of warriors in the high middle ages, and the gentrification which marked the late middle ages, were phenomena which accompanied an objectively increasing appropriation of surplus value from the rural population. There were, quite simply, *more* nobles around in the later middle ages than there had been in previous eras. And 'around' is used advisedly: they were spatially more diffused, more omni-present. Considering the class *as* a class, we can say that its members main-tained and developed dominance by sharing and diffusing it, even if as individuals they were pursuing a quite different strategy. It is perhaps for this reason that the evidence which stresses the use (and the misappropriation) of social markers comes mostly from the late middle ages. There was an increasing investment in this kind of cultural dominance.

In the last resort, however, it was an investment with diminishing returns. The last two centuries of the medieval era saw substantial movements of rebel-lion at least once in most parts of Europe (Italy, where urban dominance of the countryside gave a rather different curve to the trajectory, is probably the great exception). These were only the most visible forms of breakdown; aristocratic domination, the collective ability to choose the game and define its rules, was subverted still more by the daily effects of the market pressures created by the post-plague rise in the value of labour relative to other resources. Both kinds of pressure from below made use of some of the ideologies of domination by taking them seriously, as is well known from the grievances of 1381 and 1525. A regrouping became necessary, and it took the form of a redefinition. The old forms of social and cultural domination were reinscribed in a political order which was also in the process of being reformed. An order formerly willed by God would in future be willed not only by God but by his princes, who main-tained order, estate, and *Polizey* (in its sixteenth-century sense) for their own purposes, but in doing so increasingly defined infringements of and challenges to social and economic hierarchy as public, *political* offences.[41] The nobility became a part of the *ancien régime*, and fell along with it, or rather, was trans-formed along with it; but that is a subject for another conference.

---

[41] See H. Kaminsky, 'Estate, Nobility, and the Exhibition of Estate in the Later Middle Ages', *Speculum*, lxviii (1993), 684–709, and for more systematic surveys of the 'stratific-ation' of the late medieval and early-modern nobility, e.g. *The European Nobilities in the Seventeenth and Eighteenth Centuries*, ed. H. M. Scott, 2 vols (London, 1978); J. Dewald, *The European Nobility, 1400–1800* (Cambridge, 1996). More general surveys from which medievalists may learn much of structural and comparative interest include Oexle and Paravicini, *Nobilitas*; M. Bush, *Noble Privilege* (Manchester, 1983); M. Bush, *Rich Noble, Poor Noble* (Manchester, 1988); *Europäischer Adel 1750–1950*, ed. H.-U. Wehler (Göttingen, 1990), especially the article by O. G. Oexle, 'Aspekte des Adels im Mittelalter und in der Frühen Neuzeit', pp. 19–56.

II

Central Middle Ages

7

Princely Nobility in an
Age of Ambition (*c.* 1050–1150)

T. N. Bisson

Who could doubt that princes (*principes*) were noble in the eleventh and twelfth centuries? For admirers of their power to speak of the counts of Flanders as 'noble (or 'most noble) prince' looks on its face a redundancy. Yet the sort of semantic precision we delight in was no deterrent to writers of these post-Carolingian centuries, and it is probably no accident that they sometimes employed the superlative *nobilissimus* in reference to princes, dukes, and counts. For they more readily thought of nobility as attributive than as categorical, were eager to size people up (and down) qualitatively. Princes (that is *principes*, dukes and counts) were considered together with kings the ruling élite of Europe; and if their nobility was not exactly that of kings and queens, it lacked only the sacral attributes bestowed by consecration or coronation to distinguish it.[1]

The regality of medieval princes has not been overlooked by historians. Charlemagne's concession of Aquitaine to Louis the Pious was an archetypal structure of power, still a kingdom in the ninth century before becoming one of a cluster of principalities in which the blood or imprint of an imperial aristocracy survived. Duchies or counties could be spoken of as kingdoms in the eleventh and twelfth centuries; one or two, like Bavaria, retained some privileges of early medieval monarchy. As to France, where the Capetian kings have been habitually viewed as the makers of central government, Karl Ferdinand Werner argued in an important article that the princes not only carried on in an ages-old programme of regalian power, but even had priority over the kings in devising administrative institutions.[2]

Yet it seems likely that contemporaries experienced princely power not so

---

1 *Genealogiae comitum Flandriae*, ed. L. C. Bethmann, *MGH SS*, ix (Hanover, 1851), 304, 308; cf. p. 312; *Notae de Mathilda comitissa*, ed. P. E. Schramm, *MGH SS*, xxx/2 (1929), 974; Hugh of Fleury, *Liber modernorum regum francorum*, *PL*, clxiii, 873; Rupert of Deutz, *De trinitate*, *PL*, clxvii, 1493; etc. See generally *Kings and Kingship in Medieval Europe*, ed. A. J. Duggan, King's College London Medieval Studies, 10 (London, 1995). See also Constance Brittain Bouchard, *'Strong of Body, Brave and Noble': Chivalry and Society in Medieval France* (Ithaca, 1998), p. 26.
2 P. Wolff, 'L'Aquitaine et ses marges sous le règne de Charlemagne', *Karl der Grosse,*

much in its regality as in its nobility. And on this matter scholars have had less to say, probably because it is, and was, easy to muddle kingliness and nobility. What was, and is, understood by nobility could easily be reduced to qualitative attributes – birth, prowess, generosity, and the like – commonly shared by kings and lesser nobles. As set forth in chronicles, *vitae*, and *chansons de geste*, these attributes serve to define an aristocratic ethos that was abiding, yet inert. That (non-royal) princes of the later eleventh and twelfth centuries were essentially noble by prevailing tests requires no demonstration. What is problematic is whether the nobility attributed to them had some character of its own, either collectively in reference to the times in which they lived or individually in reference to writings in which these princes were commemorated. This essay is devoted to the nobility of some princes or princely houses, ecclesiastical as well as secular, whose ambitions and exploits were recorded in texts which, if well known in themselves, have not hitherto been examined as a class.

The texts come first, for it is only through the ideas of their authors that I can hope to characterize the princely nobility they discerned. Adam of Bremen, a canon of Hamburg church from about 1068, wrote about his archbishopric, and very centrally about Archbishop Adalbert (1043–72), towards 1072–75.[3] In 1096 Count Fulk *Richin* (1068–1109) narrated the deeds of his ancestor-counts of Anjou down to his own day.[4] A few years later a French monk was writing in Poland about the dukes (and sometime kings) of the Poles down to 1113; the inspiring hero for him was Bolesław III ('Wrymouth', 1102–38).[5] In 1115–16 the priest Donizo of Canossa composed his versified *Life* of the Countess Matilda of Tuscany (1076–1115).[6] From about 1108 until the 1120s several canons of Compostela recorded the trials and triumphs of their bishop Diego Gelmírez, who finally won recognition of metropolitan status for himself and his church in 1120.[7] The notary Galbert wrote brilliantly of Count Charles of

Lebenswerk und Nachleben, ed. H. Beumann, 5 vols (Düsseldorf, 1965–68), i, 265–306; and chapters by G. Tellenbach and K. F. Werner (notably the latter's ch. 6) in *The Medieval Nobility: Studies on the Ruling Classes of France and Germany from the Sixth to the Twelfth Century*, ed. T. Reuter, Europe in the Middle Ages, Selected Studies, 14 (Amsterdam, 1978). On Bavaria, W. Störmer, 'Bayern und der bayerische Herzog im 11. Jahrhundert: Fragen der Herzogsgewalt und der königlichen Interessenpolitik', *Die Salier und das Reich*, ed. S. Weinfürter, 4 vols (Sigmaringen, 1991), i, 503–47.

3   *Magistri Adam Bremensis gesta hammaburgensis ecclesiae pontificum*, ed. B. Schmeidler, 3rd edn., *MGH SRG* (Hanover and Leipzig, 1917), iii.

4   *Fragmentum historiae andegavensis*, ed. L. Halphen and R. Poupardin, *Chroniques des comtes d'Anjou et des seigneurs d'Amboise*, Collection de textes pour servir à l'étude et à l'enseignement de l'histoire [hereafter CTSEEH] (Paris, 1913), pp. 232–8.

5   *Galli anonymi chronicae et gesta ducum sive principum polonorum* [hereafter *Gpp*], ed. K. Maleczńyski, *MPH n.s.*, ii (Kraków, 1952).

6   *Vita Mathildis celeberrimae principis Italiae carmine scripta a Donizone presbytero qui in arce canusina vixit*, ed. L. Simeoni, Rerum italicarum scriptores, v/2 (Bologna, 1930–40).

7   *Historia compostellana*, ed. E. Falque Rey, CCCM, lxx (Turnhout, 1988).

Flanders when the shock of his brutal murder in the church of Saint Donatian at Bruges (March 1127) was fresh in mind.[8] And in the 1150s monks of Santa Maria of Ripoll were moved by the triumphant conquests of Count Ramon Berenguer IV (1131–62) to commemorate his dynastic ancestry in the house of Barcelona.[9] Other texts devoted to the deeds of noble princes could easily be added to this list, such as the versified *Deeds* of Robert Guiscard (d. 1085) or even the celebrated *Lives* of Henry IV (1056–1106) by an anonymous author and of Louis VI (prince c. 1100–1108, king 1108–37) by Suger of Saint-Denis.[10] But the observations to be drawn from the seven texts listed above can generally be validated in other sources comparable or otherwise. What may be more pertinent here is that my chosen records of two bishops and their churches, of the duke (-kings) of Poland, of counts of Anjou, Flanders, and Barcelona, and of a countess of Tuscany are far from being generically uniform. Not one of them was written to respond to the questionnaire of this Colloquium; the one of them written by a noble prince himself is hardly the most responsive to my own questions; while the two most nearly comparable compilations of *gesta*, those by the priest of Canossa and by the monks of Ripoll, have remarkably different stories to tell. Nor were the writers of these texts well stationed to influence one another. The *Historia compostellana* and the *Deeds of the Princes of Poland* were written simultaneously by French clerics working at the distant extremities of Latin Europe. The most I can claim for a connective inspiration is that at least five of the seven writers (those other than Adam and Donizo) seem to have had west-Frankish traditions of culture and power in common.[11]

The authors of these narratives were content to stress the deeds of their subjects, writing of the latter as the builders and defenders of principalities. Their nobility lay in such works, was earned by achievement such as defence of their lands against the onslaughts of 'pagans', Saracens, Bohemians, or Germans. Deeds could make up for deficient birth. The principal author of the *Historia compostellana* paused to characterize Diego Gelmírez, the son of 'worthy' castellan parents, only after having devoted a lengthy first book to

8 *Histoire du meurtre de Charles le Bon, comte de Flandre (1127–1128) par Galbert de Bruges*, ed. H. Pirenne, CTSEEH (Paris, 1891). There is a new edition by J. Rider in CCCM, cxxxi (Turnhout, 1994).

9 *Gesta comitum barcinonensium* [hereafter *Gcb*], ed. L. Barrau Dihigo and J. Massó Torrents, Cròniques catalanes, ii, Institut d'Estudis Catalans (Barcelona, 1925).

10 William of Apulia, *Gesta Roberti Wiscardi*, ed. M. Mathieu, Istituto siciliano di studi bizantini e neoellenici, Testi, 4 (Palermo, 1961); *Vita Heinrici IV. imperatoris*, 3rd edn by W. Eberhard, *SRG*, 58 (Hanover and Leipzig, 1899); Suger, *Vie de Louis VI le Gros*, ed. H. Waquet, Les Classiques de l'histoire de France au moyen âge (Paris, 1929). As texts relating to high nobility, these are in no way inferior to those cited in nn. 3–9; nor can the latter be regarded as a library of high nobility in themselves. It is not clear that contemporaries discerned a class of princes as such, let alone those I have chosen to study as a group.

11 See generally B. Guenée, *Histoire et culture historique dans l'Occident médiéval* (Paris, 1980), ch. 8; and T. N. Bisson, 'On Not Eating Polish Bread in Vain: Resonance and Conjuncture in the *Deeds of the Princes of Poland* (1109–1113)', *Viator*, xxix (1998), 275–89.

describing his prowess and vigilance in the service of Santiago and his patrimony. This tradition of modest birth, recorded in Bishop Diego's circle at the
height of his power and pretensions, can hardly be questioned; what is more
remarkable is that for all the praises heaped on him, Canon Gerald made no
claim for his nobility as such. The bishop's greatness lay in his impersonation of
Saint James and in the lordship (*patronatus, dominatio*) thereby entailed.[12] The
matter of birth works differently in the records of Anjou, Poland, and Barcelona.[13] In these cases, because the ancestor princes were themselves counts (or
dukes) it hardly mattered who *their* progenitors were. In the twelfth century it
was proclaimed that the Angevin ancestor called Ingelgarius by Fulk *Richin* was
descended from an illustrious Roman-British family, a contention that seemed
far-fetched enough to one modern scholar to suggest lowly origins for the
dynasty.[14]

What my sample texts suggest, in reality, is that princely greatness could
descend quite as well from virtuous deeds as from noble blood. Of the two traditions, the first appealed to the compilers of the *Deeds of the Princes of Poland*
and the *Deeds of the Counts of Barcelona*, the second to Adam of Bremen,
Donizo of Canossa, and Galbert of Bruges. In the cases of Poland and Barcelona, the ascription of dynastic descent from (respectively) a peasant and a
knight added ethnic resonance to familial lustre, for it implied some popular
identification in political virtue, precocious hints of Polish and Catalan identities. It is worth noting that neither of these texts insists on nobility as such, their
authors resorting easily to epithets of victory and glory and, in the discourse of
the monks of Ripoll, worthiness (*probitas*).[15]

On the other hand, Charles the Good could be described as having been born
to do his good works. The son of King Cnut IV of Denmark (1080–86) and the
princess Adela of Flanders, he was said by Galbert to have overshadowed the
kings of his mature years.[16] Likewise, Adam of Bremen and Donizo insist on the
illustrious ancestry of Archbishop Adalbert and Countess Matilda. The latter's
parents, Boniface of Tuscany and Beatrice of Lorraine, united 'in the letter B',
and 'bonitate pares, similantur nobilitate'. And Donizo speaks of

> Nobilis et fortis Mathildis, maxime doctrix;
> Ipsa tenens montes inimicos despicit omnes.[17]

But it was Adam of Bremen, the earliest of these writers, and only he, who
insisted most explicitly on his subject's nobility and who, in doing so, virtually

---

[12] *Hist. compostellana*, i and ii.
[13] Cited above, nn. 4, 5, 9.
[14] *Chronica de gestis consulum andegavorum*, ed. L. Halphen and R. Poupardin, *Chroniques des comtes d'Anjou*, pp. 26–9. See also R. W. Southern, *The Making of the Middle Ages* (London and New Haven, 1953), p. 82.
[15] *Gpp*, i. 1, 2, pp. 9–11; *Gcb* (Redacció primitiva), cc. 1, 2, pp. 3–5.
[16] *Histoire du meurtre* , p. 1
[17] *Vita Mathildis*, i. 9, lines 781–90; ii. 4, lines 459–60.

inventoried the virtues generally attributed to great princes in his day. His account is doubly remarkable in view of Adam's awareness of the likeness of his subject's ambitions to those of lay princes and of his flaws of character.

Archbishop Adalbert, said Adam, was noble in birth and deeds alike. 'Most noble in family' (he was the son of Duke Frederick and Princess Agnes), he was handsome, chaste, generous. He addressed himself humbly to the servants of God and the poor and could be overbearing with the mighty. In his excesses of arrogance, he publicly berated important men for their 'ignobility', and all for infidelity, believing it a 'most evident sign of nobility' that he spent from his own patrimony while others basely squandered what they were given. Adalbert put on feasts such as to put royal hospitality in the shade. For all his noble virtues, he might have been saintly (*beatus*), wrote Adam, save for the vice of vainglory. Ambitious in works of endowment and construction and 'in his solicitude for his diocese', he thought it a great thing and worthy of himself everywhere to leave a 'monument to his nobility'.[18]

So it seems that Adalbert himself, not only his biographer, laid claim to his nobility. This does not mean that their perceptions of princely power were out of the ordinary. If my other texts are less explicit in attributing personal excellence, they recount deeds (*gesta*) which correspond to those of Adalbert and which permit us to see that what was most characteristic of the archbishop's nobility was his lordship. It is true that Adalbert was thought to engage in a public function (*officium*), that of expanding his church's mission in Baltic lands.[19] But all princes of this age were supposed to be officers of public authority with comparable responsibilities, as the commemorative texts make clear. And the archbishop was a lord–prince in his functions, one who dominated circles of retainers lay and religious, who functioned in a court of adherents and functionaries, who held great courts, who worried about the fidelity of those about him and under him. He 'bore himself so as to prove himself equal to the rich and greater than the magnates while none the less the father of orphans and the judge of widows'.[20] Every inch a prelate mindful of the practical needs of his ministry, he felt no difficulty in deriving secular power from his religious office and his nobility, allying with the kings, avidly accepting their benefactions, creating his own military clienteles, building and managing castles, negotiating and fighting with Saxon dukes, and seeking to impose metropolitan authority on Danish and other northern churches. By turns lavish or (and increasingly) arbitrary, Adalbert indulged a taste for affectively manipulating people in his service or debt. His enjoyment of lordship became a lust for power in which the great prelate ultimately failed to secure his aims. His biographer, sobered by the conspicuous

---

18 *Gesta hammaburgensis*, iii. 2, pp. 144–5; 9, p. 150; 18, p. 161; 40, p. 183; 65, p. 212; 68, p. 215.
19 *Ibid.*, iii. 1, p. 143: 'in legatione gentium, quod primum est Hammaburgensis ecclesiae officium.'
20 *Ibid.*, iii. 24, p. 167.

desertion of the late prelate's followers and sycophants, concluded in a telling apostrophe: 'What good are they to you now, O venerable father Adalbert, those things you have ever prized, the world's glory, the crowds of people, the elation of nobility?'[21]

Altogether comparable to Adalbert's were the princely aims of Diego Gelmírez, who was elected bishop of Compostela in 1104 and promoted (precariously) archbishop in 1120. Lordship was even more essential to his nobility than to Adalbert's because the writers of the *Historia compostellana* made no claim for his illustrious birth. And while these authors fell short of Adam's literary skill in portraying character, their vast compilation proves again that princely ambitions came as easily to these Christian prelates on the frontiers of Europe as to the high-born dukes and counts. It is blatantly clear that Diego made no distinction between his impersonated (even apostolic) powers to cele-brate sacraments, consecrate bishops, or impose sworn fidelity on fighting men commended to him. If words attributed to him can be trusted, he repeatedly invoked the memory of King Alfonso VI (1069–1109), imposing 'laws, rights, peace [and] justice', as the sanctions for episcopal lordship (*dominatio*).[22] It was not simply a matter of a few castles, but more like a patronage of Galicia, whereby the invasions of pirates (including English ones) and the depredations of ill-rewarded knights were the tasks of Saint James to remedy. And from the theft of Saint Fructuosus's relics (for safekeeping in the apostolic church!) to the insistent negotiation with Queen Urraca and her allies to the imposition of stat-utes of peace to the mighty success in securing papal recognition of Saint James's claim to metropolitan status: were these not so many *gesta* of a princely prelate? 'Not so much bishops as quasi-princes', wrote Canon Gerald of Diego and his predecessor-bishops.[23]

Gerald added, writing in the preface to Book II of the 'Register of Saint James', that Compostela's power was (in some part) 'royal power which [the bishops] had from the kings'.[24] The context here was that of Christian war against the Muslims, perhaps the most potent generator of nobility in the genera-tions turning on 1100. And when this context is enlarged so as to include anti-Viking defence and Christian campaigns against Baltic and Slavic heathen peoples, it applies to most of the records here in question. It explains the origins of princely power in Anjou, Poland, and Barcelona, as represented by Fulk *Richin*, the anonymous encomiast of the Piast dukes, and the monks of Ripoll. In the case of Anjou, Count Fulk, writing in 1096, may well have had the visit of Pope Urban II to Angers in mind (as he surely was grumbling about King

---

21 *Ibid.*, iii. 66, p. 213: 'Quid tibi nunc, o venerabilis pater Adalberte, prosunt illa, quae semper dilexisti, gloria mundi, populorum frequentia, elatio nobilitatis.'
22 *Hist. compostellana*, i. 79.4, p. 124; 86.1, p. 139; see also i. 95, p. 154; ii. 1, p. 220.
23 *Ibid.*, i. 76, p. 118; 103. 1, p. 175 (piracy); i. 15.1–5, pp. 31–6 (theft of relics); i. 99–117, pp. 163–218 (primacy); and ii. 1, p. 220: 'non tantum episcopi, sed quasi principes'. See generally R. A. Fletcher, *Saint James's Catapult: The Life and Times of Diego Gelmirez of Santiago de Compostela* (Oxford, 1984).
24 *Hist. compostellana*, ii. 1, p. 220.

Philip's theft of his wife) when he wrote of the founder-counts as Christian defenders of the honour they had snatched from the 'pagans' and 'held' by the grace of Carolingian royal concession. The whole text stresses Christian probity, knightly prowess, and militant, indeed aggressive, lordship; it plausibly reckons the deeds of Geoffrey Martel (1040–60) as winning 'praiseworthy fame through the whole kingdom of France'.[25]

Likewise, the *Deeds of the Princes of Poland* tells – at far greater length – a story of dynastic lordship. From its origins in rustic virtue and the opportune conversion of Mieszko I (*c.* 963–992), it made much of the early solidarity between Otto III of Germany and Bolesław I 'Chrobry' (992–1025), whose recognition as king became a cornerstone of subsequent ducal power. It was well remembered in the writer's day that King Bolesław had first imposed peace, order, and prosperity on the Poles. Capable of disciplining and rewarding his fighting men, he won exemplary battles against the Hungarians, the Bohemians, and the Russians. He promoted Christian foundations, and secured the system of local production and supply that was a distinctive feature of early Slavic polity. And he ruled personally, through stewards (*villici*) and 'vice-lords' in the localities, through the maintenance of knights (said sometimes to feel more like the king's sons than warriors), and through 'counsellor friends' with whom he shared his table, functions, and secrets. His greatness, as depicted by the Anonymous, lay in his lordship: 'he is truly the father of his country, he the defender, he is the lord' who does not squander but spends for the public good.[26]

This regime and its collapse gave point to the novel heroism of Bolesław III, whom the Anonymous represented as the restorer of Poland 'to its pristine state'. Here again, as in the *Fragmentum* of Anjou, a model of lay nobility is powerfully implicit: much is made of this Bolesław's miraculous conception (by means of timely prayers by the monks of Saint-Gilles in Provence), his youthful precocity in hunting and arms, his vesting with the belt of knighthood in a glittering assembly at Płock. Bolesław's readiness to renew the old expansionist oppression won him the loyalties of fighting men with whom he battered Prussians, Pomeranians, Bohemians, and even the German invaders led by Henry V in 1109. This was a militant power exercised by a duke whose dazzled memorialist claimed that he ruled not a duchy but a kingdom. And while Bolesław, who had forced his inept elder brother Zbigniew from his dynastic share, never reclaimed the lapsed royal title, it is not impossible that his princely lordship was celebrated in the sung *laudes* commonly reserved for kings.[27]

---

25 *Fragmentum*, pp. 232–3, 235.
26 *Gpp*, i, pp. 1–59; (c.) 15, p. 34: 'Hic est vere pater patrie, hic defensor, hic est dominus, non aliene pecunie dissipator, sed honestus rei publice dispensator, qui dampnum rustici violenter ab hostibus illatum castello reputat vel civitati perdite conferendum.'
27 *Ibid.*, ii. 20, p. 87; ii. 1–20, pp. 63–87. Also B. Kürbis, 'Zum Herrscherlob in der Chronik des Gallus Anonymus (Anfang 12. Jahrhundert): "Laudes regiae" am polnischen Hof?', *Patronage und Klientel. Ergebnisse einer polnisch-deutschen Konferenz*, ed. H.-H. Nolte, Beihefte zum Archiv für Kulturgeschichte, 29 (Cologne, 1989), pp. 51–67.

For all his studied eloquence, the Anonymous could not conceal the rough-
ness, even crudeness, of the great Bolesław's deportment. This was a lordship of
partisan force which proved impossible to sustain during the quarter-century the
Duke had still to live when his biographer laid down his pen. By contrast,
Countess Matilda of Tuscany and Count Charles of Flanders were celebrated as
paragons of amiable regalian lordship during these very years.

Their nobility, to repeat, was extolled explicitly. Matilda was remembered as
the 'noblest Countess' in notations made independently of Donizo when she
died; while Charles, according to Galbert, overshadowed the leading kings of
the 1120s and was thought a worthy candidate to succeed Henry V in
Germany.[28] But it is clear from the memorials of their exploits that Matilda and
Charles were venerated as lord–princes who were actively engaged in the well
being of their peoples. While Matilda was praised for her shrewd dealings with
kings and popes as also for her resolute defence of the Gregorian cause, it would
seem from her diplomas and judgments that she was respected, even sought
after, for her justice. Dominating widely dispersed lands allodial and imperial,
quite the extent of a principality, she seems every inch the lord–prince, seated in
the regalian pose of her noble progenitors in the famous miniature preserved in
Vatican, MS latin 4922. Her court, said Donizo, 'replete with feasting and
largesse', was 'like a king's court'.[29]

With Charles the Good, what stands out in the commemorative tradition is a
remarkably emphatic representation of good lordship. It is true that the treach-
erous assassination of the Count elevated him to quasi-sanctity, to a pedestal
shared by no other princes of this study. But Galbert's portrayal of a prince
actively promoting peace, justice, and welfare can be verified in other records.
The panegyrist identified a cluster of qualities – 'nobility of family' and royal
blood, the fatherly protectorate of churches, generosity to the poor, affability
and honesty in baronial company, cruelty (*crudelitas* – the word stares back at
us) and wariness with enemies – which recur like a litany in his early chapters. It
is tempting to see here a Carolingian topos of regalian power, but it is a little
more than that. Galbert's platitudes are associated with descriptions of Count
Charles's reflections on the utility of peace and of his concrete directives
towards enforcing security in towns and markets, for distributing alms and
provisions in a time of famine, and for improving agricultural yields. Indeed, it
almost seems as if Galbert's lengthy evocations of justice, peace, and famine
have been prompted by his recollection of specific measures of remedy. Here is
good lordship coming close to being government: the attentive and engaged
recognition of and care for a people's needs. This is not the form of social action
traditionally identified with *gesta*, which is not to say that Charles lacked the
knightly values. But peace and order were problematic for knights, a point not

28 *Notae de Mathilda comitissa* (cited, n. 1), p. 974; Galbert of Bruges, *Histoire*, p. 1.
29 *Vita Mathildis*, ii. 5, lines 527–8; and (ed. Simeoni, plate 1). See also *Die Urkunden und
Briefe der Margräfin Mathilde von Tuszien*, ed. E. Goez and W. Goez. MGH, *Laienfürsten-
und Dynastenurkunden der Kaiserzeit*, ii (Hanover, 1998), nos. 55, 135, etc.

lost on Charles (or on his biographer). Lacking enemies on his frontiers, he kept his knights in good fettle by putting on tournaments, a minor 'sin of levity', concluded Galbert, when compared with Charles's redemptive almsgiving.[30]

Charles the Good was in no danger of losing his virtually independent princely lordship, but his untimely death without heirs followed by King Louis VI's heavy-handed intervention in the succession crisis of 1127–28 sounded an ominous new note around west Frankland. We can hear it in the mythical prologue to the *Deeds of the Counts of Barcelona*, wherein the progenitor of the great Pyrenean dynastic house seduced and then married a Flemish count's daughter. Apart from this unsubtle hint at Carolingian royal descent, the critical point of this prologue is that the counts of Barcelona won title to the *honor barchinonensis*, and assumed 'royal power' in it, by defending it without the king's aid against invading Muslims. The genealogy that follows – and possibly this alone was the work of monks of Ripoll – traces the counts descended in several lines from the sons of Guifré the Hairy (870–897) and (in its earliest form) culminates in the resumption of most of the counties in the 'worthier and longer' posterity of the counts of Barcelona. The triumphs of Count Ramon Berenguer III (1096–1131) had opened the way to his namesake son's even greater triumphs, the conquests of Lleida and Tortosa, and to the Christian occupation of New Catalonia.[31]

It was admiration, fame, and fading memory that energized this memorial of lordly *gesta* and dynastic probity. The deeds have epic resonance, as Ramon Berenguer IV, rendered 'the most famous in the whole world', captured Almería with his fifty-two knights against almost 20,000 Saracens, and captured Lleida and Fraga on the same day![32] In the different circumstances of Christian–Muslim frontiers, there was achievement here to match Charles the Good's. But in the monastic perspective, the dynastic success was forged out of Christian aggression.

Yet here too, as in the Flemish case, a new facet of lordly probity is mentioned. The counts of Barcelona, beginning with the great Ramon Berenguer I (1035–76) had attempted to legislate a new public order to take account of the emergent society of castles and knights, for which there was no provision in Visigothic law. The authors of the *Gesta comitum barcinonensium* knew this, and mentioned the event, somewhat as Galbert had spoken of Count Charles's decrees of peace. What they failed to say – and probably did not know – is that the code of feudal law known as the *Usatges of Barcelona* was *mostly* the work of Ramon Berenguer IV and his courtier-jurists, who wrote up a new code of

---

[30] Galbert of Bruges, *Histoire*, cc. 1–8. See also *Actes des comtes de Flandre, 1071–1128*, ed. F. Vercauteren, Commission royale d'histoire: Recueil des actes des princes belges (Brussels, 1938), nos. 93–124.

[31] *Gcb*, Redacció primitiva, cc. 1–8, pp. 3–12. For the contexts, see T. N. Bisson, 'Unheroed Pasts: History and Commemoration in South Frankland Before the Albigensian Crusades', *Speculum*, lxv (1990), 281–308, at pp. 293–301.

[32] *Gcb*, c. 5, p. 8.

resoundingly regalian tenor, which, covering their tracks, they attributed to
Ramon Berenguer I and the Countess Almodis.[33] What this means in the present
context is that the monk-writer(s) of the 1150s and 1160s could not represent
princely lordship in its potentially administrative aspect. Indeed, the whole
focus of this memorial-genealogy is on a form of traditional lordly nobility that
saw worthiness as innate and self-fulfilling. Historians interested in societies are
obliged by other good evidence to see the great exploits of the twelfth-century
counts as made possible by the astounding victory of Ramon Berenguer I over
his defiant castellans (1040–60), a feat unmentioned by the *Deeds of the Counts
of Barcelona*.[34] A traditional image of princely nobility was being overtaken by
realities better grasped by the canny notary Galbert than by the monks of Ripoll.

It would be a mistake to press these commemorative writings for their conformi-
ties. They are a diverse lot, if not quite miscellaneous; their perspectives bear
variously on circumstances of their times. But they are a safe indicator of the
lordly facet of nobility. For they all speak of great persons born or called to exert
power over inferiors. They all accentuate the regalian elements of lordship,
which were, indeed, what chiefly distinguished the princes from masses of
lesser people with seigneurial power. The regalian element was, indeed, their
most essentially noble attribute, even when, as with Diego Gelmírez, the prince
was of lesser birth. On the other hand, the texts I have employed routinely
underestimate the affective nature of lordship attaching to personality and associations as distinct from birth and pretence. So do most other narrative or discur-
sive texts of the eleventh and twelfth centuries, which is why we have attended
so little to the lordly realities of personal and face-to-face power, have been disposed to think of the kings and princes of this age as governors who decided,
with or without advice, on policies.

   In the reality of their day (for I dare to believe we can safely imagine it) the
power of their nobility lay in this lordship. The Polish Anonymous and Galbert
of Bruges speak of 'natural lordship', referring to territorial power, the
presumptive right of the greatest (that is, noblest) lord to the fidelities even of
people not palpably commended to them.[35] Fidelity was even more essential to
the dynastic preoccupations of lay princes. It cannot be accidental that in four of
my select memorials relating to dynastic nobility, the histories were troubled by
disruptive treachery; what is more remarkable still, these disruptions all took
place during the years between 1060 and 1082. All were related to problematic
dynastic successions. In Anjou Geoffrey Martel's nephews succeeded to power

33 Work by R. d'Abadal i de Vinyals and P. Bonnassie, set out by T. N. Bisson, *Medieval
   France and her Pyrenean Neighbours: Studies in Early Institutional History* (London,
   1989), pp. 130–40.
34 P. Bonnassie, *La Catalogne du milieu du Xe à la fin du XIe siècle: croissance et mutations
   d'une société*, 2 vols, Publications de l'Université de Toulouse-Le Mirail, Série A, 23, 29
   (Toulouse, 1975–76), ii, chs. 9–12.
35 *Gpp*, ii. 16, pp. 81, 82; Kürbis, 'Zum Herrscherlob', pp. 52–3; Galbert of Bruges, *Histoire*,
   p. 1.

in 1060, becoming the lords of competing clienteles resulting in conflicts finally won by Fulk *Richin*, who dated his 'consulship' from his victory in 1068.[36] And it was in that very year that the eldest son of Count Ramon Berenguer I of Barcelona murdered his stepmother Almodis, a tragedy surely related to her partiality to sons of her first marriage; and the troubled joint succession of Berenguer Ramon II and his brother Ramon Berenguer II ended when the former assassinated the latter in 1082. The *Deeds* refers to the murderous brothers as the 'progeny of vipers' which 'naturally . . . kill their mothers', a reminiscence of Matthew 3: 7; 23: 33 (also cited by the Polish Anonymous in reference to pagan peoples who stubbornly resisted the Polish Duke).[37] When Baldwin VI of Flanders died in 1070, his widow and young son Arnulf III were unable to prevent his brother Robert the Frisian (1071–93) from seizing power in a revolt consummated by the battle of Cassel (1071).[38] In Poland the alleged treason and execution of Bishop Stanislas at the hands of Bolesław II in 1079 brought on a crisis in which Bolesław was driven out, to be succeeded by his younger brother Władysław Hermann (1079–1102). His weak reign was filled with partisan conniving; he was unable to prevent his sons Zbigniew and Bolesław from sharing the princely lordship, with consequences that long troubled Poland in the twelfth century.[39]

All these cases betray the structural weakness of dynastic lordship. By the later eleventh century principalities had become worth fighting for in times of problematic successions. It was an age when primogeniture was coming to seem useful without by any means superseding the practice of condominium such as had prevailed in the Spanish March and which Bolesław III, perhaps mindful of his own early experience, quite intentionally devised for his successors. Lordship mattered to high nobility not least because it meant means and wealth, as was best evident when patrimonial descent failed – as in the case of Countess Matilda.

In another aspect of princely lordship, the commemorative sources are useless. They say little or nothing about implements or offices of service, leaving it to be inferred, surely justly, that fidelity and favour, as distinct from bureaucratic competence, lay indeed at the heart of such power. One must look to charters and other non-narrative matter, as also in the case of kingdoms, to see how and why great lords tried to improve on fidelitarian patrimonial service.

---

36 *Fragmentum*, p. 237; L. Halphen, *Le comté d'Anjou au XIe siècle* (Paris, 1906), pp. 133–51.
37 *Gcb*, c. 4, p. 7; S. Sobrequés i Vidal, *Els grans comtes de Barcelona* (Barcelona, 1961), pp. 92–8, 127–33; *Gpp*, i, p. 7.
38 *Genealogia comitum Flandriae bertiniana*, ed. L. C. Bethmann, *MGH SS*, ix, 307; C. Verlinden, *Robert Ier le Frison, comte de Flandre: Etude d'histoire politique*, Universiteit te Gent, Werken Uitgegeven door de Faculteit der Wijsbergeerte en Letteren, 72 (Antwerp and Paris, 1935), chs 1–2.
39 The *Gpp* has little about all this. See ii, early chapters; and *The Cambridge History of Poland: From the Origins to Sobieski (to 1696)*, ed. W. F. Reddaway *et al.* (Cambridge, 1950), pp. 41–4, 71.

In this respect, I see no reason to differentiate between the imperatives of kings and princes, so that Karl Ferdinand Werner may have been right to conclude that the counts of Blois had precedence over the Capetians in devising offices of improved patrimonial exploitation.[40] But it is far from clear from the French evidence, including Werner's, that *prévôts* anywhere were yet accountable agents. They were novel only in the sense of responding better than the old Carolingian officers to newly clustered revenues patrimonial and public; they represented new impulses in princely courts to exploit expanding wealth while rewarding commended servants. These men held shares in princely lordship.

So while it seems that princes of the early twelfth century were prepared to resist subjugation to the realms of Germany, France, and León-Castile, they were far from being a force in themselves; nor can they be viewed as bearing the promise of permanent alternative kingdoms. Expressions of nobility, no more and no less, they were the last generation of princes to feel easy about imposing the sort of submissions on lesser lords and the masses that lord–kings, abetted by the revival of biblical and legal studies, would one day demand of their successors.

Nobility was the truism of great lordship during the century ending toward 1150. It would be wrong to distinguish territorial lordship categorically from kingship. Kings had the same nobility as their descendants Matilda and Charles the Good. Henry of Huntingdon, who opined on human greatness but not on nobility as such in his *De contemptu mundi*, spoke of the 'sublimity' shared by those who lived with kings.[41] Princely regality might seem excessive to a lord–king like Henry IV, who ousted Otto of Nordheim from the dukedom of Saxony in 1071;[42] but few kings in the next century had the means or will to insist on such altitude. Princely nobility was most conspicuously on display at royal weddings, such as in Bamberg at Christmas 1114, when Matilda of England married Henry V in a dazzling court filled with the great, including five dukes 'among which the Duke of Bohemia was cup-bearer', and with countless singers and actors.[43] It is safe to imagine that nobility could be carried away from such occasions, to be matched, or more often diluted, according to the means of dukes and counts. The latter mediated, perhaps better than lord–kings, a novel absorption of knightly customs of ordained prowess. Having told of his uncle's knighting before major battles, Fulk *Richin* remembered his own knighting in a Pentecost court at Angers in 1060; and the Polish Anonymous

---

40 Werner, 'Kingdom and Principality in Twelfth-Century France', in *The Medieval Nobility*, ed. T. Reuter, pp. 256–61.

41 Henry of Huntingdon, *Historia Anglorum*, viii, *De contemptu mundi*, c. 12; ed. D. Greenway, OMT (Oxford, 1996), p. 604.

42 *Frutolfi chronica*, c. 15, ed. F.-J. Schmale and I. Schmale-Ott, *Frutolfi et Ekkehardi chronica necnon anonymi chronica imperatorum*, Ausgewählte Quellen zur deutschen Geschichte des Mittelalters, 15 (Darmstadt, 1972), p. 80: 'Otto dux Baioarie ducatum amisit. Hic itaque Saxo genere, vir amplissime nobilitatis . . . '.

43 *Anonymi chronica imperatorum . . .* , in *Frutolfi et Ekkehardi chronica*, annal for 1114, p. 262.

described the ceremonial knighting of Bolesław III together with many other young men in an Assumption Day court at Płock in 1100.[44] The prince's leadership of knights made possible, even for prelate-princes, the deeds that won fame and exercised memory. It was a measure of his nobility and lordship at once. But nobility was the sanction for power in its widest sense, as the tenants and subjects of Countess Matilda knew. Her lifetime and the generation which followed spanned a century of anxious prosperity for the princely nobility of Europe. They envied William the Conqueror and the crusader kings from Lorraine, believed in lord–kingship. Duke Bolesław III of Poland, one of the celebrated princes of his day, made no effort to reclaim the royal title his father had permitted to lapse.

---

[44] *Fragmentum*, p. 236; *Gpp*, ii. 18, p. 86. The event may have been influenced by the knighting of Henry V a few weeks earlier.

8

Words, Concepts, and Phenomena: Knighthood, Lordship, and The Early Polish Nobility, *c.* 1100–*c.* 1350

Piotr Górecki

To the memory of Aleksander Gieysztor (1916–1999)

The study of the early history of the Polish nobility is strongly affected by its well known political, constitutional, and cultural importance between the late Middle Ages and the crisis of the Polish 'republic of nobles' in the eighteenth century.[1] Throughout this period, the Polish–Lithuanian nobility had been a clearly defined group, distinguished from the rest of society in several ways: by exclusive access to political power, high office, and representative institutions; by sovereign authority over a dependent peasantry; by control over recruitment into (and exclusion from) its own ranks; by membership in large familial groups, or 'clans', within which noble status was reproduced, and among which nobles intermarried; and by the use of several ritual devices that expressed group membership, above all proper names of the 'clans', their visual counterparts the heraldic badges, and distinct cries whose meanings and functions have been debated, but which appear to have been used in battle or assembly.[2]

---

[1] For the expression 'noble republic', and for the survey of that 'republic' in the entirety, see *A Republic of Nobles: Studies in Polish History to 1864*, ed. J. Fedorowicz, M. Bogucka, and H. Samsonowicz (Cambridge, 1982); see also: N. Davies, *God's Playground: A History of Poland*, i, *The Origins to 1795* (New York, 1982), 201–55; *The Polish Nobility in the Middle Ages: Anthologies*, ed. A. Gąsiorowski (Wrocław, 1984); R. Frost, 'The Nobility of Poland–Lithuania, 1569–1795', in *The European Nobilities in the Seventeenth and Eighteenth Centuries*, ii, *Northern, Central and Eastern Europe*, ed. H. M. Scott (London, 1995), pp. 183–305; J. Topolski, *An Outline History of Poland* (Warsaw, 1986), pp. 60–118; A. Wyczański, 'The System of Power in Poland, 1370–1648', in A. Mączak, H. Samsonowicz and P. Burke, *East-Central Europe in Transition: From the Fourteenth to the Seventeenth Century* (Cambridge and Paris, 1985), pp. 140–52.

[2] For a useful general survey, see A. Gąsiorowski, 'Research into Medieval Polish Nobility: Introduction', in Gąsiorowski, *Polish Nobility*, pp. 7–20. Surveys of the individual subjects include the following: clans – J. Bieniak, 'Knight Clans in Medieval Poland', in Gąsiorowski, *Polish Nobility*, pp. 123–76; Bieniak, 'Clans de chevalerie en Pologne du XIIIe au XVe siècle', in *Famille et parenté dans l'Occident médiéval*, ed. G. Duby and J. Le Goff (Rome, 1977), pp. 321–33; clan names: J. Pakulski, 'The Development of Clan Names in Medieval Poland', in *Nobilities in Central and Eastern Europe: Kinship, Prop-*

The two historical watersheds for current study of the nobility as a distinct social group are the reunification of the Polish kingdom under the later Piasts at the turn of the thirteenth and fourteenth centuries,[3] and the generation of the fifteenth-century chronicler Jan Długosz, who, among his prolific writings on Polish history and heraldry, produced the earliest systematic treatise on the coats of arms of the most important noble 'clans' in the kingdom.[4] Both watersheds occur late in the process of the formation and self-definition of the Polish 'nobility' as a distinct social group. In the process of Polish reunification, noble 'clans' appear to have functioned as important, well-defined political agents; while the noble families whose heraldic identity Długosz began to systematize had clearly been defined (at least in part) in terms of ritual elements of status – 'clan' structure, 'clan' names, coats of arms, and the distinct cries – for some time.

Because of the historical importance of Poland's reunification as a kingdom, and of Jan Długosz's towering presence as an author and thinker, the current historiography of the Polish nobility during the three or four centuries that preceded these two watersheds has largely been a search for the origins and antecedents of those traits and features that most clearly defined it in the fourteenth and fifteenth centuries, especially in Długosz's generation – its 'clan' structure;[5] the names, heraldic images, and cries associated with that struc-

---

erty and Privilege. History and Society in Central Europe, ii, ed. J. Bak (Budapest, 1994), pp. 85–96; coats of arms: J. Szymański, *Herbarz średniowiecznego rycerstwa polskiego* [The armorial of the Polish medieval nobility] (Warsaw, 1993); battle (and other) noble cries: J. Wroniszewski, '*Proclamatio alias godlo*: Uwagi nad genezą i funkcją zawołań rycerskich w średniowiecznej Polsce' [*Proclamatio alias godlo*: concerning the origin and the function of knightly cries in medieval Poland], in *Społeczeństwo Polski Średniowiecznej* [The society of medieval Poland], iv, ed. S. Kuczyński (Warsaw, 1990), 147–70; Z. Rymaszewski, '*Godlo proclamare*', *Acta Universitatis Lodzensis, Folia iuridica*, iv (1981), 25–50.

3 J. Bieniak, *Wielkopolska, Kujawy, ziemie łęczycka i sieradzka wobec problemu zjednoczenia państwowego w latach 1300–1306* [Great Poland, Cuiavia, and the lands of Łęczyca and Sieradz concerning the problem of state unification in the years 1300–1306] (Toruń, 1969); K. Jasiński, 'Rola polityczna możnowładztwa wielkopolskiego w latach 1284–1314' [The political role of the higher nobility of Great Poland in the years 1284–1314], *Roczniki Historyczne*, xxix (1963), 215–50.

4 J. Bieniak, 'Heraldyka polska przed Długoszem: Uwagi problemowe' [Polish heraldics before Długosz: research issues], and S. Krzysztof Kuczyński, 'Herby w twórczości historycznej Jana Długosza' [Coats of arms in the historical works of Jan Długosz], in *Sztuka i ideologia XV wieku* [Art and ideology of the fifteenth century], ed. P. Skubiszewski (Warsaw, 1978), pp. 165–232; Szymański, *Herbarz*, pp. 10–11, 16, 18. Jan Długosz's treatise initiated a heraldic and genealogical genre which remained crucial well into the eighteenth century; for subsequent heraldic and genealogical works after Długosz, through the end of the Commonwealth in the eighteenth century, see W. Dworzaczek, *Genealogia* (Warsaw, 1959), pp. 109–14; Szymański, *Herbarz*, pp. 16–17.

5 J. Pakulski, 'Z metodologii i metodyki badań nad rodami rycerskimi w średniowiecznej Polsce' [On the methodology of studies of knightly kindreds in medieval Poland], *Acta Universitatis Nicolai Copernici – Historia VIII*, 54 (1973), 23–37; J. Bieniak, 'Rody rycerskie

ture;[6] and the nobility's self-definition, in terms of kinship or otherwise.[7] The historiography is concerned primarily with the degree to which those features may licitly be projected back into earlier history, and, if so, in what sense and how far. Common to this work is the treatment of the period preceding the fourteenth century as essentially a precursor of the social group clearly documented later.

Like all historical teleologies, an inquiry set out primarily in terms of origins of later, supposedly defining traits or developments, tends to get much of the story backwards, and risks anachronism. It also tends to filter out those features and issues that did not, in a logical or empirical sense, culminate in the ultimate defining traits or features of the group. Finally, it tends to underrate and distort the significance of transition. Therefore, I will begin the inquiry into the formation of the Polish nobility in terms that are accessible at the beginning rather than at the end of the process – and then take the story forward to some point of demonstrable major transition implying the existence, self-definition, and sense

jako czynnik struktury społecznej w Polsce XIII–XIV wieku' [Knightly kindreds as a factor of the social structure in thirteenth- and fourteenth-century Poland], in *Polska w okresie rozdrobnienia feudalnego* [Poland in the period of feudal fragmentation], ed. H. Łowmiański (Wrocław, 1973), pp. 161–200; Bieniak, 'Jeszcze w sprawie genezy rodów rycerskich w Polsce' [More on the origins of knightly kindreds in Poland], in Kuczyński, *Społeczeństwo*, v (Warsaw, 1992), 43–55; Bieniak, 'Możliwości i zadania polskich genealogów-mediewistów' [The possibilities and research tasks of Polish medievalists specializing in genealogy], in *Tradycje i perspektywy nauk pomocniczych historii w Polsce: Materiały z sympozjum w Uniwersytecie Jagiellońskim dnia 21–22 października 1993 roku Profesorowi Zbigniewowi Perzanowskiemu przypisane* [Traditions and perspectives of the auxiliary sciences of history: materials from a symposium held at the Jagiellonian University on October 21–22, 1993, in honour of Professor Z. Perzanowski], ed. M. Rokosz (Kraków, 1995), pp. 77–91; Bieniak, 'Rozmaitość kryteriów badawczych w polskiej genealogii średniowiecznej' [The diversity of criteria for identification of persons in Polish medieval genealogy], in *Genealogia – problemy metodyczne w badaniach nad polskim społeczeństwem średniowiecznym na tle porównawczym* [Genealogy – methodological issues in the studies on Polish medieval society in a comparative context], ed. J. Hertel (Toruń, 1982), pp. 131–48; K. Jasiński, 'Problemy identyfikacji osób w badaniach mediewistycznych' [Issues of personal identification in medieval studies], *ibid.*, pp. 9–26. For the most current generation of reconstructions of particular 'noble' families, see n. 184 below.

6 Szymański, *Herbarz*, pp. 7–21; Bieniak, 'Heraldyka', pp. 167–82, 187–92; S. Kuczyński, 'Osiągnięcia i postulaty w zakresie heraldyki polskiej' [Achievements and research goals of Polish heraldics], in Rokosz, *Tradycje i perspektywy*, pp. 93–105.

7 Conceived in terms of 'solidarity', a 'feeling of consanguinity' (*poczucie pokrewieństwa*), and 'cohesion . . . of knightly kindreds' (*zwartość . . . rodów rycerskich*) (Bieniak, 'Rody', pp. 162–3, 180–91); or in terms of 'a real existence of kindreds' (*ibid.*, p. 182); or in terms of a sense of common descent (M. Koczerska, 'Świadomość genealogiczna możnowładztwa polskiego w XV wieku' [Genealogical consciousness of the Polish high noble élite in the fifteenth century], in Kuczyński, *Społeczeństwo*, ii (Warsaw, 1982), 288–92; J. Kurtyka, *Tęczyńscy. Studium z dziejów polskiej elity możnowładczej w średniowieczu* [The Tęczyńskis: a study in the history of the Polish high noble élite in the Middle Ages] (Kraków, 1997), pp. 33–44). These elements of self-definition are of course crucial for the

of identity of that social group. A useful point of departure is the distinction made by Susan Reynolds between words or concepts on the one hand, and phenomena on the other.[8] Prior to some point in the fourteenth century, it seems that the term or concept of 'nobility' is in itself relatively unhelpful in the study of the privileged social groups as a phenomenon, whether in their early, perhaps incipient, or in their late, better defined, variant. What is helpful is to focus on the phenomenon which I will call patterns of social privilege; then inquire into the ways in which these patterns defined social groups in the Polish duchies between the twelfth and the mid-fourteenth centuries; and finally note in what sense such groups comprise a 'nobility'.

As used here, patterns of social privilege refer to (1) the activities of particular persons or groups which suggest unusual access to power or influence (within a local, regional, or supra-regional domain), and (2) the classifications of such persons or groups, as reflected in the written evidence. This approach is also indebted to Reynolds. I begin by reconstructing collective activities, then inquire into the ways in which such activities ultimately related to the definition of social groups.[9] The activities that most clearly indicate privilege in the Piast duchies between (at the latest) the twelfth century and the fourteenth fall into three broad areas: (1) making gifts to the saints, (2) waging war and facilitating peace, and (3) performance of service, above all to the Piast rulers.

1. Collective activities and group privilege

Since as far back as written evidence is available, substantial groups of donors endowed a small but expanding network of bishoprics, monasteries, and priories of canons, secular and regular.[10] The participants in these gifts included the Piast dukes (after 1320, kings), and several other categories of donors. Duke Henry the Bearded of Silesia identified their collective profile well in one of his documents for the Cistercian convent at Trzebnica, issued in 1208. He noted

nobility's sense of identity – the subject of much of this essay – but since all of them are directly documented in the post-Piast period, I base my treatment of group identity on a range of different sources.

8 S. Reynolds, *Fiefs and Vassals: Medieval Evidence Reinterpreted* (Oxford, 1994), pp. 12–16.

9 Reynolds, *Kingdoms and Communities in Western Europe, 900–1300*, 2nd edn (Oxford, 1997); for my use of her work in another context, see P. Górecki, 'Communities of Legal Memory in Medieval Poland, c. 1200–1240', *Journal of Medieval History*, xxiv (1998), 127–54.

10 The twelfth century and the first half of the thirteenth are a great age of endowment of Benedictine, Cistercian, Augustinian, and (somewhat later) mendicant orders with substantial estates that included large clusters of settlement and population, forest, hunting, fishing, and beekeeping rights, and mineral exploitation. In the course of the thirteenth and fourteenth centuries, endowment to these major ecclesiastical recipients continued, but in addition the proliferating rural and urban parish churches were similarly endowed. On the categories of ecclesiastical recipients, see J. Szymański, *Kanonikat świecki w Małopolsce od końca XI do połowy XIII wieku* [Canons secular in Little Poland from the end of the

that the nuns' estate had been formed from 'my [own] villages', from 'other villages [that] had been ecclesiastical', and from villages formerly possessed 'by clerics or by knights, in hereditary right'. Some time before 1208, Henry had 'acquired' the ecclesiastical or knightly villages from their former holders – 'some [of the villages] of the clerics and of the knights by exchange, and some by purchase, while some were given by knights for the love of God' – and in turn conveyed the entire estate on the convent.[11] The alienators of the estate included previously existing ecclesiastical institutions; ecclesiastics who disposed of their own, 'hereditary' holdings; and the 'knights'. Notably, Duke Henry paused to emphasize the pious motivation of the 'knights' in particular, and so presumably considered them an especially important category of donors.

Beneath Duke Henry's tidy division of the donors into the 'knights', ecclesiastics, and the Piast dukes themselves, his own and his cousins' charters include long and detailed lists of individual donors, and narratives of the transactions whereby their gifts were effected. Lists of donors are especially prominent features of the earliest record, stretching back to the twelfth century and into the early thirteenth – most notably in the early records of the endowment of the community of the canons regular of the Holy Sepulchre at Miechów in Little Poland compiled in 1198, and of the Cistercian monasteries at Lubiąż and Trzebnica in Silesia compiled between 1175 and 1218, and in a steady trickle of more fragmentary records thereafter.[12] The persons and activities revealed in this way help us populate, so to speak, the social group that participated in this area of collective activity.

In general, the population of donors is identified by personal names, and (less

eleventh through the mid-thirteenth century] (Lublin, 1995), pp. 95–9; J. Kłoczowski, 'Dominicans of the Polish province in the Middle Ages', in *The Christian Community of Medieval Poland*, ed. Kłoczowski (Wroclaw, 1981), pp. 73–118; Kłoczowski, *Dominikanie polscy na Śląsku w XIII–XIV wieku* [Polish Dominicans in Silesia in the thirteenth and fourteenth centuries] (Lublin, 1956); R. Bartlett, *The Making of Europe: Conquest, Colonization and Cultural Change, 950–1350* (Princeton, 1993), pp. 5–23; J. Szymański, 'Biskupstwa polskie w wiekach średnich: organizacja i funkcje' [Polish bishoprics in the Middle Ages: organization and functions], in *Kościół w Polsce* [The Church in Poland], ed. J. Kłoczowski, 4 vols (Kraków, 1966), i, 127–236; Kłoczowski, 'Les Cisterciens en Pologne, du XIIe au XIIIe siècle', *Cîteaux*, xxviii (1977), 111–34. On the estates with which such recipients were endowed, see Wacław Korta, *Rozwój wielkiej własności feudalnej na Śląsku do połowy XIII wieku* [Development of feudal great property in Silesia until the mid-thirteenth century] (Wrocław, 1964); P. Górecki, *Economy, Society, and Lordship in Medieval Poland, 1100–1250* (New York, 1992), pp. 23, 45–62, 67–114.

11 *Schlesisches Urkundenbuch* [hereafter *SU*], i, ed. H. Appelt (Vienna, Cologne, and Graz, 1963–71), no. 115 (1208), p. 81, 'et omnes villas meas in ambitu constitutas illuc dedi. Alias vero que fuerunt ecclesiastice et clericorum hereditarie vel militum acquisivi commutatione, emptione vel donatione, ecclesiasticas tantum commutatione, clericum vel militum quasdam commutatione, quasdam emptione, et quedam a militibus pro dei sunt amore donate sicut inferius patebit.' The subsequent volumes of the *SU* cited in this essay are: *SU*, ii–iv, ed. W. Irgang (Vienna, Cologne, and Graz, 1978–88).

12 Documents with substantial lists, or groups, of donors (or other alienators) for the monasteries of Miechów in Little Poland, and for the major early monasteries in Silesia, include

frequently) by family association – usually of a very close range, encompassing fathers and sons, mothers and sons, groups of brothers, and husbands and wives;[13] or by nicknames; or by locations of their most important (perhaps ancestral) estates.[14] In addition, but less regularly, they are identified by three epithets: 'count' (*comes*), 'lord' (*dominus*), and 'knight' (*miles*). Among these, the epithet *comes* seems to refer to an especially powerful sub-group of donors (and is closely associated with office, on which more below);[15] and the epithet *miles* clearly corresponds to the frequent references to the Polish 'knighthood'

the following: St Vincent's – *SU*, i, no. 19 (1139–49), p. 15; Miechów: *Kodeks dyplomatyczny Małopolski*, ed. F. Piekosiński (Kraków, 1876–86, repr. New York, 1965) [hereafter *K.Mp.*], ii, nos. 375–6 (1198), pp. 13–14, 16–18; *S.U.*, i, no. 65–6 (1198), pp. 42–4; Lubiąż: *ibid.*, i, nos. 45 (1175), p. 28; 49 (1177), p. 30; 69 (1200), p. 46; 77 (1202), pp. 50–1; 171 (1218), p. 125; 332, p. 253 (a forgery of *c.* 1295, emending no. 77 [1202]); St Mary's: *ibid.*, i, no. 58 (1180–1201), p. 35; Trzebnica: *ibid.*, nos. 83 (1202–03), pp. 55–7; 114–15 (1208), pp. 79, 81–3; 181 (1218), p. 134 (incorporates nos. 83, 114, and 115 – new alienors only); 247 (1224), pp. 180–1. A sample of documents with similar lists for other ecclesiastical institutions includes: *Codex diplomaticus et commemorationum Masoviae: Zbiór ogólny przywilejów i spominków mazowieckich*, ed. J. K. Korwin-Kochanowski (Warsaw, 1919) [hereafter *KMaz.*], no. 78 (1155), p. 75 (Czerwińsk); *SU*, i, no. 28 (1155), pp. 20–1 (diocese of Wrocław); *KMp.*, ii, no. 385 (1220), p. 27 (Mstów); *SU.*, i, no. 226 (1223), p. 165 (Rybnik); ii, no. 196 (1240), p. 124 (Henryków); *KMp.*, ii, no. 419 (1242), pp. 63–5 (Staniątki); no. 423 (1243), pp. 69–70 (*Kodeks dyplomatyczny katedry krakowskiej ś. Wacława*, ed. Staniątki; F. Piekosiński (Kraków, 1874, repr. New York, 1965) [hereafter *KKKr.*], no. 34 (1252), p. 42 (Sieciechów); *KMp.*, i, no. 44 (1254), p. 53 (Zawichost); *KKKr.*, no. 61 (1260), pp. 78–80 (Wąchock); *KMp.*, i, no. 58 (1262), p. 71 (Zawichost). In the course of the thirteenth century, consolidated lists of this type were largely eclipsed by records of gifts and other alienations by individual persons (sometimes associated with family groups, in varied ways, and of varied range – more on this below), issued in the name of, or about, such transactions; that is, the consolidated, large documents essentially fragment into much shorter and (in a formal sense) standardized records. Records of this kind number in the hundreds between the mid-thirteenth and the mid-fourteenth century; their proliferation surely reflects the rising importance of the written record, and may also reflect changes in the content and meaning of pious gifts, during the Piast period – see P. Górecki, '*Ad Controversiam Reprimendam*: Family Groups and Dispute Prevention in Medieval Poland, *c.* 1200', *Law and History Review*, xiv (1996), 213–43, at p. 218, n. 18. Insofar as such records are relevant to the group identifications with which this essay is concerned, I cite them throughout the text below.
13 I have discerned this pattern for the early thirteenth century, in Górecki, '*Ad Controversiam*', pp. 215–16 (n. 12), 220–3, and it seems to be continuous throughout the thirteenth and early fourteenth centuries – with, however, a gradual but significant change around 1300, which I discuss at nn. 157–62 below.
14 K. Mosingiewicz, 'Imię jako źródło w badaniach genealogicznych' [The personal name as a source in historical research], and J. Pakulski, 'Geneza, recepcja i znaczenie przydomków rycerskich w średniowiecznej Polsce: Uwagi problemowe' [Origins, reception, and meaning of knightly nicknames in medieval Poland: issues of research], both in Hertel, *Genealogia – problemy*, pp. 72–97 and 98–117, respectively; a case study in the meaning and functions of a nickname is Górecki, 'Communities', pp. 142–3.
15 A. Bogucki, 'Komes w polskich źródłach średniowiecznych' [The *comes* in the Polish medieval sources], *Roczniki Towarzystwa Naukowego Toruniu*, lxxvi (1971), part 3; Bieniak, 'Rody', p. 166 n. 11.

and the 'knightly villages' recorded elsewhere. Otherwise, such epithets are applied without any evident regularity; that is, the records neither explicitly explain their meaning, nor apply them to particular persons in any pattern that explains the variety of their use.

This range of donors, and the relative importance of the population called 'knights', remained in their broad contours remarkably constant throughout the thirteenth and fourteenth centuries. The thirteenth-century record from Silesia and the other Piast provinces frequently refers to 'knights', and to 'villages of the knights' (*villae militum*) as a type of estate or tenure – always on the clear assumption that the constructs of 'knighthood' and of the tenure and estate pertaining to it, were well-established and well-understood by the first years of the thirteenth century at the latest.[16] As a kind of conceptual shortcut, Polish scholars have sometimes classified the lay donors – however categorized in the evidence – outright as the Polish 'knighthood'.[17] This inference may overstate the uniformity of the donor group, and understate the fluidity of membership within the 'knighthood' itself, at any one moment and over time. An important direction in the reconstruction of privileged groups within the Polish society is a recovery, insofar as the evidence permits, of what it is that the twelfth-, thirteenth-, and early-fourteenth-century authors of the written record meant by these terms; to whom these terms referred; and how such meanings changed over time.

Another area of activity that reflected and defined social privilege was the ability to engage in the use of force against others (licitly or otherwise), and in its converse – to facilitate social peace. Use of force in medieval Polish society falls into three broad categories: (1) acts of violence; (2) exactions of a wide range of obligations from the mass of the population, nominally on behalf of the ruler; and (3) periodic warfare among dukes and their followers during what is called the period of 'fragmentation' of Poland, spanning the early twelfth and early fourteenth centuries.[18] As elsewhere in medieval Europe, these uses of

---

16 For usages that clearly assume this kind of familiarity with 'knighthood' and related constructs, see Górecki, *Economy, Society, and Lordship*, pp. 105–7, and Górecki, *Parishes, Tithes and Society*, pp. 13, 84, 105–15, 121–3, 127.

17 M. Cetwiński, *Rycerstwo śląskie do końca XIII wieku: pochodzenie, gospodarka, polityka* [Silesian knighthood until the end of the thirteenth century: origins, economy, politics] (Wrocław, 1980); Cetwiński, *Rycerstwo śląskie do końca XIII wieku: biogramy i rodowody* [Silesian knighthood until the end of the thirteenth century: biograms and genealogies] (Wrocław, 1982); J. Mularczyk, *Władza książęca na Śląsku w XIII wieku* [Ducal power in Silesia in the thirteenth century] (Wrocław, 1984).

18 On 'feudal fragmentation', see Davies, *God's Playground*, i, 61–105, especially pp. 73, 93; M. Barber, *The Two Cities: Medieval Europe 1050–1320* (London, 1992), pp. 368–73; P. W. Knoll, 'Economic and Political Institutions on the Polish–German Frontier in the Middle Ages: Action, Reaction, Interaction', in *Medieval Frontier Societies*, ed. R. Bartlett and A. MacKay (Oxford, 1989), pp. 158–60 (n. 17); T. Manteuffel, *The Formation of the Polish State: The Period of Ducal Rule, 963–1194*, trans. Andrew Gorski (Detroit, 1982); P. W. Knoll, *The Rise of the Polish Monarchy: Piast Poland in East Central Europe, 1320–1370* (Chicago, 1972), pp. 14–41; Topolski, *Outline History*, pp.

force were closely interrelated, and are difficult to differentiate from each other, and even to conceptualize adequately.[19] However, the social meaning of force in Polish society was in one respect simple: some social groups had routine access to its use, while others did not.

It is, at first glance, difficult to specify these privileged social groups. They do not seem to have been closed or formally bounded, and use of force to some extent cut across the social spectrum. For example, the earliest, unusually brutal case of violence recorded by Abbot Peter of Henryków around the turn of the twelfth and thirteenth century, was a mutual beating to death among two peasants.[20] Around the same time, an early robber had been, as Peter rather vaguely put it, a 'petty knight' (*militellus*).[21] Peter's continuator attributed to a group of specialized peasants – four *camerarii*, collectors of ducal exactions, and enforcers of ducal judgments, in the countryside – a pattern of 'oppression' of other peasants settled near Raczyce, at the turn of the thirteenth and fourteenth centuries.[22] Nevertheless, despite these incidents, use of force was the domain of groups otherwise documented as privileged; when Abbot Peter and his continuator identified the perpetrators of violent acts, it was consistently as 'knights',[23] 'lords',[24] or as descendants or ancestors of each.[25]

Apart from the violent acts recorded by Abbot Peter and his continuator, the most recurrent form of use of force in the Polish duchies was passage through regions of settlement and lordship of armed groups of travellers, who demanded

38–46; Górecki, *Economy, Society, and Lordship*, pp. 14–15; H. Łowmiański, 'Rozdrobnienie feudalne Polski w historiografii naukowej' [Poland's feudal fragmentation in the historiography], in *Polska w okresie rozdrobnienia feudalnego* [Poland in the period of feudal fragmentation], ed. Łowmiański (Wrocław, 1973), pp. 7–34.

19 'Violence', in particular, has elicited especially interesting critical attention, and been situated in the context of power and emotion, by S. D. White, 'The Politics of Anger', in *Anger's Past: the social uses of an emotion in the Middle Ages*, ed. B. H. Rosenwein (Ithaca, 1997), pp. 127–52, at 144; and by S. D. White, 'Debate: The "Feudal Revolution" II', *Past and Present*, clii (1996), 205–23, at pp. 206–7, 209, 216 – in a polemic with T. N. Bisson, 'The "Feudal Revolution" ', *Past and Present*, cxlii (1994), 6–42, and Bisson, 'Reply', *Past and Present*, clv (1977), 208–25. See P. Górecki, 'Violence and the Social Order in a Medieval Society: The Evidence from the Henryków Region', forthcoming in *The Man of Many Devices*, ed. B. Nagy and M. Sebök (Budapest, 1999).

20 *Księga henrykowska. Liber fundationis claustri sancte Marie Virginis in Heinrichow* (Poznań and Wrocław, 1949); reissued as *Liber fundationis claustri sancte Marie Virginis in Heinrichow, czyli Księga henrykowska*, ed. and trans. R. Grodecki (Wrocław, 1991) [hereafter *K.H.*, with page references to the second printing], c. 32, p. 119. On this remarkable source (and further literature), see P. Górecki, 'Rhetoric, Memory, and Use of the Past: Abbot Peter of Henryków as Historian and Advocate', *Cîteaux*, xlviii (1997), 261–94, at pp. 261–4, nn. 1, 5–6, 11, 13.

21 *KH*, c. 29, p. 118.

22 *Ibid.*, c. 165, p. 175.

23 *Ibid.*, c. 47, pp. 121–2; c. 77, p. 130; c. 78, p. 138; c. 85, p. 135; c. 111, p. 146; c. 114, p. 148; cc. 154–5, pp. 168–9; c. 158, p. 170; c. 186, p. 185.

24 *Ibid.*, c. 96, p. 139; cc. 108–9, pp. 144–5.

25 *Ibid.*, c. 52, p. 123; c. 96, p. 139; c. 108, pp. 144–5; c. 186, p. 185.

a wide range of exactions from the inhabitants.[26] A wide variety of Polish sources consistently identify roaming predatory groups as an expression of social power. Who inflicted force on whom? In his celebrated history of the Piast dynasty written in the first years of the thirteenth century, Bishop Vincent of Kraków rather unhelpfully identified the protagonists as the 'powerful' (*potentes*), acting directly and through their 'associates' (*satellites*), who demanded hospitality, fodder, and horses from 'the poor' (*pauperes*) they encountered in transit.[27] Although Vincent was directly concerned with the welfare of peasant inhabitants of ecclesiastical estates, he clearly considered predatory groups of this kind damaging to the population in general. Throughout the thirteenth and well into the fourteenth century, his ecclesiastical successors – the Polish bishops, abbots, and abbesses – and their lay and ecclesiastical friends within and outside the Polish duchies, continued to complain against a wide variety of offenders, whom they identified eclectically in different contexts as the 'leaders of the army' (*duces exercitus*), 'the army' (*exercitus*), 'knights' (*milites*), 'barons' (*barones*), 'the powerful' (*potentes*), and with other terms which, while variable and imprecise, clearly connoted an unusual degree of social power.[28]

One source of this kind of pressure was the ducal court in transit – whether on a military campaign, or in transition from one central place to another, or both. The duke was at least the nominal leader of the offending group (or groups), which typically included ducal officials, ranging from the highest (palatines and castellans), through the intermediate, and occasionally all the way down to specialized categories of peasants who exacted obligations from other peasants on behalf of the duke – such as the group of *camerarii* active in the Henryków region around 1300.[29] Another source were armed groups which cannot be clearly associated with ducal authority, but are best documented – from a perspective hostile to them – as exploiters of churches (especially during episcopal vacancies), thieves of ecclesiastical revenues (tithes above all), and usurpers of secular jurisdiction over the clergy and its peasants.[30] A third source of this conduct is the least well-documented but, as the Henryków authors suggest, perhaps the most recurrent and important: persons variously identified as 'knights', 'lords', robbers, and indeed as several categories of peasants, who, at least on a local or regional level, enjoyed sufficient power to complicate the

---

26 Górecki, *Economy, Society, and Lordship*, pp. 123–62.
27 *Magistri Vincentii dicti Kadłubek Chronica Polonorum* [hereafter *M.V.C.*], ed. M. Plezia, iv, 9, 1–4, in *MPH n.s.*, xi (Kraków, 1994), 148–9; see Górecki, *Economy, Society, and Lordship*, pp. 131–4.
28 Górecki, *Parishes, Tithes and Society*, pp. 55–8.
29 On the importance of this phenomenon, the participating groups (on both sides), its limitations in the course of the twelfth and thirteenth centuries, and the resulting patterns of immunity and lordship in Poland, see Górecki, *Economy, Society, and Lordship*, pp. 123–54.
30 On this range of issues, see Górecki, *Parishes, Tithes and Society*, pp. 55–8.

lives of others (including ecclesiastical communities) while they aggressively pursued social climbing through acquisition of land or friends, with occasional eruptions of violence.[31]

One series of documents offers an unusually detailed example of the perpetrators of grievances of this kind, and of the nature of their offences. In 1271, Bishop Thomas II of Wrocław issued a salvo of complaints against two Piast dukes, Bolesław the Chaste of Little Poland and Conrad of Masovia, and their armed followers from Little Poland, Great Poland, and Masovia, in a series of letters – three to the archbishop of Gniezno, Janusz,[32] one each to his fellow bishops Paul of Kraków, Nicholas of Poznań, Peter of Płock,[33] and two to Duke Bolesław himself.[34] The bishop was aggrieved by the damage inflicted by the dukes and their followers 'to our villages . . . and to the villages of other churches' during what he described as an unusually destructive military campaign in two regions of northern and north-western Silesia: the far western diocese of Lubusz; and the castellany of Milicz, near the boundary between Silesia and Great Poland.

Thomas described the damage and the culprits in the campaign near Lubusz as 'the duke and his barons', 'the duke himself and his [men] [*sui*]', 'the duke of Kraków and 'his [men]', the duke's followers and 'their [men]', the 'Cracovians' (*Cracovienses*);[35] in a letter to the bishop of Poznań as 'some of the knights from your diocese';[36] in a letter to the bishop of Płock as 'Duke Conrad and his barons';[37] and in the letters to Bolesław himself, as 'you and your [men]', 'you and your army', 'you and your barons', 'your knights', and to the duke 'together with your knights'.[38] On the other hand – and perhaps with a more deliberate precision – he identified the culprits in the Milicz campaign as 'knights', and in another phrase as 'the knights who cruelly destroyed our villages'.[39] Considered in conjunction, these epithets appear interchangeable, and are familiar from other contemporary documents, but there is a relatively specific and precise concern about 'knights' – as in several other contexts.

---

31 Górecki, 'Violence'. Here and below, my discussion of social climbing is indebted to the usage of that expression by E. Leach, *Political Systems of Highland Burma: A Study of Kachin Social Structure* (London, 1954, repr. 1977), and to Professor R. Inden of the University of Chicago for introducing me to that work many years ago.

32 *SU*, iv, no. 124 (1271), p. 91; no. 130 (1271), pp. 94–6; no. 136 (1271), p. 99.

33 *Ibid.*, nos. 125–7 (1271), pp. 92–3.

34 *Ibid.*, no. 131 (1271), pp. 96–7; no. 135 (1271), pp. 98–9.

35 *Ibid.*, no. 124 (1271), p. 91, line 17 (*per ipsum ducem et suos*); no. 125 (1271), p. 92, lines 8–9 (*prefatum ducem et suos barones*); no. 130 (1271), p. 94, line 29 (*per ducem Cracouie et suos*); p. 95, line 19 (*Stogneus et Rosco cum suis; post recessum Cracouiensium*); p. 96, lines 22–3 (*per Cracouienses dampna habuimus ad mille marcarum*).

36 *Ibid.*, no. 126 (1271), p. 92, line 26.

37 *Ibid.*, no. 127 (1271), p. 93, line 4.

38 *Ibid.*, no. 131 (1271), p. 96, lines 40–1, 43, 45 (*vestros vestrique exercitus; una cum militibus vestris; vobis et vestris baronibus*); no. 135 (1271), p. 98, lines 36, 40–1 (*vos et vestros; milites vestros*).

39 *Ibid.*, no. 136 (1271), p. 99, lines 16–17: 'milites qui nostras villas spoliarunt atrociter'.

In addition, he identified those culprits who were 'the most' (*maxime*) culpable by their names and sometimes by other attributes. His three letters to Archbishop Janusz identify the culprits and the offences in detail, and so provide a useful profile of the social group (or groups) in the Polish duchies which enjoyed relatively unencumbered access to the use of force. The first letter identifies thirty-eight participants of the north-western campaign,[40] the second records the destruction during that campaign in ten named episcopal villages (and identifies two additional offenders),[41] and the third identifies twenty-one participants of the disorders near Milicz.[42] The participants in the north-western campaign were above all as high ducal officials. Duke Bolesław's fourteen 'knights' included the castellan and the palatine of Kraków, Warsz and Peter, Palatine James of Sandomierz, castellans of five other important towns in Little Poland,[43] and two other high officials.[44] Likewise, eight of the twelve recruits from Great Poland,[45] and all three 'knights' from Masovia, are identified as high officials.[46] A small remainder of culprits are identified by patronymic, nickname, or given name alone;[47] and eight participants by family groups, each consisting of two brothers.[48]

On the other hand, of the twenty-one participants in the disorders near Milicz, only one is identified as an official – Ziemięta, one of the five Great Polish castellans who took part in the disturbances around Lubusz[49] – while two others are noted as palatines' sons.[50] Most are recorded by other, conventional criteria: thirteen by personal name and patronymic; five by personal name alone; two by nicknames; and one by the name of an estate, or a place of origin.[51] What is

---

40 *Ibid.*, no. 124 (1271), p. 91, lines 23–34.
41 *Ibid.*, no. 130 (1271), pp. 94–6; for the two participants, p. 95, line 19.
42 *Ibid.*, no. 136 (1271), p. 99, lines 19–25.
43 *Ibid.*, no. 124 (1271), p. 91, lines 23–5; no. 125 (1271), p. 92, lines 9–11; no. 135 (1271), p. 98, lines 41–3. On the central importance of Kraków and Sandomierz, and of the palatine and castellan, as well as the (more limited) importance of other localities, see Górecki, 'Communities', pp. 133–6, especially p. 135 n. 30.
44 *SU*, iv, nos. 124 (1271), p. 91, line 26; 125 (1271), p. 92, line 12; 135 (1271), p. 99, line 1.
45 Six castellans, one butler, one 'judge' (*iudex*): *ibid.*, no. 124 (1271), p. 91, lines 28, 30–2; no. 126 (1271), p. 92, lines 29–32.
46 *Ibid.*, no. 124 (1271), p. 91, lines 33–4; no. 127 (1271), p. 93, lines 4–5, 27–30.
47 The Little Polish list: *ibid.*, no. 124 (1271), p. 91, lines 25–8 ('Nicolaum filium Mzuy . . . Velzkam filium Michaelis, Bogufalum minorem, Laurencium'); repeated in no. 125 (1271), p. 92, lines 11–14, and no. 135 (1271), p. 99, lines 1–2; the Great Polish list: *ibid.* iv, no. 124 (1271), p. 91, lines 32–3 ('Martinum Pribislauiz . . . Ceuleyum de Ponez, item Ceuleyum Gabrielis', with the fourth identified as part of an identical list in no. 126 (1271), p. 92, line 32 (one of the castellans *cum fratre Bocenta*); the remaining participants: *ibid.*, no. 124 (1271), p. 91, line 29 (*duos filios Ianconis de Calis*).
48 *Ibid.*, no. 124 (1271), p. 91, lines 28–9, 31–2.
49 *Ibid.*, no. 136 (1271), p. 99, line 21; no. 124 (1271), p. 91, line 31.
50 *Ibid.*, no. 136 (1271), p. 99, lines 20–1 (*Bocenta filius palatini*), 23 (*Nicolaus filius palatini Sanciwy de Loda*).
51 *Ibid.*, lines 19–25. I identify patronymics in Latin form by the conjunction 'son of' between the name of the actor and another Slavic male personal name, and in Polish form

interesting about this list is the fact that at least three of the culprits led their own groups of followers: Martin Lis campaigned 'with his company' (*cum sua societate*), while Nicholas (son of a palatine), Świętomir Bożenowic, and (perhaps) several other participants listed by name were accompanied by 'their many other associates' (*et alii multi eorum socii*).[52]

Who were these followers? Bishop Thomas offered a teasing glimpse in his detailed account of damage inflicted by the campaign near Lubusz; he noted that, 'after the Cracovians' departure, Stoigniew and Rożek, with their [men] [*cum suis*]', forcibly seized a substantial group of farm animals from three peasants in one village.[53] Stoigniew and Rożek are not otherwise identified, or elsewhere listed among participants in the campaign. Evidently, after Duke Bolesław and his troops passed through the ecclesiastical villages, these two men and their own followers mopped up some of the remaining resources, that is (to risk anachronism) looted. The brief and rare appearances of these hierarchical groups help explain the complaints by the Polish clergy and its allies about companies of 'the powerful', the 'princes', the 'leaders of the armies' on the one hand, and their 'satellites' or subordinates on the other, throughout the thirteenth century and into the fourteenth.

Another activity that reflected and reinforced social privilege was the maintenance of social peace – ranging from struggles for succession to ducal office among the proliferating lineages of the Piast dynasty, all the way down to settlements of very local or very specific disputes. Throughout the thirteenth and the earlier fourteenth centuries, groups variously identified as 'the first among the princes' (*primi principum*), 'almost all the highly born' (*pene cuncti proceres*), the 'better men' (*potiores*), 'leaders' (*primates*), 'knights', 'barons', and 'the native-born', and 'certain barons and knights', repeatedly renounced, revolted against, and selected particular Piasts as rulers of their duchies, and, since the turn of the fourteenth century, as candidates for the crown of a reunited kingdom.[54]

---

by the suffix *-owic* attached to the second of two Slavic male names. Patronymics are sometimes difficult to distinguish from nicknames, so these classifications are somewhat tentative. Two examples of patronymics are *Cecholaus Coscelouiz* and *Petrus filius Vnei Cromolic* (line 20). The nicknames include *Martinus Lis* (line 19), *Tarchali Ovis* (line 22), and possibly *Thomas Cobiliz* (line 23). The geographic identification is *Iohannes de Slup* (line 24).

52 *Ibid.*, no. 136 (1271), p. 99, lines 19–20 ('Martinus Lis cum sua societate'), 24 ('Nicolaus filius palatini . . . Suantomir Boznouie [*sic*] et alii multi eorum socii.') Because it is impossible to subdivide the group preceding the phrase *et alii multi eorum socii* into clear subgroups, the number of people who were accompanied by 'their' *socii* cannot be assessed; the two names are the most conservative estimate of the size of that group.

53 *Ibid.*, no. 130 (1271), p. 95, lines 19–21.

54 *MVC*, iv, 6, 2–5; *MPH n.s.*, xi, 144–5; *Chronicle of G.P.*, c. 53 (*MPH*, ii, 552, lines 5–6), events of 1202 (*potiores terre Cracoviensis*); c. 65 (*MPH*, ii, 558, lines 18–19, events of 1232 (*primates Polonorum*); c. 72 (*MPH*, ii, 562, lines 9–10, 12, 16–17, events of *c.* 1270 (*Poloni, terrigenae Poloni*); c. 155 (*MPH*, ii, 594, lines 12–13), events of *c.* 1270 (*primates terre Cujaviae*); *Rocznik Traski* [Traska's Annals], *s.a.* 1285, and *Rocznik Kra-*

Similarly identified persons sometimes arranged peaceful succession among (or selection of) different Piast contestants to entire duchies, to portions of duchies, or to particular holdings or estates – thus forestalling revolt and violence. Abbot Peter's anonymous continuator summed up collective activity of this kind when, in or shortly before 1310, he recalled the allocation of the Henryków region to Duke Bolko I, around 1285. The monk noted that 'after the princes succeeded one another in this land, and the portion of the land [in which the monastery is situated] accrued by right of succession to the famous prince Duke Bolko, the senior knights who divided up the land assigned [a particular village] to the prince's table, to which it had belonged since long ago'.[55] Likewise, in 1296, soon after the assassination of King Przemysł II, Duke (later King) Władysław Łokietek stated that 'all the barons and nobles of the land [of Great Poland] have, in full agreement, selected us as their lord by a solemn election', and in addition that 'by the mediation of the barons of both parties', he had 'established a true peace and union of agreement' with Duke Henry of Głogów 'by means of a division of the land of [Great] Poland, in order that no dispute may arise [among us] in this land'.[56] Both authors implied that these collective functions were routine. This impression is borne out by the records of the testimonies by Polish witnesses – 'knights', 'lords', ducal and royal officials, and ecclesiastics – at the papal trials of the Teutonic Order in 1320 and 1339,[57] in which perhaps the most recurrent fact, attested to hundreds of times, is the role of Polish 'nobles', 'knights', and more open-ended groups in succession to ducal office by particular Piasts in the Polish duchies.[58] Although the

---

kowski [The Annals of Kraków], *s.a.* 1285 (*MPH*, ii, 851, lines 1–3, 7–10), events of 1285 (*milites, barones, milites Cracovienses*); *KMp.*, i, no. 109 (1285), p. 130 ('quidam barones et milites nostri terre Cracouie et Sandomirie quasi omnes nos ducem suum spreuerunt').

55 *KH, c.* 167, p. 176.

56 *Kodeks dyplomatyczny Wielkopolski*, ed. I. Zakrzewski and F. Piekosiński (Poznań, 1877–1908: subsequent volumes under different editors) [hereafter *K.Wp.*], no. 745 (1296), ii, 117.

57 The editions of these remarkable documents are: *Lites ac res gestae inter Polonos Ordinemque Cruciferorum*, i, *Sprawa wytoczona w Inowrocławiu i Brześciu Kujawskim w latach 1320–1321* [The case held in Inowrocław and Brześć Kujawski in 1320–21], ed. H. Chłopocka (Wrocław, 1970), for the earlier case only, and *Lites ac res gestae inter Polonos Ordinemque Cruciferorum*, i, ed. I. Zakrzewski (2nd edn, Poznań, 1890), for both cases. For the historical background, codicological and palaeographic analysis, and the older literature, see Chłopocka, 'Wstęp' [Introduction], in *Lites*, ed. Chłopocka, pp. ix–xxxi; E. Christiansen, *The Northern Crusades: The Baltic and the Catholic Frontier, 1100–1525* (Minneapolis, 1980), pp. 100–104, 132–45; K. Górski, *L'Ordine teutonico alle origini dello stato prussiano* (Turin, 1972), pp. 75–96; M. Biskup and G. Labuda, *Dzieje Zakonu Krzyżackiego w Prusach. Gospodarka – społeczeństwo – państwo – ideologia* [The history of the Teutonic Order in Prussia: economy, society, state, ideology] (Gdansk, 1984), pp. 139–61, 241–58, and for the trials in particular, pp. 344–8; S. C. Rowell, *Lithuania Ascending: A Pagan Empire within East-Central Europe, 1295–1345* (Cambridge, 1994), pp. 8–9, 190–1, 224–5, 232–40.

58 These testimonies were offered as one of the proofs of the Piast overlordship in those duchies, a subject contested between the Order and the Polish Kingdom, newly re-united

evidence does not describe specific – let alone formalized – mechanisms for collective governance that somehow overarched ducal rule, they do identify the importance of the groups involved in the maintenance or disruption of the dynastic order.

On other occasions, the same range of people mediated other issues that led to conflict, and served as repositories of collective memory and legal knowledge. One document, issued in 1249, helps identify such groups and their functions. It is a long notice recording the settlement of a jurisdictional dispute between the duke of Silesia (represented by the castellan of Milicz and other high ducal officials) and the diocese of Wrocław about the scope of jurisdiction over the inhabitants of the district.[59] The dispute was resolved in two phases. The first was a large assembly, which led to the selection of the preferred mode of proof: 'The matter was discussed for a long time in a full assembly in Starogomnost, on the [river] Nysa, before the barons of Silesia, and, by the express will of the duke', the gathering 'resolved' to summon of a group of particularly knowledgeable 'witnesses'.[60] The ducal court was closely involved in the selection of the witnesses. Formally, the 'choice of witnesses' belonged to the duke,[61] but on this occasion the actual group was selected by an official of the household of Bolesław's wife, Duchess Hedwig: at the assembly on the river, 'it was determined that Despryn, at that time *subcamerarius* of the lady duchess, would call forth the . . . witnesses'.[62]

Despryn's summons of witnesses opened the second phase of the dispute. The witnesses 'appeared in the church of Saint Guido in Wrocław, in the presence of Despryn and many others', and then, 'according to custom, Despryn posed to them the question of what rights pertained' to the duke and the bishop 'in the said castellany'. The witnesses 'took counsel among themselves, and unanimously responded on oath'[63] with the very detailed knowledge of ducal

under Władysław Łokietek and Casimir the Great. The size and range of witness testimony was considerable; 25 witnesses answered a total of two interrogatories in 1320–21 (*Lites*, ed. Chłopocka, pp. 23–50), while 126 witnesses responded to a total of 30 interrogatories in 1339 (*Lites*, ed. Zakrzewski, pp. 94–8, 143–407). In the present context, see above all J. Bieniak, 'Środowisko świadków procesu polsko-krzyżackiego z 1339 r' [The milieu of the witnesses in the case between Poland and the Teutonic Order of 1339], in *Genealogia – kręgi zawodowe i grupy interesu w Polsce średniowiecznej na tle porównawczym* [Genealogy: professional circles and interest groups in medieval Poland in a comparative context], ed. J. Wroniszewski (Toruń, 1989), pp. 5–35; Bieniak, 'Możliwości', pp. 80, 82.

59 *SU*, ii, no. 375 (1249), pp. 238–9; J. Matuszewski, *Vicinia id est . . . Poszukiwania alternatywnej koncepcji staropolskiego opola* [*Vicinia id est*: the search for an alternative conception of the Old Polish neighbourhood] (Łódź, 1991), pp. 71–3.

60 *SU*, ii, no. 375 (1249), p. 238, lines 8–10: 'in pleno colloquio super Nisam in Starogomnost coram baronibus Slesie eadem questione diucius agitata taliter ipsum negocium de voluntate dicti ducis expressa et de eo ipso testes eligente fuit ibi determinatum'.

61 In the words *de eo ipso testes eligente*, cited in the above note.

62 *SU*, ii, no. 375 (1249), p. 238, lines 10–11.

63 *Ibid.*, lines 20–4: 'Nominatis . . . testibus in presencia eiusdem Desprini ac plurium aliorum in ecclesia sancti Egidii in Wratislauia comparentibus et questione ipsis secun-

and seigneurial jurisdiction whose redacted summary constitutes the disposition of the charter.[64] They included six persons, 'lord Naches, an old and trustworthy man, formerly castellan of [Milicz]; Gosław, the bishop's proctor, formerly the bishop's judge in Milicz; Sulisław called the Wise; Radwan the Tooth, formerly ducal tribune of Milicz; Peter, also a former ducal tribune there; and Racław, son of Radziej, brother of Skok'.[65] Of these six men, five shared several characteristics: (1) advanced age and moral stature, traits explicitly attributed to Naches, and implicitly to Sulisław and Radwan through their nicknames; (2) past performance of high office – either for the duke, as in the case of the retired castellan Naches and the former tribunes Radwan and Peter, or, in the case of Gosław, for the bishop as his *iudex*; (3) past association in these official capacities with the castle of Milicz – the locality and district affected by the controversy; and (4) high status, implied both by this combination of traits, and by a reference to Naches with the epithet 'lord' (*comes*). The group embodied a considerable concentration of status, past official experience, and familiarity with the region whose jurisdictional arrangements were at issue between the duke and the bishop.

Mediation of this kind extended, seamlessly, down to much more local and specific legal transactions. At the latest since the beginning of the thirteenth century (and probably decades earlier), 'barons', 'knights', and similarly identified groups, routinely participated in, or witnessed, perambulations of village boundaries during gifts to the saints or property disputes, sometimes as part of broader groups of the 'neighbours' of the villages concerned.[66] Between the late twelfth century and the 1260s, Abbot Peter's legal universe was especially well-populated by persons who served as important legal resources for his monastery. An old and 'noble' man, Vincent, had been a close relative of another important person, as well as a source of expertise about the 'Polish law' of property[67] – an aged and venerable embodiment of important knowledge, like

---

dum morem a dicto Desprino facta que cui castallanorum in dicta castellania iura pertinerent, ipsi habito inter se consilio sic omnes unanimiter iurati responderunt.'
64 *Ibid.*, p. 238, line 24 – p. 239, line 23.
65 *Ibid.*, p. 238, lines 11–15: 'comitem Nachesium hominem antiquum et fide dignum et quondam eiusdem castri castellanum, Goszlaum procuratorem episcopi et quondam in Milicz domini episcopi iudicem, Sulislaum dictum Mandri, Raduanum Zamb qui quondam fuerat ducis in Milich wlodarius, Petrum eciam quondam ibidem ducis wlodarium, Radslaum Radeui fratrem Scoconis'.
66 Górecki, 'Communities', pp. 132–3, 138–40, 146–51; for the earliest evidence (and presumed origins) of boundary perambulation in particular, see G. Myśliwski, 'Powstanie i rozwój granicy liniowej na Mazowszu (XII–poł. XVI w.)' [The origins and development of the linear boundary in Masovia from the twelfth to the mid-sixteenth century], *Kwartalnik Historyczny*, ci (1994), 3–24; and G. Myśliwski, 'Boundary Delimitation in Medieval Poland', in *Historical Reflections on Central Europe: Selected Papers from the Fifth World Congress of Central and East European Studies, Warsaw, 1995*, ed. S. J. Kirschbaum (Basingstoke, 1999), pp. 27–36.
67 *KH*, c. 86, p. 135: 'qui prepositus erat vir nobilis, patruus videlicet comitis Mrozkonis et erat fundator illius claustri de Camenz'.

his contemporaries who gave testimony concerning the traditional jurisdiction in the Milicz district. A 'rather powerful knight', Albert the Bearded, built up an elaborate network of friendship and affinity within the Henryków region, and deployed it against violence by other 'knights' in the monastery's defence.[68] During one such conflict, the monks sought legal advice from a group of 'knights' based in the city of Poznań[69] – with which the monastery had enjoyed other political connections.[70]

In the course of the later thirteenth and fourteenth centuries, the roles of such groups, and the legal product of their work, became somewhat more formalized. This gradual process is reflected in records of two disputes: between Bishop Thomas II and Duke Henry IV of Silesia sometime shortly before or in 1276, and between Archbishop Jarosław of Gniezno and his suffragan Bishop John of Poznań in 1367 and 1368. The two disputes concerned very different issues. Whereas Bishop Thomas and his chapter accused the duke, as well as his 'barons, knights, and men',[71] of a wide range of grievances which span the illicit uses of force by ducal (and other) entourages,[72] Jarosław and John disagreed about the boundary line between the dioceses of Gniezno and Poznań.[73] The former dispute is recorded in a long notice by a notary named Gerardinus,[74] and in two charters issued by a group of arbitrators,[75] the latter in charters issued by Bishop John, Archbishop Jarosław, and the archbishop's (unnamed) notary.[76]

Despite the differences in issues, the two controversies were similarly resolved, by specially selected panels of arbitrators, and with analogous mandates and outcomes. On both occasions, the arbitrators were 'elected' – directly by the 'barons and knights' who had aggrieved Bishop Thomas in 1276, and indirectly by two priests appointed as proctors for this purpose by the archbishop Jarosław and his chapter in 1367.[77] On both occasions, their mandate

---

68 *Ibid.*, cc. 45–6, p. 121; c. 74, pp. 129–30; c. 106; c. 108, p. 143; c. 111, p. 146.

69 *Ibid.*, c. 116, p. 150.

70 *Ibid.*, c. 6, p. 112; c. 21, p. 116; c. 117, p. 150.

71 *SU*, iv, no. 286 (1276), p. 194, lines 16–20. The mediators repeatedly identified the bishop's opponents as 'the . . . lord duke and the barons, knights, and men of his land', and as 'the lord duke and his barons and knights': *ibid.*, no. 287 (1276), p. 196, lines 4–5, 15; no. 288 (1276), p. 196, lines 37, 39–40, p. 197, lines 24, 35–6.

72 The grievances included: (1) imposition by the duke and his followers of a variety of 'contributions, payments, and exactions . . . on the people and faithful of the lord bishop and the church of Wrocław'; (2) burdens specifically connected with the 'stationing' of ducal troops while in transit; and (3) additional holdings and obligations illicitly seized when the bishop and canons were away at the Second Council of Lyons. *Ibid.*, no. 286 (1276), p. 194, lines 22–4, 27–8, 30–3. In addition, Thomas's grievances concerned seizures of tithe revenue (*ibid.*, lines 20–2), a domain of privileged activity on which see more below.

73 *KWp*, no. 1579 (1367), iii, 298–9; nos. 1598, 1600 (1368), iii, 315–16.

74 *SU*, iv, no. 286 (1276), p. 195, lines 31–3.

75 *Ibid.*, no. 287 (1276), p. 195, lines 42–6; no. 288 (1276), p. 196, lines 31–5.

76 *KWp*, no. 1579 (1367), iii, 298 (Bishop John of Poznań); no. 1598 (1368), iii, 315 (Archbishop Jarosław of Gniezno); no. 1600 (1368), iii, 316 ('in mea publici notarii infrascripti . . . presencia').

77 *SU*, iv, no. 287 (1276), p. 195, line 46; no. 288 (1276), p. 196, line 34; *KWp*, no. 1598

was spelled out in a remarkably verbose formula – to serve as 'arbiters and arbitrators', 'friendly peacemakers', 'moderators', 'dispensators', 'good men', and so forth[78] – so as to allow the parties to settle 'for the good of the peace' and 'live in mutual friendship'.[79] The earlier group of arbitrators included four ecclesiastics and four laymen, the later only four laymen – selected, however, by two ecclesiastics. Both groups were identified in language of high status and lordship – as 'lords' (*domini*) in 1276,[80] and as 'noble, famous, and circumspect men', 'noble and famous men', and 'lords', in 1367–68.[81] In 1276, Gerardinus further described the four laymen as 'knights', one of them also a 'judge' (*iudex*),[82] while a century later Archbishop Jarosław, his notary, and Bishop John identified their four counterparts as high ducal officials, that is, palatines of Poznań and Kalisz, and castellans of Gniezno and Kamień.[83]

On both occasions, the arbitrators fulfilled their mandate – as Archbishop Jarosław's notary remarked in a loquacious description of the settlement of the boundary dispute,[84] and as Bishop John noted in his detailed account of the arbitrators' actual tasks and functions. John recalled that they had been 'given and conceded full and free power over the . . . tracing of the boundary', been instructed 'to come to the places where the boundary was being traced, and to see which place was the best [for the boundary line] among us', and, on a speci-

---

(1368), iii, 315. In the last document, the two clerics are identified as *honorabiles et discreti viri*, but otherwise without especially high office; Adam was a 'provost (*prepositus*) of Ruda', perhaps an official of a community of secular or regular canons, or merely a parish priest, at a church in that location, while Vincent was the 'parish priest (*rector*) of the church of Gostyczyna.' Their relatively low ecclesiastical office does not, in the Polish duchies, preclude their holding of other ecclesiastical offices (which may not appear in the record); for patterns of accumulation of ecclesiastical offices by parish priests in medieval Poland, see Górecki, *Parishes, Tithes and Society*, p. 86.

78 *SU*, iv, no. 286 (1276), p. 194, lines 42–4 ('tamquam in arbitros et arbitratores, amicabiles compositores, moderatores, dispensatores et bonos viros'); *KWp*, no. 1598 (1368), iii, 315 ('tamquam arbitros, compromissarios arbitratores seu amicabiles compositores limitacionis nostrarum Gneznensis et Poznaniensis dyocesum'); no. 1600 (1368), iii, 316 ('tamquam arbitros compromissarios et legitimos arbitratores et comissarios speciales').
79 *SU*, iv, no. 286 (1276), p. 194, lines 36–8 ('predicti barones et milites de predictis litibus, questionibus et controversiis ad concordiam provenire communiter et concorditer pro bono pacis et concordie conpromiserunt in viros venerabiles et discretos', who are named thereafter); *KWp*, no. 1579 (1367), iii, 298.
80 *SU*, iv, no. 287 (1276), p. 194, lines 39, 41.
81 *KWp*, no. 1579 (1367), iii, 298 (*nobiles et famosos viros et circumspectos*); nos. 1598, 1600 (1368), iii, 315–16 (*nobiles et famosi viri, domini*, in both documents).
82 *SU*, iv, no. 286 (1276), p. 194, lines 41–2. Gerardinus identified the ecclesiastical arbitrators of 1276 as 'venerable and discrete men', officials of the chapters of the episcopal churches of Wrocław and Kraków, and of the collegiate churches in Głogów and Opole, at *ibid.*, lines 38–41. In their own documents, the eight arbitrators of 1276 identified themselves by name and individual office, without general epithets.
83 *KWp*, no. 1579 (1367), iii, 298; nos. 1598, 1600 (1368), iii, 315–16.
84 *Ibid.*, no. 1600 (1368), iii, 316: 'omnia et singula . . . acta, facta, ordinata, limitata, determinata seu eciam diffinita fuerint circa limitacionem Gneznensis et Poznaniensis diocesium.'

fied date, 'to assemble in the places neighbouring with, and surrounding, the said dioceses in controversy, and determine and conclude the matter of tracing [the boundary]'.[85] The actions of the two palatines and the two castellans closely resemble boundary perambulations by (or under the leadership of) ducal officials throughout the thirteenth and earlier fourteenth centuries. Especially similar is the act of assembling the arbitrators (and perhaps some broader population) in localities adjacent to the subject of dispute – a practice analogous to, or perhaps indeed identical with, gatherings of 'neighbourhoods' to resolve more local boundary disputes throughout the thirteenth century.[86]

Finally, on both occasions the resolutions enjoyed a virtually statutory authority. In 1276, 1367, and 1368, Gerardinus, the arbitrators, and Bishop John repeatedly, and in similar words, described the terms of the resolutions as an 'agreement' (*arbitrium*), a 'pronouncement' (*dictum*), and, several times, as a 'decree' (*laudum*),[87] which, as John further noted, supervened 'any law, privilege, and statute' that might otherwise govern the subject in question.[88] The rather frantic search for the right words and phrases obscures a glimpse into an extremely interesting practice at work – the selection of *ad hoc* groups from among otherwise privileged categories of Poles, and endowment of such groups with a legislative capacity. To be sure, perhaps this glimpse, along with the other hints of formality or institutional routine in 1276, 1367, and 1368, is a distortion of the sources – an artefact of notarial involvement in the production of the documents – but, even if that were the case, the arrangements and procedures behind both resolutions demonstrably relied upon (at least some of) those

85 *Ibid.*, no. 1579 (1367), iii, 298–9.
86 The meaning, definition, and indeed the reality of the Polish 'neighbourhood' of the earlier Middle Ages is a subject of much dispute and of great interest; see K. Modzelewski, 'Organizacja opolna w Polsce piastowskiej' [The neighbourhood organization in Piast Poland], *Przegląd Historyczny*, lxxvii (1986), 177–220; Modzelewski, *Chłopi w monarchii wczesnopiastowskiej* [The peasants in the early Piast monarchy] (Wrocław, 1987), pp. 176–92; Matuszewski, *Vicinia, passim* (a very skeptical view, strongly polemical with Modzelewski). See also Górecki, 'Communities', pp. 137–40, 146–8, 152; Górecki, 'Local Society and Legal Knowledge: A Case Study from the Henryków Region', in *Christianitas et Cultura Europae: Księga Jubileuszowa Profesora Jerzego Kłoczowskiego, Część 1* [*Christianitas et Cultura Europae*: a Jubilee Book for Professor J. Kłoczowski, part 1], ed. H. Gapski (Lublin, 1998), pp. 544–50, at 549–50.
87 *SU*, iv, no. 286 (1276), p. 195, lines 3–4 ('omni laudo, arbitrio, dicto, diffinicioni, moderacioni et pronunciacioni eorum'), 10–11 ('huius compromissi et laudi et arbitrii ferendi in solidum promissa'), 16 ('latum arbitrium seu laudum'); no. 287 (1276), p. 196, lines 16–17, and no. 288 (1276), p. 197, line 34 ('presentem ordinacionem seu amicabilem conposicionem, laudum vel arbitrium'); *KWp*, no. 1579 (1367), iii, 299 ('[p]romittimus . . . obedire dictorum arbitrorum laudo, dicto, arbitrio, pronunciacioni, precepto; contra eorum preceptum, laudum, pronunciacionem seu arbitrium non . . . petemus'; a fine mandated if 'prefatum laudum seu dictum integre observatum non fuerit').
88 *KWp*, no. 1579 (1367), iii, 299: 'renunciantes omni beneficio et auxilio iuris, privilegii et statuti, rescripti, consuetudinis, apellacionis et integre restitucionis, emendacionis et correccionis seu excepcionis.'

collective activities and social groups which were otherwise crucially significant for the maintenance of social peace.

One important source of mediators, arbitrators, and unusually knowledgeable persons was the ducal court – that is, such actors were frequently also ducal officials. First, officials were present among those participants in all otherwise privileged activities where they can be individually identified.[89] Second, a high proportion of those persons within otherwise privileged groups whose life-cycles can be reconstructed typically exercised some kind of office at some phase of their lives.[90] In some instances, they carried out the privileged activities as an exercise of their office – as, for example, when ducal 'judges' (*iudices*) settled or mediated disputes, or when, as Abbot Peter recalled, a ducal 'perambulator' established or ascertained village boundaries, and testified to that fact during property disputes[91] – but by no means all the persons engaged in the other areas of privilege were officials, and of those who were, their privileged activities were typically not, on the face of the record, an exercise of their office. Performance of an official capacity intersected with other activities that defined privilege, but was not in some sense fundamental to them.[92]

Nevertheless, service to the dukes was yet another area of activity that defined privilege. Again, things are complicated because not every type of service defined privilege. Since perhaps as early as the tenth century, the Polish population had been categorized into (among other things) a wide range of statuses and tenures defined in terms of service – ploughmen, hunters, masons, wheelwrights, fletchers, tax farmers, and others.[93] From the twelfth century onward, the most important context of the diffusion and adaptation of such statuses and tenures was the expansion of settlement and lordship under ducal

89 That is, virtually every list of donors to the saints, of participants in warfare, of leaders or followers of ducal and other entourages, of mediators in ducal succession and in prevention and settlement of dispute, and, of witnesses and participants in assemblies, includes ducal officials. I cite examples of such lists above, at my discussions of these areas of collective activity, except for the collective activities of witnessing and participation in ducal assemblies, which I have, for a variety of reasons, omitted the scope of this essay, and for which provisionally see Górecki, 'Communities', pp. 130–1 n. 15.

90 For numerous examples (subject, perhaps, to some uncertainties of prosopography), see Cetwiński, *Rycerstwo . . . biogramy.*

91 *KH*, c. 106 (p. 143, Paul Slupoviz, *circuitor*); c. 162 (*quidam miles*, Jarosław of Habirsdorf, appointed as *iudex* to resolve a dispute, which was also heard by two *iudices hereditarii*); c. 185 (Nicholas of Münsterberg, a *iudex curiae*, resolves a dispute); c. 191 (*strenuus miles*, Nicholas of Münsterberg, a *iudex curiae*, resolves a dispute).

92 Górecki, *Economy, Society, and Lordship*, p. 134.

93 K. Modzelewski, 'La division autarchique du travail à l'échelle d'un état: l'organisation 'ministériale' en Pologne médiévale', *Annales E.S.C.*, xix (1964), 1125–38; Modzelewski, 'L'organizzazione dello stato polacco nei secoli X–XIII: La società e le strutture di potere', *Settimane di Studio del Centro Italiano di Studi sull'Alto Medioevo*, xxx (1983), 557–99; Modzelewski, *Organizacja gospodarcza państwa piastowskiego, X–XIII wiek* [The economic organization of the Piast state from the tenth through the thirteenth century] (Wrocław, 1975); Knoll, 'Polish–German Frontier', pp. 154–5; Górecki, *Economy, Society, and Lordship*, pp. 3, 7, 67–122.

protection. Reflecting on this process, Abbot Peter of Henryków recalled that the 'ancient dukes' had since long ago 'distributed' landed estates 'to the noble and the mediocre',[94] a broad and apparently open-ended shorthand which included groups of varied status ('middling knights', 'knights', 'ducal peasants'),[95] ethnicity (Poles, Germans, Czechs, Walloons, Jews),[96] and, far less often, specialization ('assarters', 'carpenters').[97]

Some 'serving' groups clearly enjoyed relatively high status. Individual persons are repeatedly identified as ducal (or other) *servientes*, as performing or having performed 'faithful service', or some equivalent, in the past, present, and sometimes the future.[98] Such epithets or descriptions are not applied systematically or rigorously – the same individuals are also described variously as 'knights' (*milites*), ducal officials, donors to the saints – in short, as members of the otherwise privileged groups – in expressions suggesting friendship, debt, gratitude, and trust. Quite typical is Duke Leszek the Black's grateful reference to the 'faithful knight' Stanisław of Chroberz who refused to join the major revolt against the duke in 1285, but instead 'had furnished us with a faithful, useful, and continuous service at that time and at all times, and has not ceased to do so at present'.[99] Service appears to have been a nexus of a privileged relationship, but it seems that the *fidelis*, the *serviens*, or the *servitor* were not, in medi-

---

94 *KH*, cc. 82, p. 134; 113, p. 147.
95 *Ibid.*, c. 2, p. 109; c. 29, p. 118; c. 32, p. 119; c. 34, p. 119; c. 36, p. 120; c. 38, p. 120; c. 45, p. 121; c. 82, p. 134; c. 83, p. 134; c. 85, p. 135; c. 127, p. 156; c. 128, p. 157; c. 133, p. 158; c. 138, p. 161; c. 148, p. 166; c. 151, p. 167; c. 155, p. 169; c. 158, p. 170; c. 159, p. 171; c. 161, p. 173; c. 162, p. 173; c. 167, p. 176; c. 168, p. 176; c. 183, p. 184; c. 186, p. 185; c. 189, p. 187; c. 191, p. 188; c. 192, p. 189.
96 *Ibid.*, c. 49, p. 122 (Germans, settled by Albert the Bearded); c. 55, p. 123 (Germans, Walloons of Wrocław – Albert the Bearded's family); cc. 94–5, pp. 138–9 (Menold, setted in Budzów by Duke Henry I); c. 109, p. 145 (Sibodo, a German *villicus* settled by Peter Stoszowic); c. 113, p. 147 (Boguchwał the Czech, settled by Duke Bolesław the Tall); cc. 193–4, pp. 190–1 (a Jew named Merkelin, involved in a purchase of Czelsawice).
97 *Ibid.*, c. 76, p. 130 (*duos charpentarios eosdem ville*); c. 111, p. 146 (*sectores lignorum*).
98 A sample of the documents includes: *SU*, i, no. 77 (1202), p. 50 (Godek, *servicialis patris mei*); no. 167 (1217), p. 119; no. 255 (1225), pp. 186–8 (John, *minister noster*); ii, no. 79 (1234), p. 51, line 24 ('fidelitatis ipsius erga nos intuitu et obsequii respectu'); no. 311 (1246), p. 186, line 39 ('pro fideli servicio dilectorum baronum nostrorum'); no. 352 (1248), p. 222, lines 31–2 ('Vrocowoyo militi nostro respectu servitiorum que fecit nobis et antecessori nostro'); iii, no. 32 (1252), p. 34, line 17 ('perspectis eiusdem obsequiis fidelibus et immensis'); no. 55 (1253), p. 47, line 5 (Siegfried, *noster famulus*); no. 192 (1256), p. 130, lines 42–3 (Jasso, *ministerialis noster*); no. 213 (1257), p. 144, lines 4–6 ('conspicientes fidele obsequium comitis Ianusii'); iv, no. 18 (1267), p. 25, line (Albert, *noster balistarius et minister*); no. 34 (1267), p. 34, line 35 (Cursicus, *serviens noster*); *KMaz*, no. 433 (1242–45), p. 518, lines 4–10; no. 448 (1244), p. 538, lines 25–8; no. 450 (1244), p. 540, lines 15–21, p. 541, lines 1–2; see Górecki, *Economy, Society, and Lordship*, pp. 182–5.
99 *KMp*, i, no. 109 (1285), p. 130 (for the text, see n. 62 above). I am presently working on an article which explores the ethical significance of service, among some related subjects; see also the section on identity below.

eval Poland, coherent types of status or tenure.[100] Instead, service was exactly analogous to other activities that defined social privilege: it was one of the ways in which some social groups were able to act upon, demonstrate, and enhance their relative standing and power within society.

2. Toward the definition of a privileged social group: knighthood and service

What is quite difficult to specify is the social group (or groups) which engaged in these privileged areas of activity – and which was (or were) defined by them. A variety of populations, identified with several terms, shared in these attributes of privilege, to some degree or another – and to that extent indeed they overlapped into one single privileged group. It is tempting to identify that social group as *the* Polish knighthood early on, or *the* Polish nobility later. However, to do so exaggerates the uniformity of status, identity, and other indicators of group cohesion or distinction within the population that shared these elements of privilege. It also obscures the fact that between the twelfth and the fourteenth centuries the contemporaries themselves sought to analyse and adapt these elements of privilege into meaningful and uniform categories of status and identity, and to associate the social phenomenon of the practices that defined privilege with classificatory words and concepts – which, by the mid-fourteenth century, included the ritual devices with which Jan Długosz was concerned later. For this purpose, the contemporaries drew on two recurrent constructs, or classifications, which we have seen associated with privileged activity: knighthood and service.

'Knighthood' served the contemporaries as a conceptual tool in further definition of privilege, status, and tenure. First, the term 'knight' was frequently used as a general synonym for the social groups otherwise documented as privileged, and identified in the record with a cluster of other terms of high status (such as *domini, comites,* or *barones*), or by office, or simply as participants in the kinds of activities I have outlined above.[101] Second – though here the evidence is infinitely sparser – the position of 'knight', or of a 'lord' (*dominus* or *comes*), expressed a status to which one could aspire. Abbot Peter, who was unusually sensitive to social climbing and upward mobility in the Henryków

---

100 In contrast, above all, with the German *ministeriales*, or with the English tenants 'in serjeanty'; see B. Arnold, *German Knighthood, 1050–1300* (Oxford, 1985); J. Freed, 'Reflections in the Medieval German Nobility', *American Historical Review*, xci (1986), 553–75; Freed, 'Nobles, Ministeriales, and Knights in the Archdiocese of Salzburg', *Speculum*, lxii (1987), 575–611; F. Pollock and F. W. Maitland, *The History of English Law*, 2nd edn, reissued with introduction by S. F. C. Milsom (Cambridge, 1968), i, 282–90, 323.

101 For example, as noted above, in his complaints of 1271 against Dukes Bolesław and Conrad, Bishop Thomas II of Wrocław identified the dukes' followers in general as 'knights' – interchangeably with other terms, general and specific – and similar uses of the term recur in the sources throughout the thirteenth and early fourteenth centuries; see above, nn. 35–40.

region and their political effects on his monastery, notes several deliberate moves by 'knights' (or 'lords', or 'barons') to consolidate their social standing,[102] and decries two individuals who successfully used social climbing to attain the knightly status itself.

One was Henry, an inhabitant of what later became the monastery's estate around 1200, whom Peter remembered, interchangeably, as having 'held himself out as a knight', as a 'small knight', and, in two passages, as a 'knight'[103] – as well as the eponym of Henryków, 'all the territory' around it, and of the monastery itself.[104] Henry's status was fluid; however, his social importance is reflected in the fact that he was an eponym for the central place and institution with which Peter was concerned, and that he attained knightly status through his own effort or performance.[105] Another such person was Peter, son of Stosz, active around the mid-thirteenth century. Abbot Peter remembered (and carefully described) him as an descendant and nephew of two strongmen – who, a full generation earlier, 'had hidden in [the] forest like some robbers', 'very rarely or never appeared before the . . . dukes' of Silesia, and had 'inflicted violence on the nearby peasants at their pleasure, as they wished'.[106] Peter Stoszowic continued these transgressions (this time at the monastery's expense), but the abbot referred to him with one of the epithets of lordship (*comes*).[107] At least from Abbot Peter's perspective, his difficult namesake had, over the past thirty years or so, graduated from banditry to lordship.[108] Although these glimpses of social climbing may reflect an unusual degree of social fluidity in a frontier region of the Polish duchies, they do strengthen an impression of the 'knighthood' as a status which was sufficiently defined and entrenched in

---

[102] For social climbing in the Henryków region, see P. Górecki, 'Politics of the Legal Process in Early Medieval Poland', *Oxford Slavonic Papers, New Series*, xvii (1984), 23–44, at pp. 32–3, 39–43; Górecki, 'Rhetoric', pp. 279–80.

[103] *KH*, c. 31, p. 118 ('hic Heinricus habebat se pro milite', 'predictum militellum Heinricum'); c. 34, p. 119 ('[h]ic miles Heinricus de quo superius dictum est', 'sors huius militis modica').

[104] *Ibid.*, c. 31, p. 118 ; c. 34, p. 119.

[105] For the significance of eponyms, and for the functions (memorial and proprietary) of place-names and their alterations over time, see Górecki, 'Local Society', and Górecki, 'Communities', pp. 140–6. (Regrettably, the important and suggestive remarks on these subjects by Mosingiewicz, 'Imię', pp. 85–7 had not been available to me when I wrote these articles, and I would like to correct my omission of his name from the literature on this occasion.)

[106] *KH*, c. 108, p. 144–5; for the rest of the circumstances of Peter Stoszowic, see c. 96, p. 139; cc. 103–4, p. 142, and Górecki, 'Politics', pp. 39–43.

[107] *KH*, c. 96, p. 139 (harassment *a patre comitis Petri*); cc. 108–9, pp. 144–5 (*comes Petrus; comitis Petri auctoritate*).

[108] One wonders, of course, if Peter Stoszowic himself knew the difference. For implications of perspective in cases of this kind – and, implicitly, for the fluidity of banditry and lordship in general – see above all, White, 'Debate'; White, 'The Politics of Anger', in Rosenwein, *Anger's Past*, pp. 127–53; and P. Contamine, *War in the Middle Ages*, trans. M. Jones (Oxford, 1984), pp. 249–55, 270–92, 296–302. For the Henryków region and

twelfth- and thirteenth-century Poland to be a subject of deliberate political negotiation.

Third, at the latest by the outset of the thirteenth century, 'knighthood' was a formal status (*ius*), that is, a specific bundle of privileges (and, less explicitly, obligations) for the persons to whom it pertained. Throughout the thirteenth and fourteenth centuries, that status was called 'knightly law' (*ius militare*).[109] It was broadly comparable to the 'laws' (*iura*) that specified the social positions of several other groups, including: various categories of Polish peasants and crafts-people,[110] German immigrants,[111] townspeople,[112] or, later in the thirteenth and fourteenth centuries, Jews and Armenians.[113] In contrast to some of these other social groups, the full substantive content of 'knightly' status is difficult to reconstruct because, as with the term 'knight' itself, the documents use it on the assumption that this was clear, and did not require definition. Therefore, while we do not have access to the origins or early meanings of the Polish 'knight-hood', we do have access to several specific areas of formal privilege that were associated with that status continuously throughout the Middle Ages, and to the

medieval Poland in general, see Górecki, 'Violence', and Górecki, *Economy, Society, and Lordship*, pp. 145–6, 160–1 n. 74.

109 Górecki, *Economy, Society, and Lordship*, pp. 105–8, 180, 182, 184–5, 187–8, 192, 240, 241; Górecki, *Parishes, Tithes and Society*, pp. 105, 107–9, 114, 122–3.

110 In general, see the literature cited in n. 93; for the most important particular categories, see as follows: the free peasants and the *ascriptitii* – W. Wolfarth, *Ascriptitii w Polsce* [The *ascriptitii* in Poland] (Wrocław, 1959), and Górecki, *Economy, Society, and Lord-ship*, pp. 128–9, 140–1, 144, 164, 166–77, 180–1; the 'ducal peasants': Górecki, '*Viator* to *ascriptitius*', p. 22; the *decimi*, plowmen, 'guests', and other individual statuses: K. Buczek, 'O chłopach w Polsce piastowskiej' [The peasants in Piast Poland], *Roczniki Historyczne*, xl (1974), 50–105, and xli (1975), 1–79; Buczek, 'Kto to byli żyrdnicy (żernicy)?' [Who were the *perticarii*?], *Kwartalnik Historii Kultury Materialnej*, v (1957), 454–62; D. Poppe, 'Ludność dziesiętnicza w Polsce wczesnośredniowiecznej' [The *decimi* in early medieval Poland], *Kwartalnik Historyczny*, lxiv (1957), 3–31; K. Tymieniecki, *Smardowie polscy: Studium z dziejów społeczno-gospodarczych wczesnego średniowiecza* [The Polish *smardowie*: a study in early medieval socioeconomic history] (Poznan, 1959); Tymieniecki, 'Łazęki' [The łazęki], *Słownik Starożytności Słowiańskich*, iii, 113–14; Davies, *God's Playground*, i, 76; Górecki, *Economy, Society, and Lordship*, pp. 28, 80–5, 99–101, 103, 112–13, 117, 120, 137, 176–7; Górecki, *Parishes, Tithes and Society*, pp. 104–5.

111 Bartlett, *Making*, pp. 113, 142–3, 152–3, 204–14; Hoffmann, *Land, Liberties, and Lord-ship*, pp. 61–92; Górecki, *Economy, Society, and Lordship*, pp. 193–284.

112 P. Knoll, 'The Urban Development of Medieval Poland, with Particular Reference to Kraków', in *The Urban Society of Eastern Europe in Premodern Times*, ed. B. Krekić (Berkeley and Los Angeles, 1987), pp. 63–136, at 67, 74, 81, 83, 86–9.

113 For the collective status of Jews, see two articles in *The Jews in Poland*, ed. C. Abram-sky, M. Jachimczyk, and A. Polonsky (Oxford, 1986): Aleksander Gieysztor, 'The Beginnings of Jewish Settlement in the Polish Lands' (pp. 15–21), and J. Goldberg, 'The Privileges Granted to Jewish Communities of the Polish Commonwealth as a Stabilizing Factor in Jewish Support' (pp. 31–54); and two articles in *The Jews in Old Poland 1000–1795*, ed. A. Polonsky, J. Basista, and A. Link-Lenczowski (London, 1993): J. Wyrozumski, 'The Jews in Medieval Poland' (pp. 13–22); and Stanisław Grodziski, 'The

expansion of these areas of privilege between the second half of the thirteenth and the middle of the fourteenth century.

The continuous elements of 'knightly law' included: (1) lordship – hence the routine references to 'knightly villages', or to villages held 'according to knightly law' (*iure militari*); (2) free choice of the ecclesiastical recipient of tithe revenue that was collected from such villages – a privilege routinely called the 'free tithe' (*libera decima*);[114] and (3) a specified, and relatively light, level of obligations to provide transport, hospitality, and related exactions to the Piast dukes and other powerful travellers through or near such villages – the 'knightly transport' (*conductus militaris*)[115] – a modification of one of those routine activities by the dukes and the 'knights' who accompanied them which defined social privilege in medieval Poland. These three elements of 'knightly law' appear to have been well-entrenched considerably before 1208, when Duke Henry the Bearded classified the villages acquired by the nuns of Trzebnica as having belonged to knights, ecclesiastics, and dukes. In subsequent decades, 'knightly law' and related constructs were adapted as a formal source of other legal arrangements: immunities, for instance in 1243, when Duchess Viola of Opole exempted several villages belonging to the diocese of Wrocław from 'all . . . services which are owed to us by knightly villages';[116] and dispute settlement, as when the eight arbitrators in the conflict between Bishop Thomas of Wrocław and Duke Henry of 1276 prohibited the duke from levying exactions from the bishop's peasants, except under specified circumstances, and even then only 'in the manner in which payments due from the men of the knights are gathered'.[117]

In the course of the thirteenth century, the Polish dukes (and occasionally bishops and abbots) began to express the relationship between themselves and the 'knights' in terms of service. In the process, they occasionally added another formal element to the meaning of the *ius militare*: a bilateral relationship between the 'knight' and his lord (typically the duke), centred on service, and entailing specific ethical and legal privileges and obligations. I wish to stress the very gradual nature of this particular reinterpretation of 'knightly' status. The majority of 'knights', or persons identified as beneficiaries of 'knightly law', were not, in any demonstrable fashion, associated with service. Neither service,

Kraków *Voivode*'s Jurisdiction over Jews: A Study of the Historical Records of the Kraków *Voivode*'s Administration of Justice to Jews' (pp. 199–218). For Armenians, see M. Oleś, *The Armenian Law in the Polish Kingdom (1356–1519)* (Rome, 1966).

114 Górecki, *Parishes, Tithes and Society*, pp. 105–6.

115 I would like here to correct my own misreading of that privilege as a type of activity owed *to* the knights, as it appears in Górecki, *Parishes, Tithes and Society*, pp. 130, 137 – noted, in a generous review of my work, by G. Myśliwski, *Kwartalnik Historyczny*, civ (1997), 94–8, at p. 95.

116 *SU*, ii, no. 243 (1243), p. 146, lines 45–6: 'in pouoz et in aliis nostris serviciis quod ville habent militares'.

117 *Ibid.*, no. 288 (1276), p. 197, lines 6–8: 'iuxta modum collectarum imponendum hominibus militum colligantur'.

nor 'knighthood', can at any point of the Middle Ages be reduced to the other; 'knightly law' was not, and did not become, essentially a service status or tenure. The particular knights whose status and tenure were defined in terms of service are difficult to situate within the broad framework of social privilege, and within the Polish 'knighthood'. Their proportion among the other 'knights' is impossible to assess, but in some respects they were atypical – for example, most 'knights' held estates as familial inheritances ('patrimonies', according to Polish sources) rather than as acquisitions through service.[118]

Nevertheless, on the relatively rare occasions when the contemporaries sought to articulate the details of the relationship between the dukes and members of the privileged social groups, they did so in terms of service. Two documents issued by Duke Bolesław of Masovia in 1244 provide an early example of the relationship between 'knightly law' and service.[119] Bolesław issued each document to a small group of recipients: Racibór and Albert in one case, Henry, Martin, and Wojno in the other.[120] Both documents record one specific fragment of a story, namely, deliberate resettlement of the two groups of men under ducal lordship. Bolesław noted that he had recruited ('freely received') both groups 'into my land of Masovia', and further specified that Racibór and Albert immigrated 'from Great Poland'.[121] He identified the settlers with a range of epithets: Racibór and Albert as 'these men' (*istos viros*), and then (several times) as his 'servitors' (*servitores*);[122] and Henry, Martin, and Wojno as 'good men' (*bonos viros*), his 'knights' (*milites nostros*), and, again in several passages, as 'servitors'.[123]

Each group received a modest estate, consisting of a single village – to be possessed, as Bolesław noted for Racibór and Albert, 'with full knightly law', and, for Henry, Martin, and Wojno, 'so that [they] may enjoy full knightly law,

---

118 Based on exceedingly fleeting evidence, some scholars have inferred a formal stratification within the Polish knighthood in terms of this criterion into a 'patrimonial' versus a 'created' or 'established' knightood; for a critique of this view, see Bieniak, 'Rody', pp. 166–67. I share the scepticism of this inference, because Abbot Peter's examples of several specific 'knights' (and aspiring 'knights') clearly show that inheritance and service were complementary strategies for enhancement of status by particular knights, rather than alternative bases for the creation of different categories of knighthood – see his examples of two *milites*, Albert the Bearded and Stephen Kobylaglowa (*KH*, c. 45–6, p. 121; cc. 54–5, p. 123; cc. 85–6, pp. 135–6), Nicholas, a cleric who was the offspring of parents from among the 'middling knights' in Little Poland (*ibid.*, cc. 2–3, pp. 109–10; cc. 22–4, p. 117; cc. 28–9, p. 118; c. 32, p. 119; c. 35, p. 119; c. 38, p. 120), and Boguchwał Brukał (*ibid.*, c. 113, p. 147).

119 *KMaz*, no. 448 (1244), pp. 538–9; no. 450 (1244), pp. 540–1.

120 *Ibid.*, no. 448 (1244), p. 538, line 26; no. 450 (1244), p. 540, lines 17–18, 24.

121 *Ibid.*, no. 448 (1244), p. 538, lines 25–6 ('suscepi meam in terram Mazouiam gratuite istos viros . . . de terra Poloniae'); no. 50 (1244), p. 540, lines 16–17 ('ad terram meam Mazouie et suscepi eos gratuite').

122 *Ibid.*, no. 448 (1244), p. 538, lines 25–6 ('istos viros Ratiborium et Albertum bonos meos seruitores'), 32–3 ('predictos seruitores Ratiborium et albertum'), 33 ('eisdem seruitoribus meis').

123 *Ibid.*, no. 450 (1244), p. 540, lines 17–18 ('bonos viros Henricum, Martinum, Woynonem

as all knights [do]'.[124] In both cases, Bolesław, like his Polish contemporaries, drew on 'knightly law' and on 'knights' as a general model of tenure and status. In addition, he specifically defined 'knightly law' to mean exemption from ducal justice: 'that is', he explained in the charter for Racibór and Albert, 'I have made the said servitors free and absolved from summons and trials before my palatines and . . . castellans.'[125] He defined the exemption of Henry, Martin, and Wojno from ducal justice in a nearly identical phrase, and referred to them as 'knights' specifically in that phrase.[126] He also allowed Racibór and Albert the right to receive (but evidently not impose) fines for theft and homicide.[127] He closed the disposition of their document with a particularly fulsome acknowledgement of his gratitude 'for their service, with which they have sought to furnish me faithfully and diligently everywhere', and he specifically associated the grant of the fine revenue with that service.[128]

These two documents conveniently frame two features of the relationship between social privilege, 'knighthood', and service in medieval Poland that show remarkable continuity since about the mid-thirteenth century. One is what might be called the ethical dimension of the relationship between the rulers on the one hand, and the population designated as 'knights', 'servitors', 'men', and holders of 'knightly law' on the other – cast in terms of service, fidelity, and earned reward. Bolesław's acknowledgment of Racibór and Albert's good service, and his gift of an additional reward for it, recurs explicitly in the preambles, narrations, and dispositions of ducal diplomas, sometimes in very elaborate language of debt, friendship, and entitlement. One example, among many, is Duke Leszek the Black's effusive gratitude to his 'faithful knight' Stanisław for his continued and faithful service despite the 1285 rebellion, and his gift to Stanisław 'and his posterity' of an estate and jurisdictional exemption, specifically

---

de Raygrod'), 23–4 ('supradictos milites nostros Henricum, Martinum et Woynonem'), 26 ('dictis seruitoribus meis'), 28 ('hijdem seruitores mei') – p. 541, lines 1–3 ('eosdem milites', 'prefatis seruitorijs meis').

[124] *Ibid.*, no. 448 (1244), p. 538, line 32 ('et cum omni Jure militalj'); no. 50 (1244), p. 540, lines 21–2 ('[e]t omne Jus militale habeant predicti prout omnes milites [– –]'). (The latter passage ends with a gap or erasure in the manuscript, which the editor, J. K. Kochanowski, was unable to reconstruct – see p. 540, note *g* – and therefore my gloss is somewhat interpretive.)

[125] *Ibid.*, no. 448 (1244), p. 538, lines 32–4: 'cum omni Jure militalj, sic quod predictos seruitores . . . facio liberos et solutos a citacione Judiciisque palatinorum et omnium castellanorum meorum.'

[126] *Ibid.*, no. 450 (1244), p. 540, lines 23–6: '[e]t ffacio [*sic*] . . . milites nostros Heinricum, Martinum et Woynonem . . . solutos et liberos a citacione et iudicio omnium palatinorum et Castellanorum meorum.' Although on this occasion he exempted these three men from one type of fine, he did not grant them the revenue of that fine or any other revenue from justice; p. 540, line 28 – p. 541, line 2.

[127] *Ibid.*, no. 448 (1244), p. 538, line 35 – p. 539 line 2.

[128] *Ibid.*: 'Do eciam eisdem seruitoribus meis . . . racione seruiciorum ipsorum que michi vbilibet tam soliciter quam fideliter exhibere studuerunt tollere facultatem penam pro furto et homicidio triginta marcas.'

as a reward for loyalty and service.[129] Throughout the thirteenth and early fourteenth centuries, the recipients of such documents, and of grants in return for service, consistently included (among others) 'knights', 'lords', 'men' ('noble' or not further qualified), ducal *servitores* or *ministri*, and ducal officials'[130] – in short, the range of persons otherwise documented as privileged – while the grants were consistently described as well-deserved rewards, earned by 'faithful', 'eager', or 'diligent' service, effort to serve, and the like.[131] By the fourteenth century, reward for performance of faithful service was a well-established moral claim – access to which was yet another expression, and source, of distinct social privilege for this range of persons in medieval Poland.

The other recurrent feature first reflected by Duke Bolesław's two charters of 1244 is the definition of 'knightly law' in terms of jurisdiction and economic exploitation – that is, of immunity.[132] Beginning around the mid-thirteenth century, the Polish dukes began to extend immunity to persons defined as their 'knights', their 'servitors', holders of 'knightly villages', and beneficiaries of 'knightly law' – using these terms interchangeably and cumulatively. First – like Racibór, Albert, Henry, Martin, and Wojno in 1244 – beneficiaries of 'knightly law' were fully exempted from the jurisdiction of all but the highest ducal courts.[133] Second, they were increasingly protected from ducal access to their estates and their inhabitants, and their own jurisdiction over their peasants expanded accordingly. By the turn of the fourteenth century, they acquired a very broad judicial authority, expressed in the ducal and royal charters with a

129 *KMp*, i, no. 109 (1285), p. 130; the next two footnotes provide examples, as a first approximation of the amount and content of this evidence.
130 *SU*, iv, no. 164 (1272), p. 118, line 38 ('Chwalissius noster famulus'); no. 247 (1274), p. 170, line 4 ('miles noster Heinricus'); *KMp*, i, no. 109 (1285), p. 30 ('miles noster fidelis'); *KWp*, no. 639 (1289), ii, 19 ('dilecti ac specialis ministri et servitoris nostri Petri dicti Winiarzyk'); no. 680 (1292), ii, 58 ('servitoris nostri Iacobi filii Dyrsislay'); no. 718 (1294), ii, 89 ('comitis Miroslai filii Pretpelci'); no. 795 (1298), ii, 161 ('Woyslao fideli nostro famulo'; 'Woyslaus comes'); no. 801 (1298), ii, 165 ('fideli nostro comiti Nicolao Iankonis palatino Pomeranie'); no. 1069 (1326), ii, 403 ('nobiles domini nostri fideles Pribislaus palatinus Poznaniensis et Woyslaus iudex').
131 *SU*, iv, no. 247 (1274), p. 170, line 4 ('considerantes fidelia servicia militis nostri Heinrici'); *KMp*, i, no. 109 (1285), p. 30 ('miles noster fidelis . . . nobis fidelia, utilia et continua seruicia sua tunc temporis et omnibus temporibus ostendit et adhuc exhibere non desistit'); *KWp*, no. 639 (1289), ii, 19, and no. 680 (1292), ii, 58 ('intuentes fidelia grataque obsequia'); no. 701 (1293), ii, 76 ('intuentes fidelia servicia'); no. 718 (1294), ii, 89 ('consideratis gratis obse.,uiis et fidelibus').
132 I have treated the early phase of the process of acquisition of immunity by secular recipients (through about 1250 but, I think, with implications for further developments), in Górecki, *Economy, Society, and Lordship*, pp. 182–6.
133 *KMp*, i, no. 80 (1270), p. 98 (village Dziewin, granted to Beno and Ludmila, 'imperpetuum libera est et immunis', and 'omnes incole eiusdem ville a potestate et iudicio castellani . . . et omnium iudicum ipsius omnino sunt liberi et exempti ita quod in nullo casu neque occasione strose citati teneantur respondere'); *SU*, iv, no. 247 (1274), p. 170 ('considerantes fidelia servicia militis nostri Heinrici dedimus sibi liberam opcionem locandi hereditatem suam . . . que Croscina nominatur . . . promittentes sibi quod ad ius castrense seu alia iura Polonica homines suos nullatenus trahi paciemur'); *KWp*, no. 639 (1289), ii,

standardized formula as: (1) the right to hold 'all trials, large and small', including capital offences, and to administer ordeals and other forms of inquiry;[134] (2) exclusion of ducal and other judges and officials from exercise of this jurisdiction; and (3) the right to all of its profits.[135] In addition – though here the evidence is sparser – it seems that at some point during the second decade of the fourteenth century, the peasants had formally lost the standing to seek recourse against their lords in royal courts.[136] By the fourteenth century, therefore, exercise of jurisdiction emerged as yet another activity that expressed and reinforced social privilege.

The increasing significance of service to the duke by 'knights', and by other privileged landholders, between about 1250 and 1310, at least in one region of

19–20; no. 680 (1292), ii, 58; no. 795 (1298), ii, 161; no. 801 (1298), ii, 165; no. 807 (1299), ii, 170; *KMp*, i, no. 154 (1318), p. 183; no. 1069 (1326), ii, 404; no. 1188 (1338), ii, 514.

[134] For ordeals, see: *KWp*, no. 680 (1292), ii, 58; no. 718 (1294), ii, 89 (Duke Przemysł II gives *comes* Mirosław an estate with broad jurisdiction, 'considerantes . . . quod omnia iura alciora et inferiora in bonis habet suis a nostris et suis progenitoribus ab antiquo in iure Polonico exercendi ut puta duellum, ferrum, mittere super aquam, suspendere et decollare sicut nostre castellanie et curia nostra tenet'). Note also, in the midst of a broad jurisdictional clause, the grant of right to administer torture, at *ibid.*, no. 825 (1299), ii, 186 (Duke Władysław Łokietek grants an estate to 'fidelis noster comes' Henry with 'omnes causas tam magnas quam parvas diiudicare videlicet furta, latrocinia, homicidia, et alias inferiores in civitate . . . comissas; et omnes maleficos suspendere, decollare, mutilare, rotare, cremare prefatur Heinricus vel suus scultetus iam dicte civitatis liberum arbitrium habeant dictas penas inflingere in omnibus malefactoribus'). For the ordeal in Poland in general, see R. Bartlett, *Trial by Fire and Water: The Medieval Judicial Ordeal* (Oxford, 1986), pp. 43–6. The right to administer ordeals had been one of the marks of immunity jurisdiction in medieval Poland since at least 1222; see the two documents of that year, discussed in Górecki, *Economy, Society, and Lordship*, p. 167; see also *S.U.*, ii, no. 375 (1249), p. 239, lines 11–14.

[135] An excellent example is: *KWp*, no. 801 (1298), ii, 165: 'Volumus eciam ut omnia iudicia, maiora vel minora, Polonicalia vel Theutunicalia, qualiacunque fuerint, nullus sed ipse comes Nicolaus cum sua posteritate habeat iudicare et penas iudicatas recipere integraliter et complete.' In addition to the documents cited in the preceding note, the charters that include a combination of these three elements include: *ibid.*, nos. 639 (1289), ii, 19–20; 795 (1298), ii, 161; 984 (1316), ii, 325; *KMp*, i, no. 158 (1319), pp. 187–88; *KWp*, nos. 1069 (1326), ii, 404; 1188 (1338), ii, 514 ('[i]n causis . . . criminalibus, puta furti, sanguinis, homicidii, incendii, mutilationis et alii quibuscunque prelibato Maczkoni et suis progenitis, advocato vel scultetis predictarum hereditatum iudicandi et puniendi plenam conferimus potestatem. Insuper, dum se homines civitatis et villarum antedictarum mutuo vel unus alium occiderit sibi et suis posteris penam capitis percipiendi plenam damus potestatem'). A document that concerns, on its face, only profits of justice is *ibid.*, no. 680 (1292), ii, 58: 'Et si inter ipsos [incolas] homicidium fieri contingit nullus alius set sepe dictus Iacobus et sui successores penam percipiant capitalem.'

[136] See above all the two documents concerning the peasants from Dolany: *KWp*, nos. 1027 (1322), ii, 362; 1055 (1325), ii, 384–5; the generalization is somewhat tentative, because I have not yet been able to carry out into the reign of Casimir the Great the kind of analysis of expansion of jurisdiction over the peasants in Poland which I have attempted for the earlier period in my *Economy, Society, and Lordship*.

the Polish duchies, is well reflected by Abbot Peter and his continuator. Peter viewed ducal service as only one of several significant relationships among privileged groups. Although he clearly recognized its importance whenever he noted it in his stories, he noted it relatively infrequently. In addition, his examples of service vary quite widely in terms of the status of the parties, the functions they performed, and what might be called the quality or closeness of the service relationship.[137] Forty years later, Peter's continuator clearly viewed service ducal as a routine feature of privileged tenure, and of the network of relationships among the privileged groups – affecting, above all, the dukes and the 'knights', but also other lay persons, as well as the Henryków monastery. He directly reported, or logically assumed, the obligation, performance, or avoidance of ducal service within a much higher proportion of his stories than does his predecessor. He also identified service in terms of a consistent set of obligations, assessments, remedies, and modes of entrance and exit.[138] He described local and regional 'knights' (and others)[139] as owing the dukes a level of service which was assessed in a standardized measure of a number of war-horses per estate or per unit of arable;[140] and he narrated several stories of individual 'knights' who breached their service obligation to particular Piast dukes in favour of others.[141] The overall impression, at least in this exceptional source, is that although ducal service did not displace other determinants of status, or other relationships within the socially privileged groups, it significantly increased in importance in the course of the later thirteenth century.

---

137 Abbot Peter's reports of service include: *KH*, c. 2, p. 110; c. 85, p. 135; no. 113, p. 147.
138 The continuator's reports of service include: *ibid.*, c. 127, pp. 156–7; c. 129, p. 157; c. 147, p. 165; c. 150, p. 167; c. 151, p. 167; c. 152, pp. 167–8; c. 156, p. 169; c. 160, p. 172; cc. 167–8, p. 176; c. 186, p. 189; c. 190, p. 188; c. 192, p. 194.
139 *Ibid.*, c. 127, pp. 156–7 (John Osina); c. 147, p. 165 (Stephen Kotka and his successors to perform 'full services to the lord of the land'); c. 150, p. 167 (Peter of Lubnów 'to perform the customary services from the said two hides to the prince of the land at suitable times'); c. 151, p. 167 (Cieszybór anticipates demand for ducal service); c. 152, pp. 167–8 (two men from Frankenstein perform 'full service'; several further transactions about the service, as an obligation and as an alienable estate); cc. 167–8, p. 176; c. 190, p. 188; c. 192, p. 194.
140 *Ibid.*, c. 129, p. 157 (Burchard and Jeszko 'remove themselves' to Duke Bernard); c. 156, p. 169 (Poltko refuses to perform service to the duke); c. 160, p. 172 (Siegfried Rindfleisch 'offers himself in obedience to the knights of the land', and enters service of Duke Bolesław II); c. 186, p. 189 (Alsik 'attaches himself' to the duke of Opole).
141 *Ibid.*, c. 152, p. 165 (one war-horse from holdings of two men from Frankenstein plus Nietowice); c. 156, p. 169 (Poltko's service assessed at three war-horses); c. 160 (one war-horse as service by Siegfried Rindfleisch); cc. 186–90, p. 189–92 (half a war-horse due from a total of 13.5 *mansi* in Alsik's holding). Assessment of the level of 'knightly' service obligations with a standardized measure of one warhorse recurs among a small handful of documents from other regions of Silesia – *SU*, iv, no. 57 (1268), p. 52, lines 19–20; no. 181 (1272), p. 129 – and, to my knowledge, does not recur in the other Piast duchies. Silesia therefore represents one, apparently rather distinctive, variant of the relationships between 'knighthood' and service in Piast Poland which I describe in general terms above and below in this essay. One clue to its apparent distinctness by 1300 is

3. Toward the definition of a privileged social group: identity

A crucial element of the emergence of a socially privileged group is the formation of an identity expressive of group membership. This subject is currently of
great interest among medievalists and other historians, and paradoxically for
that reason especially complicated and ambiguous.[142] I would like to begin with
the fullest possible answer to a logically straightforward but conceptually and
empirically very difficult question, namely, the ways in which members of the
privileged group (or groups) conceived of who they were. Then, I would like to
situate in that context the appearance and early uses of the ritual devices of
group membership I mentioned at the outset of this essay – the 'clan' names,
battle cries, and heraldic badges, which emerged as the classificatory criteria in
terms of which the Polish 'nobility' defined itself between the reigns of the last
two Piasts (1320–1370) and the mid-fifteenth century.

In one sense, this entire essay has been about issues of identity. Specific
persons presumably identified themselves, and were identified by others, with a
wide range of words and concepts, among which the cluster of knighthood and
service was especially important. Between the last years of the thirteenth
century and the mid-fourteenth, the repertoire of epithets used to designate

---

surely the relative importance of German knighthood in the region – a subject for which
see the brilliant work by T. Jurek, *Obce rycerstwo na Śląsku do połowy XIV wieku* [For-
eign knighthood in Silesia until the mid-fourteenth century] (Poznań, 1996).

[142] In the present context, two approaches to this amorphous subject seem especially interesting: an inquiry, long underway in East-Central Europe, about different forms of 'collective consciousness' – above all 'national', and, closely related, dynastic, noble, and
other, and about conceptions of time and space; and a much more recent emphasis, especially among anglophone medievalists, on collective (or social) memory. Some of the
approaches and findings concern remarkably similar phenomena under these rather different labels. For the Polish, Czech, and Slovak scholarship, see (in addition to n. 7
above): B. Geremek, 'Temporal Imagination in Polish Mediaeval Historiography',
Quaestiones Medii Aevi, ii (1981), 35–62; *Dawna świadomość historyczna w Polsce,
Czechach i Słowacji* [Former historical consciousness in Poland, Bohemia, and Slova-
kia], ed. R. Heck (Wrocław, 1978); *Czas – przestrzeń – praca w dawnych miastach. Studia ofiarowane Henrykowi Samsonowiczowi w sześćdziesiątą rocznicę urodzin* [Time,
space, and work in former cities: studies offered to Henryk Samsonowicz on his sixtieth
birthday], ed. A. Wyrobisz, M. Tymowski, W. Fałkowski, and Z. Morawski (Warsaw,
1991); and the remarkable series of works by Jacek Banaszkiewicz, *Kronika Dzierzwy.
XIV-wieczne kompendium historii ojczystej* [Dzierzwa's chronicle: a fourteenth-century
compendium of native history] (Wrocław, 1979), *Podanie o Piaście i Popielu. Studium
porównawcze nad wczesnośredniowiecznymi tradycjami dynastycznymi* [The legend of
Piast and Popiel: a comparative study of early-medieval dynastic traditions] (Warsaw,
1986), and *Polskie dzieje bajeczne mistrza Wincentego Kadłubka* [The legend in Polish
history by Master Vincent Kadłubek] (Wrocław, 1998). Among the anglophone studies
of social memory, see, above all, P. Geary, *Phantoms of Remembrance: Memory and
Oblivion at the End of the First Millennium* (Princeton, 1994); and J. Fentress and C.
Wickam, *Social Memory* (Oxford, 1994). For further literature, see Górecki, 'Communities', p. 128 n. 2, and 'Rhetoric', pp. 262–6 (nn. 6, 11, 17, 23), 274–5 n. 80.

privileged or important persons became more ornate and more standardized. Individuals were more routinely identified with the terms *vir*, *vir nobilis*, and *nobilis* used as a substantive noun, all accompanied by one or more adjectives indicating distinction or excellence. Now, throughout the fourteenth century, such terms, when used at all, were used in conjunction with the earlier expressions of status, such as *dominus, comes*, 'knight', and so forth, but there was a qualitative shift toward extravagant expressions of personal status and honour.[143]

Familial ties are another way in which important persons identified themselves. This subject is complicated in the present context because the three ritual attributes in terms of which 'nobility' was later defined – 'clan' names, battle cries, and heraldic devices – were evidently related to familial groups. However, looking at the evidence from the twelfth century forward rather than from the fifteenth century backward, it seems that associations of kinship and affinity, and their significance as a source of identity, varied in two respects: across different domains of activity; and over time. The two best-documented domains of activity in which familial associations mattered were (1) regional politics, that is, those patterns of association among the actors which were significant for their social position within or beyond a region; and (2) property transactions, that is, gifts to the saints and other alienations, consent to alienations of inherited estates, successions to or divisions of estates, and acquisitions of estates through purchase, gift, or service. Kinship and affinity mattered differently (as a source of identity and otherwise) within these two domains – and their significance changed in the course of the fourteenth century.

As usual, Abbot Peter of Henryków is an exceptionally helpful informant on the political significance of familial ties. He framed that significance in three ways: by classifying some of the important actors in his stories by family status; by reconstructing relationships of kinship and affinity among them; and by explicitly describing, or commenting on, the significance of these relationships. He focused on the family status of several clerics who had been crucial friends to his monastery in the course of the thirteenth century: Nicholas, the ducal notary and canon of Wrocław who had initiated the monastery's foundation shortly before 1222, whom he recalled as having been 'born', sometime after the mid-twelfth century, 'of ancestors neither very noble nor completely base, but from among the middling knights';[144] Nasław, Nicholas's successor as notary after 1227, 'born of the most noble stock in this land;'[145] and two relatives, Thomas I, bishop of Wrocław between 1232 and 1268, and his uncle

143 This generalization is based on a perusal of the documents cited throughout this essay, but not on a rigorous quantification of all of the relevant expressions and epithets.

144 *K.H.*, c. 2, p. 109: 'parentus non valde nobilibus nec etiam omnino infimis sed mediocribus militibus ex provincia Cracoviensi oriundus'.

145 *Ibid.*, c. 100, p. 140: 'Huic Nycolao successit in notaria vir quidam Nazlaus huius terre ex styrpe nobilissima natus.'

Peter, provost of Wrocław, both 'born of the noblest stock in this province',[146] and as 'most noble in name, house, and habits'.[147]

Peter reconstructed ties of kinship and affinity among a handful of actors who were especially important to the monastery's political position. Paul, bishop of Poznań between 1211 and 1248, was a member of what Peter called a 'kindred' (*cognatio*) that included the notary Nicholas and an important early settler in the region, Boguchwał.[148] He was also the godfather of Henry II the Pious, son of Duke Henry the Bearded – 'to whom he was thereby joined by a certain special familiarity'.[149] Bishop Paul's 'kindred' had been sufficiently important to serve as a focus of social climbing by other significant actors. Albert the Bearded, a 'rather powerful knight', an especially important lay neighbour of the monastery, and a brother-in-law of another important local 'knight', sought (fraudulently, yet successfully) to establish ties of kinship with Nicholas, by means of friendship, deliberate disinformation, and performance within a substantial group of nearby 'knights'.[150] Another 'neighbour' of the monastery, Siegrod, acted similarly in the 1260s. Abbot Peter was at pains to refute their carefully fabricated claims.[151]

Family membership clearly mattered in several ways – to Abbot Peter, the people he described, and the monks for whom he wrote. His classifications of Nicholas, Nasław, Thomas, and Provost Paul as 'the noble', 'the base', or 'middling knights', and in terms of degrees of 'nobility', clearly imply that by the 1260s 'nobility' was a transparent and well-established criterion of status, and that it worked as an attribute of persons and of family groups, which he interchangeably called *genera*, *stirpes*, and *cognationes*. Albert the Bearded's successful (though fraudulent) efforts to pass himself off as a member of a *cognatio* show that such groups were, among other things, sources of identity. In addition, they were periodically mobilized for legal and economic advantage of the monastery in its surrounding political universe. Bishop Paul was one of the mediators with Duke Henry of Nicholas's proposal to establish the monastery in 1222, and, six years later, helped consecrate the altar in the first cloister church; while Albert the Bearded helped the monastery against several hostile neighbours and ineffective dukes in the regional disorders after 1241.[152]

---

146 *Ibid.*, c. 199, p. 194: 'Hic idem magister Thomas erat huius provincie ex stirpe nobilissima natus.'

147 *Ibid.*, c. 200, p. 195: 'dominus Petrus nomine, genere et moribus nobilissimus'.

148 *Ibid.*, c. 21, p. 116: 'hic erat homo antiqu[u]s et reverenda persona et erat de cognatione domini Nycolai predicti'; c. 117, p. 150: 'Slesienses de cognatione domini Pauli quondam Poznaniensis ecclesie episcopi'.

149 *Ibid.*, c. 21, p. 116: 'idem dominus Paulus episcopus baptizaverat dominum Heinricum iuniorem ducem, levans eum a sacro fonte unde domino Heinrico duci antiquo barbato quadam familiaritate speciali erat coniunctus.'

150 *Ibid.*, cc. 46–7, pp. 121–2; cc. 54–7, p. 123; cc. 74, pp. 129–30; c. 108, p. 144; c. 111, pp. 146–7.

151 *Ibid.*, c. 55, p. 123.

152 For details and a broader context of alliances of this kind, see Górecki, 'Politics', pp. 32–7, 39–43.

However important they were, ties of kinship and affinity were not, either in 1260 or 1310, central or fundamental to other kinds of relationships. Rather, status and privilege were rooted in several interrelated but distinct sources, no one of which was essentially fundamental to the others – and in that sense Abbot Peter's history confirms the impression of the diplomatic evidence. In addition (and to complicate matters), familial identifications do not distinguish the otherwise privileged groups from other social strata. If anything, descent groups, which in turn lent patronymic names to the descendants as well as to places, are more clearly visible among various categories of peasants[153] than among persons otherwise identified as 'knights', 'lords', donors to the monastery,[154] robbers,[155] and their friends in the neighbourhood – in short, the privileged. Neither Peter nor his successor identify family membership, or any of its specific attributes – above all the patronymic – as a source, or expression, of a specifically 'knightly', or otherwise privileged, identity.[156]

In contrast to politics, property transactions almost always elicited the participation of close (if any) groups of relatives and affines. Furthermore even in those instances, family groups were consistently less prominent and important than other kinds of persons, above all dukes, ducal officials, and bishops.[157] However, around the year 1300 the range of familial groups participating in property transactions increased gradually. We have a subtle but marked increase in the incidence of joint transactions by familial groups of a relatively wide genealogical range, which can be classified as follows: (1) descent groups, identified in the record either in terms of a common ancestor,[158] or by means of lists of several generations of ascendants and descendants[159] – and which in addition

---

153 *Ibid.*, c. 32, p. 119: 'inter hos rusticos duo rustici existebant qui ceteros quadam potentia precellebant. Ex hiis duobus unus vocabatur Crepis alter Such unde locus iste olim dicebantur Sucuwiz.'

154 *Ibid.*, c. 31, p. 118; c. 34, p. 119; c. 36, pp. 119–20; cc. 82–3, p. 134 ; c. 85, p. 135; c. 113, p. 147; c. 119, p. 151.

155 *Ibid.*, c. 29, p. 118.

156 Above all, in the cases of Stephen Kobylagłowa and Albert the Bearded their primary holdings are not, evidently, the same as the patronymics associated with them: *ibid.*, cc. 47–8, pp. 121–2 (Ciepłowoda, Cienkowice, and Kubice), and c. 85, p. 135 (Kobyłagłowa and Głębowice/Bukowina).

157 Although I have not yet performed a rigorous quantitative survey of group involvement in property transactions through the mid-fourteenth century, the overview of the evidence seems to confirm the patterns of familial, ducal, episcopal, and other participation I have discerned through such analysis for the early thirteenth in Górecki, '*Ad Controversiam*', pp. 215–17, 221–3.

158 *KMp*, i, no. 165 (1320), p. 196 (a transfer, by 'nos Nauobius comes de Morauica et castellanus Cracouiensis, dominus Goluch canonicus ecclesie Cracouiensis, vna cum fratribus, filiis, nepotibus et consanguineis quibuslibet', of a convent 'quod eadem per progenitores nostros videlicet nobilem quondam uirum Secechonem in ciuitate . . . Cracouiensi . . . sit constructa'). For descent and ego-centered family groups, see R. Fox, *Kinship and Marriage: An Anthropological Perspective* (Cambridge, 1983).

159 *KWp*, no. 833 (1300), ii, 192 (a sale of several holdings by 'comes Nicolaus vexillifer Brestensis una cum suis fratribus, filiolis et nepotibus Swantoslao, Iaroslao, Przeslao,

may have included godchildren;[160] (2) ego-centred sib groups, recorded at their cores as brothers, paternal uncles, and nephews;[161] and (3) groups that were clearly large and extended, but which are difficult to categorize as familial (or otherwise) because of the inadequacies of the evidence.[162]

To be sure, records of this kind are not typical in the fourteenth-century evidence; most property transactions apparently continued to involve smaller and closer family groups. However, isolated as they perhaps are, such records are, on their face, quite important. Their appearance indicates either that the structure of family groups involved in property transactions was undergoing a change – that is, that the family groups participating in property transactions were, at least sometimes, larger than they had been before – or, more cautiously, that property transactions provided the participants with an occasion to identify, appreciate, and (perhaps) commemorate an expanding range of relatives and affines by means of the written record. In either event, property transactions reflect an expansion (however slight and gradual) in the range and breadth of socially significant family groups around the turn of the fourteenth century.

Finally, Abbot Peter, his continuator, and their contemporaries of the thirteenth and the fourteenth centuries sometimes identified specific persons with nicknames, that is epithets attached to other, presumably given names.[163] Nicknames are relatively rare, and, when they do appear, their uses seem untidy and eclectic. Specific persons may or may not be identified by a nickname in

Vito, Floriano, Sulislao, Paulo et Nemsta'); nos. 1007–8, 1010 (1319), ii, 344–5, 347 (a sale to the Łekno monastery, by 'comes Martinus . . . una cum omnibus nostris confratribus subnotatis, scilicet Nicolao filio quondam comitis Nicolai . . . patrui nostri, tum Philipo, Beniamin fratribus nostris, Nicolao filio Ianchonis filiolo nostro', amplified as 'Philippus et Beniamin fratres uterini, Nicolaus dictus Zareba, nec non pueri iam dictorum').

160 *Ibid.*, no. 900–901 (1306), ii, 249–50: 'de consensu nostroum filiolorum videlicet filii Sandivogii . . . et filii Nicolai . . . et de consensu filiorum comitis Olbrachti', reiterated as 'de consensu . . . meorum filiolorum videlicet Martini filii fratris mei Sandivogii . . . et Nicolai filii fratris mei Nocolai . . . et de expresso consensu filiolorum meorum Sandivogii, Nicolai et Gotpoldi, filiorum fratris mei Albrachti'.

161 *Ibid.*, no. 947 (1311), ii, 289: 'ego Gerhardus de Prendekow . . . cum Gisen filio meo, cum Gisen patruo meo, cum Barteken, Gerhardo Ottoni avunculis meis nostrisque legitimis heredibus . . . recepimus' an estate from the Cistercian monastery in Paradyż.

162 *Ibid.*, no. 868 (1303), ii, 223 ('comes Unislaus et Iohannes heredes de Gwoszewo una cum Alberto ceko herede de Kamones'); no. 1050 (1325), ii, 380 (gift of an estate for the Byszów monastery, 'collata per comitem Wit de Lubow et filios eius videlicet Petrum, Nycolaum, Bodzetam et Iohannem nec non per dominum Andream archidyaconem . . . et per fratres et filiolos suos Albertum iudicem . . . et germanum suum Cristinum, Mathiam et Bodzetam filios comitis Petri, et per Andream filiolum suum.'

163 For a somewhat different working definition, see Pakulski, 'Geneza', pp. 100–101, 105. The following are among the nicknames excerpted from the primary source quotations cited above in this essay: 'the Wise', 'the Tooth' (*SU*, ii, no. 375 [1249], p. 233, lines 11–15); 'the Gaul' (*ibid.*, iv, no. 286 [1276], p. 194, line 41); 'the Czech' (*KH*, c. 113, pp. 147–8); 'the Blind' (*KWp*, no. 868 [1303], ii, 223); Lis, Ovis, Kobylic, Słup, Łodzia (*SU*, iv, no. 136 [1271], p. 99, lines 19, 22–4); Winiarzyk (*KWp*, no. 639 [1289], ii, 19); Zaręba (*ibid.*, no. 1010 [1319], ii, 347).

conjunction with a patronymic, along with other expressions of status and identity, in any combination. Nevertheless, the formation and meanings of nicknames, their group specificity, and above all their identifying functions over time, do cohere in ways that can best be reconstructed from the work of Abbot Peter and his continuator.

Their stories suggest that at the time they were established, associations of this kind were to a large degree random – and that it is difficult to subsume the initial production of any one nickname under some kind of an overarching linguistic or symbolic system.[164] Nevertheless, considered analytically, all surviving nicknames appear to have derived from three sources.[165] The first was a place-name, that is, the name of the designee's principal (perhaps ancestral) estate, connected to the given name with or without inflection – as when Abbot Peter identified the 'knight' Stephen as 'Kobylagłowa', or 'of Kobylagłowa',[166] or the 'knight' Albert as 'of Ciepłowoda'.[167] Abbot Peter designated with this type of nickname only persons he otherwise identified as 'knights' or 'lords;' as far as he was concerned, it was therefore an attribute specific to the 'knighthood'.

A nickname could also refer to a trait, with or without implicit value judgment or irony.[168] An early settler named Boguchwał earned a nickname for himself 'among the neighbours' because he habitually helped his wife operate a domestic hand-quern – which, here as elsewhere, was apparently women's labour, and so, as Peter carefully explained, it elicited an ironic epithet deriving from the Polish word related to a grindstone.[169] A 'ducal peasant' named Kwiecik, contemporary with Boguchwał, had been very severely maimed by sword cuts, and, 'because [he] lacked one hand and had no use of the other, the Poles at that time called him "the Stump" '.[170] Facial hair elicited attention, and Abbot Peter consistently referred to Duke Henry, and to 'rather powerful

---

164 By which I mean that any one nickname could be drawn from a variety of sources that were highly circumstantial and accidental – but not that their subsequent meanings and functions do not conform to patterns, or are chaotic, a point on which I follow Pakulski, 'Geneza', p. 115.
165 For classifications refracting this typology into further categories, see Pakulski, 'Geneza', pp. 102–8.
166 *KH*, c. 85, pp. 135–6; c. 87, p. 136.
167 *Ibid.*, c. 45, p. 121.
168 Pakulski, 'Geneza', p. 105.
169 *KH*, c. 113, p. 147; Górecki, 'Communities', pp. 142–3. On milling as women's labour, R. Holt, *The Mills of Medieval England* (Oxford, 1988), p. 2; on ironic surnames for men who perform women's labour, M. Segalen, 'Mentalité populaire et remariage en Europe occidentale', in *Marriage and Remarriage in Populations of the Past*, ed. J. Dupâquier, E. Hélin, P. Laslett, M. Livi-Bacci, and S. Sogner (London, 1981), pp. 67–77, at p. 69; on both subjects, in the context of Henryków, M. Dembińska, 'Day ut ia pobrusa a ti poziwai' ['Let me grind and you rest'], *Kwartalnik Historii Kultury Materialnej*, xxv (1977), 499–502.
170 *KH*, c. 84, p. 134; Górecki, 'Communities', pp. 144–5.

knight' Albert as 'the bearded', 'with beard', or 'the beard'.[171] Toward the end of the thirteenth century, the namesake (and presumably descendant) of the knight Stephen Kobylagłowa, who 'was in the habit of hunting what belonged to others in nightly roamings just as a cat roams about and hunts at night', earned himself a nickname that meant a feral female cat.[172]

Third, nicknames were derived from other kinds of words, with or without apparent intrinsic meaning. These typically appear in combination with other kinds of nicknames. Thus, Abbot Peter consistently referred to the gender-bending Boguchwał with an ethnic epithet, 'the Czech' (*Bohemus*), and he introduced the 'bearded' knight, Albert, as 'nicknamed Łyka', but referred to him by his facial hair thereafter. In the very phrase explaining Stephen Kotka's feline nickname, Peter's continuator also referred to him with the geographic nickname, Kobylagłowa.[173] This aggregation of nicknames, and variation in their meanings and transparency, recur throughout the thirteenth and earlier fourteenth centuries in the (always scarce) records of this type of identification.

The stories of Boguchwał and his descendants, and of the two knights named Kobylagłowa, shed light specifically on the relationship between nicknames and identity. Boguchwał had initially earned one of his nicknames through a social response to an unusual trait or activity – transgression of gender roles through performance of women's labour. Immediately after explaining this basis of his nickname, Abbot Peter added that 'this is why all of his descendants are called Brukalice', and elsewhere he further referred to one of Boguchwał's sons as 'Racław of Brukalice'.[174] Therefore, this nickname subsequently worked as a patronymic, and as a name of a descent group. Although Peter frequently notes the triple function of patronymics as designations of localities, descent groups, and particular persons, in this story he further shows that a patronymic could be derived from a nickname – and thus from the trait that nickname expressed.

In this case, the nickname, referring to a personal trait, was generated, or produced, by a local community in which the designee lived and acted. Once produced, it may have functioned as a socially based marker of identity. Thereafter, it – and the trait or attribute for which it was a shorthand – may have 'stuck' to the designee as a personal attribute, been reproduced over generations, and thus served both the original designees and their descendants (or perhaps otherwise recruited groups) as an identifying device, memorializing the

---

171 Duke Henry: *KH*, c. 21, p. 116; c. 40, p. 120; c. 56, p. 123; c. 94, p. 139; cc. 97–8, p. 139; c. 101, p. 140; c. 108, p. 145; Albert: *ibid.*, c. 46, p. 121; c. 74, p. 129; c. 106, p. 143; c. 108, p. 144 ; c. 111, p. 146.

172 *Ibid.*, c. 147, p. 165; for the text, please see the next note.

173 *Ibid.*: 'Fuit autem heres dicte hereditatis nomine Stephanus de Cobulagloua cognomento Kotka. Qui ideo Kotka dictus fuit quia sicut kattus noctis tempore discurrit et venatur predam suam, sic iste per nocturnos discursus res alienas crebrius venabatur.'

174 *Ibid.*, c. 113, p. 147 ('[q]uod videntes vicini . . . appellabant eum Bogwal Brucal inde est quod sua posteritas tota vocatur Brucaliz'); c. 115, p. 148 ('quidam iuvenes Bogussa et Paulus filii quondam Ratzlai de Brucaliz'); c. 119, p. 151 ('filii quondam Razlai de Brucaliz').

person to whom they originally referred. In the case of the two Stephens of Kobylagłowa, an attribute of this kind eventually gave rise to a visual image. In 1278, a charter issued by (or in the name of) the second Stephen Kobylagłowa was confirmed by his own and his uncle's seals, both of which carried an image of a horse's head – an almost exact iconographical counterpart of the meaning of the words *kobyla głowa*, that is, of the name of the estate, the common nickname of the two Stephens, and of one of the nicknames of the younger of them.[175] In very different ways, the early story of Brukał and his idiosyncratic activity, and the late story of the Stephen Kotka and his estate with a distinctive name, show how their contemporaries deployed and configured words, personal attributes, proper names, and symbols to define one another and themselves.

Associations and functions of this kind shed – in exceedingly hypothetical fashion – unexpected light on the most difficult and intractable issue of the definition of a single privileged group in medieval Poland: the formation of 'clan' names, battle cries, and heraldic devices, that is, the formal bases for self-conscious inclusion into and exclusion from the Polish 'nobility' since some point in the fourteenth century. Sources produced in the later thirteenth and the fourteenth centuries gradually begin to identify specific persons in two ways that are rather new, and that increase in frequency over time: (1) with nicknames which, although used in ordinary fashion, correspond to some of those 'clan' names in terms of which the Polish nobility routinely defined itself later; and (2) by membership in the 'clans' themselves – that is, in large groups usually called 'houses' (*domus*), 'stocks' (*genus*), extended families (*cognationes*), 'clans' (*genealogiae*), and the like, each of which had its own proper name – which, of course, is what historians call the 'clan' name.

In the first case, individual designees are identified by 'clan' names used plainly as second names ('Martin Lis'), or through conjunctions suggesting a place or group ('Sędziwój of Łodzia'), or through simple amplification ('John, called Doliwa');[176] or the designees are groups rather than individuals, as in 1327, when King Władysław Łokietek referred to a family group of eight 'noble men . . . called Pałuki',[177] or in 1352, when a notice of an assembly of ninety

---

175 Cetwiński, *Rycerstwo . . . : biogramy*, p. 183 n. 769.

176 *KWp*, no. 613 (1271), i, 572 (*Martinus Lis, Sanciwy de Loda*); 'Rocznik Świętokrzyski' [Annals of the Holy Cross monastery], ed. A. Rutkowska-Płachcińska, *s.a.* 1333, 1348, 1348, in *MPH n.s.*, xii (Kraków, 1996), 62, c. 102 ('Iohannes episcopus Poznaniensis dictus Doluwa'), p. 66, cc. 106–7 ('obiit . . . Iohannes . . . episcopus Cracoviensis cui succedit Schirzyk per electionem canonicam', 'obiit Schirzyk'); *KMp*, i, no. 199 (1335), p. 237 (*Paulus Rola*); 'Kalendarz Krakowski', *s.a.* 1335, 1348, 1357, in *MPH*, ii, 916, lines 16–18 (*Johannes Doliwa, Johannes Lyodzia*), 923, lines 33–4 ('dominus Petrus dictus Szirik episcopus Cracoviensis'), 914, lines 11–12 ('d[omi]nus Jacobus custos Gneznesis et canonicus Cracoviensis dictus Szirik'); *K.Wp*, no. 1313 (1352), iii, 21–2 ('Pribco dictus Lys', 'Iacussius et Mathias filii Pribconis Lys').

177 *KWp*, no. 1086 (1327), ii, 417: 'nobiles viri Vincenctius cum suis filiolis Kelcznone, Paluka, Vigloz, Virbanta' with 'nobilibus viris suis fratribus videlicet Zbiluto, Svantoslao, Slavniconi dictis Paluky'.

named men included a record of a smaller family group 'called Lis'.[178] In the second case, individuals are identified as members of 'clans' explicitly. Writing at the turn of the thirteenth and fourteenth centuries, the Poznań clerics recalled in a passage of the *Chronicle of Great Poland* that, around 1220, Duke Casimir the Just of Little Poland had appointed as his deputy in Pomerania 'a certain brave man of Kraków, from the family of Griffin, by the name of Bogusław',[179] and that in 1248 Duke Przemysł I of Great Poland had imprisoned 'Thomas, castellan of Poznań, and Tomisław, and Sędziwój, his son, the butler, from the family of Nałęcz'.[180]

In addition, we have ephemeral and rather vague associations of 'clan' names with the kinds of broad groups of leaders and followers which I have noted earlier in connection with military campaigns.[181] Thus, in 1271, Bishop Thomas II of Wrocław noted that a group of 'companions' engaged in the Milicz campaign had been led by 'Martin Lis', and that 'Nicholas, son of palatine Sędziwój of Łodzia', among others, led a following of 'many other associates of theirs;'[182] while some decades later the Poznań clerics recalled that the 'knights' Thomas, Tomisław, and Sędziwój 'from the family of Nałęcz' had been imprisoned in 1248 because they had plotted on behalf of one duke against another 'together with their associates'.[183] The terms used to designate such groups (*societas, socii, consortes*), seem especially vague – but in conjunction, they do suggest networks of kinship, patronage, or some other kind of alliance, which were at least on occasion designated with 'clan' names, and which may have been coextensive with, or segments of, familial groups; however, as in other contexts, such groups may have related to a wide variety of kinds of association discussed elsewhere in this essay, including office, membership in armed entourages, or service.

The (partial) overlap of nicknames (applied to individuals or groups) with at least some of the 'clan' names which became an important element of noble identity in the course of the fourteenth and fifteenth centuries has understandably prompted historians to assume that the individuals so identified were members of the 'clans', that they and those 'clans' represent the earliest visible trace of the Polish 'nobility', and that the 'origins' of that nobility can be recon-

---

[178] *Ibid.*, no. 1313 (1352), iii, 21–2 (Andrew, Martin, and Przybko *dicti Lys*, and later in the list of participants, Jacus and Matthew, 'sons of Przybko Lis').

[179] *MPH*, ii, 554, lines 9–12: 'virum strenuum de cognatione Griffonum, Cracoviensem, Boguslaum nomine'.

[180] *Ibid.*, ii, 566, lines 1, 20–8, especially 21–4, 26–7: 'Thomam castellanum Posnaniensem et Thomislaum ac Sandzivogium filium ejus pincernam de congatione Nalancz'. For other examples of a correspondence between nicknames (applied to individuals, groups, or both) and 'clan' names, during and beyond the period relevant to this essay, see Pakulski, 'Geneza', pp. 105–10 (the names include: Ogon, Lis, Zaremba, Nałęcz, Pałuka).

[181] See the text at nn. 52–3 above.

[182] *SU*, iv, no. 136 (1271), p. 99, lines 19–20 ('Martinus Lis cum sua societate'), 23–4 ('Nicolaus filius palatini Sanciwy de Loda, Suantomir Boznowie et alii multi eorum socii').

[183] *MPH*, ii, 566, lines 26–7: 'prefati milites cum suis consortibus'.

structed by reconstructing the ties of kinship and affinity among the ancestors of persons so identified as far back as the evidence allows. As a result, perhaps the most important direction of recent Polish studies on the 'nobility' (or its early constituent groups) prior to the mid-fourteenth century has been meticulous prosopographic reconstitution, all the way back to the twelfth century if not earlier, of those particular families ('clans') which in the course of the fourteenth century clearly became identified, and identified themselves, in terms of common names, their visual counterparts, and distinctive cries.[184]

For all of its interest, validity, and importance, the 'genealogical' approach suffers from two limitations. First, it is reductionist; that is, it subsumes the formation of a population which at some relatively late point came to express, experience, and strengthen its bundle of privileges in very particular ways, under the study of family and kinship. However, throughout the twelfth, thirteenth, and the fourteenth centuries, privilege in Polish society had been expressed by, and had reinforced, a wide variety of ties and relationships, of which the familial were not in any demonstrable sense the most important. To complicate matters, it is not clear that for most of the period with which this essay is concerned such ties, relationships, and activities defined one single social group – 'knightly', 'noble', or otherwise – and therefore that one such social group can be reconstructed through prosopographic retrogression, however methodologically sophisticated. The dramatic transition spanning the mid-thirteenth and the mid-fourteenth centuries was the definition of a single group of high status, partly in terms of several criteria that had defined privilege since much earlier ('knighthood', service, lordship, jurisdiction, and use of force), and partly in terms that seem new, and that include 'clan' membership and its visual and oral expressions.

Thus, the second difficulty with the 'genealogical' approach is the fact that it obscures that very real transition in the significance of familial ties – paradoxically, perhaps, given its emphasis on the primordial 'reality' and significance of kinship. I would therefore like to suggest an explanation for the shift in significance of 'clan' names and their oral and visual counterparts couched not in terms of the early formation and function of 'clans', but in the production and

---

184 Among others, the major prosopographical reconstructions of particular noble families include: J. Pakulski, *Nałęcze wielkopolscy w średniowieczu. Genealogia, uposażenie i rola polityczna w XII–XIV wieku* [The Nałęcz clan of Great Poland in the Middle Ages: genealogy, endowment, and political role between the twelfth and the fourteenth centuries] (Warsaw, 1982); the following articles, in *Genealogia – studia nad wspólnotami krewniaczymi i terytorialnymi w Polsce średniowiecznej na tle porównawczym* [Genealogy: studies on familial and territorial communities in medieval Poland in a comparative contexts], ed. J. Hertel and J. Wroniszewski (Toruń, 1987): J. Bieniak, 'Ród Łabędziów' [The Łabędź clan] (pp. 9–32), B. Śliwiński, 'Ród Lisów. Problem pochodzenia wojewody krakowskiego, Mikołaja, i biskupa krakowskiego, Pełki' [The Lis clan: the problem of the origins of Palatine Nicholas of Kraków, and of Bishop Pełka of Kraków] (pp. 33–52), and J. Wroniszewski, 'Ród Rawiczów w wiekach średnich' [The Rawicz clan in the Middle Ages] (pp. 75–92); Kurtyka, *Tęczyńscy*.

function of nicknames. Perhaps at some point a proper name, reflecting the name of a locality, or a personal trait, or something else, attached to a person or a small group of relatives as a nickname – that is, became his, her, or their individual or distinguishing attribute. Subsequently, that attribute was reproduced through succession, in a manner, and with the social meaning, which was analogous to a patronymic. Perhaps in the course of the thirteenth and fourteenth centuries, we can observe the use of specifically that type of attribute by the socially privileged groups in the process of further self-definition, and further reinforcement of the traditional areas of privilege. Persons and groups otherwise routinely identified – and presumably self-identified – as 'knights', 'noble and illustrious men', bishops, palatines, castellans, or ducal 'servitors' – began, among other elements of identity, to define themselves (individually and in groups) with reference to an attribute of that kind.

The earliest expression of that kind of attribute documented in the written record is the proper name of the *genealogia* – and in the thirteenth and fourteenth century we first glimpse such names in their double function as nicknames and as names for descent groups. Presumably during the same period, these proper names acquired visual counterparts in the form of heraldic symbols; and the individual lineages within each *genealogia* in turn identified themselves by yet another device that had a proper name, the cry used for battle, assembly, and other purposes. In their particulars, each of these relatively late attributes of privilege is sparsely documented until well beyond 1350. However, in a cumulative sense it is clear that by 1350 they constituted a complicated grammar of group membership and identity, and that they were deliberately used to express, reinforce, and above all defend the claims to formal social privilege by the persons who used them.[185] In his mid-century legislation, King Casimir the Great clearly defined the Polish 'nobility' as one complex personal attribute, incorporating 'knightly law', military service to the king, and the personal possession of these three ritual elements.[186]

The most telling symptom of the significance, and the vulnerability, of that

---

[185] Disentangling that grammar – and especially tracing the relationship between the three ritual elements – is one of the central subjects of the current inquiry into the early nobility among Polish scholars (complicated, I believe, by an excessive and essentialized emphasis on the centrality of kinship); see Pakulski, 'Geneza', pp. 110–17 (especially for the functions of nicknames in this context), and Bieniak, 'Heraldyka', pp. 167–81.

[186] For the equivalence of these terms in the king's Statute for Great Poland, see *KWp*, no. 1261 (c. 1360), ii, 587 (§20: '[q]uod barones et nobiles nostri . . . quanto melius et efficaciter poterint teneantur militare et armis se instruere et servire'), 593 (§39: '[m]ilites et nobiles ad expeditionem bellicam sunt obligati. Sed quia in armata militia honor regis et defensio totius regni dependet, tenentur igitur quilibet miles secundum quantitatem et possessionem suorum bonorum et redituum ad rem publicam certis armatis hominibus servire et prodesse dummodo bona ipsorum sint libera et iure militari instituta'), 594 (§46, which specifies a procedure *de probatione nobilitatis*, that is, '[s]i quis inculpatus fuerit quod non haberet ius militare', the procedure must be followed 'more consueto ad obtinendum suum ius militare'; §47, in which a provision for dower and dowry is made '[s]i quis militum aut nobilium de hoc seculo migrabit').

group from the fourth decade of the fourteenth century onward was the frequency and intensity of litigation about the 'privilege of knighthood', or the 'privilege of nobility' – clearly used as interchangeable categories – with which members of the group challenged one another, which they routinely framed in terms of access to the right to use one or more of the ritual attributes of 'nobility', and which therefore emerged as yet another practical expression of group privilege.[187] The importance of this type of litigation suggests that, like the other elements of privilege, status, and identity in medieval Poland, the attribute of 'nobility' was not merely held and reproduced, but that it required sustained aspiration and effort. The systematizations of this social and political practice after the death of the last Piast – in the contexts of litigation, group participation in representative assemblies, negotiations relating to royal succession, diplomatic and military relations, the late medieval and early modern court culture, and learned historical and heraldic constructions such as Jan Długosz's – are all subsequent chapters of this continuing story.

---

[187] *Ibid.*, no. 1261 (*c.* 1360), ii, 594 (§46), cited above; a superb case is *KMp*, i, no. 199 (1335), pp. 237–8 (it concerns an *inculpatio* of one person by another *pro defectu milicie*, an elaborate proof by the accused of *miliciam et nobilitatem suam*, which is also called a *probacio milicie*, and a conclusion that the accused 'cum tota prole ex eo emanata et emananda ius nobilitatis et milicie perpetuis temporibus obtinere et nostris subditis terrigenis et nobilibus uniuersisque fidedignis in omnibus iuribus esse parem').

9

Nobles and Nobility in the Narrative Works of Hartmann von Aue

Martin H. Jones

1. Hartmann von Aue

Hartmann von Aue occupies a position of signal importance in the history of German literature, being the earliest in that group of narrative poets, which includes also Wolfram von Eschenbach, Gottfried von Straßburg, and the poet of the *Nibelungenlied*, whose works, together with outstanding achievements in the lyric, have led to the years from *c.* 1180 to *c.* 1230 being regarded as the classical period of German literature in the Middle Ages. In a development which can be traced back to the middle of the twelfth century, the Church's monopoly of literature in the vernacular was emphatically broken at this time, and lay society in the form of the secular aristocracy found its own distinctive literary voice in the poetry of the classical period. Though profoundly indebted in many ways, both practically and intellectually, to the literate culture of the clerics, the vernacular literature of Hartmann and his fellows was a literature written for and largely about the secular nobility, reflecting its chivalric and courtly character. It is symptomatic of the change in the domain of letters at this time that in Hartmann we have the first narrative poet in German who identifies himself as a knight.

Hartmann was the author of a substantial number of lyrics and of a didactic poem, *Die Klage*, which treats the theme of love in the form of a dialogue between the body and the heart, but the high regard in which he was held by poets in the Middle Ages and continues to be held today by students of literature rests principally on his four narrative works: the chivalric romances, *Erec* and *Iwein*, which are the earliest examples of Arthurian romance in German, and two shorter poems of religious character, *Gregorius* and *Der arme Heinrich*. None of these works can be dated precisely, but it is generally accepted that they were composed – in the order *Erec*, *Gregorius*, *Der arme Heinrich*, *Iwein* – in the first half of the classical period, that is, from *c.* 1180 to *c.* 1205. It is with aspects of these four works that the present essay will be concerned.[1]

For information about Hartmann himself, we are largely dependent upon

---

[1] Hartmann's works are cited in the following editions: *Hartmann von Aue: Die Klage. Das (zweite) Büchlein aus dem Ambraser Heldenbuch*, ed. H. Zutt (Berlin, 1968); *Erec von*

what he tells us in his works, particularly in the prologues to them, and upon inferences which can be drawn from the works.[2] His social status is to an extent clearly defined in his description of himself in line 5 of *Der arme Heinrich*: 'dienstman was er ze Ouwe' ('he was a serving knight at Aue'). The word *dienstman* is the equivalent of the term *ministerialis* which occurs in Latin legal and other sources of the time to designate men of unfree status who performed primarily military and administrative duties in the service of a lord. As ecclesiastical and secular lords built up their retinues in the course of the eleventh and twelfth centuries in order to protect their estates and administer their affairs more effectively, there was a rapid expansion in the number of men belonging to this category in Germany; there was also increasing diversity among them with respect to the wealth, privileges, and influence which they acquired through the performance of their ministerial offices, so that by Hartmann's time it is not possible to deduce from the term *dienstman/ministerialis* alone what that status signified in concrete terms for the manner of life lived by any individual.

In the prologue to *Der arme Heinrich* Hartmann also refers to himself as 'ein ritter' (line 1, 'a knight'). Although *ritter* was frequently used with reference to men of ministerial status, it could be applied to free-born nobles as well. In addition to being thus socially more inclusive than *dienstman*, through its association with the verb *rîten* ('to ride'), the word *ritter* carried in it a sense of the military equestrian character of the life led by men designated in this way. It is noteworthy that in *Der arme Heinrich*, Hartmann describes himself as a *ritter* first and then as a *dienstman*, and that in the prologue to *Iwein* he refers to himself only as a *rîter* (line 21). If this suggests that he attached greater importance to his status as knight than to that of *ministerialis*,[3] it would accord well with his advocacy of chivalry as a model of behaviour and the intimate knowledge of the mentality of knights evident particularly in the Arthurian romances.

Both of Hartmann's references to himself as a knight are directly linked with mention of his education. In *Der arme Heinrich* we read:

Hartmann von Aue, ed. A. Leitzmann, continued by L. Wolff, 6th edn, prepared by C. Cormeau and K. Gärtner, Altdeutsche Textbibliothek, 39 (Tübingen, 1985); *Gregorius von Hartmann von Aue*, ed. H. Paul, 14th edn, revised by B. Wachinger, Altdeutsche Textbibliothek, 2 (Tübingen, 1992); *Hartmann von Aue: Der arme Heinrich*, ed. H. Paul, 16th edn, revised by K. Gärtner, Altdeutsche Textbibliothek, 3 (Tübingen, 1996); *Iwein. Eine Erzählung von Hartmann von Aue*, ed. G. F. Benecke and K. Lachmann, 7th edn, revised by L. Wolff, 2 vols (Berlin, 1968). Translations from these texts are my own, but I have consulted existing translations, in particular *The Narrative Works of Hartmann von Aue*, trans. R. W. Fisher, Göppinger Arbeiten zur Germanistik, 370 (Göppingen, 1983).
2   All the narrative works except *Erec* have a prologue. In the *Ambraser Heldenbuch*, which alone preserves *Erec* in nearly complete form, the start of the text is lacking.
3   See W. H. Jackson, *Chivalry in Twelfth-Century Germany: The Works of Hartmann von Aue*, Arthurian Studies, 34 (Cambridge, 1994), p. 75.

Ein ritter sô gelêret was
daz er an den buochen las
swaz er dar an geschriben vant. (lines 1–3)

(A knight was educated in such a way that he could read whatsoever he found written in books.)

The passage in *Iwein* is virtually identical, beginning 'Ein rîter, der gelêret was/ unde ez an den buochen las' (lines 21–2, 'A knight who was educated and read in books'). In the context of Hartmann's time, this was a self-description which was no doubt worthy of repetition, for it was a relatively rare individual who combined firsthand knowledge of the military life with an education which afforded the benefits of literacy. The implication that he had a command of Latin, contained in the statement 'he could read whatsoever he found written in books', is fully consistent with the mastery of the rhetorical arts which Hartmann displays in all his works, with the theological knowledge which he demonstrates in *Gregorius*, for instance, and with the learned allusions which are particularly abundant in *Erec*. The education that is made evident in these ways was ordinarily available only through attendance at a monastic or cathedral school, but precisely where Hartmann acquired it and under what circumstances, it is impossible to determine. That Hartmann could also read French may be inferred from the fact that he certainly had French sources for the Arthurian romances – *Erec* and *Iwein* are adaptations of Chrétien de Troyes's *Erec et Enide* and *Yvain* respectively – and for *Gregorius*, which is based on the anonymous *Vie du pape saint Grégoire* (middle of the twelfth century), and, although in this case no precise source has been identified, probably for *Die Klage*, too. As someone who had a foot in both chivalric and clerical worlds, Hartmann epitomizes the interplay of the two otherwise often antagonistic cultures out of which sprang the poetry of the medieval German classical period.

Hartmann repeatedly associates himself with a place named 'Ouwe' (= modern German Au/Aue).[4] This is, however, not especially helpful in localizing him, since the word *ouwe* signifies 'water', 'water meadow', 'meadow' and it occurs widely as a place-name or as an element in place-names. Linguistic studies have placed Hartmann in the Alemannic dialect region, which in terms of political geography means the old duchy of Swabia in the south-west corner of German-speaking lands, but even with this delimitation there is a superabundance of possibilities to explain the toponym 'von Ouwe/von Aue', and in spite of strenuous efforts to establish the claims of several such places, none can command full credibility.[5]

4 In *Die Klage* (line 29) and in *Gregorius* (line 173) he refers to himself as 'von O(u)we Hartman', in *Der arme Heinrich* (line 5) as 'dienstman [. . .] ze Ouwe', and in *Iwein* (line 29) as 'ein Ouwære'.
5 For details see C. Cormeau and W. Störmer, *Hartmann von Aue. Epoche – Werk – Wirkung*, 2nd edn (Munich, 1993), pp. 32–6.

Evident as the association of Hartmann with 'Ouwe' is, it is not entirely clear what its nature was. When Hartmann refers to himself as being 'von Ouwe' or as an 'Ouwære', it could mean that he was a member of a (ministerial) family that had property in and named itself after Ouwe, or it could mean that he was in the service of a lord who had property in and named himself after Ouwe. The prologue to *Der arme Heinrich* seems to point in the direction of the second alternative with Hartmann's description of himself as 'dienstman [. . .] ze Ouwe', but the issue is complicated by the fact that the hero of this story, Heinrich, is described as a lord who had his seat in Swabia (lines 30–1), who was in birth 'fully [or 'almost'] the equal of princes' ('wol den vürsten gelîch', line 43),[6] and who 'was born [of the family] of Aue' ('und was von Ouwe geborn', line 49). In itself this is not problematical – it could imply that Hartmann, as a *dienstman* in the service of the family 'von Ouwe', was purporting to tell a story about one of the forebears of his lord's family. However, in the opinion of most Hartmann scholars, the story's outcome is such as to make this unlikely, for the princely or prince-like Heinrich von Ouwe enters into marriage with the daughter of one of his tenant farmers in gratitude for her saving his life, an alliance which, it is generally believed, would have entailed a reduction of the social status of the von Ouwe family henceforth.[7] It is regarded as implausible that Hartmann's lord would have welcomed a story imputing such a decline in the family's standing, and most modern commentators prefer an alternative interpretation, namely that Hartmann wished to suggest that the story relates to one of his own forebears by the name of Heinrich and offers an explanation for a putative decline in his own family's status from that of free nobles to that of *ministeriales* which has the virtue of ascribing that decline to high moral motives. In this reading, 'Ouwe' is the seat of Hartmann's own family, once free nobles but now of ministerial status.[8]

Finally, there is the question of Hartmann's relationship to patrons. Nowhere in his narrative works does he refer to a patron or to the poet–patron relationship,[9] but in general it is assumed that, like other poets of the time, he was dependent upon a court of considerable standing for sponsorship. Among the Swabian nobility of his time, three families above all have been considered to qualify as potential patrons of Hartmann, the Staufer, the Welfs, and the

---

6   The statement is made ambiguous by the adverb 'wol' which ranges in sense from 'fully, certainly' to 'nearly, almost'. See H. Henne, *Herrschaftsstruktur, historischer Prozeß und epische Handlung: Sozialgeschichtliche Untersuchungen zum 'Gregorius' und 'Armen Heinrich' Hartmanns von Aue*, Göppinger Arbeiten zur Germanistik, 340 (Göppingen, 1982), p. 233.
7   This matter is discussed more fully later in this essay.
8   See V. Mertens, *Gregorius Eremita: Eine Lebensform des Adels bei Hartmann von Aue in ihrer Problematik und ihrer Wandlung in der Rezeption* (Munich, 1978), pp. 154–6 and 161–2.
9   In Hartmann's lyrics there is reference to the death of his lord, but there is no clue as to his identity. Hartmann wrote two crusading songs; whether he actually participated in the crusade is uncertain.

Zähringer, but there is nothing concretely to link him with the courts or members of any of these families or with their dependants.

2. The narrative works

Virtually all the leading figures of Hartmann's narrative works are of high birth – Erec and Iwein are the sons of kings, their wives are respectively the daughter of a count and a queen; Gregorius is from the ducal house of Aquitaine, his mother/wife is the duchess of Aquitaine; while Heinrich is a Swabian lord whose status is princely or comparable to that of princes – and all the works represent the life of the secular nobility in some measure. The fullest picture is to be found in the Arthurian romances. The stories of Erec and Iwein are similarly structured, each showing a bipartite scheme of action which involves three major scenes at Arthur's court and two cycles of adventures undertaken by the protagonist which fall between these scenes. In the first cycle of adventures, originating in an incident which occurs while they are at Arthur's court, the heroes accomplish a chivalric exploit which leads to their marrying and assuming a lordship: Erec is installed as regent by his ageing father when he returns home with his bride, while Iwein (more problematically) acquires his wife and her kingdom after slaying her husband in combat. The success of the heroes in their initial exploits is celebrated by the Arthurian court, but they prove to be inadequate to the demands of their new station in life and are disgraced. Erec is so taken with the pleasures of the marriage bed that he neglects chivalry and his lordly duties, bringing himself and his court into disrepute; it falls to his wife Enite to reveal this to him, and she is made to accompany him during the second cycle of adventures, on which Erec now launches himself in order to restore his reputation. Iwein, on the other hand, is so taken up with demonstrating his prowess on the tournament circuit in the company of the Arthurian knights that he breaks his word to his wife Laudine, failing to return to her at the end of the period for which she grants him leave of absence, and jeopardizes the security of the realm; for this he suffers public condemnation before Arthur's court, which causes him to go mad and live like a wild man in the forest, until his sanity is restored and he can enter upon a series of adventures which serve to rehabilitate him. The second cycle of adventures in each of the works is longer than the first and composed of incidents which in one way or another have a bearing on the heroes' failings, so that in proving themselves masters of the challenges they confront, they simultaneously prove themselves worthy of the position of honour and privilege which they had initially gained but then lost. Erec establishes a right relationship with Enite and is crowned in succession to his now deceased father; Iwein eventually finds the forgiveness of Laudine and is reinstated as her husband and lord of her lands.

Although both Erec and Iwein assume the role of the knight errant for much of the time and have encounters in the forest world of adventure with beings typical of that realm (for example, the giants in *Erec*, the wild man in *Iwein*), most of the action of both romances is set in or near castles and involves members of the nobility. Thus in *Erec*, apart from scenes at the courts of Arthur and of Erec himself, there are the following locations associated with the nobility: the market town below the castle of Tulmein, home of Duke Imain; the market town below the castle of Count 'Galoain';[10] the castle of King Guivreiz where Erec and Enite spend a night after their first encounter with him; the castle of Count Oringles at Limors; the castle of Penefrec belonging to Guivreiz where Erec and Enite spend two weeks; the castle at Brandigan, the seat of King Ivreins and scene of Erec's final adventure. The situation in *Iwein* is little different, with a high proportion of the action being sited at the courts of Arthur and Laudine.

In this wealth of scenes many aspects of the life of the noble class are depicted, often in great detail and often in highly idealized fashion. When Erec returns to Arthur's court with his bride-to-be, more than forty verses are given to reporting how Enite is sumptuously dressed for her first appearance at court (lines 1532–77); then, like a dutiful court correspondent, Hartmann names many of the 140 knights who are present at the Round Table and witness her entry (lines 1628–97). The report of the wedding of Erec and Enite runs to over 300 verses (lines 1887–2195), with mention of many of the noble guests by name, descriptions of their fine clothes, and their hunting exploits as they proceed to Arthur's court. Even more space is given to the tournament that is held immediately afterwards, producing an account which not only glorifies Erec but also renders the character of the event in unprecedented detail (lines 2222–808). Guivreiz's castle at Penefrec is situated in the middle of a lake, whose waters provide abundant fish, while its shore all around for a distance of two miles is enclosed by a wall and divided into three sections by further walls to contain game of different kinds, creating a veritable huntsman's paradise (lines 7121–87). *Iwein* opens on the scene at Arthur's Whitsuntide festival when, after feasting, the knights of the court take their leisure as they choose: conversing with the ladies, strolling, dancing, singing, running races, jumping, practising archery, telling stories of love and of heroism, seeing to weapons, sleeping (lines 62–75). Later, Hartmann conjures up a vignette of gracious courtly living when he describes how Iwein enters a castle and finds an elderly couple sitting in a garden listening as their daughter reads to them in French (lines 6435–70).

Very different impressions of court life and lordly behaviour are, however, conveyed in some episodes in both works. This is particularly so in the events which occur at the castle of Count Oringles in *Erec* (lines 6178–665). Oringles saves Enite from committing suicide when Erec appears to have died. He takes her (and the seemingly dead Erec) to his castle, urges her to abandon her mourning, and proceeds to woo her. She rejects his advances, but, undeterred by this and by the opposition of his knights, who regard his behaviour as disgraceful, Oringles summons bishops, abbots, and priests and insists on being

[10] This count is not named by Hartmann. The convention in Hartmann scholarship is to refer to him by the name of the corresponding figure in Chrétien's work.

married to her that same day. When Enite, grieving over Erec's body, twice ignores Oringles's summons to join him at table, he himself drags her away. He forces her to sit opposite him, so that he can ogle her, and urges her to eat. Her refusal to do so enrages Oringles, he loses self-control and strikes her. When his men reproach him for this, he becomes even more furious, insists on his right to treat his wife as he will, and silences their protests. Seeing the opportunity to join Erec in death, Enite tries to provoke the count into killing her. He strikes her repeatedly, but her cries arouse Erec from his state of unconsciousness, and he charges into the court, kills Oringles, and sends the whole company fleeing for their lives. In *Iwein*, the court of Laudine emerges as a hotbed of vicious rivalries after Iwein's failure to return to her punctually. Lunete, Laudine's servant and confidante, who had urged her to marry Iwein, is accused by the steward and his two brothers of having betrayed their queen with this advice, and Lunete faces the certainty of being burned at the stake unless she can find a knight to champion her cause against her accusers. She explains the hostility of the steward and his fellows as long-standing envy of the special favour which she enjoyed with Laudine; now they have succeeded in turning her mistress against her (lines 4109–35). When Iwein tackles the three traducers of Lunete in combat in order to save her life, further light is shed on the politics of the court, as a group of young ladies pray that God will preserve Lunete, for she has represented their interests to the queen and they fear for the future without her as their advocate (lines 5204–16). Iwein's final adventure sees him involved in a dispute over inheritance. The Count of the Black Thorn has recently died, and his elder daughter has forcefully deprived her sister of her share in the patrimony (lines 5625–38). Iwein successfully asserts the rights of the younger daughter by fighting as her champion in a judicial combat at Arthur's court.

Unflattering as the images of life among the nobility projected by such incidents may be, they do not constitute a focused critique of the social élite. Those who fall short of the conduct expected of them are seen to receive the punishments they deserve: Oringles is killed by Erec; Laudine's steward and his brothers are defeated by Iwein and suffer the death at the stake that they intended for Lunete; the elder daughter of the Count of the Black Thorn is compelled by King Arthur to concede to her sister her rightful share in the inheritance. It is the heroes, employing the forceful means available to them as members of the nobility, who right the wrongs perpetrated by aberrant members of their class; the nobility in effect polices itself. The same applies to the failings of Erec and Iwein themselves, except that in their case the corrective mechanisms are internal to them. They are guilty of errors of youth and inexperience, and the crises to which these errors give rise are the spur to inner amendment and greater achievement. Both these men are innately equipped with the personal qualities which ensure that their hereditary claim to high station in life is ultimately supported by actions which qualify them to enter into their birthright. That is to say, in the terms of the debate about the nature of nobility which was conducted throughout the Middle Ages, nobility of virtue or achievement (*nobilitas morum*), evident in the reformed conduct of the heroes, comes through to vindicate the claims of nobility of birth or blood (*nobilitas carnis*).[11] Hartmann's Arthurian romances are much concerned with setting priorities and finding the right balance between different aspects of the noble life, but they do not invite a questioning of that way of life in itself.

The situation is rather different in Hartmann's socially more diverse and generically more complex shorter narratives. *Gregorius* is the story of a double incest: the hero is born of the young duke of Aquitaine and his sister and when grown to manhood unwittingly commits incest with his mother. None the less Gregorius's ultimate destiny is to become Pope in Rome. His career is a kaleidoscope of ways of life: nobly born but sent out Moses-like upon the water, he is raised in ignorance of his origins in the family of a poor fisherman; taken into a monastery at the age of six, he proves to be a superlative scholar and appears destined for a monastic career, until he discovers that he is a foundling and determines to leave the monastery to become a knight; his travels as a knight take him back to Aquitaine where he liberates his mother, who now rules the country after her brother's death, from oppression, marries her and becomes duke of Aquitaine; the revelation of their incest leads him to abandon the secular world and to adopt an extreme form of penance chained to a bare rock in a lake; seventeen years of this eremitical existence culminate in his being fetched to Rome where, attended by miracles which mark his sanctity, he is consecrated Pope. This is a story of extremes of guilt, penance, and grace whose didactic thrust is to warn against the sins of presumption and despair. The route to Gregorius's final destination is most obviously via the monastery and the rock, but the episodes set in the courtly environment of Aquitaine occupy over forty per cent of the work's length and do more than provide the context in which the two acts of incest occur. They paint a picture of aristocratic life at moments of particular danger and strain: the old duke's death leaves his young son and daughter, Gregorius's parents, orphaned and open to the temptations of awakening sexuality, while the condition in which Gregorius finds his mother – the country devastated, she besieged in her capital – exposes the difficulties of a country which lacks a lord to conduct its affairs. The characters act in what seems to be the best interests of the country, but this leads them into grievous sin. Whether this constitutes an indictment of aristocratic life is a question which is keenly debated and calls for careful and detailed assessment.

Der arme Heinrich is also the story of a nobleman who is displaced from his position in the world. Seemingly a paragon of courtly perfection, high-born and virtuous, Heinrich is, at God's command, stricken with leprosy, making him repulsive to his peers. He seeks medical advice, only to be told by a doctor in

---

[11] A detailed account of views on the nature of nobility and the relative claims of *nobilitas carnis* and *nobilitas morum* in the twelfth and thirteenth centuries will be found in K. H. Borck, 'Adel, Tugend und Geblüt: Thesen und Beobachtungen zur Vorstellung des Tugendadels in der deutschen Literatur des 12. und 13. Jahrhunderts', *Beiträge zur Geschichte der deutschen Sprache und Literatur* (Tübingen), c (1978), 423–57; see also M. Keen, *Chivalry* (New Haven and London, 1984), pp. 143–61.

Salerno that there is but one cure for his condition: the heart blood of a virgin freely given. Thinking it impossible to find such a cure, Heinrich gives away his possessions except for one farm, to which he withdraws. There he is well looked after by the free-born peasant in gratitude for Heinrich's generous treatment in the past which has ensured the family a prosperous living. For three years he lives there, enjoying the attention in particular of the peasant's young daughter (she is eight years old when Heinrich comes there), before the nature of the cure that he has been told of comes to light. The maiden immediately seizes on the idea of offering her life for Heinrich's health and overcomes her parents' and Heinrich's initial opposition to this. She and Heinrich travel to Salerno. When she is on the point of being killed by the doctor, Heinrich is moved by the sight of her innocent beauty to stop the sacrifice and to accept that his diseased condition is God's will and unalterable. This inner transformation in Heinrich elicits God's intervention to cure him of his leprosy. Heinrich is restored to his possessions and former position in the world and, with the agreement of his vassals, marries the peasant's daughter. Materially speaking, the aristocratic world plays little part in *Der arme Heinrich*, by contrast with the other works. For most of the period of time that it covers the story is set in the peasant's farm, though that too is little realized in concrete detail. The work crystallizes the issues, which include the significance of the remarkable maiden's role, with a rare refinement. For Heinrich the essential problem is his relationship to God, an issue of universal and timeless import, but his noble status, the fact that he receives comfort from the peasant and his family, and the conclusion of the work, his marriage to the maiden, are more than accidents of local colour and lend the work a distinct social relevance.

From this brief account of Hartmann's narrative works it will be clear that, in their different ways, they provide plentiful material for the subject in hand, more indeed than can be dealt with in this essay. I propose, therefore, to concentrate on three areas, which can be characterized in a general way as follows: the 'noble poor'; nobility and knighthood; nobility and religion.

3. The 'noble poor'

Examples of persons of noble birth who live in reduced circumstances, deprived of the material advantages which characterize the noble style of life, occur throughout Hartmann's works. In the two religious stories the heroes themselves experience impoverishment: Gregorius abandons society and takes on a life of absolute poverty as a penitent beggar to atone for the sin of incest (lines 2745–50), while Heinrich adopts a life of relative poverty when, having been stricken with leprosy, he divests himself of nearly all his estates and riches in acts of charity and donations to the Church and withdraws to the one farm he retains as he prepares himself for what appears to be his inevitable death (lines 246–60). In both these instances, impoverishment is deliberate and motivated by religious considerations. Altogether different are the instances of impoverished noble persons found in the Arthurian romances; here the deprivation suffered is entirely involuntary and comes about through no fault of those afflicted. It is the latter examples of the 'noble poor' (this is Hartmann's phrase) that are to be considered more closely.

In the episode at Pesme Avanture in *Yvain*, Chrétien presents a scene of three hundred noble ladies who have to endure degrading sweatshop conditions of work. The ladies have been sent to the castle where Yvain comes upon them as the tribute agreed by their foolish young lord in order to release himself from the obligation to fight two giants who control the castle, and they labour to produce needlework which is sold at a great profit but for which they receive scandalously low wages and meagre rations, leaving them emaciated, shabbily clothed, and filled with a sense of shame at their condition. Yvain liberates the ladies by overcoming the giants in combat and restores them to their rightful place in society.[12]

In his retelling of this episode Hartmann follows Chrétien closely, but makes two significant additions. First, he introduces the notion of the shame felt by the ladies when they become aware that Iwein is observing them:

> wârens ê riuwevar,
> ir leides wart nû michels mê.
> in tete diu schame alsô wê
> daz in die arme enpfielen,
> wan in die trähene wielen
> von den ougen ûf die wât.
> daz ir grôzen unrât
> iemen vremder hete gesehen,
> dâ was in leide an geschehen.   (lines 6222–30)

> (If before they had looked sad, their suffering now grew much greater. Their shame pained them so much that their arms drooped, for tears fell from their eyes onto their clothes. That a stranger had seen their great misery caused them suffering.)

When Iwein joins the ladies in their workroom, their sense of public humiliation is evident again, as they blush with shame and weep to hear his offer of service to them (lines 6299–302). Secondly, Hartmann incorporates into the scene an observation about the sense of shame exhibited by the ladies in their degrading condition. Iwein is moved by their plight and asks them to tell him of their station and their families, for he cannot believe that they were born poor:

> ist iuch disiu armuot an geborn,
> sô hân ich mînen wân verlorn.
> ich sihe wol daz iu wê tuot

---

12 *Chrestien de Troyes, Yvain*, ed. T. B. W. Reid (Manchester, 1942; repr. 1967), lines 5185–337. The episode has attracted considerable interest as an example of 'social realism' in which Chrétien reflects conditions in the contemporary clothing industry. Chrétien gives precise details of the ladies' wages and the profits gained from their labour.

diu schame der selben armuot,
und versihe michs dâ von:
swer ir von kinde ist gewon,
dern schamt sich ir sô sêre niht
als man hie an iu gesiht.   (lines 6307–14)

(If you were born into this poverty, then I have been much mistaken. I see clearly that the shame of this poverty pains you, and this
makes me certain: anyone who is used to it [poverty] from childhood does not feel such great shame on account of it as one sees
here in you.)

Underlying Iwein's assumption about the ladies' status is the idea that a
noble person who becomes impoverished experiences greater inward suffering
on account of his or her poverty than does a person who has been accustomed to
poverty from birth. A somewhat similar idea is expressed in *Gregorius* when
Gregorius urges his mother, after the discovery of their incest, not to abandon
her place in the world but to remain as duchess of Aquitaine, living ascetically
and devoting her wealth exclusively to godly works: this will be a severe
penance for her, he argues, since it is harder on the spirit of one who enjoys a
life of luxury to renounce it than it is for one who has never experienced such a
life (lines 2716–20).[13] It does not follow from this that Hartmann displays indif-
ference to the situation of those born poor – indeed, in *Gregorius* he evokes
sharply the hard life of the poor fisherman who has to wrest a living from the sea
(lines 1201–9), and in *Der arme Heinrich* the poor are deemed to be worthy
objects of Heinrich's charity when he disposes of his worldly goods (lines
251–5). Rather, it is the case that Hartmann is conscious of the particularly
severe emotional trauma experienced by those of great estate who lose their
social position.

The most striking example of impoverished nobility is to be found in *Erec*,
where Hartmann takes the opportunity presented by the episode in Chrétien in
which the hero first meets the woman who is to become his wife to develop the
psychological dimensions of that condition. Overall the context and substance
of the episode are much the same in Chrétien and in Hartmann. Erec has
suffered an offence to his honour but is unable to avenge it immediately because
he is unarmed. He pursues the knight responsible for his disgrace to a town,
where, as Erec learns there, the annual contest for the sparrowhawk is to be

---

13 The idea is not peculiar to Hartmann, being found in German literature in the earlier *König
Rother* (ed. T. Frings and J. Kuhnt [Halle (Saale), 1968], lines 1389–98) and later in
Wolfram von Eschenbach's *Parzival* (*Wolfram von Eschenbach*, ed. K. Lachmann, 6th
edn [Berlin and Leipzig, 1926; repr. 1965], lines 170,29–171,6). On the passage in *König
Rother*, see N. F. Palmer, 'The Middle High German Vocabulary of Shame in its Literary
Context: A Study of *blûc, blûkeit, bliuclîche*', in '*Das unsichtbare Band der Sprache*':
Studies in German Language and Linguistic History in Memory of Leslie Seiffert, ed. J. L.
Flood *et al.*, Stuttgarter Arbeiten zur Germanistik, 280 (Stuttgart, 1993), pp. 57–84, at pp.
70–2.

held; the sparrowhawk should be awarded to the fairest lady present, but, as has
happened in the two previous years, the knight whom Erec has pursued proposes
to seize it for his lady, although she is not the fairest, relying on the absence of
anyone courageous enough to challenge his claim to it. This presents Erec with
an opportunity to confront the knight and to avenge the wrong done to him, but
he needs first to make good his deficiency in arms and armour and to find a lady
on whose behalf he can claim the prize of the sparrowhawk. These requirements
are met when he finds lodging with an elderly, impoverished nobleman who
provides him with armour and weapons and agrees not only to allow his
daughter to be championed by Erec in the contest but also to be betrothed to
him. Erec is victorious in the combat which follows his challenge to the knight
and celebrates his marriage at Arthur's court; later he makes over two castles in
his kingdom to his bride's father, restoring him fully to the noble way of life.

In retelling this episode after Chrétien, Hartmann introduces a number of
changes which affect its significance in the work as a whole and its immediate
impact.[14] Of particular interest here are the modifications which are made in the
presentation of Enite's family, above all of her father Koralus, and their circumstances. In Chrétien, the heroine's father, Liconaus by name, is a *vavasor*
(member of the lower nobility)[15] who has suffered a decline in his fortunes as a
result, it seems, of over-reaching himself in military ventures (lines 515–17).[16]
However, he maintains a house, a very poor one, to be sure, but none the less in
the town – Erec first sees him reclining on the steps before it; he is very prompt
to greet Erec and offer him hospitality when he rides into the courtyard; he
keeps a servant who cooks for the family; and altogether he is able to provide a
level of comfort and sustenance which gives no cause for embarrassment: Erec
sits with the family on beds which are covered with embroidered quilts and rugs,
their meal includes meat and fowl, and they are all able to eat their fill (lines
373–89, 477–500). When Erec asks why Enide is so shabbily dressed, Liconaus
explains that he has lost his estates in the wars, but that Enide could be much
better dressed if he had permitted her to accept the generosity of her uncle, who
is lord of the town, or had acceded to the wishes of local lords who wished to
marry her. He has not done so because he has greater ambitions for his daughter,
rating her qualities so highly that he thinks her worthy of a king or count (lines

[14] Of the many discussions of this episode in Hartmann, I note only N. F. Palmer, 'Poverty
and Mockery in Hartmann's *Erec*, v. 525ff. A Study of the Psychology and Aesthetics of
Middle High German Romance', in *Hartmann von Aue: Changing Perspectives. London
Hartmann Symposium 1985*, ed. T. McFarland and S. Ranawake, Göppinger Arbeiten zur
Germanistik, 486 (Göppingen, 1988), pp. 65–92, which has much of relevance to the
present subject, and W. Freytag, 'Zu Hartmanns Methode der Adaptation im *Erec*',
Euphorion, lxxii (1978), 227–39, which provides a detailed comparison of Chrétien's and
Hartmann's texts at this point.
[15] See G. Burgess, *Chrétien de Troyes: Erec et Enide*, Critical Guides to French Literature,
32 (London, 1984), p. 23.
[16] References are to *Les romans de Chrétien de Troyes, I, Erec et Enide*, ed. M. Roques, Les
Classiques Français du Moyen Age, 80 (Paris, 1977).

509–36). Informed by Liconaus about the sparrowhawk contest, Erec obtains from him the loan of arms and armour which are new and of the finest quality, and then, explaining that he is the son of the mighty King Lac, he asks if he may be Enite's champion and marry her in the event of his victory. With this, Liconaus's patience is wondrously rewarded, his ambitions for Enide are fulfilled, and the betrothal is agreed amid scenes of immediate and unqualified joy (lines 666–90).

The differences in detail between this portrayal of the heroine's family and of her father's dealings with Erec and that in Hartmann's account are considerable. Koralus is in rank far superior to Chrétien's *vavasor*. He is a count who formerly enjoyed great wealth and honour but has been dispossessed of his inheritance by men mightier than he with superior military force and under circumstances which, it is stressed, reflect no discredit on him ('vil gar unlasterlîche', line 403) and did not arise from any villainy on his part ('dehein sîn bôsheit', line 406). In addition, Koralus's descent into poverty is much more precipitous than that of Liconaus. His home is no house, however mean, in the town, but a ruined building far outside which Erec thinks must be uninhabited when he approaches it (lines 250–69).[17] He is not on public view before his home, but sits out of sight inside. He has no servants; in place of Liconaus's furnishings there is only straw covered with a white sheet for them to sit on; and as for food, good will has to substitute for it (lines 308–12, 366–95). The armour and arms that Koralus makes available to Erec are relics from his fighting days, long past (lines 589–606); when Erec makes his challenge for the sparrowhawk it is evident that they are old-fashioned, unwieldy, and no match for his opponent's equipment (lines 744–50).

By upgrading Koralus's status while at the same time downgrading the conditions under which his family live, Hartmann obviously intensifies the sense of the impoverishment which they have suffered by comparison with that of Liconaus's household. He also focuses more directly on how this condition is borne by 'dise edeln armen' (line 432, 'these noble poor') – the term is coined by Hartmann to describe Koralus, his wife Karsinefite, and Enite.[18] There is a moving account of how the elderly couple come to terms with their drastically reduced circumstances. They endure their poverty 'mit listen' (416, 'resource-fully'); as far as they can, they conceal their need of material things 'mit zühten' (419, 'with gracious good breeding'), so that no one might be aware of it; indeed, very few people know that they have been so completely overcome by poverty (421–3). It is a picture of hardship borne with dignity and restraint,

---

17 Erec is without the means to pay for lodging and hopes to sleep in the apparently empty building. The emphasis placed by Hartmann on Erec's own (relative) poverty at this point is another distinctive feature of his account. For observations on the significance of this innovation, see Palmer, 'Poverty' (n. 14), at pp. 72–4.

18 Interesting reflections on this term and related ones are to be found in T. R. Jackson, 'Paradoxes of Person. Hartmann von Aue's Use of the *Contradictio in Adiecto*', in *Hartmann von Aue: Changing Perspectives. London Hartmann Symposium 1985*, ed. T. McFarland and S. Ranawake, pp. 285–311.

without complaint or self-pity – indeed, of hardship nobly borne. And yet behind this brave front there lies a pain that cannot be assuaged, the feeling of shame and disgrace which afflicts Koralus and compared with which all his material deprivations are as nothing:

> dem wirte was diu arbeit
> die er von grôzer armuot leit
> dâ wider süeze als ein mete
> dâ engegen und im diu schame tete.   (lines 424–7)

> (For the host the hardship which he suffered on account of great poverty was as sweet as mead by comparison with that which shame caused him.)

Hartmann does not specifically identify the source of Koralus's feeling of shame here, but the depth of the mental anguish to which poverty makes Koralus susceptible is evident when Erec proposes that he, the son of King Lac, will marry Enite if he is successful in the sparrowhawk contest. In complete contrast to Liconaus's joy at this proposal, in which he sees his waiting game in the matter of his daughter's marriage vindicated, Koralus is profoundly distressed. His eyes cloud over with a deeply secret, private sorrow ('von jâmer vil tougen', line 526), his heart is moved to tears, and he is barely able to express his thoughts (lines 525–31). Then, in what is by far his longest speech thus far (lines 532–59), Koralus calls on Erec not to mock him with this talk of marriage. His present condition has been laid upon him by God, whose power over the destiny of man he acknowledges. His life has turned out differently than was to have been expected, but he accepts this as God's will. Erec should desist from his mockery, for Enite is disqualified by her poverty from marrying him:

> ir getuot ze wîbe
> mîner tohter wol rât,
> wan si des guotes niht hât.   (lines 547–9)

> (You can well do without my daughter as your wife, for she has no wealth.)

What of course is implicit in Koralus's reference to Enite's lack of wealth is his own inability as her father to provide her with the dowry that she would normally be expected to take into marriage. Unthinkingly, with his proposal of marriage, Erec has exposed the full extent of Koralus's social degradation, has made it 'public' knowledge. In the matter of marriage, always a central concern in the life of the nobility and one in which issues of rank and wealth were paramount, Koralus is powerless to act on behalf of his daughter, has no hope of being able to arrange a suitable match for her.[19] While Koralus and Karsinefite can bear

---

[19] Support for the highlighting of the father–daughter relationship at this point is to be found in Enite's later (bitter) reflection that her parents had thought they had done well for her in giving her in marriage to Erec, for whose apparent death she holds herself responsible (lines 5974–82).

their poverty with quiet dignity, drawing on the resources of self-discipline inculcated by their good breeding (*zuht*), the reminder of the lack of prospects for Enite causes the breakdown of Koralus's emotional defences. He represents himself as helpless before the mystery of God's dispensation which has humbled him, and it is in God's name that he twice appeals to Erec not to mock him ('durch got', lines 533 and 545). Finally, as if to restore some vestige of dignity to himself but in so doing highlighting again the extent of his fall, he tells Erec that there was a time when he and Erec's father called one another companions and that they were knighted together in Lac's country (lines 550–6).

Painful as it is for him, Koralus feels the obligation to draw to Erec's attention what he believes to be the impediment to Enite's marrying one of his rank, but this is no obstacle for Erec, who is not distracted by the poverty of Koralus's material condition from appreciation of the family's nobility. Swiftly overcoming his own embarrassment at having been the cause of such anguish to Koralus, Erec insists on the absolute sincerity of his wish to marry Enite, firmly setting aside the objection of her poverty and proclaiming that it would be base of him to be influenced by mercenary motives in this matter (lines 560–81). This suffices to reassure Koralus that Erec is in earnest, and joyfully he turns his attention to equipping him for the contest on the coming day, Erec's victory in which leads in due course to the reinstatement of Koralus and his wife to their former dignity (lines 1806–37).

With reference to Enite's family, Hartmann indicates to his audience what he believes to be the right response to the plight of the noble poor:

> swen dise edeln armen
> niht wolden erbarmen,
> der was herter dan ein stein. (lines 432–4)

> (Anyone who did not take pity on these noble poor was harder than a stone.)

In *Iwein*, too, the immediate reaction of the hero to the account of the ladies' history is one of pity (*erbarmen*, lines 6407 and 6415). In his adaptation of both these episodes Hartmann has sought to bring out the pathos of the characters' condition of impoverishment, to lead his audience to experience their pain with them. In the case of Koralus in particular it can be observed how Hartmann has elaborated the situation by psychological insight, conveying a sense of the inner vulnerability of those whose normal expectation was to enjoy the pomp and circumstance of the noble life. In the figure of Koralus, Hartmann gives shape to an apprehension which is inseparable from the possession of rank and power: fear of its loss and how that can be coped with. To use Hartmann's phrase, it would have taken one harder than a stone not only to be unmoved by the picture he presents of poverty nobly borne but also, seeing Koralus reduced to tears and hearing his talk of having been humbled by God, not to reflect that but for the grace of God there go I.

4. Nobility and knighthood

Excellent research has been done in recent years on the sociology of knighthood as it is reflected in the works of Hartmann, much of it evaluated and enhanced by W. H. Jackson in his book *Chivalry in Twelfth-Century Germany: The Works of Hartmann von Aue*, which very much represents the state of the art. A quotation from the conclusions of that book will set the context for the remarks that I wish to make on the subject of nobility and chivalry:

> Knighthood was still, in the German empire around 1200, a military func-
> tion, intimately connected with mounted warfare. This function is amply
> documented in the knight's use of force in Hartmann's works, and in Hart-
> mann's presentation of shield, sword, and lance as the characteristic mili-
> tary attributes of knighthood. Knighthood also acquired broader
> connotations of a prestigious social nature during the twelfth century, in a
> gradual redefinition of the upper levels of German society which involved
> movements in two directions: on the one hand a downward percolation of
> aristocratic principles and lifestyle from the old, free nobility into the
> expanding category of *ministeriales*, and on the other hand an expansion
> and an upward movement of the term *ritter*, 'knight', as it spread beyond its
> early sense of professional warrior, including serving vassal, to be accepted
> as an honouring term by great nobles. It is an oversimplification to locate
> the origins of German knighthood exclusively either in the old, free nobility
> or in the newer category of *ministeriales*. Rather, the new order drew ele-
> ments from both sources. As a result of these movements, knighthood was
> often viewed in the twelfth century as a military and social community, an
> *ordo*, that included the high nobility and the lesser *ministeriales*.[20]

One notable respect in which Hartmann's works reflect the social developments described here is in the use of the term *ritter* for all levels of the aristocratic hierarchy from kings downwards. This is a particular feature of *Erec*, in
which the word *ritter* is used more frequently and with reference to a wider
range of men of noble status than in any earlier German work.[21] The attribution
of the term entails expectations regarding conduct, so that nobility is seen to
manifest itself in the fulfilment of the chivalric way of life and its ideals. This is
the case in both *Erec* and *Iwein*, where the heroes demonstrate their aptitude to
rule by their personal commitment to the practice of arms in a variety of causes.
In so far as these causes consist, for example, in the defence of the weak and
oppressed and in the upholding of justice, there is no conflict between the
expectations made of the knight and the expectations made of a lord, but a
potential source of conflict lies in the expectation, indeed it might be said the
requirement, that the lord-cum-knight maintain an active commitment to the
exercise of arms and to the upholding of his personal honour as a fighting man.
    The issue can be seen to some extent focused in the figure of King Guivreiz

---

[20] Jackson, *Chivalry*, p. 282.
[21] See Jackson, *Chivalry*, pp. 73–83.

in *Erec* – or more precisely in the contradictory reactions of modern scholarship to this figure. Guivreiz plays an important role in Erec's career, doing combat with him on two occasions and becoming a close friend and companion. They first meet when Erec is seeking to rehabilitate his reputation after neglecting to fulfil his responsibilities as king on account of his preoccupation with his wife. Guivreiz challenges Erec to combat in the name of adventure, as he is in the habit of doing with knights who pass by (lines 4588–603); he never misses any opportunity to undertake chivalric exploits, and he has achieved an unparalleled reputation for prowess (lines 4304–18). Some critics have seen Guivreiz's devotion to combat as an example of irresponsible and mindless aggression unbecoming in a lord, whereas others, myself included, have argued that he embodies the principle of active knighthood which seeks through regular exposure to martial challenges to maintain the prowess and reputation on which lordship is seen ultimately to reside in this work.[22]

Whichever view one takes of Guivreiz, it is certainly the case that Erec's failure to rule successfully in his father's stead at the first attempt has less to do with an excessive interest in sex *per se* than with the loss of understanding that it is incumbent on him to maintain his excellence in the profession of arms personally and to make his court a place where others are enabled to do so too. He has a residual awareness of this responsibility in that he enables his knights to attend tournaments elsewhere, though he does not take part in them himself; but this is not enough, and the time comes when knights and squires – 'ritter unde knehte' (line 2975) – who had previously found activities to their liking at his court desert it and no one else is attracted there by the prospect of chivalric activity. Erec is judged to have gone to ruin and his court stands in disrepute. Only the most vigorous demonstration of his prowess in the subsequent course of the action can eradicate this stain.

The example of Erec's failure is cited in *Iwein* at a comparable point in the action of that work, that is to say, at the time when Iwein has married and become the lord of his wife's kingdom. Gawein, the leading knight of the Arthurian court and Iwein's good friend, takes him aside and urges him to consider carefully how he should conduct himself. He begins by warning Iwein not to neglect his chivalry because he now has a wife and to avoid Erec's error (lines 2787–98). His specific recommendation is that Iwein should continue to go tourneying as he did before:

> Ir hât des iuch genü̈gen sol:
> dar under lêr ich iuch wol
> iuwer êre bewarn.

---

22 For a concise review of the differing attitudes to Guivreiz, with references to the relevant literature, see Jackson, *Chivalry*, p. 123. My own evaluation of Guivreiz is contained in the essay 'Chrétien, Hartmann, and the Knight as Fighting Man: On Hartmann's Chivalric Adaptation of *Erec et Enide*', in *Chrétien de Troyes and the German Middle Ages*, ed. M. H. Jones and R. Wisbey, Arthurian Studies, 26 (Cambridge and London, 1993), pp. 85–109, at pp. 99–109.

ir sult mit uns von hinnen varn:
wir suln turnieren als ê.
mir tuot anders iemer wê
daz ich iuwer künde hân,
sol iuwer rîterschaft zergân.   (lines 2799–806)

(You have enough to make you content. All the same I wish to
advise you how to preserve your honour. You should come away
from here with us: we shall go tourneying as before. Otherwise, if
your knightly activity ceases, it will always grieve me to be
acquainted with you.)

Gawein then launches into a passage without counterpart in Chrétien's *Yvain* in
which he conjures up the image of a lord who has become completely absorbed
in the business of managing his estates and has abandoned all aspirations to
knighthood. The passage deserves to be quoted in full, so that the caricature and
the force of Gawein's argument can be appreciated.

vil maneger beschirmet sich dâ mite:
er giht ez sî des hûses site,
ist er êlîche gehît,
daz er danne vür die zît
sül weder rîten noch geben:
er giht er sül dem hûse leben.
er geloubet sich der beider,
vreuden unde cleider
die nâch rîterlîchen siten
sint gestalt und gesniten:
und swaz er warmes an geleit,
daz giht er ez sîn wirtes cleit.
er treit den lîp swâre,
mit strûbendem hâre,
barschenkel unde barvuoz.
und daz ist ie der ander gruoz
den er sînem gaste gît:
er sprichet 'sît der zît
daz ich êrste hûs gewan
(daz geloubet mir lützel ieman)
sone wart ich nie zewâre
des über ze halbem jâre
ichn müese koufen daz korn.
hiure bin ich gar verlorn
(mich müet daz ichz iu muoz clagen):
mir hât der schûr erslagen
den besten bû den ich hân.
ich vürhte ich müeze daz hûs lân.
etewie ernert ich den lîp,
wan daz ich sorge um mîn wîp:
diene weiz ich war ich tuo.

dâ hœret grôz kumber zuo,
swer daz hûz haben sol:
jane mac nieman wizzen wol
waz ez muoz kosten.
ich wære wol enbrosten
der werlt an andern dingen,
möht ich dem hûse geringen.'
Sus beginnet er trûren unde clagen
unde sînem gaste sagen
sô manec armez mære
daz im lieber wære
wærer nie komen dar.
der wirt hât wâr, und doch niht gar.
daz hûs muoz kosten harte vil:
swer êre ze rehte haben wil,
der muoz deste dicker heime sîn:
sô tuo ouch under wîlen schîn
ob er noch rîters muot habe,
und entuo sich des niht abe
ern sî der rîterschefte bî
diu im ze suochenne sî.   (lines 2807–58)

(Many a man excuses himself, saying that it is the custom of the household that once one is married, one should henceforth neither ride out on knightly exploits nor entertain; he says he has to devote himself to his household. He gives up both social pleasures and clothes which are fashioned and cut in the knightly manner, and the warm clothes that he puts on he claims are the clothes he should wear as master of the household. He goes about looking wretched, with tousled hair and legs and feet bare. And the first thing he says to his guest after welcoming him is always: 'Since the day I first took over the household (nobody believes me), I have never been able to avoid having to buy grain every half year. This year I am in a terrible way (it pains me to have to tell you this): a hailstorm has destroyed the best farmland that I have. I fear that I shall have to give up the household. Somehow or other I should myself survive, but I worry about my wife: I don't know what to do with her. Anyone who has a household has great troubles. No one can know what it will cost. I could meet the other demands of society if only I could cope with running the household.' So he begins to moan and complain and to tell his guest so many sad stories that he would rather never have come there at all. The master of the household is right, yet not entirely. A household must cost a great deal, and anyone who wants to manage it respectably, in a proper manner, has to be at home all the more often. Yet from time to time he should show that he still has the spirit of a knight and not fail to attend and take part in tournaments.)

Although Gawein concludes by acknowledging some justification in the

position of the lord concerned with house and estates, he presents a case which
Iwein finds persuasive for continuing to engage actively in chivalry by participating in tournaments, and he secures permission from his wife to do so for a
year. The problem which then arises is that he overstays this period of leave.

Viewing it specifically within the context of the work, one may be inclined to
regard Gawein's advocacy of the tournament as the standpoint of the bachelor
knight which it is grossly irresponsible of him to urge upon Iwein at this juncture. However, with respect to the relationship between nobility and knighthood,
we may detect beneath the humour of his argument signs of a very real tension
within the nobles' way of life between the need to secure the economic basis of
their lifestyle and the obligation to engage in chivalric activity as a means both
of maintaining military effectiveness and of enhancing their reputation for
prowess.[23] It is, of course, well known that the tournament was an aspect of
chivalric life which polarized opinion within aristocratic society itself (not to
speak of the criticism it provoked among churchmen), creating a division
between those who held it to be a dangerous and expensive waste of energy and
those for whom it was – or so they hoped – the route to glory and riches.[24]

A further respect in which the relationship of nobility and knighthood may be
considered concerns the idea that social developments of the twelfth century
encouraged the creation of a chivalric community encompassing men of diverse
rank from the highest nobility to the unfree *ministeriales*. If such a community
existed, what were its implications? Did the conception of knighthood as an
order defined by function rather than by birth mean that it was possible for merit
in the form of chivalric prowess to be thought to override considerations of
rank? In other words, could nobility of virtue or achievement gain recognition in
this context as superior to nobility of birth? Such issues have been considered
important for attempts to determine whose interests were paramount among
Hartmann's audiences – those of the old established nobility, wedded to the
principle of birth, or those of the *ministeriales*, for whom the aspiration to noble
status would, in default of noble birth, be based on the principle of merit.[25] One
narrative situation in which these issues can become live ones is the conclusion
of a combat between two knights who do not know one another, when the act of
surrender by one party, involving the naming of himself, can have consequences
for the relative status of the two men henceforth. Comparison of two combats in
Erec is of interest here.

In the final adventure of the work, Erec decisively overpowers the noble
knight Mabonagrin, but Mabonagrin refuses to acknowledge defeat or to name

---

[23] For a more detailed analysis of the passage, which brings out a range of further aspects,
see Jackson, *Chivalry*, pp. 217–26.

[24] A detailed account of the social (and literary) background of the tournament is given in R.
Harvey, *Moriz von Craûn and the Chivalric World* (Oxford, 1961), pp. 112–217.

[25] A leading study of these questions in the German context is G. Kaiser, *Textauslegung und
gesellschaftliche Selbstdeutung: Die Artusromane Hartmanns von Aue*, 2nd edn (Wies-
baden, 1978). For a summary of objections to Kaiser's interpretation of *Erec* as a work
favouring ministerial aspirations, see Jackson, *Chivalry*, pp. 81–2.

himself, insisting that he will not do so unless he first learns that his opponent is of noble birth (lines 9338–44). For if his opponent is not of noble birth – if he is 'ein unadels man' (line 9349) – then Mabonagrin would rather die than surrender. His position, which is not anticipated in this form in Chrétien, is that it is more honourable to die not having surrendered to a man who is not of noble birth than to live by surrendering to such a man. For Mabonagrin, therefore, there is no question that the merit shown by Erec in overcoming him can compensate for any possible deficiency in his birth. This poses a dilemma for Erec, who has no wish to kill Mabonagrin but is fully aware of the implication of his identifying himself first, namely that he would appear to admit defeat (lines 9325–32). However, in an act of extraordinary magnanimity, he does reveal his name and lineage and is able to receive the surrender which Mabonagrin offers when he learns of Erec's high birth. On the evidence of this combat alone, it appears that nobility of virtue is not considered a criterion which can take precedence over nobility of birth, though it does attest to the social heterogeneity of the category of men known as knights.

Earlier, in the first of his combats with King Guivreiz, Erec also emerges as the victor. He is poised to kill Guivreiz when the latter pleads for mercy and, in a passage without precedent in Chrétien, offers his surrender and submission to Erec in recognition of his prowess and setting aside any consideration of his lineage:

> vil gerne sicher ich dir.
> nû emphâch mich ze man.
> und wizzest daz ich nie gewan
> deheinen herren mêre.
> wan daz dir diu êre
> geschiht von dîner manheit,
> ich wære des tôdes ê bereit
> ê ez immer ergienge:
> dehein edel dich vervienge.
> sus ist ez mir unmære:
> swer dîn vater wære,
> sô edelet dich dîn tugent sô
> daz ich dîn bin ze herren vrô.   (lines 4447–59)

(I very gladly surrender to you. Now accept me as your man. And know that I have never acknowledged anyone as my lord. Were it not for the fact that you have gained this honour by your prowess, I should be prepared to die rather than that this should happen. However nobly you might be born, it would not help you. As it is, it is immaterial to me: whoever your father might be, your prowess ennobles you to such a degree that I am glad to have you as my lord.)

Erec responds to this by sparing Guivreiz, without insisting on his surrender or homage but only asking to know his name.

It has rightly been pointed out that caution needs to be exercised in evaluating

Guivreiz's words here. For Guivreiz shortly asks Erec if he would not mind revealing his rank, as it would be easier for him to bear defeat if he knew it had come about at the hands of a man of noble status, and he is greatly relieved to learn that he has been overcome by a social equal (lines 4513–56); it can, therefore, be said that in the upshot, when all is revealed, the prowess which is praised here is seen to be the prowess of the man nobly born, and there is no breaking of the aristocratic mould.[26] Furthermore, viewing these events within the context of Erec's own progress, it is evident that recognition of his prowess is precisely what is called for at this point, his combat with Guivreiz being the first properly chivalric encounter with a social equal since he set out from his kingdom to re-establish his reputation as a knight.[27] Such considerations make it clear that it would not be appropriate to build too much on the sentiments expressed by Guivreiz in the immediate context of the combat, to load them with too much weight of ideological or sociological significance regarding, for example, the composition of Hartmann's audiences. Yet, in spite of this caveat, it remains the case that for a moment at least the idea that prowess can confer nobility, rendering questions of birth irrelevant for a community of knighthood based on excellence in the exercise of arms, is allowed to hang in the air and would surely not have gone unnoticed by Hartmann's audiences, sensitive as they would have been, in the German context, to the differences in status existing among those known as knights.

5. Nobility and religion

Hartmann's shorter narratives come into consideration here. I shall begin with *Gregorius*, commenting not on the scenes set in the aristocratic world, but on the moment in the text when Gregorius, having discovered that he is a foundling and not the son of the fisherman in whose family he has been raised, resolves to leave the monastery for the life of chivalry. Gregorius's decision to abandon the life for which he appears destined – there has, it should be noted, been no formal commitment to the monastic life either by Gregorius himself or in the form of oblation – is made the subject of reflection in that he announces his intention to the abbot and is engaged by him in extended debate. This is a passage of the text in which Hartmann expands significantly upon his source, emphasizing the momentous choice facing Gregorius at this juncture and examining the merits of

---

26 See G. Zink, '*Geburt* bei Chrétien und bei Hartmann', in *Dialog: Literatur und Literatur-wissenschaft im Zeichen deutsch-französischer Begegnung. Festgabe für Josef Kunz*, ed. R. Schönhaar (Berlin, 1973), pp. 22–31, at p. 29; R. Pérennec, *Recherches sur le roman arthurien en vers en Allemagne aux XIIe et XIIIe siècles*, Göppinger Arbeiten zur Germanistik, 393, 2 vols (Göppingen, 1984), vol. I, pp. 107–11; Jackson, *Chivalry*, pp. 80–1.

27 See my essays 'Chrétien, Hartmann, and the Knight as Fighting Man', at pp. 107–8, and 'Schutzwaffen und Höfischheit. Zu den Kampfausgängen im *Erec* Hartmanns von Aue', in *Spannungen und Konflikte menschlichen Zusammenlebens in der deutschen Literatur des Mittelalters. Bristoler Colloquium 1993*, ed. K. Gärtner *et al.* (Tübingen, 1996), pp. 74–90, at pp. 83–5.

the two ways of life between which he is poised. Gregorius's desire to become a knight predates the knowledge of his true origins in the aristocratic world, made known to him only in the course of the conversation, and is revealed to the abbot as a wish which he has secretly cherished while he has been a scholar in the monastery. Gregorius vividly evokes the image that he has had of himself as a knight, displaying a knowledge of the chivalric life which astonishes the abbot and convinces him that Gregorius is not by disposition a monk: 'dû bist, daz merke ich wol daran,/ des muotes niht ein klôsterman' (lines 1635–6, 'you are, I see clearly from this, by inclination not a monk'). What speaks through Gregorius's vision of himself as a knight is the voice of his aristocratic heritage; he was born of and into the aristocratic world, and although removed from it at infancy, raised as a fisherman's son, and trained as a monk, that heritage remains a determining force upon him and leads him finally away from the monastery.

Before that point is reached, however, the exchanges between the abbot and Gregorius include a weighing-up of the relative merits of the monastic and chivalric ways of life. Gregorius concedes to the abbot that the monastic life is the sweetest, the finest that God has given to the world, but with the proviso that one is called to it (lines 1507–10). If one is not, if one is rather called to knighthood, then that is better than leading a life as a monk without a vocation ('ein betrogen klôsterman', line 1535). The sense of vocation is ultimately what Gregorius's decision rests on. The argument is finely balanced, as the abbot insists on the certainty of Gregorius falling into sin if he leaves the monastery for knighthood, while Gregorius shows himself inspired by an ideal of service and aspiration as a knight. It is difficult to know who has the advantage in this debate, and one may be inclined to conclude that they are both right, from their different points of view, the abbot with his experience of life and Gregorius with his youthful optimism. There are good reasons within the narrative economy of the text why the position should be left ambiguous – who can foresee what is right for Gregorius, what God might intend for him? But the point to be emphasized in this context is that Hartmann has here presented an issue of choice between two ways of life – the Church or the secular world – such as must have confronted many of the nobly born in his audience; in laying out some of the arguments involved and perhaps particularly in highlighting the importance of a sense of vocation, he may be seen to be reflecting and even informing debate on this question.

Finally, I turn to *Der arme Heinrich*, the narrative part of which begins with a lengthy description of Heinrich before he is stricken with leprosy and removes himself from the aristocratic world (lines 29–74). It is a remarkable portrait of an ideal figure of courtly society – honourable, humane, cultivated, throughout which there runs as a central theme that he is noble not just by birth but also by his good qualities of character or virtues:

> er hete ze sînen handen
> geburt unde rîcheit;
> ouch was sîn tugent vil breit.

swie ganz sîn habe wære,
sîn geburt unwandelbære
und wol den vürsten gelîch,
doch was er unnâch alsô rîch
der geburt und des guotes
so der êren und des muotes.
[. . .]
im was der rehte wunsch gegeben
von werltlîchen êren;
die kunde er wol gemêren
mit aller hande reiner tugent.   (lines 38–46, 56–9)

(He had birth and wealth; also his good qualities of character were
numerous. However complete his possessions were, however
impeccable his birth and fully [or 'almost'] the equal of princes, yet
he was not nearly as rich in birth and possessions as he was in honour and disposition. [. . .] He had been granted all that could be
wished for in the way of worldly honours; he knew how to increase
these with all kinds of excellent qualities of character.)

Here is a man in whom any possible tension between the claims of nobility of
birth and nobility of virtue appears to have found a harmonious resolution, with
noble birth being seen as the springboard for noble action. One may imagine
that for an aristocratic audience the figure that Hartmann drew here would
appear to embody perfection, to represent the fulfilment of their own highest
aspirations. And yet, and this is one of the shocking and challenging features of
this text, it is precisely such a man that God brings low with the socially alienat-
ing disease of leprosy. Hartmann does not make it easy for his audience to know
how to interpret this, invoking as analogies on the one hand Absalom, a symbol
of pride which met its fall, and on the other Job, whose calamity was a testing by
God, not a punishment (lines 84–90, 124–45). In the event Heinrich's case
seems to lie closer to that of Job in so far as God restores him to health and
wealth, but that is contingent upon change in Heinrich, change which involves
rejection of the world into which he was born and of which he was such an
adornment. For, as may have been suspected from the outset by those sensitive
to the references to the world in the portrait of him (for example, in line 57
quoted above), Heinrich is too much of this world and unmindful of the fact that
all he has depends on God's graciously sustaining it. This attachment to the
world runs deep, for although Heinrich abandons the noble life utterly, giving
away all his possessions but the one farm, he still hankers after the world. When
confronted with the maiden's willingness to die for him, he initially rejects this
opportunity, but the temptation proves too strong; his clinging to the world is
seen for what it is when he is prepared to contemplate the death of another for
his own restoration to health. In reality his only way back to the world is through
the absolute rejection of it in the final refusal of the sacrifice.

Beyond this relativization of worldly values which might already give an
aristocratic audience grounds for reflection, there is the sociological dimension

of this work, the fact that Heinrich finds one who is prepared to sacrifice herself for him not among his peers, all of whom find him loathsome (lines 120–7), but in a peasant family. The maiden's attitudes are in themselves not unproblematic, but this does not alter the fact that it is through her that Heinrich is led to the change of heart that makes his redemption possible. Most significantly, the maiden is not set aside when Heinrich is restored to health and his former place in society. In the only scene in the work which is actually located in a courtly environment, a scene familiar from secular narrative, in which a lord's advisers are gathered to consider the choice of a marriage partner for him, Heinrich announces that the only one he will ever marry is she through whom he has, by God's hand, been restored to health (lines 1492–1508). The question of the suitability of this match in a social as opposed to a moral sense, given the great difference in status between the free nobleman Heinrich and the daughter of a free peasant, is not addressed other than in Heinrich's simple statement: 'nû ist si vrî als ich dâ bin' (line 1497, 'now she is as free as I am'). This line has been the subject of extensive debate, including consideration of the status of the peasant, who is from the outset described as *vrî* (269 'free'), and of the circumstance that Heinrich gives the peasant the farm to hold in his own right after he returns to society (lines 1437–45).[28] But there appears to be no way round the fact that for Hartmann's time the maiden cannot be said in social terms to be free in the same sense as Heinrich is free and that the marriage that he contracts with her would have been regarded as a *mésalliance*, with severe implications for the social standing of his offspring – in short, that this is a marriage that would be likely to shock and challenge the assumptions of noble audiences no less than the downfall of Heinrich.[29]

Heinrich's equation of his own status with that of the maiden in respect of freedom is, in social terms, untenable, but it has been persuasively argued that it invokes a concept of freedom deriving from spheres other than the social, namely the notion of the equality of all mankind before God as propagated in contemporary writings on the Christian idea of freedom and on natural law.[30] Borck traces one tradition of such thinking, based on St Paul's assertion that

28 See, for example, Henne, *Herrschaftsstruktur*, pp. 232–41.
29 The classic study of the legal aspects of the situation is F. Beyerle, 'Der "Arme Heinrich" Hartmanns von Au [*sic*] als Zeugnis mittelalterlichen Ständerechts', in *Kunst und Recht: Festgabe für Hans Fehr*, Arbeiten zur Rechtssoziologie und Rechtsgeschichte, 1 (Karlsruhe, 1948), pp. 28–46. Beyerle finds no example of a marriage comparable to that between Heinrich and the maiden in German records of the twelfth and thirteenth centuries. The fourth conclusion of his study is: 'Die Gleichsetzung von edelfrei und freibäuerlich im Armen Heinrich (V. 1497) entspricht nicht sozialer Wirklichkeit der Zeit, gehört vielmehr zur religiösen Grundidee dieses Gedichts' (p. 46).
30 See K. H. Borck, 'Nû ist si vrî als ich dâ bin. Bemerkungen zu Hartmanns *Armen Heinrich*, v. 1497', in *Medium Aevum deutsch: Beiträge zur deutschen Literatur des hohen und späten Mittelalters. Festschrift für Kurt Ruh zum 65. Geburtstag*, ed. D. Huschenbett *et al.* (Tübingen, 1979), pp. 37–50, and H. Freytag, 'Ständisches, Theologisches, Poetologisches. Zu Hartmanns Konzeption des Armen Heinrich', *Euphorion*, lxxxi (1987), 240–61.

'where the spirit of the Lord is, there is freedom' (2 Corinthians 3: 17, 'ubi autem spiritus domini, ibi libertas'), through to the reform movement of the eleventh and twelfth centuries, arguing that it is on that tradition that Hartmann draws, while Freytag cites from Latin and vernacular texts to construct a background of legal thought about the original freedom and equality of all mankind as the creatures of God. Viewed in this light, Heinrich's statement reflects a concept of the dignity of all mankind in the sight of God which implicitly runs counter to the aristocratic notion of nobility conferred by birth, just as it is explicitly opposed to that notion by some ecclesiastical and legal authors.

In *Der arme Heinrich*, Hartmann tells the story not of a world lost and regained, but of a world transformed, and a vital part of that transformation is Heinrich's union with the maiden in defiance of contemporary marriage practices among the nobility. Heinrich's experience of the loss of his worldly status, it is implied, gives him understanding not only of his own dependence on God's grace but also of a community of humanity in which differences of rank are of no consequence. It is the sense of that community to which his statement 'nû ist si vrî als ich dâ bin' gives expression, and in his marriage to the maiden it takes on concrete form.

The three topics considered in this essay do not add up to an exhaustive treatment of the subject of nobles and nobility in Hartmann, but in them we see something of the character of his work as a whole. They reflect his status as a knight and his literate education, and whether or not his sensitivity to the condition of the noble poor has anything to do with his personal or family history, it illustrates the compassionate quality which he brings to the depiction of a wide variety of human situations. Respectful of the existing order and its hierarchical distinctions, Hartmann has no agenda for social change – even where he is at his most radical, in *Der arme Heinrich*, the new dispensation which he hints at is contained within the world of the contemporary nobility – but is concerned more with the individual destiny and inner life of his leading characters. Yet out of the complexity of his own identity as an educated knight there arises a reflectiveness which expresses itself in a gentle stretching of the aristocratic imagination at certain points – through exposure of the particular vulnerability of those of noble rank and a sympathetic portrayal of the emotional consequences of poverty, through the idea that knighthood may constitute a fraternity which transcends social distinctions, and finally through the suggestion that outside the confines of court and castle there may lie a humanity no less worthy than that which resides within them.

10

A Noble in Politics: Roger Mortimer in the Period of Baronial Reform and Rebellion, 1258–1265[1]

D. A. Carpenter

Few nobles played a more decisive part in the downfall of Simon de Montfort than the great Marcher baron Roger Mortimer of Wigmore. After the battle of Lewes in May 1264, Roger's continued resistance did much to undermine the Montfortian regime.[2] After the Lord Edward's escape from Hereford in May 1265, Roger and his wife gave him safety and succour at Wigmore. And at the battle of Evesham in the following August, Roger led one of the royalist lines of battle, the others being commanded by Edward himself and the earl of Gloucester. According to some modern historians, Roger blocked the bridge out of Evesham thus preventing Montfort's escape. According to others, he was stationed with Edward and Gloucester up on the hill above the town and was fully engaged in the main battle.[3] Indeed, in a newly discovered contemporary account, it was Roger himself who struck Montfort the fatal blow.[4] Certainly, after the great earl's body had been mutilated, his head began a horrible journey to Wigmore where it was presented 'To Dame Maud de Mortimer [Roger's wife] who foully abused it'.[5]

Historians have appreciated that a personal feud between Montfort and the

---

1 I am most grateful to Paul Brand, Margaret Howell, and Jon Crump (who is writing a thesis on the Mortimers) for commenting on a draft of this paper.

2 There are good accounts of Roger's career in G. E. Cokayne and others *The Complete Peerage*, 13 vols (London, 1910–59), ix, 276–81 and (by T. F. Tout) in *The Dictionary of National Biography*, xiii, 1029–32. Tout, however, inevitably relied on the printed sources (chiefly the chronicles) then available. There is also an outline of Roger's career in C. Hopkinson, 'The Mortimers of Wigmore 1214–1282', *Transactions of the Woolhope Naturalists' Field Club*, xlvii (1991), 28–46, at pp.33–43. For the family as a whole, see B. P. Evans, 'The Family of Mortimer' (University of Wales, PhD thesis, 1934). The period between 1258 and 1265 can now be studied in two fine new books: J. R. Maddicott, *Simon de Montfort* (Cambridge, 1994), and M. Howell, *Eleanor of Provence* (Oxford, 1998).

3 D. A. Carpenter, *The Battles of Lewes and Evesham, 1264/1265* (Keele, 1987); D. C. Cox, *The Battle of Evesham: A New Account* (Evesham, 1988). Cox's version is to be preferred.

4 O. de Laborderie, J. R. Maddicott, and D. A. Carpenter, 'The Battle of Evesham: A New Account', forthcoming in *EHR* for April 2000.

5 *The Metrical Chronicle of Robert of Gloucester*, ed. W. A. Wright, 2 vols, RS 86 (1887), ii, 765.

Mortimers underlay the events of these last years. They have been less able to explain Roger's wider conduct between 1258 and 1265. In 1258, after all, he had been ostensibly at least a leading member of 'the common enterprise': he was one of the twelve chosen by the barons to draw up the reforms and one of the council of fifteen set up to govern the realm. In 1261 he had resisted the king's overthrow of the Provisions of Oxford and recovery of power, thus in effect standing shoulder to shoulder with Simon de Montfort. Yet in 1263 Roger was conspicuously absent from the faction (although it contained several Marcher barons) which brought Montfort back to England and helped him reassert the Provisions of Oxford. At the end of 1263 he willingly swallowed the bait dangled by the king and plunged into the feud which had its bloody denouement at Evesham. In changing tack between 1258 and 1263 Mortimer was not, of course, alone. Hugh Bigod, the justiciar of 1258, trod a similar path. Such conduct has no single or simple explanation. The following paper does not claim to have sifted even the case of Roger Mortimer to the bottom; but it does offer some nuggets which, I hope, when everything else has been taken out, will still be seen to gleam as gold.

Roger Mortimer entered his inheritance in February 1247. He offered not the statutory £100 relief but a fine of 2000 marks, almost certainly because he was still under age and buying himself out of a period of royal wardship.[6] Roger was to pay off the fine in five years (at an annual rate of £266), but he managed it in four, a testimony both to his efficiency and his resources.[7] If his income (and this is only a guess) was between £400 and £500 a year, then he would certainly have been in the top half of any table of England's wealthiest men, although of course he was less wealthy than the greatest earls who measured their income in thousands of pounds rather than hundreds.[8] The ancestral manors and fees of the Mortimers were scattered through much of England but the chief bases of their

---

[6] *Excerpta e Rotulis Finium, 1216–1272*, ed. C. Roberts, 2 vols (Record Com., 1835–36), ii, 7–8.

[7] Public Record Office E 372/ 91, m. 10d; E 372/ 94, m. 27d. Henceforth unless stated all manuscript references are to documents in the Public Record Office.

[8] Sidney Painter, having obtained figures for the incomes of twenty-seven major landholders between 1260 and 1320, found the median income to be £339 and the average (inflated by the incomes of the great earls) £668. He gives a figure of £485 for the income of Mortimer of Wigmore. This is based on the assignment of dower to Edward Mortimer's widow in 1304 (*Cal. Close Rolls 1302–7*, pp. 175–6) and takes no account of the lands in Ireland for which see *Cal. Inq. Post Mortem*, ii, no. 446. I am unable to follow the basis of Painter's calculations and would put the figure much higher. Mortimer income must have very considerably increased between 1250 and 1300 however. See S. Painter, *Studies in the History of the English Feudal Barony* (Baltimore, 1943), pp. 173–6. In the fourteenth century Radnor and Gwerthrynion were valued at £314 and Maelienydd at between £160 and £334 but again these figures bear little relationship to what was received in Roger Mortimer's early years: R. R. Davies, *Lordship and Society in the March of Wales, 1282–1400* (Oxford, 1978), p. 196. For magnate incomes, see also C. Dyer, *Standards of Living in the Later Middle Ages* (Cambridge, 1989), ch. 2.

power lay in the marcher counties of Shropshire and Herefordshire.[9] Their chief castle and *caput* of their honour was at Wigmore some twenty-three miles north of Hereford.

In the years after 1247, as throughout his life, Roger Mortimer strove to consolidate and increase his power in what historians call the Middle March, the lands – essentially Elfael, Gwerthrynion, and Maelienydd – between the Wye valley above Hereford in the south and the Severn in the north.[10] The Mortimers had long struggled to control this crucial area and had not always been successful. Ralph Mortimer, Roger's father, had been forced to accept Llywelyn the Great's overlordship of Maelienydd (which lay immediately to the west of Wigmore) and, coming to terms, had married Llywelyn's daughter Gwladys.[11] On Llywelyn's death in 1240, however, the tide had turned. Ralph, with support from the crown, had then extinguished or subjected the native rulers in both Maelienydd and Gwerthrynion; in the latter case the process, as Beverley Smith has shown, can be followed in a series of charters preserved in the Mortimer Cartulary.[12] Roger (the fruit of the marriage with Gwladys, and thus a grandson of Llywelyn) continued where his father had left off and built a new castle at Cefn-llys to consolidate Maelienydd's conquest.[13] In all this he was helped by his own marriage (which took place before he inherited) to a marcher heiress: Maud de Braose.[14] Maud was a granddaughter of William Marshal and thus had claims to a share in the much divided Marshal inheritance.[15] More importantly, she and her three sisters were the sole heirs of their father, one of the greatest of all the marcher barons, William de Braose. Maud's portion was the lordship of Radnor which lay just to the south west of the lordship of Wigmore and thus further tightened Roger's grip alongside the Middle March.[16]

---

9   Some impression of this can be gained from *The Book of Fees*, 3 vols (London, 1920–31), ii, 814, 963; iii, 426; *Placita de Quo Warranto* (Record Com., 1818), pp. 266, 270, 271, 273, 675, 677, 681, 684.

10 For the area, see J. Beverley Smith, 'The Middle March in the Thirteenth Century', *Bulletin of the Board of Celtic Studies*, xxiv (1970–72), 77–93 and J. J. Crump, 'The Mortimer Family and the Making of the March', *Thirteenth Century England VI*, ed. M. Prestwich, R. H. Britnell, and R. Frame (Woodbridge, 1997), pp. 117–26.

11 *Royal Letters of the Reign of Henry III*, ed. W. W. Shirley, 2 vols, RS 27 (1862–66), i, no. cv; Crump, 'The Mortimer Family', pp. 123–4. As Crump shows, however, Llywelyn did concede to Hugh the manors of Norton and Knighton in Shropshire over which there had previously been dispute.

12 Smith, 'The Middle March in the Thirteenth Century', pp. 83–4; Crump, 'The Mortimer Family', pp. 125–6.

13 *Annales Cambriae*, ed. J. Williams ab Ithel, RS 20 (1860), p. 100; *Brut Y Tywysogyon or The Chronicle of the Princes. Peniarth MS 20 Version*, ed. T. Jones (Cardiff, 1952), pp. 112, 210.

14 *Close Rolls 1242–7*, p. 484. Roger's father had long held the wardship of Maud and her lands: see *Book of Fees*, ii, 800.

15 These included lands in Leinster, the start of the Mortimer involvement in Ireland. See *Cal. Inq. Post. Mortem*, ii, no. 446. For a division of Marshal lands and fees between Maud and her sisters, see *Cal. Patent Rolls 1247–58*, p. 8; *Close Rolls 1251–3*, pp. 221–3.

16 Much of Maud's inheritance appears in *Cal. Inq. Post Mortem*, ii, no. 446.

In these years between his accession and the revolution of 1258 Roger's relations with the court were distant to say the least. He was knighted by the king at Whitsun 1253 and then went on the royal expedition to Gascony.[17] Yet in all these years Roger only once entered the circle which attested royal charters, in September 1257 when the king passed through Worcester on his journey back from his war in Wales.[18] By itself this does not show that Roger was at odds with the king. He was probably too young to be a major player at court. In any case, busy with his own affairs, that was probably the last thing he wanted to be. Yet there are, in fact, good reasons to think that Roger was a man with grievances. One concerned affairs in Wales. Here Roger was badly hit by the revival of Gwynedd's power under Llywelyn ap Gruffyd. Indeed in 1256 Llywelyn had destroyed his hold of Gwerthrynion.[19] Henry III was not unsympathetic. In 1256 he made Roger presents of game and timber and pardoned him a 100 mark forest amercement.[20] Henry's own campaign against Llywelyn next year was, however, a depressing failure. Another was planned for 1258 but Roger must have suspected that unless it was better led the result would be much the same: he would be left to his fate. Still there were worse things than that: the great marcher barons were used to fighting their own battles. And at least Roger was no worse off than many others who were suffering at Llywelyn's hands. Although significant, therefore, Roger's grievance over events in Wales paled before his other complaint against the court: this was highly individual and highly unique and, we will suggest, dominated much of Roger's conduct in the years after 1258. Roger, in short, believed that Henry III and Richard of Cornwall had disseised him of the manor of Lechlade in Gloucestershire unjustly and without judgment by an act of arbitrary will (*per voluntatem*).

Lechlade was the inheritance (or so the Mortimers liked to think) of Roger's grandmother, Isabel Mortimer, the daughter of Walkelin de Ferrers (see Table, p. 187).[21] Widowed in 1214 on the death of Roger Mortimer, and again in 1235 on the death of her second husband, Isabel lived on till 1252. She seems to have lived, moreover, very much at Lechlade. Certainly she founded a hospital there

---

[17] *Annales Monastici*, ed. H. R. Luard, 5 vols, RS 36 (1864–69), i, 152; *Cal. Patent Rolls 1247–58*, p. 232.

[18] All statements about Roger's attestation of royal charters are based on the manuscript analysis of the witness lists of Henry III's charters preserved at the Public Record Office.

[19] *Brut*, p. 110. For Wales and the Marches in these years, see two (very different) classic works: J. E. Lloyd, *A History of Wales from the Earliest Times to the Edwardian Conquest*, 2 vols (London, 1911), ii, ch. 20 and R. R. Davies, *Conquest Coexistence and Change: Wales 1063–1415* (Oxford, 1987), ch. 12.

[20] *Close Rolls 1254–6*, pp. 300, 342; E 372/ 100, m. 15. The amercement had been imposed on Roger's father.

[21] Much of what follows comes from two cases about Isabel's inheritance which will be discussed in detail below. There are brief references to Lechlade in Evans, 'The Mortimer Family' (pp. 78–9, 135). I am grateful to Clive Knowles for sending me photocopies of the relevant pages.

The Mortimers and Lechlade

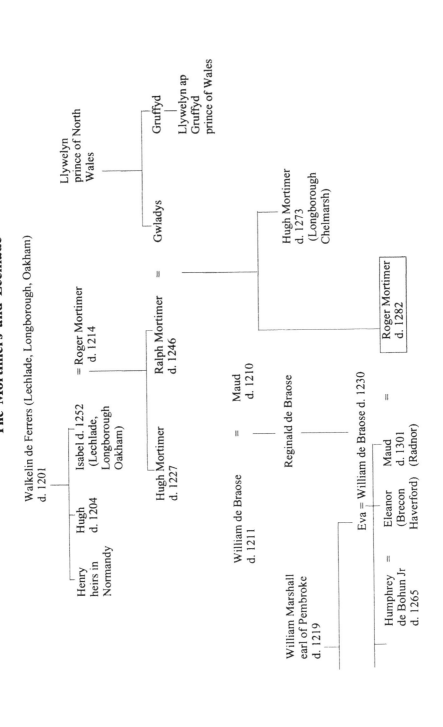

and was buried in its chapel.[22] Situated at the highest navigable point of the
Thames, with the Cotswolds to the north and the Marlborough downs to the
south, Lechlade had a bridge over the river, 600 acres of rich meadow land and
an annual value, according to an extent in 1252, of £48. It was indeed a fitting
place for long years of active widowhood.[23] For the family there was only one
snag. How secure was Isabel's title? Might it not be argued that Lechlade was in
fact the inheritance of her elder brother, Henry, and his descendants? In that
case it should escheat to the crown as part of the 'lands of the Normans', the
lands forfeited in England by those, like Henry and his descendants, who had
chosen the French allegiance in and after 1204.[24] That Isabel held the manor was
simply due to the king having graciously conceded her a life interest.

It seems certain that the Mortimers were well aware of this threat: a government inquiry into Isabel's lands in Rutland had stated ominously that 'her heirs
were beyond the sea'.[25] Consequently they took preventive measures. Eight
weeks before she died, Isabel summoned her grandson Roger to her (according
to Roger's later testimony) and put him in possession of Lechlade. It was to no
avail. The 'lands of the Normans' were the great bank on which the thirteenth-
century kings drew for patronage. Lands which the bank might seize were
constantly ferreted out by government agents and freelance investigators, the
latter usually courtiers eager to be paid out what they had themselves paid in.[26]
And a very big courtier indeed was eyeing up Lechlade, none other than the
king's brother, Richard, earl of Cornwall. In 1243 when Richard had taken the
queen's sister, Sanchia, as his second wife, he was promised by the king lands
worth £500 a year. In the early 1250s around half of the land still had to be
found.[27] Lechlade would make a nice contribution, all the more so since it was
in the same county as Richard's abbey at Hailes, which had been consecrated in
1251. Accordingly, on 29 April 1252, some three weeks after Isabel's death, the
escheator was ordered to take Lechlade into the king's hands.[28] A month later

---

22 *Cal. Charter Rolls 1226–57*, p. 296; Mortimer Cartulary: London Brit. Libr., MS Harley
1240, fol. 44v; W. Dugdale, *Monasticon Anglicanum*, new enlarged edition by J. Caley,
H. Ellis, and B. Bandinel, 6 vols in 8 (London, 1817–30), vi, 684; *Complete Peerage*, ix,
273.

23 *Cal. Inq. Misc.* , i, no. 457. By 1276 it was valued at £98: *Cal. Inq. Post Mortem*, ii, no.
203. For the background, see *The Earliest English Legal Reports I*, ed. P. A. Brand,
Selden Soc. 111 (1995), pp. 21–7.

24 For Isabel's branch of the Ferrers family and its Norman and English properties, see
Magni Rotuli Scaccarii Normanniae, ed. T. Stapleton, 2 vols (London, 1840), ii,
cxxii–cxxv; Sir Maurice Powicke, *The Loss of Normandy, 1189–1204* (2nd edn, Manchester, 1961), p. 338.

25 *Book of Fees*, ii, 1151.

26 For the lands of the Normans, see N. Vincent, *Peter des Roches: An Alien in English Politics, 1205–1238* (Cambridge, 1996), pp. 29–31.

27 H. Ridgeway, 'Foreign Favourites and Henry III's Problems of Patronage, 1247–1258',
EHR, civ (1989), 599–600. In this article Ridgeway shows how Henry was under far more
pressure to find patronage in the 1250s than he had been in the 1240s.

28 *Close Rolls 1251–3*, pp. 82–3.

the king issued a charter granting the manor to Richard and his heirs by Sanchia.[29]

The king was evidently informed of the situation at Lechlade and expected trouble. Trouble was what he got. On 29 April itself the sheriff of Gloucestershire was ordered to help the escheator deal with any resistance to the seizure of the manor. Later, in June 1252, Roger Mortimer was summoned *coram rege* to explain why 'by force and arms' he had intruded himself into Lechlade, an escheat (so the writ alleged) of the lands of the Normans.[30] All those who had abetted him were to appear as well. Evidently Roger had either resisted the escheator's attempt to take possession, or had subsequently repossessed the manor, perhaps both. Yet outraged though he was Roger gave way. What happened when he appeared *coram rege*, if he did, is unknown. He seems to have escaped punishment but he did not recover, or attempt to recover, the manor. Perhaps, a measure of his good sense, he realized the odds were just too great. The king was pliable but there was no chance that Earl Richard would give way, and had not the judges themselves recently whispered in the ear of William of Horton, the St Albans abbey legal expert, that there were two dominant people in the realm against whom they did not dare give judgment; one was John Mansel, the other, of course, was Richard of Cornwall.[31]

Roger then passed the matter over and waited for better times. He did, however, accompany Henry III on his expedition to Gascony in 1253–54, while Richard of Cornwall remained behind to assist the queen in the governance of the realm. If, as seems quite likely, Roger hoped thus to bend the king's ear over Lechlade, he was to be grievously disappointed. Instead salt was poured into his wounds. Almost as soon as Roger was out of the kingdom the king's serjeant and attorney, the ubiquitous Laurence del Brok, began a legal action to recover another part of Isabel's 'inheritance', namely the manor of Longborough, situated north of Lechlade high up in the Cotswolds and also worth some £50 a year.[32] The reason a legal action this time was necessary was because the manor did not escheat with Isabel's death; it had a tenant who had sat there evidently rather longer than Roger's eight weeks, namely Roger's younger brother, Hugh de Mortimer.[33] It was against Hugh, therefore, that Laurence del Brok brought his case and Hugh promptly called Roger Mortimer to warrant him his pos-

29 *Cal. Charter Rolls 1226–57*, p. 392; *Close Rolls 1251–3*, pp. 95–6; N. Denholm-Young, *Richard of Cornwall* (Oxford, 1947), p. 168. Denholm-Young does not comment on the circumstances of Lechlade's acquisition. At this time Richard and Sanchia were also granted another of Isabel's manors, that of Oakham in Rutland valued at an annual £116 (*Close Rolls 1251–3*, p. 92). See below p. 190.

30 *Close Rolls 1251–3*, p. 220.

31 *Gesta Abbatum Monasterii Sancti Albani*, ed. H. T. Riley, 3 vols, RS 28/4 (1867–69), i, 316.

32 *Close Rolls 1253–4*, p. 67. In 1276, however, it was valued at £37: *Cal. Close Rolls 1272–9*, p. 268. For Laurence, see P. A. Brand, *The Origins of the English Legal Profession* (Oxford, 1992), pp. 64–5.

33 Hugh appears as Roger's brother in Just 1/ 300C, m. 14d and as his uncle in Just 1/ 1188,

session. But Roger was in Gascony. All he could do, when he heard the case was due to be heard during the Michaelmas term of 1253, was to obtain a writ ordering the judges not to place him 'in default for his absence'. This was on 7 October, the day after the case had been due to start or restart. On 8 October, Roger did better and the king ordered the case to be postponed altogether until the following May.[34] It hardly helped. In May 1254 the case did indeed recommence before the council in England. Roger, still in Gascony, appeared (presumably through his attorney) and argued that Longborough was part of Isabel's inheritance and he was the heir. He failed to convince. The council's judgment was that the manor should be taken into the king's hands as an escheat of the lands of the Normans.[35] Before the end of the month the queen had authorized a grant of the manor to, surprise surprise, Richard of Cornwall; the two at this time were working hand in glove in charge of the government and Longborough was less then eight miles from Hailes. Richard's determination to make the best of all possible advantages is amply demonstrated by the argument he now advanced, namely that Longborough was actually simply part of Lechlade; only if an inquiry showed it was not should it be valued and the value deducted from the annual sum he was receiving until the king gave him his promised lands.[36] On this particular point Richard seems to have been foiled, but he got his way on the main issue. Longborough was valued but it was also in April 1256 granted by royal charter to Richard and his heirs by Sanchia.[37] For Roger there was no compensation. Through the loss of Lechlade and Longborough, Mortimer income had been reduced by a £100 a year. Indeed if one included Oakham in Rutland as well, a hugely valuable manor held by Isabel which was also granted to Richard and Sanchia (although here Isabel's title was more clearly only one for life), then the losses amounted to over £200 a year, a very large slice indeed of Mortimer resources.[38] For Roger it was worse even than that. Having failed to warrant Longborough to his brother Hugh, he was forced to compensate him for its loss. Accordingly land worth £50 a year was granted to Hugh from Roger's

m. 2. Since Hugh the uncle had actually died back in 1227, brother is certainly correct. I am grateful to Jon Crump for helping me on this point. See also below n. 51.

[34] *Close Rolls 1251–3*, pp. 177–8. The order for adjournment was recorded on the roll dealing with the business coming before the council in the Hilary term of 1254: KB 26/152, m. 1. I have been unable to find any reference to the case in the records of the Michaelmas term.

[35] KB 26/151, mm. 30d, 31. For the judgment (which does not appear on the badly damaged roll), see *Close Rolls 1253–4*, p. 67.

[36] *Ibid.*

[37] Denholm-Young, *Richard of Cornwall*, p. 168. Richard's fee seems to have ceased after 1256, by which time he may have received the £500 worth of land promised with Sanchia. *Cal. Liberate Roll 1251–60*, p. 292 for the last payment.

[38] For Oakham, see *Rotuli de Oblatis et Finibus*, ed. T. D. Hardy (Record Com., 1835), pp. 398–9; *Book of Fees*, ii, 1151; *Close Rolls 1251–3*, p. 92; *Cal. Charter Rolls 1226–57*, p. 392; Denholm-Young, *Richard of Cornwall*, p. 169. Roger never seems to have sought its recovery.

manor of Chelmarsh in Shropshire.[39] The queen offered but one compensation. She postponed Roger's amercement for losing the Longborough case until he got back from Gascony![40]

By 1258, therefore, Roger Mortimer was a man full of discontents. He was disillusioned by the king's failure in Wales; he was enraged by the appalling injustice over Lechlade and Longborough. Yet Roger played little direct part in the upheavals of that year. He seems to have been absent from the April 1258 Westminster parliament where the revolution began, for he was not a member of the baronial confederation formed on 12 April and attests none of the numerous royal charters enrolled during the month. On 15, 16 June during the Oxford parliament, he received gifts of game from the king, but he attested neither the royal charter issued of the fifteenth nor those on the fifth, twelfth, fourteenth, seventeenth, nineteenth, twentieth and twenty-first.[41] It may well be that the open war with Llywelyn kept Roger to his castles in the March. If so it is all the more testimony to his power and influence that at Oxford he was still chosen as one of the baronial twelve and one of the council of fifteen.[42] Potentially he was now for the first time at the very centre of government. What would he do with his power? The answer was to come next year

In April 1259 the justiciar Hugh Bigod left London and journeyed to the west. By the twenty-first he had reached Lechlade and there for a few days he stayed and heard a series of Gloucestershire pleas.[43] One of those pleas was Roger Mortimer's for Lechlade itself. Indeed it was surely to hear this plea on the spot that Hugh had gone to Lechlade in the first place.[44] Roger's great campaign to recover the manor had begun. It was to last until the collapse of the council's power at the end of 1260, providing an angry and unsolvable sub-plot to the whole of this first phase of baronial reform.[45]

Roger began the case by bringing a simple action of novel disseisin against

---

39 Just 1/ 300C m. 14d. I owe this information and the reference to Jon Crump.
40 *Close Rolls 1253–4*, p. 70. For the queen's role in this period, see Howell, *Eleanor of Provence*, ch. 5.
41 *Close Rolls 1256–9*, pp. 233–5.
42 *Documents of the Baronial Movement of Reform and Rebellion*, ed. R. F. Treharne and I. J. Sanders (Oxford, 1973), pp. 100–101, 104–5, chaps. 3, 9.
43 Just 1/ 1188, mm. 1–3d and (for the date) Just 1/ 873, m. 26. See E. F. Jacob, *Studies in the Period of Baronial Reform and Rebellion 1258–1267* (Oxford, 1925), p. 40; R. F. Treharne, *The Baronial Plan of Reform 1258–1263* (Manchester, 1932), pp. 145, 146 n. 1; A. H. Hershey, 'Success or Failure? Hugh Bigod and Judicial Reform during the Baronial Movement, June 1258–February 1259', *Thirteenth Century England V*, ed. P. R. Coss and S. D. Lloyd (Woodbridge, 1995), p. 84.
44 Assizes of novel disseisin were usually heard in the counties to which they belonged. One would expect Roger to have paid for a writ initiating an action of this type before the justiciar but I can find no trace of this on the fine rolls.
45 Just 1/ 1188, mm. 1, 2, 2d from where all the following details come. Changes in the ink show that the record was made in stages as the case went along. The proceedings are partly printed but with many important omissions in *Abbreviatio Placitorum* (Record Com., 1811), pp. 145–6.

Richard of Cornwall and his officials for disseising him of Lechlade back in 1252.[46] Richard, of course, was now king of Germany, but he had returned to England in January 1259 and remained there for most of the time the case was in progress.[47] He did not, however, in April 1259 (or later) appear in person. Instead his representative simply pointed out that Lechlade had been seized by the sheriff on orders of the king and then been granted to Richard by a royal charter. Richard himself had carried out no disseisin. Since all this clearly touched the king the case was adjourned till Easter, when it was to come *coram rege* so that Henry himself could be consulted.[48] Sure enough at the end of April 1259 the king came before his council at Westminster and acknowledged that he had seized the manor as an escheat after Isabel's death (she only holding from the king for life). He then agreed to warrant the manor to Earl Richard (who thus went 'without day') and asked Roger Mortimer to show his right. Roger replied that Isabel held the manor hereditarily and had granted it to him before her death as her nearest heir. As the king was 'not advised' how to reply the case was adjourned again, this time to come *coram rege* at the beginning of July. When it did, little progress was made and a new side issue appeared. Why had Roger never come to the king to do homage for the manor? Roger's reply was that he held it not from the king but from the Ferrers earls of Derby. The case was adjourned to come again *coram rege* on 13 October.

13 October 1259 was of course the day the great parliament opened at Westminster, the day indeed of the protest of the 'community of the bachelry of England' about the selfish conduct of the barons. This was not perhaps the best moment to re-open the suit for Lechlade and in fact it was postponed till 4 November. Roger then came before 'the whole council of the king' and was asked if he wished to say anything new to clarify his seisin (this was once more the issue) and show why he ought to be restored to the manor. The council was clearly trying to be helpful and Roger was ready with his response. He now explained more fully than before how he had come into possession. Isabel's father Walkelin de Ferrers had had two sons, Henry the elder and Hugh the younger. Walkelin, wishing to advance his younger son, had granted him Lechlade. It was to be held from Walkelin and his heirs in hereditary right. After Walkelin's death (in 1201) Hugh had done homage to his elder brother, Henry, as his lord and sought his confirmation. He had then remained in possession all his life and (in 1204) had died in seisin without heirs of his body. On this Isabel had succeeded as his heir 'because Henry who was then alive could not be both

[46] Technically the case was for one messuage and two parts of the manor together with half an acre. It is not entirely clear why Roger did not demand the other third of the manor but it may be because of claims of Hugh Mortimer's widow to hold it in dower (see below p. 193 n. 51).
[47] Richard was absent in Germany from 18/19 June to 24 October 1260: Denholm-Young, *Richard of Cornwall*, pp. 103–5.
[48] The specified reason why it touched the king was that in default of heirs by Sanchia, Lechlade would revert to the crown.

lord and heir'.[49] Isabel, in her turn, had retained possession until she rendered the manor to Roger 'as her grandson and nearest heir'. So, Roger concluded, he sought the return of the seisin he had thus received. Afterwards he was to ready to answer concerning his right.[50]

The reply to all this was given by the king's attorney, Laurence del Brok, now back on the case. He drew attention to the earlier and parallel action over Longborough in 1254, where the court had ruled that the manor was indeed an escheat of the lands of the Normans. This was because Henry had heirs living in the allegiance of the king of France in Normandy and, so long as that was the case, Isabel could not be Hugh's heir.[51] Her tenure was merely one for life by concession of the king. Roger countered, in his turn, by pointing out that the action over Longborough had been one of right, while this one over Lechlade was simply about seisin. It was not necessary for him to show that Isabel *was* Hugh's heir. He merely observed (by way of explanation) that it was 'as his heir' that she had gained seisin. Not surprisingly the case was postponed yet again, this time to the parliament due to meet in February 1260.

This, of course, was the famous Candlemas parliament of 1260 which Simon de Montfort tried to hold in defiance of the king's prohibition. He may perhaps, on this occasion, have had Roger's support. As it was, the record of the case noted its postponement because the parliament had been adjourned from 9 to 23 February. Then on the twenty-third the case was adjourned again until 25 April 'because of the absence of the king and because the king has forbidden the justiciar and the magnates from holding a parliament in his absence, nor shall anything be decided about the state of the kingdom until his return from the parts across the sea'. In April all that was done was to postpone the case again so that meanwhile the rolls could be searched for the record of the Longborough

---

49 Henry (so Roger said) also had no heirs of his body to whom the inheritance could come. In the pleadings in 1204 Roger had given more details about Henry's childless English marriage (KB 26/ 151, m. 30d). However Henry subsequently had children in Normandy.

50 Oakham too had been held by Walkelin de Ferrers but he never granted it to Hugh. It thus passed to Henry de Ferrers and was forfeited on his defection. Isabel's fine with King John was merely for possession of the manor: see the references in n. 38 above and *Magni Rotuli Scaccarii Normanniae*, ed. Stapleton, ii, cxxiii–cxxiv.

51 Laurence at this point also alleged that on the death of Hugh Mortimer (about whose identity more in a moment) his widow (a gap in the record is left for her name) had impleaded Isabel for a third of Lechlade as her dower. Isabel had replied that she could only give dower for the term of her life since she only had a life interest in the manor. As a result of this admission, Richard of Cornwall had immediately seized that third of the manor into his hands when given it by the king. For the truth of all this, Laurence placed himself on the rolls of the bench. However, no order was subsequently made to search for them and no more is heard of this argument. Roger countered it in part by saying that he was at present making no claim for the third in question. In all this Laurence describes Hugh as Isabel's son and Roger's uncle. That Hugh had died in 1227. Yet Laurence also says that it was against this same Hugh that the 1253–54 case was brought. Clearly this is impossible and Laurence is here conflating Hugh, Roger's uncle, with Hugh, Roger's younger brother (who died in 1273). It is hard to believe that Laurence was really confused over this and I wonder whether the mistake is that of the enrolling clerk.

action. By 8 July, when the case came again before the council, that record had indeed been found and it prompted a fresh investigation, this time into the 1000 mark fine which (so the king alleged) Isabel had made to be allowed to hold Hugh's lands for life. The case accordingly was adjourned till 20 October so the fine could be found. On 20 October Roger appeared and sought seisin as before, only for the case to be prorogued from day to day until 2 December. By that time Isabel's fine had been discovered. It had been made in 1204 and was for 300 marks not one thousand.[52] Roger at once claimed that it gave her a 'free tenement and fee . . . as sister and heir of Hugh de Ferrers'.

Roger Mortimer had now been litigating for more than a year and half without results and must have been hugely fed up. The importance he attached to the affair is revealed by a total change in his itinerary. The statements in the record of the case about his appearances cannot be taken at face value. In practice he was probably represented by an attorney. But what does prove his presence at court are his attestations to royal charters. Before 1259, as we have seen, he had attested hardly a single one. In 1259, by contrast, he witnessed charters in February, May, June, July, October, and November. In November indeed he was appointed with Philip Basset to attend on the justiciar during the king's absence in France.[53] In 1260 Roger attested in May, July, August, November, and December.[54] It was not simply, one may suspect, that he had suddenly become a committed reformer. He also wished to bring all his influence to bear on the Lechlade case.

Perhaps Roger also believed that the situation in Wales now permitted his presence at court. If so he was much mistaken. It is true that a truce with Llywelyn had been arranged during the 1258 Oxford parliament and it was renewed in August 1259 to last for another year.[55] But in January 1260 Llywelyn had invaded the lordship of Builth, which the Lord Edward had entrusted to Roger's custody. Surely from that point onwards Roger's station was in the March, yet he was at court in May 1260 and again in July. On 17 July Builth fell into Llywelyn's hands. This created a scandal and the king issued a letter patent which said that both he and Edward (Edward in his father's presence at Westminster) had exonerated Roger from all blame. The letter went on to explain that Roger had been at Westminster only because summoned to parliament to treat with the king and council on the urgent affairs of the realm.[56] Just how contentious this letter was, is shown by a remarkable note about it on

---

[52] *Rotuli de Oblatis et Finibus*, p. 209; *Pipe Roll 6 John*, ed. D. M. Stenton, Pipe Roll Soc., n.s., 18 (1940), p. 148.

[53] *Documents of the Baronial Movement*, pp. 156–7.

[54] In 1260 no charters were enrolled until after the king's return to England towards the end of April.

[55] Lloyd, *Wales*, ii, 722–3, 726. For Roger's role in negotiating the truces: *Foedera*, I, i, 387.

[56] It is a good example of the accuracy of the information given by the witness lists of royal charters that Roger attests on 18 July but not on the sixteenth. He had (according to the statement in a letter patent) arrived at Westminster on 17 July: *Foedera*, I, i, 398 (*Cal. Patent Rolls 1258–65*, p. 85).

the patent rolls. This stated that on 20 July, the day news arrived of Builth's fall, the letter had been read in the prior's chamber at Westminster before the earls of Gloucester, Norfolk, Hereford, and Warwick, together with Hugh Bigod, the justiciar, Philip Basset, John Mansel, and Robert Walerand, all members of the council of fifteen. They had accepted the letter and ordered its issue. No mention was made here of Edward and in fact his position, so he quickly claimed, was totally misrepresented. A further note had thus to be added to the roll. It explained that Edward had come before the magnates of the council and protested against 'the exoneration' (*remissio*) which the letter had given to Roger Mortimer.[57] Roger had arrived at Westminster on 17 July a few days after the case over Lechlade had recommenced before the council.[58] This was the session at which the previous plea over Longborough was inspected and it was decided to seek the text of Isabel's fine. It is difficult to believe that Roger's presence was unconnected with his prosecution of the suit. If so, it had contributed directly to the loss of Builth.

Roger's breach with the heir to the throne (who held all the king's lands in Wales) was a serious matter, although essentially (given Edward's limited influence in 1260) one for the future.[59] For the moment, in December 1260, Roger's chief concern was his failure to make any progress over the Lechlade case. That failure is not difficult to explain. One reason was political and centred on Richard of Cornwall. Although the king had taken over the defence, it was still Richard who would be the loser by Roger's victory. And presumably victory over Lechlade would carry victory over Longborough in its wake. Perhaps it might even begin to throw doubt on Richard's title to Oakham. More than once, Philip Basset appeared in court on Richard's behalf to say that it would be quite wrong for him now, having gone 'without day', to lose seisin 'without writ' when he had enjoyed it for so long. Whatever the rights and wrongs of that, the last thing the council wanted to do was to make an enemy of the king of the Romans.

The other problem lay in the very complexity of the case. Roger's attempt simply to recover seisin may reflect the fact that it was far better to defend one's right in possession than to seek one's right out of it. But it may also indicate Roger's doubts about whether he could indeed win an action over right in the first place. His case over seisin would have been stronger had he indeed been disseised by Richard of Cornwall, rather than by the king, but Roger did not persist with this claim. If, on the other hand, the king had disseised him it was far from clear that he had done so unjustly. A reasonable argument could be advanced for saying that Lechlade was fairly repossessed as an escheat of the

---

57 *Foedera*, I, i, 398 (*Cal. Patent Rolls 1258–65*, p. 85). See also *Documents of the Baronial Movement*, pp. 232–3, ch. 21[2]. The note also said that the letter had been sealed on the council's authority in the absence of the chancellor. It actually bears the date 30 July, not 20 July, which may reflect resistance to its issue.
58 It came before the council on the quindene of John the Baptist (8 July).
59 For Edward in these years, see M. Prestwich, *Edward I* (London, 1987), ch. 2.

lands of the Normans. Inevitably here the case spilled over into questions of right. Roger's claim that Isabel *was* Hugh's heir, because the elder brother Henry might not be lord and heir at the same time, was a good one, but it was not conclusive. It had been overridden during the Longborough action in 1254, with the decision that Isabel was *not* Hugh's heir so long as Henry had heirs of his own. Since those heirs were in the faith of the king of France it followed that the manor was an escheat of the lands of the Normans. Unfortunately it is not clear on what grounds the lord and heir argument was rebutted in 1254. The reasons for the judgment are lost, as is much of Laurence del Brok's pleading.[60] Paul Brand, however, suggests to me that the thinking might have been along the following lines: the initial presumption would always be that the better right belonged to Henry as the elder brother. On the other hand he could indeed be prevented from inheriting by the lord and heir rule. In this particular case, however, while momentarily in possession before the rule came into operation, Henry would have forfeited as a result of having taken the French allegiance. His descendants thus remained the heirs (if in a state of forfeiture) because the stage at which they would have been disqualified by the lord and heir rule had never been reached.

In these circumstances a great deal depended on the terms of the fine Isabel had made with King John in 1204, after Hugh's death and Henry's defection, for seisin of Lechlade and Longborough. Roger, as we have seen, claimed that it gave her free tenement and fee as Hugh's heir. If so, Henry had clearly been cut out and it was game set and match to the Mortimers. But in fact King John had been careful not to commit himself. He had given Isabel the manors 'which were of Hugh de Ferrers her brother of the gift of Walkelin his father of whom she is the heir, as she says, provided she stands to right if anyone wishes to speak against her'.[61] 'As she says': John was making no acknowledgment of Isabel's right.[62]

The fact was that the outcome of ambiguous and important cases of this kind depended on political clout and Roger's clout, big though it was, was insufficient to knock out Richard of Cornwall. There was one other factor here. In bringing an action which in effect accused the king of unlawful disseisin Roger

---

[60] (KB 26/ 151, mm. 30, 30d, 31). Laurence referred to the result of the 1254 case in 1259 (Just 1/ 1188, m. 2) but did not go into details.

[61] *Rotuli de Oblatis et Finibus*, p. 209; *Pipe Roll 6 John*, p. 148. John's acceptance of the fine should be seen in the context of a series of favours to Isabel's husband, Roger Mortimer, around this time: see Crump, 'The Mortimers', pp. 121–2.

[62] The fine, on the other hand, did not explicitly support the king's line that Isabel only held for life. For royal letters in 1235 which recognized that Isabel held both Lechlade *and* Oakham in hereditary right, see *Close Rolls 1234–7*, p. 102 (see also *Book of Fees*, i, 50). However Isabel and Roger Mortimer had offered 700 marks simply 'to have the manor of Oakham' (*Rotuli de Oblatis et Finibus*, pp. 398–9, 416). The issue was not much affected by the question of whether Lechlade was held from the Ferrers or the king. An investigation by the Exchequer ordered in December 1260 seemed to come down in favour of Ferrers' overlordship. Even if that was indeed the case, however, the manor would still have come into the king's hands as 'lands of the Normans'.

was very much on his own. Henry had denied and delayed justice but he had not, during his personal rule, committed the blatant disseisins which (so it was believed) had disfigured Angevin governance before 1215 and his own in 1232–33. In 1215 or 1234 Roger would have been supported by many others with similar grievances. The issue of disseisin *per voluntatem regis* was highly live. Now no great issue of royal conduct seemed to be raised by his case, especially when the rights and wrongs of the matter were so hard to sort out.

In December 1260, therefore, Roger Mortimer cut a rather lonely figure. He had been disowned by the Lord Edward, obstructed by Richard of Cornwall, and let down by his colleagues on the council, however much they had supported him over Builth. His loyalty, as the king prepared his bid to recover power, was very much up for grabs. The king made at least some effort to grab it. On 14 December he granted robes to Roger and some other councillors as members of the royal household.[63] The council grabbed more decisively. On 28 December, in what was its last recorded act, it commissioned an inquiry into whether Roger had been in seisin of Lechlade by Isabel's gift and 'as his right and inheritance as her grandson and right heir as he says'.[64] This was to be carried out by jurors of the county of Gloucester, meeting at Cirencester, and the results were to be returned to the council on 23 February. There had clearly been a huge argument over this inquiry. The letter which set it up was attested not by the king but by the justiciar Hugh Despenser. In the record of the Lechlade case the names of the presiding judges (Robert de Brus and William of Englefield) and when and where they were to meet were written over erasures.[65] The inquiry did not guarantee Roger victory but it took him a long way in that direction. After all, the jury was clearly being invited to say that he was the right heir and thus that the manor was not an escheat of the lands of the Normans.[66] Richard of Cornwall, on the other hand, who had been invited to attend the inquiry, was evidently furious, and he was now at court, masterminding his brother's bid for freedom. On 20 January, therefore, by which time the council's control had disintegrated, a fresh order was sent to the judges: they were to proceed in such a way that the king incurred 'no damage or disinheritance for the king does not remember that the inquiry proceeded from him or by his order'.[67] This was to cut Roger adrift as far as the court was concerned (in fact as far as is known the inquiry never took place), and adrift he seems to have been throughout the year. In July 1261, as part of the changes designed to secure royal control of local government, he was removed as castellan of Hereford and he waited till the last possible

---

63 *Close Rolls 1259–61*, p. 317. For earlier efforts by one side or the other to conciliate Roger, see *Cal. Liberate Rolls 1251–60*, p. 504; *Close Rolls 1259–61*, p. 306; *Cal. Patent Rolls 1258–66*, p. 86 although the annual fee mentioned was never paid.

64 *Cal. Patent Roll 1258–66*, p. 181.

65 Just 1/ 1188, m. 2d.

66 Lechlade was within the abbot of Cirencester's liberty of Cirencester, a liberty with return of writs: Just 1/ 1188, m. 1.

67 *Cal. Patent Rolls 1258–66*, p. 181. The note indicating that the original commission was authorized by the council was also apparently added at this time: C 66/76, m. 21d.

moment in December 1261 before accepting the Treaty of Kingston which in effect restored the king to power.[68]

We now come to the most crucial and puzzling period of Roger's career. On 16 December 1261 he was listed with Simon de Montfort and several others who would prove Montfortian stalwarts (Hugh Despenser, Henry Hastings, John fitz John, Nicholas Seagrave, and Geoffrey de Lucy) amongst those who had not yet put their seals to the Treaty of Kingston. This does not prove that Roger was part of Montfort's affinity (for Roger Bigod, earl of Norfolk, who certainly was not was also on the list) but it does suggest that in 1261 they had taken the same political stance.[69] Yet, as we have said, when Montfort returned to England in April 1263, Roger stood aside and by the autumn was firmly in the royal camp. This was despite the fact that, thanks in part to government impotence, Roger had suffered fresh blows in Wales: in December 1262 an uprising supported by Llywelyn had destroyed his hold of Maelienydd.[70] It was also despite the fact that many of those who sponsored Montfort's return were former members of Edward's affinity, who had quarrelled with their lord, several of them indeed Marcher barons. Mortimer's experience was not dissimilar. If never part of Edward's inner circle (he was not listed as one of the prince's followers in the agreement with the earl of Gloucester in March 1259), he had certainly enjoyed the prince's favour and had then been cast out.[71] If in 1263 he had thrown in his lot with such Marcher rebels as Roger Clifford and Hamo Lestrange (both ex-Edwardians) and also with John fitz Alan, whose son had married Roger's daughter, it would not have seemed surprising.[72] Yet he did not. How can we explain it? It is here that I would like to pull some Lechlade rabbit out of the hat and I will say at once that I cannot do so, or not directly. It is true that in June 1262 the king promised to give Roger justice over Lechlade without delay.[73] But Roger knew only too well the value of such promises and nothing seems to have come of this one.

I would suggest, therefore, that there is another although in some ways related explanation for Roger's conduct and it is this. John Maddicott has rightly drawn attention to how deeply Henry III resented the grants to Simon de Mont-

[68] *Ibid.*, p. 163.

[69] *Close Rolls 1261–4*, p. 95.

[70] *Annales Cambriae*, p. 100; *Brut*, pp. 112, 210.

[71] For Edward's grant of rights in Elvael to Roger in 1258, see *Cal. Charter Rolls 1226–57*, p. 7. He had also, of course, entrusted him with Builth. On the other hand Roger does not attest a charter of Edward until March 1264. I am grateful to Robin Studd for allowing me to use his calendar of the witness lists to the Lord Edward's charters.

[72] For the marriage contract (made in 1260) between Roger and fitz Alan, see CP 25(1) 283/15/378.

[73] *Cal. Patent Rolls 1258–66*, p. 215. In return for this promise Roger agreed to stand to right against anyone who wished to accuse him of trespass. Probably this was related to his intervention in 1262 in the quarrel between John de Braose and Walter of Clifford over Corfton castle just north of Ludlow when he had seised the castle briefly for himself: *ibid.*, pp. 175, 231, 211.

fort of several royal manors in 1259.[74] There are good reasons for suspecting that they came to be resented equally deeply by Roger Mortimer. Three of the manors in question were Lugwardine, Marden, and Dilwyn. Worth together an annual £123, these lay between Hereford (where Roger had been constable in 1260–61) and Wigmore.[75] They were surrounded by manors held by Roger himself and his tenants.[76] They were thus right in the middle of Roger's sphere of rule. Roger must have feared the impact which the sudden arrival of such a powerful and charismatic figure as Montfort would have in the region. Would the great earl prise away Roger's tenants and do so the more easily perhaps since some held not from the honour of Wigmore but from the newly acquired honour of Radnor?[77] If Roger had such fears they proved, as we shall see, well justified. There was also another reason for Roger's resentment: jealousy. After all here was Montfort, as early as May 1259, securing a settlement of his grievances (the manors were to fulfil the king's promise to convert Eleanor de Montfort's *maritagium* into land). He had got his way, moreover, both by blackmail, refusing otherwise to make the renunciations required by the Treaty of Paris, and in contravention of the councillor's oath not to consent to alienations of the royal demesne.[78] Roger himself as a member of the council (for the concessions were made with the council's consent) had witnessed the charters making the grants to Montfort. Yet he himself had been forced to go on campaigning for another year-and-a-half over Lechlade and had still got nowhere. He had accepted, however reluctantly, the council's decision to do something for Montfort. But Montfort and the council had done nothing in return for him.[79]

It is true, of course, that these feelings had not prevented Roger standing on the same side as Montfort in 1261. But in 1261 Montfort had still been only one of several great baronial leaders: the earls of Gloucester and Norfolk also resisted Henry's attempt to overthrow the Provisions. In 1263 it was quite different. Everyone recognized that Montfort was now in charge. If Roger joined up he must submit to the great earl's leadership. It was that which he could not stomach. Roger, therefore, stood aside and by October when he was at

---

74 Maddicott, *Simon de Montfort*, pp. 188–90.
75 *Cal. Charter Rolls 1257–1300*, pp. 18, 20, 34–5, 46, 52–3, 98–9.
76 *Book of Fees*, ii, 814.
77 *Ibid.*, ii, 800, 802, 804, 805, 806, 1481.
78 *Documents of the Baronial Movement*, pp. 196–9, chaps. 9–11 where Simon's replies to the accusations are also found.
79 Another explanation of Roger's stance might be that he was alarmed by Montfort's growing links with Llywelyn. But that alliance was not really concluded until early 1264 and it did not prevent another Marcher baron, Humphrey de Bohun junior (lord of Brecon), who had also suffered at Llywelyn's hands, from remaining a Montfortian. See *The Chronicle of William de Rishanger of the Barons' Wars*, ed. J. O. Halliwell (Camden Soc., 1840), p. 20 and also *Cal. Patent Rolls 1258–66*, pp. 305–6 which shows that Roger, as late as 20 January 1264, was attempting to negotiate a truce with Llywelyn. In 1259 there had been friction between Roger and Humphrey over their respective shares of the Braose inheritance (*Cal. Patent Rolls 1258–66*, p. 13).

Windsor with the king (now free of Montfortian control) he had clearly rallied to the royal standard.[80] On 16 December he was one of the king's party who agreed to submit the quarrel to Louis IX's arbitration.[81] The great feud between Roger and Simon de Montfort was about to begin; it was a feud in which Lechlade returned to play a substantial supporting part. The precise date is uncertain but it was quite probably on 16 December, or a day or so later, that Henry III (at Windsor) gave Lugwardine, Marden, and Dilwyn to Roger Mortimer.[82] There was, of course, no possibility of peacefully enjoying the revenues. Rather, Roger's brief was to do exactly what he did do. As the Montfortians complained only a few days after the event, he invaded the manors with a considerable army, threshed the corn, collected the Christmas rent, carried off Montfort's chattels and extorted an oath of fealty from the tenants. At the same time he attacked the nearby lands and castle of Henry of Pembridge, one of his major Herefordshire tenants (of the honour of Radnor), who had deserted (as Roger would have seen it) to the Montfortians.[83] In all this, the king was getting in his revenge before Louis IX pronounced his verdict and commanded all sides to be at peace. He may also have hoped that the attack would prevent Montfort going to Amiens for the arbitration.[84] Roger, for his part, must have weighed carefully the consequences of his action. He could seize the bases of his hated rival but retaliation might be swift and brutal. Nor, it is clear from later events, was he being offered the manors on any kind of permanent basis. He was simply to have them during the war. Roger, therefore, needed support and reward. Accordingly, on 18 December 1263, he and his heirs were granted £100 a year from the farms of the royal manors of Norton and Bromsgrove in Worcestershire, this to last until the king provided land of equivalent value. In return, Roger issued a charter surrendering his rights in Lechlade.[85] The great case was over. The king had waited a long time before reaching a settlement. Both he and the reforming regime had paid dearly for their delay. But at least the king had found a time when his money was supremely well spent. Roger had emerged from the Lechlade case if not with total victory, then at least with a settlement very much to his advantage. Indeed the £100 a year was sufficient to compensate him for the loss of Lechlade and Longborough as well. Not surprisingly

---

[80] *Cal. Patent Rolls 1258–66*, p. 291.

[81] *Documents of the Baronial Movement*, pp. 282–3.

[82] *Annales Monastic*, iii, 226. For this and what follows, see Maddicott, *Simon de Montfort*, p. 257.

[83] *Documents of the Baronial Movement*, pp. 266–7 and 277 n. 14; *Book of Fees*, ii, 814. After the war Roger forced Henry to sell him Pembridge: Mortimer Cartulary: London Brit. Libr., MS Harley 1240, fol. 75.

[84] The Canterbury/Dover annals say that 'the barons of England' were unable to go to Amiens because of the Mortimer's war in the March: *The Historical Works of Gervase of Canterbury*, ed. W. Stubbs, 2 vols, RS 73 (1879–80), ii, 233. Montfort himself, however, was prevented from going by a broken leg.

[85] *Cal. Patent Rolls 1258–66*, pp. 302–3. If Lechlade ever returned to the king's hands it was be given to Roger while whatever he held in its place was to be returned to the king.

Roger plunged enthusiastically into his feud with Montfort and remained absolutely loyal for the rest of the war.[86]
    The remainder is briefly told. Early in 1264, as soon as the results of Louis's
arbitration were known, Montfort indeed took his revenge. He sealed an alliance
with Llywelyn and sent his sons Henry and Simon to the march with a large
army. They laid waste Roger's lands and sacked the castles of Radnor and
Wigmore.[87] In the process they probably insulted and maltreated Maud
Mortimer, who was quite probably in command of one of the castles, as she
certainly was later in 1265. Perhaps Maud defended Wigmore or Radnor with
the vigour her great-grandmother, Maud de Braose, had shown in defending
Painscastle in the 1190s, after which it was thenceforth named after her: Castle
Maud? Maud Mortimer was lady of Radnor in her own right. Throughout
Roger's life she may well have played an important part in family affairs. On 1
January 1253 she received a belt as a new year's present from Queen Eleanor.
Was she at court lobbying over the Lechlade case?[88] In nearly twenty years of
widowhood after Roger's death, Maud busied herself in the administration of
her estates. Perhaps she was hardened by memories of her ancestors: her father
had been hung for an affair with Llywelyn's wife; her great-grandmother, the
fabled Maud, had been starved to death by King John in the dungeons of
Windsor castle. Maud Mortimer was a dangerous woman to offend. It was all
the more extraordinary therefore that Montfort should release Roger after the
battle of Lewes. Roger had fought the battle alongside Edward and had ended
the day with the prince and the king in the priory, surrounded by Montfort's
forces. As the price for Henry and Edward's surrender, Montfort had agreed that
Roger and other Marchers should go free. He doubtless calculated that with the
king and his son in captivity, Roger would not dare cause trouble. But in fact, as
Roger saw quite well, the threat to harm the royal captives was one which could

---

86 The precise date of Roger's attack on Montfort's manors is unclear. The Dunstable annals
    (*Annales Monastici*, iii, 226) imply that it took place before the national quarrel was
    referred to Louis (on 16 December). However Roger was at Dover with the king on 3
    December (*Gervase of Canterbury*, ii, 229) and was probably at Windsor on 16 Decem-
    ber. (That is the date of the letter which he sealed referring the quarrel to Louis IX: *Docu-
    ments of the Baronial Movement*, pp. 282–4). Both the Canterbury/Dover annals and the
    baronial *Gravamina* prepared for Louis state that Roger's attack was in breach of the
    agreement over arbitration, that is it was later than 16 December: *Gervase of Canterbury*,
    ii, 232; *Documents of the Baronial Movement*, pp. 266–7. My own view is that Roger left
    Windsor as soon as the deal over Lechlade was finalized on 18 December and hurried to
    the March. The attack on Montfort's manors thus took place around Christmas. This
    would have left time for the details to be included at the end of the baronial *Gravamina*. It
    was not till 31 December that the Montfortians (in London) appointed proctors to repre-
    sent them at Amiens (*The Chronicle of Rishanger*, pp. 122–3). The king himself did not
    leave England till 2 January: *Gervase of Canterbury*, ii, 232.
87 John Giffard was also involved in the attack on Roger: *Annales Monastici*, i, 179; iii, 227;
    Flores Historiarum, ed. H. R. Luard, 3 vols, RS 95 (1890), ii, 486; *Gervase of Canterbury*,
    ii, 233; Maddicott, *Simon de Montfort*, pp. 263–4; F. M. Powicke, *Henry III and The Lord
    Edward* (Oxford, 1947), p. 456 n. 2.
88 E 101/ 349/ 13. I owe this reference to Margaret Howell.

not be carried out. Thus, as we saw briefly at the start of this discussion, Roger
was left free to work Montfort's downfall. Maud Mortimer herself was more
than the passive recipient of Montfort's head. When Edward escaped from
Hereford it was she who was in command at Wigmore. As Robert of Gloucester
put it:

> What need of a long tale? He escaped thus,
> And to the castle of Wigmore the way soon he took.
> There was joy and mirth enough when he came thither,
> With the lady of the castle, dame Maud de Mortimer.
> Soon the word was sent to her lord Sir Roger . . . .[89]

Between 1263 and 1265 Roger Mortimer had proved to Edward both his
absolute fidelity and his fighting qualities. He was indeed, as Wykes put it, a
miles robustissimus.[90] In 1270 Edward appointed Roger to the small committee
which was to look after his affairs during his crusade. When Roger died in the
middle of the second Welsh war in 1282, Edward wrote an emotional letter to
his son:

> As often as the king ponders over the death [of Roger], he is disturbed and
> mourns the more his valour and fidelity; and his long and praiseworthy
> services to the late king and himself recur frequently and spontaneously to
> his memory. As it is certain that none can escape death, the king is consoled
> and [Roger's son] ought to be consoled on his part because there is a good
> hope that his father, after the trials of this life, has now a better state than he
> had.[91]

Not surprisingly, given this record of valour and fidelity, Roger reaped his
reward. After the first Welsh war of 1277, in which he played a notable part,
Edward granted him in hereditary right Kerry, Cydewain, and Llywelyn's castle
at Dolforwyn.[92] Roger's hold of Maelienydd and Gwerthrynion were also now
assured. In England Roger did not retain Lugwardine, Marden, and Dilwyn.
After the war they were granted by royal charter to Edmund, Henry III's second
son.[93] That, however, gave Roger his chance. On 1 August 1270 Edmund sold
Marden to Roger and his heirs for 1000 marks cash down. Three days later, as
he was about to set out on his crusade, Edward confirmed the gift. So did his
father Henry III.[94] Thus Roger, despite all the restrictions on alienation of the
royal demesne, had prised a royal manor from the crown, something even
Montfort had failed to do since he had only held Marden and the rest 'in

[89] *Metrical Chronicle of Robert of Gloucester*, ii, 757–8; for the translation, see J. Stevenson,
The Church Historians of England, 5 vols (London, 1853–58), v/i, 371.
[90] *Annales Monastici*, iv, 446.
[91] *Cal. of Various Chancery Rolls 1277–1326* (London, 1912), p. 257.
[92] *Cal. Charter Rolls 1257–1300*, p. 211.
[93] *Cal. Patent Rolls 1258–66*, p. 529; *Rotuli Hundredorum*, 2 vols (Record Com., 1812, 1818), i, 185.
[94] Mortimer Cartulary: London Brit. Libr., MS Harley 1240, fol. 56. Edmund made his own grant on 1 August. The Mortimers were to hold the manor directly from the crown.

tenancy'.[95] Roger and his successors also retained the £100 a year from the farms of Norton and Bromsgrove, which had been granted as compensation for the loss of Lechlade. In practice they may have acted as lords of the manors. Finally in 1317 they were given them by Edward II in hereditary right in return for a rent of £10 a year.[96]

There was even a sequel to the Mortimer tenure of Lechlade itself. Here Richard of Cornwall was no absentee landlord.[97] Indeed he turned Isabel Mortimer's hospital into a small Augustinian priory. Eventually, however, his son by Sanchia, Edmund, earl of Cornwall, granted both Lechlade and Longborough to Hailes abbey,[98] only then for the abbot and convent (in 1318) to give Lechlade to the royal favourite, the elder Hugh Despenser, in return for a grant of land elsewhere. One is bound to wonder whether this was a move in the great feud between the Despensers and the Mortimers which had begun with the death of Hugh's father at the battle of Evesham. If so, the Mortimers had their revenge. After the executions of Hugh Despenser and the next tenant, Edmund earl of Kent, Roger Mortimer, earl of March, secured a grant of Lechlade (and other earldom of Kent properties) for Geoffrey Mortimer, one of his younger sons. That grant, of course, did not survive Roger's fall a few months later in 1330. Lechlade passed back to the Kents where it stayed for the rest of the century.[99] But at least the Mortimers had not given up easily.

The story of Roger Mortimer has several points of interest. It shows the importance of women as heiresses and hints at the role which they could play as wives and widows. It shows how the policies of a Marcher baron could be influenced by interests outside the March. And it shows the importance of property disputes in determining political allegiances. To say that Roger Mortimer was uninfluenced by the political ideas and idealisms which lit up the period of reform and rebellion may be unfair.[100] It is conceivable that his own sense of injustice gave him for a while a wider commitment to a movement which was designed to give justice to everyone. Yet in the end (much more clearly than with Montfort) it is difficult not to think that Roger's allegiance was up for sale to the highest bidder. That leaves open some intriguing possibilities. If the council, with Montfort in the lead, had secured Lechlade for Roger, might he not have sided with the great earl in 1263 rather than against him? If so the history of the next few years would have been very different.

95 On 20 June 1265 (when he was at Hereford) Montfort had actually returned the manors to the sheriff who was to answer for the issues at the Exchequer *Cal. Patent Rolls 1258–65*, p. 434.

96 *Victoria County History of Worcestershire*, 4 vols (London, 1901–24), iii, 22, 182; *Cal. Charter Rolls 1300–1326*, p. 366. The grant was to a younger son (John) of Roger Mortimer, the future earl of March.

97 I owe this point to Margaret Howell.

98 *Cal. Charter Roll 1257–1300*, p. 349; *Cal. Charter Rolls 1300–1326*, p. 2. A rent of 100 marks a year had to be paid for Lechlade, however.

99 *Cal. Patent Rolls 1317–21*, p. 212; *Cal. Charter Rolls 1327–41*, pp. 4, 176; *Cal. Inq. Post Mortem*, x (London, 1921), 42. I am grateful to Nigel Saul for helping me on this point.

100 See Maddicott, *Simon de Montfort*, pp. 166–70, 251–6.

11

King Magnus and his Liegemen's 'Hirdskrå': A Portrait of the Norwegian Nobility in the 1270s

Steinar Imsen

1. Hirdskrå and nobility

The composite noun *hirdskrå* is made up of Old Norse *hirð* and *skrá*. The term *hird* in the Hirdskrå itself, like the almost contemporary *Konungs skuggsiá* (the King's Mirror), was believed to derive from the Old Norse *hirða*, which means to guard, watch over, or herd. But this is wrong. Norse *hirð* is borrowed from Anglo-Saxon *hîred* or *hîrd*, which means household, retinue, brotherhood, or company.[1] Despite the false etymology, Old Norse *hirð* in fact corresponds to this original meaning of the word, since it refers partly to the royal retinue or the king's liegemen as a group, partly to the royal household or court.[2]

The noun *skrá* means parchment or book, and to *skrá* or to *skrásettia* means to put on parchment or enter in a book. *Hirdskrå* then can be understood as a document or book containing written customs, by-laws, and statutes concerning the king's liegemen and the royal household. Such a codex was compiled during the reign of Magnus Håkonsson (1263–80), and should be seen as part of a comprehensive project of legislation, which comprised a common civil code for the whole realm, 'the Landlaw' (1274), and a codex for the city of Bergen (1276) that soon afterwards was also adopted in Trondheim, Oslo, and Tønsberg. King Magnus's hirdskrå, the Hirdskrå as we call it today, must have been finished before August 1277, probably as early as the summer of 1274.

According to the Hirdskrå itself, there was already an older, now lost, law-

---

[1] H. Falk and A. Torp, *Etymologisk ordbok over det norske og danske Sprog* (Facsimile edn: Oslo, 1991); J. R. Clark Hall, *A Concise Anglo-Saxon Dictionary*, 4th edn (Cambridge, 1975); cf. L. Hamre, 'Hird', *Kulturhistorisk Leksikon for nordisk Middelalder* (*KLNM*), vi (Copenhagen, 1961) col. 568.

[2] The term and institution of *hird* appear in Danish sources as well, most frequently in documents before 1200. Thereafter *hof* (court/household) and *herremænd* (pl., lat. *homines dominorum*), probably influenced by German usage, are substituted for *hird* and *hirdmen*, i.e. the members of the hird. By the end of the thirteenth century the Danish *herremænd* had been turned into a real noble class. In Sweden too there are references to *hird* in the sources from the early Middle Ages, but it is too poorly documented to allow us to say much about it: Herluf Nielsen, 'Hird (Danmark)', *KLNM*, vi, cols 577ff.; cf. N. Lund, *Lið, leding og landeværn* (Roskilde, 1996), pp. 26, 62, 221f., 231, 237, 242, 288.

code for the royal hird, which historians associate with the reigns of King Sverre (1177–1202) and his grandson Håkon IV Håkonsson (1217–63), King Magnus's father. This former *hirdskrå* was certainly embodied entirely or in part in King Magnus's compilation, which contains *hird*-custom dating back at least to the eleventh century.[3] The Hirdskrå has been transmitted in nine almost complete versions from the fourteenth century, most of them from the first half of the century. In addition we have many fragments, some dating back to the end of the thirteenth century, and later copies and translations.[4]

The socio-juridical concept 'nobility' is not to be found in Old Norse legal terminology.[5] The German concept of *Adel* was introduced to Scandinavia around 1520, and a noble estate (*adelsstand*) was established in Norway only in the second half of the sixteenth century. It is somewhat anachronistic therefore to talk about a Norwegian nobility in the Middle Ages. Nevertheless we can identify a group of men who may be distinguished from the rest of society by being called the king's *håndgangne menn*, which literally means 'men who have gone to the hands of the king'. Henceforth I will refer to them as liegemen. We should note that the concept of vassalage, like nobility, is not to be found in Norwegian laws from the Central Middle Ages, or in other relevant contemporary sources. The royal liegemen constituted what I choose to call a Norwegian nobility in the Middle Ages. Socially they were rather heterogeneous, but being members of the same exclusive community they shared some common rights and filled some common functions in society.

The Hirdskrå is a main source for our knowledge of the Norwegian hird in the thirteenth century. Even though in many respects it depicts an ideal, and therefore should be treated with caution, Norwegian historians agree that it is a treasure-chest of information about the role and position of the Norwegian nobility. By focusing on the Hirdskrå I intend to highlight some structural and functional aspects of the class of royal liegemen in Norway in the last decades of the thirteenth century: how they were organized, their internal relations, and their relationships with king and kingdom.

---

[3] According to tradition King Olav Haraldsson (1015–30), Norway's national saint, was the author of the very first hirdskrå, on which later versions were based. Likewise the Danish *Lex Castrensis* 'Vederloven', which is a parallel to the Norwegian hirdskrå, and which was written down around 1200, has been ascribed to King Olav's rival Cnut (*Den danske rigslovgivning indtil 1400* [Copenhagen, 1971], i, 2; cf. *ibid.*, pp. 3ff, 5ff., 25ff., 34ff). However we should treat the traditions about the origin of these law-codes with caution. Our Hirdskrå as well as the Danish *Lex Castrensis* are certainly products of the political situation and systems in Scandinavia in the Central Middle Ages.

[4] All references here are to the edition in *Norges gamle Love* (*NglL*: Christiania and Oslo), ii (1848), 387–450.

[5] The word *nobiliores* occurs twice in an agreement (*compositio*) from 1273–1277 between King Magnus and Archbishop John the Red, but it is used in a very general sense, meaning the best and wisest men of the realm (*NglL*, ii, 458, 463, cf. *ibid.*, p. 470).

2. The members of the royal hird

The hird was organized in corporations, so-called *lǫguneyti* (n.), that is, literally speaking, 'law-communities' or 'law-fellowships', the members of which were called *lǫgunautr* (m.), that is fellows sharing the same rights and duties. There were three such corporations, which to some degree differed with regard to rank, rights, and service/duties. The so-called *hirðmen*, which I will refer to as the hirdmen proper, constituted the main corporation and ranked above the other two corporations, called *gestir* (guests), and the *kertisveinar*. However the hirdmen proper were not a homogeneous group, but were divided by rank, privileges, and seniority. At the top was an élite group called *hirðstiorar*, which means hird-leaders.

Next to duke and earl, which ranked above all other liegemen, we find the so-called *lendmen*.[6] Their number has been estimated to between 12 and 15 in the 1270s.[7] Chapter 18 in the Hirdskrå says 'the king shall lead the lendman to the highest seat of dignity in the hird'. A new lendman was automatically regarded as a royal councillor. The name lendman (ON, *lendr maðr*) means a man who has been granted (royal) land. The Hirdskrå stipulates a lendman's benefice (ON, *veizla*, f.) to an annual income of 15 marks silver, which indeed was not an impressive income. The Old Norse *veizla* means contribution or payment, for which I will use the English term benefice. The Latin *feudum* never occurs in Norwegian legal or administrative sources from the Central Middle Ages, but the German *len* was introduced during the second half of the thirteenth century in Norwegian administrative terminology. *Lén* in Old Norse denotes the economic output of the local royal office called *sysla* (f.), the holder of which is called *syslumaðr* (m.). I have not observed *len* used synonymously with the king's grant of *veizla* to his liegemen.[8]

Among the members of the hird the lendmen alone had title to royal benefice by virtue of dignity. The other hirdmen were paid for their service. The lendmen were also granted the right to keep an armed bodyguard of forty men, called housecarls, 'to protect themselves and help the king'. Like the other members of the hird they also enjoyed the privilege to be judged by their peers (*privilegium fori*), but in cases of treason only. Although the dignity of lendman was not hereditary, at least in principle, it seems to have circulated among the members of an exclusive group of outstanding families, which almost a century after the

---

6 Dukes however were appointed only twice in Norway during the Middle Ages, and apart from Orkney, earls are found in mainland Norway rather exceptionally. According to the Hirdskrå, dukes and earls might be a threat to the unity of the Kingdom, and the king is warned against appointing earls. The dignity of duke was reserved for members of the royal family.

7 G. Storm, 'Om Lendermandsklassens Talrighed i 12. og 13. Aarhundrede', *Historisk Tidsskrift*, viii (1884), 129–88.

8 Cf. E. Hertzberg, *Lén og veizla i Norges sagatid* (Göttingen, 1873), pp. 310–18. There was also an older concept *lán* in Norwegian legal terminology, related to the thirteenth- to sixteenth-century *len*, which is not relevant to our problem (*NglL*, v, 377; cf. p. 396).

title of lendman had been abolished still made up the core of the Norwegian nobility.

From 1277 the lendmen obtained the right to call themselves barons, and to be addressed as *herra*. However the new title never replaced the older lendman title. Their dignity was removed by a royal decree of 1308. Norwegian historians have discussed whether the dignity of lendmen vanished as a result of the royal decision of 1308 or if it was caused by structural changes within the Norwegian nobility at the beginning of the fourteenth century. We cannot know for certain, but during King Håkon V's reign (1299–1319) the traditional ranks among the hirdmen proper were substituted by a two-level system: knights and squires.[9] By 1350 the corporations of guests and kertisveins had disappeared too. This rather late formal restructuring of the Norwegian nobility gave it an appearance much closer to the situation in Sweden and Denmark. We should notice the rather archaic or traditional character of the Norwegian nobility in the thirteenth and early fourteenth centuries.

The holders of hird-offices like chancellor, stallar (ON, *stallari*, Anglo-Saxon, *steallare*), and merkesman (ON, *merkismaðr*) enjoyed the same rights as lendmen, even though they might be recruited outside their exclusive circle (cc. 21–3). The chancellor, who also was included among the hird-leaders, enjoyed lendman's rights, but his benefice of 15 marks silver was to be paid from administrative fees, defining his status as civil servant rather than vassal.

Next in rank after lendmen, stallar, merkesman, and chancellor came the so-called 'skutilsveins' (ON, *skutilsveinn*, m., cc. 24–5), which is derived from Anglo-Saxon *scutel* (a dish). *Skutilsvein* denotes a (young) man who serves at the table. The Hirdskrå does not say anything explicitly about their rights. They did not have title to royal benefices or a seat in the king's council; neither were they allowed to keep housecarls. But according to the Hirdskrå, the king should consult them at the appointment of 'drottsete' (ON, *dróttseti*, m.) and 'munnskjenk' (ON, *skenkjari*, m.), who were responsible for provisions of food and drink to hird and royal household respectively. And of course the skutilsveins were not excluded from appointment to the highest offices in the hird, at least not in principle. Together with the lendmen and the hird-officers the skutilsveins formed what was called the leading segment of the hird, the so-called *hirðstiorar* (hird-leaders). In 1277 the skutilsveins obtained the title of 'ridder' (knight) and, like the lendmen, the right to be addressed as 'herra'.[10] After the restructuring of the Norwegian nobility in the first decades of the fourteenth century, the knights constituted the highest level among the king's liegemen.

Below the level of the hird-leaders we find the ordinary hirdmen. Little is

9 *NglL*, iii, no. 25. O. J. Benedictow, 'Konge, hird og retterboten av 17. Juni 1308', *Historisk Tidsskrift*, li (1972); A. Holmsen, 'Kongens rett, kongens makt og kongebrevet av 17/6 1308', *ibid.*; L.Hamre, 'Litt omkring Håkon Vs hirdskipan 17. juni 1308', *Historisk Tidsskrift*, lxxii (1993).

10 *Islandske annaler indtil 1578*, ed. G. Storm (Christiania, 1888), pp. 29, 50, 69, 140, 195, 259.

said about their rights, but all the more about their service and duties (cc. 27–42). As already mentioned, nobody below the rank of lendmen was entitled to royal benefice, but the text suggests that loyal hirdmen, of whatever rank, could expect royal grants, subsidies, and gifts. Moreover membership of the hird gave exclusive right to royal office, regardless of rank, and this right was probably the most important privilege of the hirdmen. Of course, to belong to the hird must in itself have been prestigious, especially for minor hirdmen out in the rural communities. The status of hirdman certainly gave them precedence over their fellow farmers.

Tax exemption is not mentioned at all in the Hirdskrå. But from the agreement between King Magnus and Archbishop Jon the Red in 1277, we know that lendmen and skutilsveins had been granted tax exemption for themselves and two members of their household. All other members of the hird, guests and kertisveins included, enjoyed freedom from tax for themselves together with one member of their household, just like the ordinary parish clergy. In practice, tax exemption for ordinary hirdmen was restricted only to the farm on which they lived.[11] Compared with their colleagues in Denmark and Sweden, who had obtained extensive tax exemptions at about this time, the Norwegian nobility enjoyed only symbolic immunity.[12]

With regard to *privilegium fori*, all disputes and feuds between hirdmen could be treated at the hird-assembly (ON, *hirðstefna*, f.) or by the king himself. Matters concerning discipline were also to be treated in the *forum internum* and, as already noted, in cases of treason, members of the hird were granted the right to be judged by their peers (*judicium parium*, cc. 20, 40, 42). However the main rule was that '. . . all cases which the king's liegemen had to defend in local society, had to be tried at the local court, by a local assize, and according to the law of the land'. Documents from the fourteenth and fifteenth centuries bear witness to complete concordance of principle and practice at this point. Norwegian nobility enjoyed only limited jurisdictional privileges, which were almost as symbolic as their tax exemptions.

As already said, guests and kertisveins constituted separate corporations in the hird (cc. 42–7). The guests were the king's bodyguard and police. The Hirdskrå ironically states that 'They are called guests because they have a lot of places to visit where they don't feel welcome' (c. 43). Thus they fulfilled the functions of the original hirdmen, the housecarls of King Cnut and King Olav Haraldsson in the early eleventh century, and which are very well documented in older Scandinavian and English sources.[13] In King Magnus's time, only the lendmen's followers were called housecarls.

The guests were also to have a ship of their own, which was to sail close to

---

11 *NgIL*, ii, 472. Cf. K. Helle, *Norge blir en stat 1130–1319* (Oslo, Bergen, and Tromsø, 1974), p. 202; and A. Holmsen, *Nye studier i gammel historie* (Oslo, Bergen, and Tromsø, 1976), p. 164.

12 Jerker Rosén, 'Frälse', *KLNM*, iv (Copenhagen, 1959), cols 670ff.

13 C. Warren Hollister, *Anglo-Saxon Military Institutions on the Eve of the Norman Con-

the king's in the royal flotilla, and in spite of inferior rank the Hirdskrå says that they should 'share duties and respect with the other members of the hird'.

The kertisveins were to perform the service of pages, and according to the Hirdskrå they were to be recruited among the 'better and respectable families'. Their name is derived from Old Norse *kerti* (n.), that is 'candle' or 'torch', which they should tend at the royal table. Like the skutilsveins, the kertisveins' prime duty was to serve at the table, and like the guests they were to have their own ship in the royal flotilla, and 'share all duties and respect within the hird' as all other hirdmen.

The Hirdskrå does not say anything explicitly about the social background of the members of the hird, though what is said about the kertisveins would seem to indicate recruitment of young men to this service from 'better families'. The most prominent members of the hird were probably more or less born into royal service, even though membership in principle was not hereditary. The king alone could grant membership in the hird, which was given on an individual basis. In addition to those few who were predestined to become royal liegemen, the majority of ordinary hird-members were probably recruited among the richest and most respected farmers. Thus the royal hird was based on a relatively broad segment of what we might call a Norwegian yeomanry–gentry, with a rather fluid line of demarcation to the ordinary farmers. This is very well documented in the sources from the beginning of the fourteenth century, and the King's Mirror from about 1250 takes for granted that better off farmers should aspire to royal service and membership in the hird.

3. The hird as guild or brotherhood

Even though the hird was split into corporations and segregated by rank and seniority, all its members had one thing in common: they were royal liegemen. It was their exclusive relationship to the king which gave them what we might call noble status. They were not like ordinary people, which in Old Norse are called *almugi* (m.), that is 'common men', or *þegn* (m.), which means a free subject. Thus the Hirdskrå already in its opening states: 'Now, since the people owe their king obedience, loyalty, and devotion to duty, this holds even more for us who are his liegemen, and have been elected among our countrymen to guard the king and render service in person.' It was the hirdmen's special relationship to the king and their duty to serve him which justified their privileges and position. On the other hand, the distinction between noble and non-noble may have been much less sharp in Norway than in most other European countries since noble privileges were rather modest compared to the neighbouring countries, and since the majority of the hirdmen came from the better off among the farmers. Access to royal service seems to have been fairly open in Norway in

quest (Oxford, 1962), pp. 12–18. N. Hooper, 'The Housecarls in England in the Eleventh Century', *Anglo Saxon Studies*, vii (1984). Cf. Helle, *Norge blir*, p. 210.

the thirteenth century, partly as a consequence of the civil wars, which lasted about a century from 1130 onwards. An outsider from the Faroe Islands, Sverre, and his followers, the so-called birchlegs, were victorious in the end, and King Sverre's male descendants ruled Norway until 1319. Especially during Sverre's and the first decades of his grandson Håkon IV's reigns, many newcomers entered royal service. Such 'upstarts' even replaced some of the old lendman-families during the first years of King Sverre's reign.

The act of *håndgang* was necessary to enter the hird, therefore all liegemen whatever their rank were referred to as the king's *håndgangne menn* (ON, *handgenginn men*). Norwegian *hånd* means hand. Central elements in this act were the king's hands and the royal sword. Everybody in the hird, except the kertisveins, are also referred to as royal swordkeepers (ON, *sverðtakari*, m., c. 31, cf. cc. 11, 12, 16, 20, 27, 43, 47). Likewise guests were to swear the same oath of fealty as the hirdmen proper. As far as I can see, the Norwegian act of *håndgang* was an ordinary act of homage, which constituted the special personal tie between the individual member of the hird and his lord, the king. However it was also framed by a ceremony, which underlined the newcomer's entrance into a fraternity as well. (The word *hirðbróðir* [hird-brother] occurs several times.) The king is depicted as patron and leader of a brotherhood, in which all relationships are conditional on each member's relation to him. The Hirdskrå is permeated with guild analogies. The common drinking, the metaphors of drinking, the ceremonies of drinking, the common table, the seats around the table, the etiquette of feasting, the equipment for drinking and eating, all this remind us constantly of the guild. The organization of hird and service in the hird also underline this. I have already explained Old Norse *skutilsvein* and *kertisvein*, which are associated with service at the royal table. The skutilsveins also had a special relation to the drottsete and the munnskjenk, who were responsible for provisioning the royal household and the serving of food and drink at the common table. Thus the Hirdskrå seems to take for granted that these hird-offices should be reserved for skutilsveins.

The symbolic table-service of the skutilsveins is also reflected in their installation ceremony, which was to take place after the king had finished his meal, but before he left the table. The candidate would then be led to the king's seat, either by the drottsete or by the munnskjenk, and a chalice with cover would be placed in front of the king, who then 'was to be given what is to be given', as the text says (c. 24). Thereafter the candidate was to take hold of the stem of the chalice and kiss the king's hand. Finally the new skutilsvein would step aside and fill the king's cup from the chalice.

Like any other guild, the hird provided for its members in case of illness or age. Thus c. 53 tells us that all hirdmen were obliged to help their fellows 'to the monastery' if they could no longer care for themselves, which meant to pay for their sustenance at St John's hospital at Varna. All members of the hird had therefore to give one third of their tithe to this hospital (c. 21). In a royal amendment from 1261 (c. 55) King Magnus undertook to finance one half of the cost of sustenance at Varna for all members of his hird.

Unconditional loyalty and solidarity among the members of the hird was fundamental, and the sanctions against those who broke this code were severe. Everybody had to attend a fellow hirdman's funeral, or his execution, if he had been sentenced to death. 'Public' or open discussions within the hird were absolutely forbidden.

Chapter 38 about how to share booty is unique. It carries the flavour of the Viking age and gives a glimpse of older days' warrior kingship and the hird as a war-band. Under certain circumstances the common interests of the band are given priority even over the king's interests. The king for instance could not count on special treatment in the distribution of booty. If he wanted some precious objects, he had to pay the full price. Booty was in principle regarded as common property, and only those items which the king or others could document a legal title to, and which had been taken from them by the enemy at an earlier date, could be claimed back without any compensation to the war-band.[14] Chapter 38 is certainly among the oldest parts of the Hirdskrå. It is indeed a relic of an earlier age, in a document which therefore reveals the times and mentalities of the Viking weapon brotherhood, the civil wars, and also the Christian monarchy, and the polished courtly ideals of the thirteenth century.

We must therefore conclude that the hird, even though it had been Christianized and modernized, had deep roots in a Viking past. In the 1270s it was still a community, which included the king, who as patron and leader of the hird, was not placed outside and above it. Except some few prerogatives, such as the right to decide the salary of his men and other such matters, there is no single paragraph in the Hirdskrå which gives the king 'sovereign' rights to rule the hird without the consent of its members. Yet we must add that the Hirdskrå is characterized by a pronounced monarchic tendency.

4. The hird as government

The hird and its members' duty to guard and serve the king is central to an understanding of this body (c. 1). Service was not restricted to the hird as corporation and the king as patron of the guild. The hirdmen also served the king as ruler of the realm. Hird-service went beyond the security of the monarch and ceremonial duties; it was above all a governmental service: the hird was also in its way a body of government. In their oath of fealty all members of the hird bound themselves to observe their king's pledge to his subjects. What services

---

[14] P. Brown, *The Rise of Western Christendom* (Oxford, 1996), p. 86, tells a story, which reminds me of c. 38 in the Hirdskrå. When the Franks, after having conquered Soissons in 486, were about to share the booty, King Chlodvig (Clovis) wanted to put aside a couple of valuables for the bishop, among which was a precious decanter. One of his soldiers, however, could not accept this, and, taking his axe he smashed the decanter to pieces, saying to his king, 'you are not allowed to take a greater share of the booty than what you are entitled to'.

and duties were required of the royal liegemen within what we may call a Norwegian state around 1270?

Household and retinue, which were the two formal *loci* of the hird, had been the basis of royal rule in Norway, at least since the end of the Viking age. The household had been the seat of the royal administration, wherever the king resided – and until the thirteenth century he was a peripatetic monarch – and his housecarls were his armed force. This system was not peculiarly Norwegian, but rather Scandinavian. We find it in England after 1016 as well as in Denmark and Norway, and it was of course related to the old Germanic system of *comitatus*.[15]

This old tradition permeates the Hirdskrå. The armed hirdmen, the king's retainers, were understood to be the core of the royal armed force (c. 35, cf. cc. 32–4). They were expected to protect him, and they should see to it that his orders were carried out. Yet in contrast to most other European countries the Norwegian defence was not based on the feudal levy, but on the militia, first and foremost the coastal militia called 'leidang' (ON, *leiðangr*, m.). All free men were obliged to participate in this naval defence-system, which was organized on a communal basis. From the mouth of the Göta river (the border separating Denmark, Norway, and Sweden until 1645) up to the Arctic sea the country was divided into so-called 'skipreids' (ON, *skipreiða*, f.), communal units, which were responsible for manning and equipping a warship. This was still the situation in 1300. It was a leidang-fleet which sailed to defend the Hebrides against the Scots in 1263, and Norwegian leidang-fleets threatened Denmark time and time again in the 1280s and 90s.

Seen from a military point of view then, the hird was rather insignificant. King Magnus intended to remedy this. In the winter of 1273 he summoned hird-leaders and the hird from Southern Norway to Tønsberg, and the following summer he continued negotiations in Bergen with hird-members from Western and Northern Norway. These talks resulted in two royal statutes, which aimed at establishing a professional army based on the hird. According to c. 36 in the Hirdskrå, King Magnus's statutes had received the consent of the hird-leaders, and a fragment of King Magnus's Saga reports that the decisions were passed by a hird-assembly in Bergen. From now on all lendmen and others who received a royal benefice equal to 15 marks silver were to pay and equip five men, armed as hirdmen, for three months of military service. The 'sysselmen' (ON, *syslumaðr*, m., *syslumen*, pl.), who were the Norwegian equivalents of the English sheriffs, were to keep a number of men in proportion to their 'lén', that is the income from their office, called 'sysla'. The sysselmen had to arm their men in accordance with the standard norm of hirdmen, guests, and kertisveins. The number of armed men in the coastal districts was stipulated in proportion to the

---

15 S. B. Chrimes, *An Introduction to the Administrative History of Medieval England* (Oxford, 1966), pp. 2–8, 21–24; G. O. Sayles, *The Medieval Foundations of England* (London, 1966), pp. 172–79; A. E. Christensen, *Kongemagt og aristokrati* (Copenhagen, 1968), pp. 29–39; N. Lund and K. Hørby, *Samfundet i vikingetid og middelalder 800–1500* (Copenhagen, 1980), Dansk social historie, ii, 192–95.

estimated number of men in the leidang. From inland Southern Norway, which
was not part of the coastal defence system, the meeting of Tønsberg agreed on a
fixed number of men from each 'sysle', or shire.

In other words this 'professional' army, equipped according to hird-standard,
and financed by the holders of royal benefices and offices, was to supplement
the leidang. This involved a considerable increase in the military and financial
burdens on lendmen and sysselmen. The Bergen assembly therefore added that
it was 'necessary not to put further burdens on the shoulders of the king's men,
so that they should not be forced to spend their private means or to exhaust royal
lands and income to accomplish this task'.

The new army was far from impressive. The Norwegian historian Andreas
Holmsen has calculated the number of armed men to about 1200. 'There were
roughly between 40 or 50 sysselmen', he says; and continues:

> In addition come 12 to 15 lendmen, many of whom were sysselmen as well.
> The total number of men who were to finance the new army did not exceed
> 60, which meant an average number of 20 fully armed, equipped, and pro-
> visioned warriors each. The burdens were graduated according to the
> income accruing from benefice and office. These were the resources which
> were to cover all the extra costs involved in the military reforms. No finan-
> cial compensation or subsidies from the king are mentioned, and the tax
> exemption, which the hirdmen were granted some few years later, would
> barely cover the cost of feeding two men for one month, if we follow the
> royal cost scale. The lendman's immunity would only cover the upkeep of
> the 20 men for a couple of days. The military obligations the lendmen and
> sysselmen took on in 1273 were no burden to the king himself.[16]

Yet the reforms seem rather to point to royal weakness than to royal power. The
decisions taken in Tønsberg and Bergen were probably never implemented, at
least not in full.

According to the Hirdskrå, retinue and household were still the basis of royal
administration in the 1270s, at least in principle, and were assumed to be so in
the future as well. King Magnus's hird, however, was radically different from
that of Cnut and Olav at the beginning of the eleventh century. Since then the
royal hird had been transformed to meet new challenges and new circumstances.
Norway was about to be politically united in the thirteenth century. What we
may call a state-building process had been going on since the second half of the
twelfth century, and a 'national' aristocracy arose as a consequence of this and
of the civil wars. Let us try to view King Magnus's hird in this context.

Different from the original hird, which consisted of the king's retainers and
household servants only, its high medieval successor comprised all the royal
vassals throughout the kingdom, including the tributary provinces overseas. At
the latest from the end of the twelfth century we find two categories of hirdmen:
those who served at court, called 'bordfaste', literally 'fixed to the table', and

16 Holmsen, *Nye studier*, p. 165.

therefore resident, and all the others, the non-resident hirdmen, who were the majority. They lived in the countryside, representing the monarchy as 'sysselmen' (sheriffs), 'lensmen' (ON, *lénsmaðr*, m., *lénsmen*, pl.), who were responsible to the sysselmen and assisting them in the collection of taxes, fines, etc., and 'lagmen' (ON, *lǫgmaðr*, m., *lǫgmen*, pl.), that is, the royal judges. In addition, we must include many local hirdmen, who did not have any royal office, but who filled important positions in local public life and who were available for royal service.

All this is reflected in the Hirdskrå. We see here royal government as a function of the household within the framework of the hird, which also constituted the political and administrative network of the country. The most important regulations concerning royal central administration are to be found in the chapters dealing with the hird-leaders (18–26). I have already noted that the chancellor is included in this group, but as far as I can see he was not a liegeman. He was a professional civil servant, who had to swear an oath of office at his appointment, but who did not perform the act of homage, and as already remarked, he was paid by administrative fees.[17]

The other hird-officers, such as stallar, merkesman, and below them the drottsete and the munnskjenk were chosen among the hird-leaders. They were installed in office by investiture-like ceremonies. In the case of the stallar, the Hirdskrå specifies that the king must announce publicly that he wants this man as stallar, and that he will grant him the honour and privileges pertaining to the stallar according to age-old custom. Then two skutilsveins are to lead the candidate to the king's seat, and finally the king himself is to take him by the hand and lead him to the 'stallar-seat', which symbolizes his office. According to the Hirdskrå, the stallar was next in rank after the lendmen and the chancellor. It was his duty to speak on behalf of the king at all hird-meetings, and to communicate the royal will to the hird. Moreover, the stallar was obliged to follow the king on all his journeys, and act as royal prosecutor in all matters. The stallar was also obliged to attend all hird-meetings and to act as negotiator and conciliator in disputes and quarrels between the hirdmen. Finally he was responsible for horses and transport. As the king's spokesman to the hird and as mediator in the hird, the stallar combined the roles of royal officer and representative of the brotherhood.

The same double character is also evident in the merkesman's office. He was

---

[17] The chancellor belonged primarily to the administrative staff and was totally dependent on the king. His office must be somewhat older than the Hirdskrå, perhaps dating from the reign of Håkon IV. Cap. 27 states that the chancellor shall be one of the most prominent royal councillors. He should be responsible for keeping the royal seal and draw up all royal charters. Furthermore he should register royal property and income, and also the land, which the king had bestowed upon his men. And he should see that all royal rent was exactly registered, and properly assessed and collected. The chancellor was also obliged to take on royal errands or missions when requested. In other words he combined the functions of Head of the Royal Bureaucracy and Chancellor of the Exchequer. At King Magnus's death the chancellor was still the only 'professional' among the royal officers.

to carry the royal standard in war as well as in peace. Besides, he was to serve with the stallar at all meetings in the hird and assist him in internal hird-matters, and in general he was to be at the king's disposal. About his installation the Hirdskrå says that when the king wants to appoint a merkesman he shall summon the hird-assembly. After having announced publicly that he wants this man as his standard-keeper, and that he will give him all privileges and honours belonging to the office of merkesman, the king shall take the standard and present it formally to the merkesman. Receiving the standard the merkesman shall kiss the king's hand.

The lendmen too were installed in their dignity by an investiture-like ceremony. Once again the Hirdskrå specifies that the king himself should take the candidate by hand and lead him to his new 'seat of honour' at his right hand, where all the other lendmen were seated. I find it reasonable to presume that this 'seat of honour' at the king's right hand side symbolizes the lendman's position as royal councillor. Likewise we have already seen that the skutilsveins' installation in court service is symbolized by the presentation of the chalice before the king. Taken together the chapters about the hird-leaders portray them collectively as 'Government'.

The hird as defined in the Hirdskrå is therefore in the nature of a palimpsest. We can dimly perceive the old war-band and the flock of house-servants, which still had been a reality during King Sverre's reign and the civil wars two generations earlier. Ancient hird-custom and functions such as guard-duty, escort, and daily service in the royal residence still account for a substantial part of King Magnus's hird-code. It must also be seen as a concession to traditional equality among the members of the hird, whatever their rank, that everybody was obliged to perform such duties, at least in principle and mostly on ceremonial and festive occasions. Thus there is also an element of theatre here.

Nevertheless the new Hirdskrå makes it clear that in 1270 the old weapon-brotherhood was a theme of the past, and that the war-band had not only been transformed into a Christian corporation or guild, but had also become a political–administrative body. Court and guild, hird and king, were tied together by the act of 'håndgang' and mutual obligations. But entrance to the hird, either to ordinary hird-service or to greater eminence, was entirely at the king's will. Concepts such as realm or nobility did not have any meaning without him. Autonomous hird-power is inconceivable, as the hird is a function of kingship. The Hirdskrå is then, as we have already said, a pronouncedly monarchic document. However, in governing his hird, as in governing his kingdom, the king had to observe some formalities. In principle his authority rested on the consent of the ruled. It followed that the members of the hird had a right to co-operate in all matters concerning hird and government. In this sense the authority rested in the hird and was articulated jointly by the king and his liegemen of all ranks. We must add that a strict hereditary principle of succession to the throne was established in the new law of succession, which comprises the first part of the Hirdskrå. The law of succession was also embodied in the Landlaw and was sanctioned with it by the provincial 'þing'-assemblies in 1274.

Chapter 36 is the most comprehensive of all the 56 chapters of the Hirdskrå, and also the most ambitious. We have already mentioned the military reforms, which were agreed in meetings in Tønsberg and Bergen in 1273. The same hird-meetings passed a series of statutes which aimed at wide administrative and jurisdictional reforms. The relationship between the king and his local office-holders, the sysselmen, must have been on the agenda in Tønsberg. We find in this chapter a formula for a letter of obligation, which the sysselman was to sign and seal at his appointment to office. This must be a result of talks between the king and his liegemen. Such a document is said to be necessary '. . . so that nobody should have any doubts about royal property and royal income in his district', that is the shire. For this reason the sysselman was to send annual reports and accounts to the chancery, and never violate the rights of the people. In general he promised to perform his business properly and according to law; implicitly he could be removed from office in case of abuse. What is important here is that this letter established an official and juridical nexus between king and sysselman, not a personal one.

As already shown the relationship between hird-leaders and lord, or should we say monarch and corporation, is based on some kind of personal reciprocity. The only exception was the chancellor, who was a servant of the Crown and not a vassal. The regulations concerning the hird-leaders and their governmental functions (cc. 12–26) are probably older than c. 36. I find it reasonable to assume that they have been taken from the former hird-code of Sverre and Håkon IV. According to c. 36 the relationship between the king and his local officials, even though they were mostly recruited among the hird-élite, were to be based on legal and bureaucratic principles. The Tønsberg- and Bergen-meetings also adopted rules for how the judges should record their sentences, and how sysselmen should act as prosecuting authority and police. In their capacity as sysselmen then, the royal liegemen were regarded as public servants, not vassals. The Bergen and Tønsberg meetings besides conceding an increase in the military burdens also consented to the principle that royal estates and their revenues should be managed through bureaucratic control. The whole chapter reeks of officialdom in contrast to what we might call the 'feudal' flavour of the rest of the Hirdskrå. The Hirdskrå is therefore an equivocal document with an unresolved tension, or even a contradiction, between c. 36 and the rest of the law-code, between a traditional concept of kingship and a modern principle of royal service and an exalted monarchy. This contradiction was ignored during King Magnus's reign, but it broke through the surface after his death when the lendmen took over the rule during the minority of Magnus's eldest son Erik. Håkon (V) who succeeded his brother Erik in 1299, abolished in 1308 the dignity of lendmen and started to build a central bureaucracy outside the hird and free from his liegemen. This is, however, another story. King Magnus himself seems almost miraculously to have obtained acceptance of his plans for the modernization of the army and the royal administration.

Returning to the hird, it is necessary to seek some clarification as to who had the authority to make laws for the hird. In the first place we can observe some interesting differences between the prologues of King Magnus' Landlaw and of the Hirdskrå. The introduction to the Landlaw is constructed like that of a normal royal charter with a protocol (*intitulatio*, address, and *salutatio*) and a text, which clarifies the background of the legislative process, the king's mandate to carry it out, and the outline of the new law-code. The law-code ends with a normal *sanctio* and eschatocol. Such information is totally lacking in the Hirdskrå. There is no *inscriptio*, no address, no *salutatio*, no *sanctio*, no eschatocol, and nothing is said about the legislator or his mandate, and of course not a single word about the outline of the law-code. The prologue of the Hirdskrå is very brief and gives very general grounds for the work. The main section is about the religious origin of kingship and the moral obligation of the hirdmen to serve their king. Thereafter comes a reference to the civil wars in the twelfth century, which argues for the following statute about strict hereditary succession to the throne, not for the need of a new hird-code as such. This paragraph is almost identical with the introduction to c. 3 in the Landlaw, which too contains the law of succession to the throne.

Neither does the Hirdskrå say anything about who had instigated the work, at least not explicitly. However, in both Landlaw and Hirdskrå we meet an acting 'We'. In the Landlaw this 'We' is identical with his majesty's plural. We are told that the provincial 'þing'-assemblies had 'sentenced' King Magnus to carry out this work. The 'We' of the Hirdskrå on the other hand is more ambiguous. Sometimes it can be understood to be the collective 'We' of the hirdmen, sometimes it seems also to include the king – the entire hird-corporation expressed in the collective 'We'. This is in line with how the law presents itself in the opening sentence: 'Here begins the hird-code of the king of Norway and his liegemen.' His majesty's 'We' is found only in the statutes, which have been embodied in the compilation, such as in c. 36. However these statutes, which were published in the name of the king, were results of talks with the most prominent liegemen and had been agreed to by representatives of the hird.

The Hirdskrå then presents itself as an internal hird-document, parts of which, but probably the whole, had been sanctioned by the hird-assembly (ON, *hirðstefna*, f.). A fragment of Magnus Håkonson's saga illustrates this point. We are told that on 1 of July 1273 the king summoned the 'hirdstevne' (hird-assembly) and 'accounted for what customs he wanted with regard to carrying weapons and other things'.[18] Formal hird-resolutions in matters of this sort are mentioned in c. 55 of the Hirdskrå. Hird-resolutions however required royal advice and probably royal sanction as well. Though the Hirdskrå thus presents itself as a collective product, it certainly included royal participation. The King was leader of the hird, and there is reason to believe that he has initiated the work, which probably was carried out in co-operation with leading – and trusted – hird-members.

There has been a widespread view among Norwegian historians that the

---

[18] *Norges Kongesagaer*, ed. F. Hødnebø (Oslo, 1979), iv, 357.

Hirdskrå was a purely royal product, and that the king was sovereign in all matters concerning the hird. This cannot be the case. I conceive the Hirdskrå as the result of an understanding between king and his liegemen rather than as an expression of royal will. We must remember that the king in all legislative matters was dependant on the consent from those implied, the representatives of the rural communities at the provincial assemblies or the hirdmen at the hird-assembly. Yet we must take note of those elements, which do not easily fit into this interpretation. One is the very strong monarchic ideology, which permeates the text. Another is the radical nature of the royal prerogatives, for instance the king's sovereign right to decide on matters concerning payment and subsidies to the members of the hird or to bestow marks of distinction to whoever he wanted. In principle he was free to appoint whomever he wanted to any office in the hird. Yet, we must keep in mind that the king could not admit new members into the hird without consent from his liegemen, who had a legal title to protest and, on certain grounds, even to prevent an applicant from becoming a member of the hird. Even though it was not easy to block entrance to the hird, c. 30 makes clear the liegemen's right to participate in vital hird-decisions.

Practically none of Håkon V's many statutes concerning the nobility and government are embodied in any of our Hirdskrå-manuscripts,[19] which is striking as the oldest and best Hirdskrå-text in our possession stems from King Håkon's reign and probably belonged to the royal family.[20] According to Lars Hamre, King Håkon acted much more independently than did his father in traditional hird-matters.[21] King Håkon restricted himself to most often consulting a few members of his council when making statutes concerning the nobility and government. His famous statute of 1308 revoking the dignities of earl and lendman and defining the duties of the crown officials, bears no traces whatsoever of co-operation with any of his councillors, or anybody else but his clerk Torgeir who wrote the document. As already hinted, his reign seems to mark a turning point in the history of the hird and the hird-nobility.

5. The end of the hird and the Hirdskrå

The Hirdskrå expresses an ideal. What is probably an almost contemporary source, the King's Mirror, confirms the Hirdskrå-portrait of the Norwegian nobility. The King's Mirror is also a normative source, and like the Hirdskrå the King's Mirror is more concerned with how things ought to be than how they really were. Nevertheless, the Norwegian historian Knut Helle holds that '. . . even though the Hirdskrå and the King's Mirror are normative, and portray the hird from the point of view of the king, i.e. as royal court and monarchic service organization, they also to some extent reflect reality. In combination with

---

19 There is only one exception in an Icelandic copy from the 1360s (*NglL*, ii, 450 n. 28).
20 The original manuscript is now in the Arnamagnæan Institute (Catalogue no. AM 322 fol.) in Copenhagen. For the hirdskrå manuscripts, see G. Storm in *NglL*, iv, 502–14.
21 Hamre, 'Litt omkring Håkon Vs hirdskipan'.

evidence from other sources the Hirdskrå and the King's Mirror give a fairly trustworthy picture of the hird-organization, its functions and its position in society.'[22]

There is reason to believe that the Hirdskrå lost much of its importance soon after King Magnus' death. During the reign of King Håkon V the monarchy, or to be more precise, the royal administration was separated from the hird. Secondly, the old lendman-élite disappeared, and the nobility was restructured in accordance with continental patterns. Thirdly, in 1319 Norway entered the first of a series of Scandinavian unions, which lasted for centuries and which entailed that the kings resided abroad for long periods, and after 1380, more or less permanently. With the king and court in foreign parts, the hird was no longer a functional body. The Norwegian nobility that survived was a reduced body, much smaller in number than the former hird-nobility, and it was now an exclusive nobility of blood, not a nobility of service. During the fifteenth century, as a consequence of demography, inter-marriage, and the politics of the Scandinavian unions, men of Swedish, Danish, and German descent replaced the old Norwegian aristocracy.

However the system of local hirdmen survived outside Norway proper, namely in its tributary provinces, the so-called 'skatlands': Iceland, the Faroe Islands, Shetland, Orkney, and Jemtland. There hirdmen continued representing the Norwegian Crown. It is reasonable to suppose that together with a peculiar system of provincial self-rule inherited from Norway, the link between king and local hirdmen made possible the continuation of a Norse political tradition in the Atlantic until the end of the Middle Ages.[23] In Iceland after 1320 the rule of the country was almost completely entrusted to Icelanders, all of whom were royal hirdmen, and the governor, whether he be an Icelander or a foreigner, was now given the title of hird-leader, which he kept until the sixteenth century.[24] Likewise in Jemtland throughout the fourteenth century local hirdmen operated in important administrative and political positions. We meet hirdmen in the Faroe Islands as late as 1479. In Orkney hirdmen still played a prominent role in public life in the fifteenth century. Until the middle of the sixteenth century the provincial assembly at Kirkwall with its leading body of 24 so-called 'roithmen' (ON, raðmen) was called hirdmanstein, which means hirdman's stevne (hirdman assembly).[25] The name hird then, which was imported from the British Isles during the Viking age, survived in Norway's western provinces until the early-modern period, and was finally abolished by Scottish authorities after 1550, in what was to become the Northern Isles of Britain.

[22] *Under kirke og kongemakt 1130–1350. Norge Historie* (Oslo, 1995), iii, 173.
[23] S. Imsen, 'Public Life in Shetland and Orkney c. 1300–1550', *New Orkney Antiquarian Journal*, i (Kirkwell, 1999).
[24] R. B. Wærdahl, *Skattland og kongemakt 1262–1350*, NTNU (Trondheim, 1998).
[25] J. Storer Clouston, 'The "Goodmen" and the "Hirdmen" of Orkney', *Proceedings of the Orkney Antiquarian Society*, iii (Kirkwall, 1924–25).

III

Late Middle Ages

12

The Nobility of Medieval Portugal
(XIth–XIVth Centuries)

Maria João Violante Branco

Over the last twenty years Portugal has witnessed a notable revival of historical studies in general, and of the study of medieval history in particular.[1] So far as the study of nobility is concerned, the starting point for the modern research is José Mattoso's work on the Lineage Books of the late thirteenth and fourteenth centuries. Mattoso's critical editions of the texts[2] have provided a new lease of life for studies of the Portuguese nobility, especially when considered in combination with other types of material. By combining the material of these lineage books with information derived from the royal Enquiries of the thirteenth and fourteenth centuries,[3] and with the patrimonial documentation of monasteries and other houses, of the royal chanceries and episcopal sees, Mattoso has laid the foundations of a prosopographical study of the nobility of the Entre-Douro e Minho from the tenth to the twelfth century,[4] and enabled scholars to begin to

1 J. Mattoso, 'Perspectivas actuais sobre a nobreza medieval portuguesa', *Revista de História das Ideias*, xix (1998), 7–37, where the author analyses the latest data on nobility and even reshapes some of his earlier conceptions. For previous approaches, J. Mattoso, 'Perspectivas actuais da investigação e da síntese na historiografia medieval portuguesa (1128–1383)', *Revista de História Económica e Social*, ix (1982), 145–162, gives a fairly good panoramic view of this last century's production; should be compared with T. Veloso, 'Para uma bibliografia crítica de História Medieval de Portugal: algumas notas', *Ler História*, xxi (1991), 24–34, and H. Baquero Moreno, L. M. Duarte, and L. C. Amaral, 'História da Administração Portuguesa na Idade Média – um balanço', *Ler História*, xxi (1991), 35–45.
2 *Portugaliae Monumenta Historica a saeculo octavo post Christum usque ad quintum decimum, nova série*, i, *Livro Velho/Livro do Deão* [*LV/LD*]; ii/1–2, *Livros de Linhagem do Conde D. Pedro* [*LL*], ed. J. Mattoso and J. Piehl (Lisbon, 1980).
3 Good examples of such work are O. Bethencourt, L. Krus, and J. Mattoso, 'As inquirições de 1258 como fonte da História da Nobreza – o julgado de Aguiar de Sousa', *RHES*, lx (1982), 17–74, or I. Gonçalves (dir.), 'O Entre Cávado e Minho, cenário da expansão senhorial no século XII', *Revista da Faculdade de Letras de Lisboa*, 4th ser., ii (1978), 399–440, or even J. A. Pizarro, 'A nobreza do julgado de Braga nas Inquirições do reinado de D. Dinis', in *IX Centenário da Dedicação da Sé de Braga. Actas do Congresso*, i (Braga, 1990), pp. 185–245.
4 The first results of this work were his pioneer articles 'As famílias condais portucalenses

perceive the structural contours of the subject.[5] Thanks to Mattoso, it is now possible to propose some important conclusions on subjects such as the different hierarchies of nobility,[6] marriage strategies, kinship, property, and the mental structures which formed and informed these noblemen, as well as the system of values according to which they acted.[7]

Some of the fruits of this process have been born in the form of MA and PhD theses which have proliferated since the 1980s, notably on such subjects as the history of specific families or individuals,[8] and the rôle and influence of such

---

dos séculos X e XI' and 'A nobreza rural portuense nos séculos XI e XII', in J. Mattoso, *A nobreza medieval portuguesa: A família e o poder* (Lisbon, 1981), pp. 101–57, 159–251.

[5] As was the case with Mattoso's own papers on the structure of the medieval family in northern Portugal in the same collection of studies quoted in the previous note, and again in 'Problemas sobre a estrutura da família', in *Portugal Medieval-Novas interpretações* (Lisbon, 1985), pp. 241–57.

[6] An intense work on the self-titulation of the noblemen has been carried out mainly by Mattoso himself. In fact the status of 'cavaleiro' as a noble category is not always clear. In the Reconquest frame, the 'cavaleiros–vilãos' of the *concelhos*, who serve the king in the war and come out from the oligarchy of the *concelhos*, assume a role and a social standing which is often difficult to define. The denomination of *cavaleiro* as the same as *miles* is therefore one of the subjects for doubt. The definition of the real contents of the different denominations for noblemen, 'filii benenatorum', 'boni homines' (another expression also used for non-noblemen), 'ricos-homens', 'infanções', 'filhos de algo', 'nobiles', 'barones', and others, have been thoroughly examined in both their diachronic and synchronic evidence, in their geographical and political context, and have provided some new results. For all this see J. Mattoso, *Ricos-homens, infanções e cavaleiros: A nobreza medieval portuguesa nos séculos XI e XII* (Lisbon, 1982) and the exhaustive discussion of the subject and comparison with the Spanish data in the last revised edition of his *Identificação de um País: Ensaio sobre as origens de Portugal (1096–1325)*, 5th edn (Lisbon, 1995), pp. 104–25.

[7] On these last subjects, see L. Krus, *A concepção nobiliárquica do espaço ibérico (1280–1380)* (Lisbon, 1996), and *Passado, memória e poder na sociedade medieval portuguesa: Estudos* (Redondo, 1994).

[8] B. V. Sousa, 'Os Pimentéis. Percursos de uma linhagem da nobreza medieval portuguesa (seculos XIII–XV)', unpublished PhD thesis, Universidade Nova (1995), has studied this family and its social ascendancy. Its story contains in itself the elements which most of these lineages share. Other work on specific families and individuals has been done, like the important works of Leontina Ventura, with 'O cavaleiro João Gondesendes: Sua trajectória politico-social e económica', *RHES*, xv (1985), 31–69, 'D. João Peres de Aboim: Da Terra da Nóbrega à Corte de Afonso III', *RHES*, xviii (1986), 57–73, and, with A. Oliveira, 'Os Briteiros (séculos XII–XIV): Trajectória social e política', *RPH*, xxx (1995), 71–102, or J. A. Pizarro, *Os patronos do mosteiro de Grijó (Evolução e estrutura da família nobre: Séculos XI a XIV* (Ponte de Lima, 1995). Other works, like L. Rosa, 'Quadros de Organização do Poder Nobre na Baixa Idade Média. Estrutura familiar, património e percursos linhagísticos de quatro famílias de Portalegre', *A Cidade, revista cultural de Portalegre*, vi (1991), 47–65, or J. P. Cumbre, 'Os Melo. Origens, trajectórias familiares e percursos políticos (séculos XI–XV)', unpublished MA thesis, Universidade Nova (1997), also shed new light on old problems. Many MA and PhD theses are being written on specific branches of certain famílies. In the Universidade Nova of Lisbon, there are currently lines of research on the collective memory of the nobility, the history of

noblemen and women in and on religious houses.[9] Court society[10] and the institution of the *Morgadio*,[11] as the apotheosis of the agnatic system in the territorial sphere, have been the subject of much work, too.

Although the source materials are vast, the best part of what we know comes from the elements in the lineage books. The purpose of such books is aptly summarized in the prologue of the latest of these books, that of D. Pedro Afonso, the cultivated bastard son of King Dinis,[12] dating from 1340:

5.   And because no friendship can be as pure in nature as the one of those who come from the same blood, because these come faster to the things by which friendship is preserved, it had to be declared in this book, by titles and allegations, so that each one of the *fidalgos* might easily know (his relations) and thus friendship is discovered and not lost between those who should keep it. And what moved me to this were seven things:

6.   The first one was to accomplish and keep what I just said.

7.   The second was so that these *fidalgos* might know of whom they descend from father to son, and the transversal lines.

8.   The third was so that they may all act as of one heart, and so fight their enemies who are the destruction of Jesus Christ and his Faith and because they come from the same lineage, whether it is in the fourth or fifth degree or further up they must not make distinctions, any more than those who are as close as cousins and third degree relatives, for it is better to love a person's distant relative, if he is good, than a close relative, if he is dead. And men who are not good, do not care about the lineage they come from except for brothers and cousins in first and second and third degree. And from fourth degree upwards they do not care. And such men do wrong both to themselves and to God, because a men who has a relative in the fifth or sixth degree or further up, if he is of great power, must serve him, because he comes from his blood. And if he is his equal he should help him. And if

families, and on noble households, whose results will surely provide much material. It is expected that in some years' time the panorama will be much changed.

9   For a general but up to date approach to this subject, see the synthesis of M. H. Coelho and R. Martins, 'O monaquismo feminino cisterciense e a nobreza medieval portuguesa (séculos XIII–XIV)', *Theologica*, 2nd ser., xxviii/2 (1993), 481–506, as well as M. A. Marques, 'A evolução do monaquismo feminino até ao século XIII, na região de Entre Douro e Tejo: Notas para uma investigação', in *A mulher na Sociedade Portuguesa: Actas do Colóquio* (Coimbra, 1986), pp. 5–30.

10   R. Costa Gomes, *A Corte dos reis de Portugal no final da Idade Média* (Lisbon, 1995). L. Ventura, 'A Nobreza de Corte de Afonso III', 2 vols, unpublished PhD thesis, Univ. Coimbra (1992), as well as giving an account of the court, provides extremely important data on the structural organization of the nobility of the late thirteenth century.

11   L. Rosa, *O Morgadio em Portugal: sécs XIV–XV* (Lisbon, 1995).

12   For the identity of Conde D. Pedro with the son of D. Dinis and his authorship of the book of lineages as well as of the *Crónica Geral de Espanha de 1344*, see *Crónica Geral de Espanha de 1344*, ed. L. F. L. Cintra, i (Lisbon, 1951), 'Introdução', pp. cxxvii–clxc.

he is lesser than himself, he should do good to the other, and they all should be of one heart.

9.   The fourth was so that they might know the names of those of whom they come from and some of the good things they did.

10.   The fifth was so that the kings could know it and favour the living with graces because of the worthiness and the works and the great efforts they have received from their ancestors in conquering this land of Spain for them.

11.   The sixth was for them to know how they can be married without sin, according to the precepts of the Church.

12.   The seventh was so that they may know of which monasteries they are natural patrons.[13]

What this amounted to was a *memorandum* for the correct behaviour and collective self-consciousness of the Portuguese nobility. It is to be noted that it was the nobility itself which assumed responsibility for the perpetuation of its own dynastic memory and of the defence of its political and social supremacy.

The *Livro de Linhagens do Conde D. Pedro* is the last of the three medieval lineage books which have come to our knowledge. All three belong to the period from 1280 to 1340. The so called *Livro Velho* is the earliest. Written *c.* 1286–90 in the monastery of Santo Tirso it is incomplete. Its prologue sets out to tell the story of the five main 'lineages' which have made Portugal: Sousa, Bragança, Maia, Baião, and Riba Douro, but only the part concerning the Sousa family and a section of its treatment of the Maia have reached us. It proposes to explain, therefore, how these five families were the makers of the kingdom.

The second of these books, called *Livro do Deão* on account of the anonymous dean to whom reference is made in the prologue, is a much more complete work. It describes twenty-three of the thirty families mentioned in its prologue. The *Livro do Deão* was finished around 1343 and reiterated the view that the new kingdom owed its existence to the noble families of Portugal. It also introduced the notion of the noble superiority on account of its priority over the Portuguese monarchy. The *Livro de Linhagens do conde D. Pedro* is the longest, and adopts a different approach, altogether. In fact, it starts with narrative texts drawn from the Navarrese *Liber Regum* retracing human history from the time of Adam and Eve, by way of the Egyptian and Roman empires to the Navarrese, Aragonese, Castillian, English, and French kingdoms. Finally, it explains the descent of the Portuguese kings from the French line and the origins of the nobility of Castile, León, Portugal, and Galicia. Emphasized is the process by which they built up their prestige and power from the fight against

---

[13]   *LL*, Prólogo, pp. 56–7: my translation.

the infidel, and again, how it was *to them* that the Portuguese kings owed their existence.[14]

These lineage books, generally ignored except by Portuguese medievalists, are very rich sources and present various features which distinguish them from the most part of the other Western genealogies.[15] Unlike the usually terse and short genealogies common elsewhere in the West, these are detailed colourful narratives of the different families, their names, and connections, contain many anecdotes and explain the successive marriages and the descent of each of the members of each line.[16] They are full of tales of loyalty and treason, illegitimacy and kidnapping, fierce battles, and less noble episodes of nervous saddle soiling in a tight corner,[17] and of running away from battle fields and cheating their kings.[18]

But most of all, the lineage books are full of names and kinship data, full of lineages and collaterals, full of myths and genealogical self-legitimating

---

[14] For all these elements see Krus, *A concepção nobiliárquica*, pp. 15–16, and Mattoso in the introduction to his edition of the *LV*, i, 12–18; and of the *LL*, ii/1, 7–9.

[15] Cf. J. Mattoso, 'Os livros de linhagens portugueses e a literatura genealógica europeia da Idade Média', in *A nobreza medieval*, pp. 35–53.

[16] Nothing or hardly anything is known about the cultural tradition preserved on these books as far as the genealogies in themselves are concerned. As Count D. Pedro himself declares, he had to work very hard to recollect the stories and the genealogies he compiled. This might indicate that there was, at that time, an effective social use of this type of recounting, but the fact is that, apart from the attested inspiration from the *Liber Regum* and from the Alfonsine works (either historiographical or legislative), as well as from the French Arthurian romance literature and the *gestae*, nothing much is known about the ancestors of the genealogical data given by Count D. Pedro and the *Livros Velhos*. Cf. J. Mattoso 'As fontes do nobiliário do Conde D. Pedro', in *A nobreza medieval*, pp. 55–98, where he analyses all the retraceable narratives.

[17] *LD*, 14Y5. This episode gave this men a nickname which would preserve for eternity his weakness in a moment of panic.

[18] The narrative of the fight of Ázere, Braga, and Guimarães (*LL*, 25G3), in 1219, in which Martim Sanches (a bastard son of King Sancho I who had gone to serve the king of León and was by then fighting against the Portuguese forces) refuses to begin hostilities against his half brother, the leper-king Afonso II until he is withdrawn from the battlefield and Martim Sanches can no longer see the Portuguese flags, is described as vividly as the numerous episodes of almost anecdotal violent fighting within the nobility itself, and between them and ecclesiastics, or between them and kings. The accounts of the cases of treason to kings and of lack of moral coherence alternate with the natural description of the good relations between Moors and Christians, of Moors becoming Christians, and of unions with Moorish women, almost as much as the praise to the good Christian warriors who kill many infidels. A typical episode is the case of Simon Curutelo, in the milder version of the *LL*, persecuted for having said a bad word to Nuno Velho in front of Alfonso VI. The king told Nuno Velho's son, Pero Velho, to vindicate his father. The old man, seeing a breach in Simon's helmet, wanted to warn his son that he could strike him through the breach near the eye; but he pointed to his own eye with such vehemence, while his son was distracted with something else, that his eyeball came out of its socket. When they finally settled the offence, the old knight had to see several doctors to regain the perfect use of his eye (*LL*, 51C3). The most interesting treason 'cycle' is conveyed with the stories of those who should have maintained their loyalty towards King Sancho

constructions,[19] full of the nobility's concept of itself at the end of the thirteenth and the beginning of the fourteenth centuries, and of the part the nobility considered itself entitled to play in the kingdom it maintained it had created.

All this makes these Lineage Books an irreplaceable source of knowledge of the *mores* of the nobility both within the kingdom of Portugal and beyond. Marriage strategies, birth 'statistics' and all the rest we may derive from their information concerning the interrelationship of the different families and the part they played in political society. How they deployed their influence near the king or within a military order, in the territorial lordship or in the *Reconquista*, becomes much clearer from the study of the roughly five thousand noblemen mentioned in the *Livro de Linhagens*.[20]

The *ethos* and rules of nobility had already been defined and we know how eager the nobles were to realize and implement them and to exploit the power that rights and privileges provided. Moreover, in the specific context of the Lineage Books it is also possible to observe the process of verbalization by means of enunciating the names and the glories of their ancestors. This process has been fully studied by scholars of the medieval romance in respect of the role of the enunciation of a name and of its magical effect in relating an individual to the group. Only by knowing the name, the roots and therefore the lineage to which an individual belonged was it possible to be invested with a personality, and to assume a distinct identity.[21] Genealogies, and especially these type of genealogy, share these preconcepts: the consciousness of belonging to a particular group was thus elevated into a principle by its being recorded in writing.

In a country in which the chronicle tradition was both weak and dominated by churchmen, the secular narratives inserted into the lineage books provide the possibility of perceiving the nobility on its own terms. The preoccupation with preserving noble status and prestige and its reaffirmation[22] by writing it down in a time when the oral tradition was decaying is indeed very significant.

II, from whom they had received the castles, but instead became the vassals of the 'usurpator', according to the compiler's point of view.

[19] As is the case with the mythical origins of some families like the Velosos and the Marinhos, derived from unions between nobles and semi-pagan deities, like the mermaid who could not speak or the lady with the goat's feet. For the origins of such myths in their relation with similar *topoi*, see L. Krus, 'A morte das fadas: a lenda genealógica da dama pé de cabra', *Ler História*, vi (1985), 3–34, and idem, 'Uma variante peninsular do mito de Melusina: a origem dos Haros no Livro de Linhagens do conde D. Pedro de Barcelos', in *Passado Memória e Poder*, pp. 171–95.

[20] More exactly, 4738 names and 776 families, as counted by Krus, *A concepção nobiliárquica*, p. 16.

[21] Carlos Carreto, *Figuras do Silêncio: Do Inter/Dito à emergência da palavra no texto medieval* (Lisbon, 1996), pp. 325–47 makes a deep analysis of this very theme in French romance. See also his 'Nome, escrita e genealogia. O poder dos signos na narrativa de linhagens', in *Poder e Sociedade: Actas das Jornadas Interdisciplinares*, ii (Lisbon, 1998), pp. 401–25.

[22] See L. Krus, 'O discurso sobre o passado na legitimação do senhorialismo português dos

It is also important to bear in mind how all three books were compiled in times of tension between the kings and the nobility. But what motivated such tensions, and how was it that these men came to occupy the status and positions they enjoyed?

Within the Iberian Peninsula, the nobility had always had to defend their posses- sions from the Moors for real life-and-death purposes: fighting Islam and defending or enlarging their patrimony. The *Reconquista* theme has always served a wide variety of purposes, from the ninth century, when its ideology was developed by ecclesiastics for the benefit of the kings of Oviedo,[23] until the cen- tral decades of our own century, when various Spanish and Portuguese his- torians launched their own 'crusade', in order to prove the non-existence of feudalism in the Spanish kingdoms, a non-existence attributable, allegedly, to the Reconquest itself. As the guiding principle which propelled every form of life in the Iberian Peninsula and which held every part of society together in har- mony while aiming to defeat the enemies of Faith, the idea of Reconquest has been required to account for the supposed dependence of the nobility on their kings, and, therefore, for the latter's retention of their authority intact. Further- more, it has been proposed that the constant struggle against the infidel served to instil a sense of comradeship into nobles and kings alike, thereby frustrating the fratricidal tendencies characteristic of nobilities north of the Pyrenees, and favouring the processes of centralization from which the cause of monarchy in Hispania was destined to benefit.

The centralized sanctified kingship of Spain, together with the non-existence of feudalism in Iberia, was a crown jewel for Spanish and Portuguese medieval- ists of the middle of this century, and the mission of enhancing national pride and superiority they were asked to fulfil, but has been proved wrong from all the works elaborated in more recent years.[24]

Although it may be thought that recent Spanish and Portuguese historians discovered feudalism when all historians elsewhere were discovering that it never existed in the way we once thought we could conceive it,[25] the truth is that the study of the nobility and its social and economical practices as illuminated

finais do século XIII', in *Passado, Memória e Poder*, pp. 197–207, and 'O rei herdeiro dos condes: D. Dinis e a herança dos Sousas', *ibid.*, pp. 59–99.

23 On the issue of the 'Invention of the Reconquest' see, in the chapter with that same title, P. Linehan, *History and the Historians of Medieval Spain* (Oxford, 1993), pp. 95–127.

24 For a thorough analysis of the problem and its latest developments see Mattoso, *Identifi- cação de um País*, pp. 81–7, as well as his four articles on Portuguese feudalism concen- trated in one of the collected studies volumes, J. Mattoso, *Fragmentos de uma composição medieval* (Lisbon, 1987), pp. 115–47.

25 A sharp criticism of the Spanish pro-feudal fundamentalists has been made by Linehan, *History and the Historians*, pp. 191–203, and also in 'The Church and Feudalism in the Spanish Kingdoms in the Eleventh and Twelfth Centuries', in *Chiesa e mondo feudale nei secoli X–XII: Atti della dodicesima Settimana internazionale di studio, Mendola, 24–28 agosto 1992* (Milan, 1995), pp. 303–29.

by works of economic history and on the terminology used to describe the social relationships has revealed a structure of relationship every bit as 'feudal'[26] as anywhere else in Europe, and the same sort of problems, too.

The conquest of the territory from the Moors did not imply such drastic differences between these men and their equals in the rest of the medieval world. As elsewhere, men organized themselves into a hierarchical system ruled by *amor* and *vassalage* oaths liable to be fractured by the usurpation of land and jurisdiction, and the murder of royal officials. The power and autonomy of these lords, undeniable in theory, must indeed seem the greater to the extent that they operated remote from central power. In this analysis, the effect of the Reconquest emerges as the very opposite of the fanciful construct of an earlier generation of historians. Certainly, the nobility served the kings. But they did so on their own terms, serving Muslim and Christian lords indifferently, as self-interest dictated.

Yet it would be wrong to ignore the fact that the kingdoms of Christian Spain were continuously being extended during our period, and to neglect the importance of this for the peninsular nobility. To start with, they owed most of their property, wealth, influence, and prestige to the fight. Moreover, the opportunities created by the constant availability of new lands to the military minority, and the sort of contacts established with their confessional enemies served to promote an acculturative society with specific characteristics. Let us now consider the course of this process on the Portuguese side of the Peninsula.

The beginnings of the so-called 'Portuguese nobility' are traceable back to the times of the Astur–Leonese kings. The kings of Oviedo granted the newly conquered territories as tenures to the very highest nobility, assigning them vast regions to administer, govern, and populate. It was at this time that Coimbra and Oporto were established as counties, each of them protecting rivers which roughly circumscribed the frontier line.[27] But these high Galician noblemen showed much more interest in poisoning unfriendly kings than in providing for the territories entrusted to them. The counts of Coimbra and Oporto were above all king's men, curialists, and resident at court. The real administration of their estates they left to a lower rank of the nobility, later to be known as *infanções*, who, as the count's delegates, not only saw to territorial administration but also to judicial business, acting as judges for their lords. Of course they did not fail to build fortunes for themselves, and, consequently, to develop a territorial bond to the places to which they were attached. In the mid-eleventh century, a series of events would catapult this middle-rank provincial nobility into new prominence.

[26] For the feudal vestiges in the terminology of its own time see J. Mattoso, 'A difusão da mentalidade vassalática na linguagem quotidiana', *Fragmentos*, pp. 149–63, and Ventura, 'A Nobreza de Corte de Afonso III', pp. 170–6, 227–40.

[27] For the whole process see A. Andrade, L. Krus, and J. Mattoso, *O Castelo e a Feira: A Terra de Santa Maria nos séculos XI a XIII* (Lisboa, 1989), pp. 117–73, and M. J. Branco Silva, 'Portugal no reino de Leão: Etapas de uma relação (866–1179)', in *El reino de León en la alta Edad Media, iv: La Monarquía (1109–1230)* (León, 1993), 537–625.

The Galician dynasties of the Leonese kings were unable to protect themselves against both internal dissent and Islamic threats, and, in 1035 the throne of León came to the hands of the Navarrese Fernando I. Being well aware of the tradition of regicide and deposition associated with the outgoing dynasty and unwilling to maintain the same entourage as his predecessors, Fernando I changed his staff from the Portuguese–Galician counts to the second-rate *Infançōes* nobility, and Mozarabic élites, and gave them direct control in the regions over which they already enjoyed delegate powers at one remove. This adjustment was quite easy to implement, as it coincided with the biological extinction of the lineages of the comital families.[28]

The disappearance of the descendants of these lineages, famously symbolized in the battle of Pedroso (1071) where Count Nuno Mendes died, would mark the final extinction of the comital families (preserved only by the marriage of the daughter of the count to Sisnando, the new governor of the newly reconquered Coimbra) and their replacement by the families of *infançōes*, which, as well as inheriting the social uses and practices of their predecessors, were also immediately attached to the region.

Court office and military responsibilities provided new opportunities for enhancing the prestige of these newly advanced lineages. Therefore, when, later, Alfonso VI of León nominated his son-in-law Henry as count of Portucale (combining the previous counties of Oporto and Coimbra), the new lord of the region took into account the relevance of these men and the power they wielded. Coming from Burgundy, and representing the 'French connection' in the Alfonsine court, he had to deal carefully with the well-entrenched nobility he found, especially in the region between the rivers Douro and Minho, where the earliest occupation had taken place, and where the frontier had been firmly settled for more than two hundred years already. So he created a personal court in the image of the Leonese, and to this he attached the most important members of the old nobility. The nomination of these men as the count's *maiordomus*, *armiger*, and *notator* kept his small scale 'kingdom' functioning, and gave the nobility of the place reason to be satisfied and appeased.[29]

When Count Henry died, in 1112, his widow Teresa (the illegitimate daughter of Alfonso VI) began to rule, intervening in the dynastic fights of the Leonese kingdom as her husband had previously done. She then had to deal with a powerful group of privileged noblemen. It is therefore not surprising that when Teresa embarked on her Galician adventures and alliances with the Travas, and started to lose both territories and power in a suicidal war against both her sister Urraca and her nephew Afonso,[30] these men felt threatened. First of all, they were not interested in the kingdom of León, as both Henry and Teresa were, and

28 Cf. Mattoso, *Ricos-Homens Infançōes e cavaleiros*, pp. 30–94, and Branco Silva, 'Portugal no reino de Leão', pp. 554–76, and the bibliographical references there given.
29 T. S. Soares, 'O governo do conde Henrique de Borgonha', *RPH*, xiv (1975), 383–8 and H. B. Ruas, 'Se partio ayrado del rey', *RPH*, iv (1955), 5–7.
30 B. Reilly, *The Kingdom of León and Castile under Queen Urraca, 1109–1126* (Princeton,

secondly, they were apprehensive of the effects of Galician influence[31] on their recently acquired political power.

The political bad luck or clumsiness of Teresa, and two consecutive interventions by Urraca and her son in 'Portuguese' territory, with heavy losses on the Portuguese side, gave them the motive to rise in rebellion, with Afonso Henriques as their standard bearer. It was they who not only sustained the ambitions of Portugal's first king, but also helped him win the fight of 1128 in which he assumed power.[32] From having been mere delegates of the counts, these men had grown into first rank curialists. Having done so, they most likely expected to be rewarded in the political field. What they surely did not anticipate was the king's distancing of himself from them, a process which began in 1130 when Afonso Henriques astutely moved his 'capital' from Guimarães to Coimbra and by doing so evaded the old nobility's control.

Leaving their 'physical' sphere meant escaping their powerful schemes and the southward movement of the new king and his court implied the promotion of a second-generation nobility who supported the new king unconditionally, because they were his creation. The king himself owed nothing to these nobles, whereas his debts towards the nobility of the Entre-Douro e Minho were considerable.[33]

The men who served Afonso Henriques were, therefore, mostly second sons of the old lineages, or lesser lineage men, who needed to earn and expand their own power, and whom border fights provided with the perfect opportunity for extending their power basis. The war against Islam, which would be held as the legitimate basis for the king's claim to his right to rule the kingdom, also served the interests of these men and their vassals. Coimbra was also the source of ideological support for the new king in the diocese of Coimbra and the monastery of Santa Cruz. In that sense, it could be said that the king's decision to move from Guimarães to Coimbra was the only logical one.[34]

Supported by nobles he could control and by the military orders (especially the Templars in these years) he then progressed with the occupation of the territory which confirmed him in his power. Towards the old nobles he adopted a new policy: he granted them prominent places in his *curia*, but deprived them of real political influence.

1982), pp. 87–117, retraces the par course of Teresa during the years which preceded her son's rebellion. See also T. S. Soares, 'O governo de Portugal pela infanta-rainha D. Teresa (1112–1128)', *Colectânea de Estudos em honra do Prof. Damião Peres* (Lisboa, 1974), pp. 99–109.

[31] J. Mattoso, 'A nobreza medieval galaico–portuguesa. A identidade e a diferença', *Ler História*, i (1983), 5–12.

[32] J. Mattoso, 'A Primeira tarde portuguesa', in *Portugal Medieval: novas interpretações* (Lisbon, 1985), pp. 11–35.

[33] J. Mattoso, 'A realeza de Afonso Henriques', *Fragmentos*, pp. 213–32, for the king's strategy.

[34] See Andrade, Krus, and Mattoso, *O castelo e a Feira*, pp. 145–160 where the role of Coimbra as a cultural and political centre is enhanced.

In this, he was initiating a practice which would be followed at least throughout the first dynasty and which was based upon the distinction between the settled and senior nobility of the north and the restless middling nobility of the south. The old nobility enjoyed immense powers in their northern estates, ruled as independent lords within their own lands, and schemed to control the monarchs. Lower rank nobles were very much more concerned to remain close to the king, and his service, and to enlarge their landed holdings by means of royal grants. The old nobility would soon be driven into opposition and the king be moved to attack their growing privileges. This process of action and reaction would establish the pattern according to which events would move during the centuries under consideration. The never-resolved disputes of the kings of the first dynasty and their nobles would provide the dynamic of Portuguese society, which expressed itself in client faction and court intrigue.[35]

Realising that most noblemen were exceeding their jurisdictions, the kings would soon start to try to subject them and their properties to review. Hence the royal Enquiries and also the general laws, in the issuing of which the monarchs would implicitly and also sometimes explicitly confirm their own authority within political society, thereby further alarming the noblemen who regarded their privilege as immune from kings they considered as their own creation.[36]

All this helps to explain why the Books of Lineage were compiled at moments of political tension, and is reflected in the ideology which fills their pages. Tension between the kings and the old conservative nobles, who frequently supported rival candidates to the throne (such as the king's brothers or sons) in order to neutralize the monarch's attempts to master them, in both the political and the economic fields, pervaded all the power relationships between kings and nobles throughout the first dynasty. In broad terms, the gestation of a two-level nobility was associated with the geographical dispersal of the respective lineages, alternatively supporting or fighting the kings. Even so, all continued to gravitate towards the king's court in order to maximize their opportunity of securing royal favours. The court service in high and middle officiality catapulted many families who had already gained their territorial positions, but lacked the nobility derived from the king's service. The part they would assume in every moment of crisis and the marriages they made with royal or highly placed families were to play a part, too, in their search for influence in political affairs.[37]

Even if in this quest they often forgot the loyalty they owed to their own

---

35 J. Antunes, A. R. Oliveira, and J. G. Monteiro, 'Conflitos Políticos no reino de Portugal entre a Reconquista e a Expansão: Estado da questão', *Revista de História das Ideias*, vi (1984), 25–160.

36 M. J. Branco, 'The General Laws of Afonso II and his Policy of "Centralisation": A Reassessment', in *The Propagation of Power in the Medieval West*, ed. M. Gosman, A. Vanderjagt, and J. Veenstra (Groningen, 1997), pp. 79–95.

37 L. Ventura, 'A Nobreza. Da Guerra à Corte', in *Nova História de Portugal*, dir. J. Serrão and A. H. Oliveira Marques, iii, *Portugal em Definição de Fronteiras (1096–1325)* (Lisbon, 1996), pp. 206–24.

kings and regularly alternated in the service of other peninsular kings, both Christian and Muslim.

So far, I have been discussing the 'external' mechanisms by which this nobility ascended to power. I now turn to the internal mechanisms of that same ascent, as well as to the strategies it adopted in pursuit of its social aims.

Within a group such as this, within which privilege and fortune are transmitted by blood as much as codes of conduct and physical characteristics, kinship (natural or artificial) and matrimonial strategies are the most efficient and obvious mechanisms whereby the group maintains and reproduces itself both biologically and socially. The view has been taken that in Portugal, where feudal bonds are so difficult to discern, it is in the bonds of kinship structures and alliances that the basis of noble solidarity may be said to have been rooted.[38] Here, where the nobility can be traced from the ninth century, there is evidence for the gradual adoption of the practice of patrimonial transmission along agnatic lines.[39] The establishment of this system has been confidently ascribed to the mid-twelfth century,[40] and this seems to be confirmed by the contents of the lineage books. It has been accepted that the agnatic system and its practices, initially adopted by the royal house, were soon imitated by the principal families of the kingdom, anxious to follow the royal model.[41] However, the reality does not seem to have been so clearly *linear*.

Although it seems that the main tendency was in favour of *linearization* of the succession through the eldest son, and although it has to be recognized that what is at issue is the multiplication of simultaneous vertical successions rather than the simple persistence of cognatism,[42] it is none the less necessary to insist that in Portugal, as in the rest of the Iberian Peninsula,[43] at least, this process was neither rapidly nor completely achieved. In fact, the persistence of cognatic elements over many years is undeniable.

It may more readily be conceded that the reservation of the symbolic and territorial patrimony of the lineages to the first born was one of the reasons for the frequent disposal of second sons in cathedral churches or convents, military

---

[38] Such is the belief of most of those who have dealt with the nobility. See, for example, Mattoso, *Identificação de um País*, i, 209–216; B. V. Sousa, 'A família nobre medieval portuguesa: Balanço historiográfico e perspectivas de investigação', forthcoming paper presented to the École des Hautes Études en Sciences Sociales de Paris in December 1997, pp. 2–3, and Ventura, 'A Nobreza de Corte de Afonso III', i, 177–240.

[39] J. Mattoso, 'Notas sobre a estrutura da família medieval portuguesa', in *A nobreza medieval*, pp. 393–9.

[40] Mattoso, *Ricos-Homens, Infanções e cavaleiros*, pp. 109–11.

[41] *Ibid.*, pp. 112–13.

[42] See Sousa, 'A família nobre', pp. 9–11.

[43] Spanish scholars have reached identical conclusions when analysing the Castilian model as well, as may be seen by the work developed by I. Beceiro Pita and R. Cordoba de la Lave, *Parentesco, Poder y Mentalidad: La nobleza castellana-siglos XII–XV* (Madrid, 1990).

orders, or royal service in the reconquest or the royal bureaucracy, or even as settlers, as recorded in the *Repartimiento* which followed the conquest of Seville in 1248.[44] And the same would go for daughters, condemned either to marry or to live the rest of their days in the family home or enter a convent. Genealogical literature and both monastic and royal records mention numerous such cases of second sons and daughters.[45]

And yet, it is equally the case that there were occasions in which the succession of the family name passed through the maternal line and the children adopted not the father's name, but the mother's.[46] Similarly, there are many examples of records of partible inheritance from which we may conclude that equitable division between all the children was frequently the norm. The eldest son might receive a slightly larger share, the *melhoras*,[47] but the main practice was a division of patrimonial goods by which all heirs profited.[48] Indeed, according to a law of the late thirteenth century, noted by Vasconcellos Sousa,[49] all children had to receive equal shares. In short, we have to acknowledge that the system in place was a mixed one, in principle agnatic but retaining many residual cognatic elements.

The late introduction of the *Morgadio* regime by which the agnatic system was definitively institutionalized, as well as the (again late) lay lordships, seem to provide confirmation of these considerations.[50] In the same sense, recent studies of female religious communities have revealed numerous cases of

---

44 The Portuguese settlers in that process have been identified by H. David, 'Os portugueses nos livros de "Repartimiento" da Andaluzia (século XIII)', *Revista da Faculdade de Letras: História*, 2nd ser., iii (1986), 51–75, and H. David and J. A. Pizarro, 'Nobres portugueses em Leão e Castela (século XIII)', *Revista de História*, vii (1987), 135–50. They match the traced profile.

45 Cf. Mattoso, *Ricos-homens, Infanções e Cavaleiros*, pp. 104–13, and for the case of the second-sons his 'Cavaleiros andantes: a ficção e a realidade', in *A nobreza Medieval*, pp. 353–69.

46 As was the case with Martim Afonso de Resende, who inherited his mother's prestige, the *nucleus* of property and especially, the family name. B. V. Sousa, *Os Pimentéis*, pp. 300–2.

47 The same process is detectable in Castile, as it is perfectly described in I. Beceiro Pitta and R. Cordoba, *Parentesco, Poder y Mentalidad*, pp. 232–4 and through the references there given.

48 For this processes see, for all, B. Sousa, *Os Pimentéis*, pp. 393–401, where the whole problematic is reviewed and where new data are proposed. The very recent PhD thesis of J. A. Pizarro, 'Linhagens medievais portuguesas: Genealogias e estralégias (1279–1325)', 3 vols, Univ. of Oporto (1997), firmly confirms those elements.

49 *Ordenações Afonsinas*, Livro iv, Tit. cvii, as cited by Sousa, 'A família nobre', p. 11.

50 For this, check the very relevant elements produced by L. Rosa, 'Estrutura familiar e mecanismos de reprodução do poder: morgadios e dimensão horizontal da linhagem do século XIII ao XV', in *Actas do Encontro 'A Construção Social do Passado'* (Lisbon, n. d.), pp. 93–115, as well as her already quoted work on the *Morgadio*. For the Castilian case, see B. Clavero, *Mayorazgo, propriedad feudal en Castilla, 1369–1836* (Madrid, 1974).

women of the high or middling nobility who were professed nuns, receiving patrimonial goods in their convents and sharing them with the rest of their brothers and sisters, and administering them totally independently, *pleno iure*.[51] All of which confirms what is known to have been the case in neighbouring kingdoms, where progress towards a pure agnatic system was very slow and gradual.

The most striking feature of the matrimonial strategies of the group of families whose fortunes we may follow is a marked endogamous tendency. I am not talking of endogamy in the strict sense of the term, but rather, in accordance with the results of the works of José Mattoso,[52] Leontina Ventura,[53] Luis Krus,[54] and Bernardo Vasconcellos,[55] in the sense of marriages within a limited number of families. There seems to be no doubt about the intentions which lie behind specific strategies in the interrelationship of certain families. This is very obvious from the many cases known of successive marriages of an individual with several sisters of the same lineage, marriages of two brothers of one line with two sisters of another, and marriages within the same family or families over several generations.

José Mattoso constructed a series of highly informative charts of such endogamic unions for his *Identificação de um País*.[56] This work provides a graphic account of what I have just described. The classification proposed by

---

[51] The proliferation of these studies has brought up surprising elements, as the unexpected independence of these women in their administration seems to be widespread. For Portugal, see F. Andrade, *O Mosteiro de Chelas, uma comunidade feminina na Baixa Idade Média: Património e Gestão* (Cascais, 1996); M. J. Branco and H. Vilar, 'Vivência religiosa e propriedade no mosteiro de Arouca no dealbar do século XIV: o exemplo de Margarida Pires de Portocarreiro', in *Poder e Sociedade*, pp. 273–91; M. H. Coelho, *O Mosteiro de Arouca do século X ao século XIII*, 2nd edn (Arouca, 1988); R. C. Martins, *Património Parentesco e Poder: o Mosteiro de Semide do século XII ao século XV* (Lisboa, 1992); J. S. F. Mata, 'A comunidade feminina da Ordem de Santiago: a comenda de Santos na Idade Média', unpublished MA thesis, Univ. of Oporto (1991); A. M. Rodrigues, 'O Património das donas de Santos durante a Idade Média', in *As Ordens Militares em Portugal. Actas do I° Encontro sobre Ordens Militares* (Palmela, 1991), pp. 115–30; M. L. S. Santos, 'O Domínio de Santa Maria do Lorvão no século XIV. Gestão feminina de um Património fundiário', unpublished MA thesis, Universidade Nova of Lisbon (1997); *idem*, 'Um mosteiro na estratégia senhorial: Lorvão no século XIV', in *Poder e Sociedade*, pp. 293–302. For another female patrimony, M. H. Coelho and L. Ventura, 'Vataça: Uma dona na vida e na morte', in *Actas das II Jornadas Luso-Espanholas de História Medieval*, i (Porto, 1987), pp. 159–94.

[52] *A nobreza medieval*, pp. 381–4

[53] 'A Nobreza de Corte de Afonso III', pp. 196–227.

[54] Andrade, Krus, and Mattoso, *O Castelo e a Feira*, p. 23. They detected, only in the region of Santa Maria da Feira, a percentage of endogamic unions for the three first generations of settlers of 67%.

[55] *Os Pimentéis*, pp. 335–51, where the alliances of the Pimentéis with the Pereiras expose such strategies in a very eloquent form.

[56] Mattoso, *Identificação de um País*, pp. 244–5. All the conclusions reached here come out

the same author, dividing the nobility into court nobility, prominent families, and regional nobility, allows the detection of the frequency of such movements. The first-born of the highest lineages married almost exclusively within their own family circle; the regional lineages also seem to have preferred matrimony with their equals. This is very clear for the twelfth century, but a little less so for the thirteenth century, when second sons or collaterals began to assume a more active part in establishing matrimonial alliances within the circle of the most important families. This development was surely related to the role of the second-rank nobility during the crisis which followed Afonso III's accession to the throne, and to the support this king sought and which he received from promoting such men. Ascending to a higher rank by serving the king and receiving large benefices as reward for such service, the next logical step for them would be to 'marry well'. But these strategies did not always work. They were subject to the vagaries of contingency and biological survival.

The *infanções*, who replaced the counts in the political field, would also mimic their social customs, marriage strategies included. In fact, they also used marriage as a means of maintaining the stability of alliances or of enabling lesser nobles to ascend socially. This was achieved through what has been called 'the circulation of women',[57] meaning that the female members of families, while circulating through the *nucleus* of noble families by marriage, were, in a sense, the motor and the *means* whereby alliances, peace, and prosperity were achieved and kept. And also, frequently, the only *form* through which the family could subsist. Marriages into lineages in which the feminine element predominated could prove very profitable. Such was the case with the Riba de Vizela, a minor lineage whose males benefited from successive marriages within the same branch of the Maia family, which was itself afflicted by a lack of male heirs. The result was that, in two generations, the Riba de Vizela inherited not only the patrimony of the Maia but also its traditions and prestige, which they assumed as their own, as if they were the true, biological heirs, despite the fact that they retained the name of Riba de Vizela.[58]

It would be wearisome to list the many similar cases by which the artificial kinship created by marriage and sealed by biological reproduction proved an efficient means of preserving alliances and perpetuating lineages in danger of extinction. Family strategies seem to be the same all over, and Portuguese nobles do not constitute an exception, except, perhaps, in respect of *mobility*, a characteristic which distinguished the 'Portuguese' nobility on both the geographical and the social plane.

Firstly, there was mobility within the group, in the hierarchy of the nobility

of the many studies which have been made, and they are given in *Identificação de um País*, pp. 210–16, where the most recent research is reviewed.

57 Expression first used by Mattoso in his *A nobreza Medieval*.

58 Mattoso, *Identificação de um País*, pp. 162–4; L. Krus, 'O tema das origens da nobreza portucalense no relato fundacional da linhagem dos senhores da Maia (finais do século XIII)', in *A Memória da Nação*, ed. D. Curto and F. Bethencourt (Lisbon, 1991), pp. 71–9.

itself, both upwards and downwards. The desire to advance to a higher rank, by means of a good marriage, is a permanent characteristic of the middling nobles, whether they had become powerful in the king's service and now wished to marry into court nobility or old nobility families, or just seek gains made in war or by illegitimate usurpation of royal rights.[59] Then, mobility in the sense of the different places these men often occupied during their careers, advancing from the status of mere warriors or military knights or regional lordship or the rule of some religious house to more prestigious and profitable service at court: a process capable of projecting families from provincial obscurity to the very summit of the social hierarchy. Next, there was the mobility of those who operated on the wider peninsular stage: those noblemen, generally members of high nobility, or of the royal family itself, who sought their fortunes in the service of whichever peninsular king would offer them better terms. Treasons and internoble faction were as much the weapons of such men as marriage into the highest lineages of Castile, León, and Galicia, if not with royal bastards or even legitimate offspring. This happened quite commonly with the royal *infantes*, who, once deprived of the hope of inheriting the throne, took themselves off to neighbouring courts, with whose lords they generally shared blood bonds. The *peninsularity* of the old high nobility is undeniable and some of the members of these lineages were so closely connected with the nobility of the other Spanish kingdoms that it seems difficult to assign them a specific identity. We probably should not even try to do so, as they themselves seem to have regarded themselves as Hispanic rather than as Portuguese or Castilians or Galicians, as the lineage books so well underline.[60]

Finally, there are those for whom mobility was a consequence of marriage, as they took possession of estates far away from their place of origin. The royal Enquiries are extremely useful in allowing us to observe such middling nobles enlarging the properties received by marriage by means of various devices (amadigo, usurpation, patronage) in order to create vast dominions.[61] Movement was generally towards the south, as was logical, but there were also cases of those who went north. Some of these enjoyed impressive careers. One such was the recently studied family of the Pimentéis, whose rise contained all the elements already mentioned, and which, as soon as its patrimonial basis was

---

[59] See B. Sousa on the characteristic 'open' situation of the Portuguese nobility as late as the thirteenth and fourteenth centuries, *Os Pimentéis*, pp. 20–2. In the same vein, although regarding the access to nobility instead of the circulation within it, see M. C. Gerbert, 'Accès à la noblesse et renouvellement nobiliaire dans le royaume de Castile (de la Reconquête au XVéme siècle)', *Arquivos do Centro Cultural Português*, xxvi (1989), 359–87.

[60] Once again, revert to Krus, *A concepção nobiliárquica*.

[61] Several of such examples in Ventura, 'A Nobreza de Corte de Afonso III', pp. 639–41; an excellent example is given by the members of the family of the future master of the order of Santiago, Paio Peres Correia, whose rise was propelled by each and every one of such ways and means, in order to improve their social and economic status. Paio Peres Correia, the general master, is himself yet another example of those noblemen whose careers have known no settled frontiers, borders, or lords.

secure, invaded the political sphere, placing its members in the king's court, the military orders, and the ecclesiastical hierarchy. Its matrimonial strategy and calculation at all times were the basis upon which the success of this family, one of the most distinguished and powerful lineages of the fourteenth and fifteenth centuries, was founded. This is remarkable if we consider how the origins of the Pimentéis were obscure and darkened by the adulterous bastardy of its remote ancestors. Yet, from the time of the marriage of Vasco Martins Pimentel with Maria Anes de Fornelos,[62] the history of the family was one long success story, with its members coming to occupy positions of the highest trust at the Portuguese, and after that, the Castilian court.

It has been suggested above that women played a crucial rôle in the nobility enhancing strategies under discussion; yet it has often been frequently maintained that, once married, these women became mere objects in the hands of their husbands, lacking both juridical existence and economic capacity. But the thesis of the non-entity of the medieval woman does not bear scrutiny. Take, for example, the supposed inability and (or impossibility) of such women to administer their resources and organize their own lives. To be sure, a superficial analysis of the Portuguese documentation related to patrimonial administration reveals that in the vast majority of transactions in which women sell, buy, exchange, or rent property, they do so together with their husbands, always as one of a couple, even if it is the woman who is the vendor or the purchaser. Yet on further analysis, it will be found that, in many cases, women acted alone, as widows, for example, when sharing the wealth received from their husbands with their sons and daughters, or, as we previously saw, in the case of religious women, nuns or *devotae* or *familiares*, administering their patrimonies in total freedom and independence from male control. Or – though this is more rare – of women who appear to have been unattached and to have acted simply as single women.[63]

The issue of the administration of the patrimony of Portuguese noble women,

---

62 B. Sousa has brilliantly shown the ascending movement of this family and its mechanisms, and dismantled very accurately the manipulation of this 'family-staining' episode in the lineage books in order to hide the 'sin' and transform the adulterous relation into a union which took place only after the husband's death. Cf. *Os Pimentéis*, pp. 67–79.

63 For a general overview of the situation, although diminished by the chronological impossibility of taking in consideration the results from the latest researches as quoted above, see M. H. Coelho and L. Ventura, 'A mulher como um bem e os bens da mulher', in *A Mulher na Sociedade Portuguesa: Visão Histórica e Perspectivas Actuais. Colóquio* (Coimbra, 1986), pp. 51–90. These cases are profusely illustrated in the works quoted in n. 51 above. It might also be observed that in patrimonial charters in which men appear as the first vendors or purchasers, it is very uncommon for them to act without their wives. These deeds needed the authority of both man and wife in order to be valid. Yet it has never been proposed that men had no juridical existence just because they appear in the documents in the company of their wives.

and the closely related matter of dowry, deserves to be compared and contrasted with the case of northern societies.

According to the text of Alfonso X's *Partidas*, as represented by the early Portuguese translations, the woman should never lose control of her dowry.[64] After marriage, and for as long as the union lasted, the dowry should be administered by the husband. Yet the woman never lost the right to her landed wealth, which represented her reserve, and in the case of divorce or widowhood, was always legally hers to keep. So, the law itself proclaimed the right of women to keep their possessions intact throughout the marriage. Likewise, the abovementioned law in the Ordenações Afonsinas,[65] according to which the patrimony of the father had to be divided in equal shares amongst his sons and daughters, also protected the right of sisters to receive inheritances in the same juridical sense as their brothers.

Most of what we know about the mechanics of these processes comes from the study of religious houses. We are far less informed about lay noble woman,[66] despite the patrimonial documentation referred to, and the partition deeds and charters of *arras*, by which the husband granted his future wife a dowry. And the case of the queen's household, at the heart of the king's court, is of its nature too exceptional to serve as a wider generalization.[67]

So we are left with the female religious houses, monasteries administered by these noble ladies whose practices provide ample material for study at an institutional level. Recent study of such monasteries has provided numerous surprises. Unlike their male counterparts, their female inhabitants retained their family names, whether the house was Augustinian, Benedictine, Cistercian, or Mendicant.[68] And they also retained the right to administer their own wealth. The distinction between their personal patrimony and the convent's is clear, and

---

[64] According to *Partida* IV, tit. XI, law XVII, the woman should always maintain control over her inherited wealth, even during the marriage. If she gives her wealth to her husband, he should limit himself to administering it, but without taking full possession of it. *Partida* IV, tit. XI, law XXVI states that in case of separation, the husband should keep the *arras* and the woman should receive her dowry, and compensations should be given to settle the increase in the fortunes which might meanwhile have occurred. In this way, the woman's situation is preserved and assured. For the Portuguese use of these texts and their translation and introduction in the 15th-century compilations, see G. B. da Cruz, 'O Direito subsidiário na história do direito português', *RPH*, xiv (1975), 195–7.

[65] Ordenações Afonsinas, Livro IV, tit. CVII: see reference in n. 49.

[66] The work of I. S. Ferreira, 'No silêncio das Palavras. Mulheres nos livros de linhagens', unpublished MA thesis, Universidade Nova (1995), although with innovative aspects, cannot shed light on this specific subject.

[67] Studied by R. C. Gomes, *A Corte dos reis de Portugal no final da Idade Média* (Lisbon, 1995), pp. 46–62. This author was able to retrace the families of servants of the queen's household and the role of certain 'dynasties' of bishops, as well as of almost every other sort of officials in the queen's service, which emulated their male counterparts.

[68] All this is profusely demonstrated in the work done on female monasteries, quoted in n. 51. For Chelas and similar cases in Portugal and Spain, see Andrade, *O Mosteiro de Chelas*, pp. 22–5. The same features appear in the Cistercian Celas de Coimbra and Odi-

those personal goods only passed to the convent after their death. All of this of course was contrary to every rule, both religious and secular, especially if we consider the enormous volume of mortmain legislation issued by the kings throughout the thirteenth and the fourteenth centuries prohibiting religious houses from buying or inheriting property: laws which were probably as frequent as the exemptions to them issued by the same kings.[69]

In whatever sense the cloister is to be seen as a haven for women from the traditional scheme of things, it certainly provided them with greater freedom and autonomy than they would have enjoyed in the world.[70] The documentary evidence reveals a society in which nuns buy and sell, share and exchange land, and bequeath it in wills to close or distant relatives or to the convent. Other ladies preferred not to take vows but to live in the vicinity of religious houses, leading a pious life, but controlling their own affairs to the same extent and operating either in their own name or through proctors[71] – just like men. Houses such as these could also be said to display endogamous characteristics, in that in

velas of Lisbon. See M. R. Morujão, 'Santa Maria de Celas de Coimbra, um mosteiro feminino da Ordem de Cister', in *Actas do Congreso Internacional sobre San Bernardo e o Cister en Galicia e Portugal*, i (Ourense, 1992), pp. 583–7, and H. Vilar and M. J. Branco, 'A fundação do mosteiro de Odivelas', *ibid.*, pp. 589–601. Moreover, this seems to be the case also in the other peninsular kingdoms. P. Linehan, in *The Ladies of Zamora* (Cambridge, 1997), shows that the Dominican ladies behaved just like their neighbours of Portugal and acted as lay lords in respect to their patrimonies. The same applies to their Allariz colleagues, as well as for other female houses, as has been amply shown by numerous works. See, generally, C. Rodrigues Nuñez, *Los conventos femeninos en Galicia: El papel de la mujer en la sociedad medieval* (Lugo, 1993), and also *I Congresso Internacional del monacato femenino en España, Portugal y America, 1492–1992*, 2 vols (León, 1993), in which papers, although the chronological frame is somewhat different, the same features are recognizable.

69 In fact, the mortmain legislation which began to be issued early in the thirteenth century would become much more strict than its first representatives. The prohibition of the Church's inheriting property from their dead members would soon become the general interdiction of buying property and receiving grants in mortmain. But the fact is that the monarchs also used to give every house several charters of protection which included exemptions from such laws. On this subject, see the remarks of I. Gonçalves, *O Patrimónío do Mosteiro de Alcobaça* (Lisboa, 1989), p. 27. Alcobaça was the only religious house completely exempt from such legislation. As a sample, see the cases of Arouca as alluded to in Vilar and J. Branco, 'Vivência Religiosa', p. 287, and of Odivelas, *idem*, 'A fundação do mosteiro de Odivelas', p. 599, where the royal privileges permitted the nuns or *devotae* of Arouca or Odivelas to buy and receive donations from whomever it might be by a period of time or in a specific case. See also J. F. Mata, 'O mosteiro de Santos sob a protecção régia (secs XIV–XV)', in *Poder e Sociedade*, i, 303–15, and Filomena Andrade, *O mosteiro de Chelas*, pp. 44–6, where she lists similar exemptions granted to that monastery.

70 As Santos, 'Um mosteiro na estratégia senhorial', p. 300, proposes, when she states that belonging to a convent also emancipated women from men's dominion, and allowed them to act with much more independence.

71 Cf. the lists of proctors of the monastery and of individual nuns, presented by Andrade, *O*

most cases there seems to have been a tendency for members of the same families to congregate in the same houses. Thus at Lorvão,[72] Arouca,[73] Semide,[74]
and many others, at any one time there would be grandmothers, sisters, cousins,
and nieces of the same lineages in residence.

This phenomenon may be attributable to previous patronage of the house by
particular families, just as the royal *infantas* were at Lorvão, Arouca, and Celas
de Coimbra,[75] for example. At all events, the relationship of these religious
houses with the area in which they were situated was identical to that of the
ladies' male relation. As rich institutions and landlords, they would continue to
prosper until the sixteenth century.

Of course, away from the convents, we encounter women of a different sort.
Such epithets as 'long neck' or 'hot legs' which we find in the lineage books
conform to the traditional image of women as helpless victims of males, passive
as a rule, except when represented as modern Eves and the root of all evils. Even
so, in real life we can cite the case of certain royal ladies whose careers tell a
different story. Take that of Teresa Sanches, for example. The daughter of King
Sancho I, she had married Alfonso IX of León. Repudiated on grounds of
consanguinity, after giving him three children, she returned to Portugal, and
became patron of Lorvão, expelled the male community and introduced the
Cistercian rule in place of the Benedictine.[76] A woman of vast wealth, after her
father's death she received a considerable dominion *iure hereditario*.[77] From
then on, she administered her inheritance vigorously, fighting for her alleged
rights both in Portugal, where a challenge from her brother the king led to civil
war and the military intervention of her former husband, the ruler of León, and
at the papal court.[78] The record is that of a woman running her affairs in total
freedom and as the owner of extensive powers, not only dealing with noble
faction, wars, and diplomacy, and protecting Dominicans and Franciscans, but
also granting charters of privilege to little villages, and rents and benefices to

---

mosteiro de Chelas, pp. 132–5, and by Santos, *O Dominio de Santa Maria do Lorvão*, pp.
157–60.

[72] Santos, 'Um mosteiro na estratégia senhorial', pp. 295–8, reveals the existence not only of
a significant concentration of members of the same family in the same house but also the
contemporaneous existence of members of the same branch of the same family in several
different houses which maintain the pattern for at least three generations.

[73] Coelho, *O Mosteiro de Arouca*, pp. 44–7, and Vilar and J. Branco, 'Vivência religiosa',
pp. 280–2, 291.

[74] Martins, *Património, Parentesco e Poder*, pp. 41–82.

[75] For these see M. Cocheril, 'Les infantes Teresa, Sancha, Mafalda et l'Ordre de Cîteaux au
Portugal', *RPH*, xvi (1976), 33–49. The life of Mafalda in Arouca has been studied in a
modern way by M. H. Coelho, *Arouca, uma terra, um mosteiro, uma santa* (Arouca,
1989).

[76] M. A. Marques, 'Innocêncio III e a passagem do mosteiro de Lorvão para a ordem de
Cister', *RPH*, xviii (1980), 231–83.

[77] T. Veloso, 'A questão entre Afonso II e suas irmãs sobre a detenção dos direitos senhori-
ais', *RPH*, xviii (1980), 197–229.

[78] M. J. Branco, 'The General Laws of Afonso II', pp. 80–1, 91–2.

her ecclesiastics.[79] She issued *privilegios* modelled on those of the royal chancery, had a complex staff to assist her, and still managed to acquire for herself a reputation for sanctity and the epithet of *beata*[80] as soon as she died. And her sisters and half-sisters led similar lives.[81] We describe such women as exceptional, in the sense of exceptions to the rule. But were they? Or is it not rather lack of information on our part that makes them appear so? Noble men and women all shared the exceptional status which allowed them to benefit from immunity and privilege.

[79] Teresa Sanches would surely have been considered a great 'feudal' lord by last century's historians, if it were not for the fact that she was a woman. In fact, it seems to me that her importance has not been recognized until now, precisely because of that. In my present research, I intend to emphasize her actions and the government of her estates during the period when she fought her brother, the king, and headed the resistance to him in the civil war, supported by the papacy and the king of León. In a time when dynastic succession was still not a perfectly accepted form of acceding to the throne, and in a territorial area in which women used to accede to royalty by their own right, the struggle of the king with his sisters is much more serious than has been proposed.

[80] For her 'sanctity', although it is a romanticized view, D. Yanez Neira, 'Tres princesas lusitanas en el Cister – Teresa, Sancha y Mafalda, vistas por los historiadores españoles', *Brigantia*, xii/1–2 (1991), 93–125.

[81] Not only Sancha and Mafalda, but also Branca, as well as Constança Sanches, one of Sancho I's bastards, whose career as a territorial entrepreneur extended over fifty years. The impressive number of documents in the Portuguese archives, which prove this assertion and illustrate the life of this very influential although somewhat shadowy woman, who deals in her own exclusive name, during the reigns of four kings (father, brother, and nephews), deserves a monographic treatment, which has not yet been done.

13

Noblewomen, Family, and Identity in Later Medieval Europe

Jennifer C. Ward

In 1261, a parliament was held at Nikli, summoned by the *baili* of Morea in the aftermath of the Latin defeat at Pelagonia at the hands of the Byzantines two years earlier, when William de Villehardouin, prince of Achaia, was taken prisoner, and required to surrender three of his strongholds, Monemvasia, Mistra, and Maina. The parliament was attended largely by women, the wives of those who owed military service, although there were at least four men there as well. It was agreed to accept the terms laid down by the victorious Greeks, and the daughters of the marshal and constable were selected to go as hostages to Constantinople. This parliament was an extraordinary happening in the later medieval world, the usual pattern being for women summoned by right of tenure to send a male representative. At Nikli the husbands were necessarily absent because of death in or imprisonment after the battle, and, although the chronicle accounts only give men's speeches in the debate, the women had an important say in the final decision.[1]

The whole episode raises important questions as to how women saw their identity in the medieval world. Did women, particularly of the higher nobility, see themselves as having a political role in later medieval Europe, and was this role inextricably linked with the position and circumstances of their families? Did the role change over time, and were there differences between the various parts of Europe as a result of law and custom, social ideas, and political decisions? In considering these questions, twentieth-century historians have to be mindful of a number of contradictory considerations which had to be faced by the medieval nobility. It was taken for granted that most noblewomen would be married, and, although the widow often enjoyed independence in her personal and business decisions, the presence of a husband was regarded as an invaluable support to a woman in safeguarding her property; when Margaret de Neuilly failed to secure her inheritance of Akova, she was advised by her friends to

---

[1] *The Chronicle of Morea*, ed. J. Schmitt (Groningen, 1967), pp. 290–9; *Livre de la Conqueste de la Princée de l'Amorée*, ed. J. Longnon (Paris, 1911), pp. 120–3; *A History of the Crusades*, ed. K. M. Setton, 6 vols (Madison, 1955–89), ii, *The Later Crusades, 1189–1311*, ed. R. L. Wolff and H. W. Hazard, pp. 246–8; P. Lock, *The Franks in the Aegean 1204–1500* (London, 1995), p. 305.

remarry, so that with the help of a powerful husband she would be able to secure her rights.[2] From the point of view of the upwardly mobile, the value of marriage to an heiress as the means of gaining estates and political alliance was universally accepted, and not only in the Middle Ages; unfortunately, there were never enough heiresses to go round. However, from the viewpoint of the family, the importance of a continuous male dynasty was a constant preoccupation. Parents hoped for the birth of a male heir – and preferably for the birth of more than one son, since expectation of life was uncertain; the birth of daughters rather than sons could be significant for securing alliances, but proved expensive for the provision of dowries, and signalled the end of the dynasty. Any head of a noble family wanted to ensure the continuation of the dynasty, but at the same time to keep the family patrimony intact. Contradictions also arose over the position of the widow. She could play an important role in providing for family continuity during minorities, but she had to be provided with dower, and a long-lived and frequently remarried widow could seriously cramp the style of the heir when he came of age. All these considerations were in the minds of the nobility in the later Middle Ages; the question arises as to how far women's roles were affected by them.

The developing legal frameworks governing tenure and inheritance had a major impact on the position of women. On the one hand, there are significant contrasts between geographical areas. On the other, there came to be increasing similarities across Europe as a result of the emphasis on primogeniture and the use of the entail. By the thirteenth century, in many areas, including England, Scotland, Northern France, Burgundy, and the Low Countries, the succession of the eldest son by primogeniture was usual, but in the absence of a son daughters might inherit; the custom varied as to whether the succession went to the eldest, or to all the daughters in equal shares. However, in some areas such as Burgundy and the Limousin, a woman's dowry counted as her share of the inheritance, and she could only claim a share of the family lands by surrendering her dowry. The widow's dower normally consisted of a life tenure of half or one-third of her husband's lands. Although the preference was for a male fief-holder, it was accepted that women could hold fiefs, and carry out the obligations either in person or by substitute. The emphasis therefore came to be on the nuclear rather than the extended family; cousins and more distant relations normally only had a claim if there were no immediate descendants of the deceased fief-holder.[3] A similar situation obtained in the lands of the Latin

---

2 *Chronicle of Morea*, pp. 474–502; *Conqueste de la Princée de l'Amorée*, pp. 197–211; Lock, *Franks in the Aegean*, pp. 302–5. Margaret failed to win her case even with the help of her new husband, John de St Omer, although William de Villehardouin subsequently granted her one third of the barony. Margaret had failed to put in her claim within the prescribed time of a year and a day of the lordship becoming vacant, because she was one of the hostages sent to Constantinople in 1261.

3 R. Boutruche, *La Crise d'une société: Seigneurs et paysans du Bordelais pendant la*

Empire; a daughter might inherit lands and rights if there was no son to inherit, and she could perform homage and be invested with the fief.[4]

It was thus usual in the thirteenth century and later to find women in these areas holding and inheriting land. In thirteenth-century lists of vassals in England, names of men and women are found alongside each other in the lists of knights' fees in 1242–43, although the numbers of women were relatively few; in Norfolk, Walter fitz Robert had forty-two male tenants and six female, and the Earl Warenne sixty-nine men and five women.[5] In Champagne, the ratio of women fief-holders remained throughout the century at about twenty per cent, and this included women who were holding by inheritance, as well as by dower, wardship, and escheat.[6] An analysis of acts of homage in the Limousin about 1300 revealed 10.81 per cent acts of homage by single women, wives, and widows. This covered a wide range of vassals, from officeholders like Eustachie, *vicomtesse* of Comborn, to women with only small areas of land. Widows primarily acted as guardians for their children. Although husbands were in overall charge of the family lands, three instances were recorded of married women doing homage without their husbands, as when Margaret, wife of Itier de Montvalier, did homage for property that had been held by her father and brother.[7]

Women's landholding is partly explained by the frequent extinction of the male line in medieval noble families, giving daughters and sisters the prospect of inheritance. In the case of the Vendeuvre family of Champagne, Hulduin I divided his large estate between his two sons about 1170. In the elder line, the lands had to be divided between his two great-granddaughters because their brother had gone into the Church, while in the younger line a granddaughter inherited. In a comparatively short space of time, the estate had passed to three new families. The transmission of lands and claims through women because of the failure of male heirs occurred frequently in the Latin Empire. Margaret de

Guerre de Cent Ans (Paris, 1947), p. 287; M.-T. Caron, *La Noblesse dans le Duché de Bourgogne 1315–1477* (Lille, 1987), pp. 194–201, 216–18; T. Evergates, *Feudal Society in the Bailliage of Troyes under the Counts of Champagne, 1152–1284* (Baltimore, 1975), pp. 71, 130; R. Hajdu, 'Family and Feudal Ties in Poitou', *Journal of Interdisciplinary History*, viii (1977–78), 117–39; R. Hajdu, 'The Position of Noblewomen in the Pays des Coutumes, 1100–1300', *Journal of Family History*, v (1980), 122–44; J. Hudson, *Land, Law and Lordship in Anglo-Norman England* (Oxford, 1994), pp. 108–18; M. Parisse, *Noblesse et chevalerie en Lorraine médiévale* (Nancy, 1982), pp. 164–72; J. Verdon, 'Notes sur la Femme en Limousin vers 1300', *Annales du Midi*, xc (1978), 319–29; R. L. Wolff, 'Baldwin of Flanders and Hainaut, First Latin Emperor of Constantinople: His life, death and resurrection, 1172–1225', *Speculum*, xxvii (1952).

4   Lock, *Franks in the Aegean*, pp. 302–5.
5   *Book of Fees*, 3 vols (London, 1921–31), ii, 902–7.
6   Evergates, *Feudal Society*, p. 71.
7   Verdon, 'Notes sur la Femme', pp. 319–29.

Neuilly's claim to the barony of Akova came through her uncle Gautier de Rosieres who died childless.[8]

Women were less likely to be visible where it was customary to divide lands among the sons or even among cousins and other male relatives, although even here they were by no means completely excluded. Aristocratic custom in Germany and parts of Lorraine throughout the later Middle Ages favoured partible inheritance among the male members of the family. Rights of heiresses were sometimes accepted, and they transmitted their rights to their husbands and male heirs. However, there are instances of women's rights being questioned, as when the succession of Mahaut, daughter of Simon III, to the county of Sarrbrücken was said to be contrary to the custom of Germany and the church of Metz.[9] As elsewhere in Europe, marriage could provide an opportunity of securing land and status; the marriages of the sisters of Duke Louis I of Bavaria to the margrave of Vohburg, the count of Wasserburg, and the count palatine of Ortenburg resulted in the acquisition of those counties by the dukes in the first half of the thirteenth century. The concentration of the lordships of Jülich, Berg, Kleve, and Mark on the lower Rhine between the fourteenth and early sixteenth centuries came about as a result of marriage and inheritance.[10]

Emphasis on masculine inheritance is also found in Southern Europe. The noble clans of northern and central Italy saw male succession as perpetuating the family lineage, the eldest son inheriting the principal house and tower, and the rest of the property being divided among the other male heirs. The dowry contributed by the bride's family to the marriage was returned to her when she was widowed, together with the dower settled on her by the husband at the time of the marriage. However, the dower was increasingly limited or abolished in the course of the later Middle Ages, thus preventing the dispersal of property outside the dynasty.[11]

All these legal customs governing inheritance continued into the early modern period. As a result, a minority of noblewomen were able to exercise considerable power as heiresses and widows. The lands which they inherited from their parents, together with estates derived from their husbands, gave them rights and political power in their own localities, and sometimes at the centre as

---

8 Evergates, *Feudal Society*, pp. 207–9; *Chronicle of Morea*, p. 474; *Conqueste de la Princée de l'Amorée*, p. 197.

9 Parisse, *Noblesse et Chevalerie*, p. 186; Mahaut succeeded her elder sister Laurette, and was succeeded by her son Simon.

10 B. Arnold, *Princes and Territories in Medieval Germany* (Cambridge, 1991), pp. 151, 239, 242; E. Ennen, trans. E. Jephcott, *The Medieval Woman* (Oxford, 1989), pp. 239–40.

11 M.-C. Gerbet, *La Noblesse dans le Royaume de Castille: Etude sur ses structures sociales en Estrémadure (1454–1516)* (Paris, 1979), pp. 170–1; J. Heers, trans. B. Herbert, *Family Clans in the Middle Ages* (Amsterdam, 1977), pp. 55–7, 101, 104–5; D. Herlihy, *Medieval Households* (Cambridge, Mass., 1985), p. 154; C. E. Meek, 'Women, Dowries and the Family in Late Medieval Italian Cities', in *'The Fragility of her Sex'? Medieval Irish Women in their European Context*, ed. C. E. Meek and M. K. Simms (Dublin, 1996), p. 138; D. Nicholas, *The Growth of the Medieval City* (London, 1997), p. 197.

well. Rowena Archer has commented on the 'rich old ladies' of later medieval England who derived their considerable wealth from inheritance, together with jointure and dower; one of them, Margaret de Brotherton, was created duchess of Norfolk in her own right by Richard II. Joan de Bohun, countess of Hereford, held county and local office in the early fifteenth century.[12] These women can be compared with the noblewomen who exercised political control in various parts of France and the Low Countries; Mahaut countess of Artois (d.1329) as a widow governed the county which she had inherited from her father in 1302, intervening in the affairs of town and country and vigorously defending her rights. About one hundred years earlier, Blanche of Navarre, widow of Count Theobald III of Champagne, ruled the county on behalf of her son between 1201 and 1222, her son Theobald IV having been born posthumously. Jeanne and Margaret, daughters of Count Baldwin IX, ruled as countesses of Flanders for much of the period between 1206 and 1278.[13]

However, at the same time as women such as these were playing a political role based on their landed wealth and status, there was from the later thirteenth century a growing emphasis on primogeniture and the male entail among the higher nobility, and as a result women were excluded from estates which they would earlier have enjoyed and where they would have exercised power as land-owners. Women's rights over property appear to have declined progressively in northern and central Italy where preference was put firmly on male succession, a distant kinsman as heir being preferred if there was no son who could take over as head of the family. Moreover, the wife's authority over her land and goods was weakened, and her rights to her dowry called into question.[14] In Sicily, the trusts of the later fourteenth century showed that major baronies were passing to the eldest male heir, and both alienation and female succession were forbidden.[15] The attempt to insist on impartibility and male inheritance in Germany in the Golden Bull of 1356 was largely a failure; where this happened, as in the duchy of Württemberg at the end of the fifteenth century, it was largely due to family accident rather than imperial privilege; when Württemberg was

---

12 *Rotuli Parliamentorum*, 6 vols (London, 1783), p. 355; *Calendar of Patent Rolls, 1399–1401*, pp. 60–1; *ibid. 1401–5*, p. 129; *ibid. 1408–13*, pp. 204–5; R. E. Archer, 'Rich Old Ladies: The Problem of Late Medieval Dowagers', *Property and Politics: Essays in Later Medieval English History*, ed. A. Pollard (Gloucester, 1984), pp. 15–35; R. E. Archer, 'The Estates and Finances of Margaret of Brotherton, *c.* 1320–1399', *Historical Research*, lx (1987), 264–80.

13 *Recueil de documents rélatifs a l'histoire de l'industrie drapière en Flandre: Première partie. Des origines à l'époque Bourguignonne*, ed. G. Espinas and H. Pirenne, 4 vols (Brussels, 1906–24), i, 61–2, 79–82, 125–6; J.-M. Richard, *Mahaut Comtesse d'Artois et de Bourgogne (1302–29)* (Paris, 1887), pp. 28–47; Evergates, *Feudal Society*, p. 3; D. Nicholas, *Medieval Flanders* (London, 1992), pp. 151–7.

14 J. Larner, *Italy in the Age of Dante and Petrarch* (London, 1980), pp. 67–9; T. Dean, *Land and Power in Late Medieval Ferrara* (Cambridge, 1988), pp. 109–11; Meek, 'Women, Dowries and the Family', pp. 136–8.

15 H. Bresc, *Un monde Méditerranéen: Economie et société en Sicile, 1300–1450*, 2 vols (Rome, 1986), ii, 680–1.

created a duchy in 1495, inheritance by primogeniture in the male line was laid down, and it was the extinction of one dynastic line the following year which enabled the other to take over without the danger of further partition.[16]

Similar trends are found in other parts of Europe. In Andalusia and Estremadura, emphasis was put on primogeniture as a means of enhancing the position of the head of the family, with the entail being used to preserve the unity of the patrimony; the earliest examples of such practice among the higher nobility date from the late thirteenth century. In Estremadura, all children were entitled to a share of the parents' property, unless in the case of daughters they had already received a dowry, but the parent was allowed by law to give more to one child. This particularly advantaged the eldest son who was regarded as becoming the head of the lineage. In addition, in the fourteenth and fifteenth centuries, the higher nobility made use of the entail, which had to have royal consent, to give a further advantage to the eldest son. The parent in his or her will was allowed to dispose of twenty per cent of property in religious and charitable bequests. Of the remaining eighty per cent, one-third could be entailed on one child who would also receive his legal share of the family property. Emphasis was put on primogeniture and the preservation of the patrimony, and some founders of entails specified that no daughter was to inherit, although she could transmit her rights to a son.[17]

The nobility of the British Isles pursued similar policies. In England, several members of the higher nobility created male entails in the fourteenth century, in some cases to provide for younger sons or daughters' dowries, but often to ensure male succession to the family patrimony. Thomas de Beauchamp, earl of Warwick, made detailed provision for his family in 1344–45, and it is significant that the lands settled upon himself and his three eldest sons were all to descend in tail male; by far the largest group of lands were settled on the earl and his eldest son Guy. Male entails were also created by John de Vere, earl of Oxford (d.1360). Such arrangements did not necessarily ensure peaceful succession, as evidenced by the entail set up by Thomas Lord Berkeley in 1349 for the core of his estates. On the death of his grandson in 1417, his only child Elizabeth and her husband Richard Beauchamp, earl of Warwick, refused to accept her cousin James as heir, and the feud was energetically pursued by both them and their daughters, only being settled much later in 1609.[18]

Similar developments occurred at about the same time in Ireland. During the fourteenth century earldoms were created in tail male, and from the late thir-

---

[16] F. L. Carsten, *Princes and Parliaments in Germany from the Fifteenth to the Eighteenth Century* (Oxford, 1959), p. 2.

[17] Gerbet, *Noblesse dans le Royaume de Castille*, pp. 197, 206–10, 213–26. Entails could be created for younger sons, or for daughters if there were no sons, but these were rarer than the entail for the eldest son. Very occasionally, the property was divided equally among the children, as in the will of 1435 of Isabel de Guzmán, wife of Pedro de Zúñiga; yet it has to be pointed out in this case that the eldest son had in addition one entail from his mother's family and two from his father's.

[18] *Women of the English Nobility and Gentry 1066–1500*, ed. and trans. J. Ward (Manches-

teenth century male heirs were increasingly favoured. The concept of lineage was paramount, and both Thomas fitz Leones in 1287 and the Rochefort family of Ikeathy in County Kildare in 1299 wanted to avoid female succession and the consequent fragmentation of the family estate. As the 1299 settlement stated, in the event of there being no male heirs in the main line, the barony of Ikeathy should pass to the noblest and strongest men who possessed the blood and name of the Rocheforts, so that it should never be divided and never pass to daughters.[19]

The importance of the male kindred was increasingly stressed in Scotland in the late Middle Ages, and male entails were created. However, because of the number of sons born to the higher nobility in the late fourteenth and fifteenth centuries, it would have been rare for daughters to succeed, even if the entail had not been in place. The emphasis on agnatic lineage was reflected in the fact that the woman kept her natal family name when she married, and did not become fully a member of her marital kin.[20]

In France, there seems to have been a degree of convergence between North and South in the later Middle Ages, with the North showing growing concern for younger sons, and the South an increasing desire to preserve the unity of the patrimony. The importance of the male heir was emphasized in the will of Armand VII de Polignac in 1343. After stating that the establishment of the heir was the top and bottom line of any will, he stated that he wanted to be succeeded by his eldest son if he had one, or alternatively by a nephew; if he had daughters, they were to be provided with dowries, but there was no place for them in the succession.[21] Some families like the Albret manipulated local custom in order to ensure the eldest son's inheritance. Bernard-Ezi II in his first will of 1341 left his patrimony to his eldest son, some fiefs to the next son, and lands to another son, his wife and executors having to choose which son would be the best

ter, 1995), pp. 108–9; G. A. Holmes, *The Estates of the Higher Nobility in Fourteenth-Century England* (Cambridge, 1957), pp. 47–9; K. B. McFarlane, *The Nobility of Later Medieval England* (Oxford, 1973), pp. 136, 145, 273–4; C. Given-Wilson, *The English Nobility in the Late Middle Ages* (London, 1987), pp. 140–4; C. D. Ross, 'The Household Accounts of Elizabeth Berkeley, Countess of Warwick, 1420–1', *Transactions of the Bristol and Gloucestershire Archaeological Society*, lxx (1951), 81–3.

19 *Calendar of Documents relating to Ireland*, ed. H. S. Sweetman, 5 vols (London, 1875–86), iii, nos. 453, 525; *Justiciary Rolls, or Proceedings in the Court of the Justiciar of Ireland, 1295–1303*, ed. J. Mills (Dublin, 1906), pp. 325–6; A. J. Otway-Ruthven, *A History of Medieval Ireland* (London, 1968), pp. 106–7; R. Frame, 'Power and Society in the Lordship of Ireland 1272–1377', *Past and Present*, lxxvi (1977), 11, 25–6.

20 A. Grant, *Independence and Nationhood: Scotland 1306–1469* (London, 1984), pp. 127–30, 139–41; J. Wormald, *Court, Kirk and Community: Scotland 1470–1625* (London, 1981), pp. 28–30; J. Wormald, *Lords and Men in Scotland: Bonds of Manrent, 1442–1603* (Edinburgh, 1985), p. 79.

21 P. S. Lewis, *Later Medieval France: The Polity* (London, 1968), pp. 193, 204–5; A. Jacotin, *Preuves de la Maison de Polignac*, 5 vols (Paris, 1898–1906), ii, 1–11. In the Latin wording of the will, the establishment of the heir was described as 'caput et fundamentum' of any will.

layman; two other sons were consigned to become clerks, and two to become knights of the Order of St John of Jerusalem.[22]

Why did this Europe-wide development occur? Was it simply the continuation of earlier trends, or was it encouraged by other factors? It is tempting to regard war and violence as a factor in this development. Many of the areas where male entails were established suffered from war, rebellion, and disorder in the fourteenth and fifteenth centuries. It might therefore have been considered advisable to have a lord in charge who was capable of military leadership, especially in frontier and unstable areas;[23] women were involved in war preparations, defending castles, and accompanying campaigns, but they did not participate in the actual fighting. Yet it has to be remembered that entails are found in stable as well as unstable areas. Other factors are more likely to have been influential. The growth of a cash economy and the realization by the later thirteenth century that land was a finite resource encouraged the conservation of the patrimony and the use of money for dowries. In parts of northern Italy, the growth of office-holding by the nobility in the towns from the late twelfth century restricted the roles open to women, because they would never be eligible for such a position; at the same time, it was a vital means for a family to acquire power.[24] The general growth of education and of professionalism in government may also have encouraged the eclipse of wives' roles as counsellors to their husbands and the view that their role was primarily domestic; however, the evidence on this is sparse, and Christine de Pisan, in *The Treasure of the City of Ladies*, expected the princess to counsel her husband informally.[25]

The main reasons for the growing emphasis on male succession lie in state-building and royal policies, and in the significance of lineage. For rulers, interventions in marriage and inheritance were an important way of extending control, exercising patronage, acquiring lands, and providing for their own family. The rights of the ruler were laid down in custom and legislation, and where possible exercised in practice. In the *Liber Augustalis* of 1231, the Emperor Frederick II insisted on his right to control succession and marriage; no count, baron, or knight was to presume to marry without the emperor's permission, or to give his daughters, sisters, or nieces in marriage, or to arrange for his sons to marry wives who held property.[26] The Capetian kings of the thirteenth century used marriage to extend their territories and to bind vassals to the

---

22 Boutruche, *Crise d'une société*, pp. 386–8.
23 R. Frame, 'Power and Society in the Lordship of Ireland 1272–1377', *Past and Present*, lxxvi (1977), p. 20, stressed the need for strong leadership and solidarity at a time of insecurity in fourteenth-century Ireland.
24 J. Larner, *The Lords of Romagna: Romagnol Society and the Origins of the Signorie* (London, 1965), pp. 22, 35–9, shows how nobles were taking up the position of podestà in the towns.
25 Christine de Pisan, trans. S. Lawson, *The Treasure of the City of Ladies* (Harmondsworth, 1985), pp. 50–2, 62–5.
26 J. L. Huillard-Bréholles, *Historia Diplomatica Friderici II*, 6 vols (Paris, 1852–61), iv, 134.

Crown; thus in 1258 Louis IX arranged a marriage between his son John of Damietta and Yolande, the eldest daughter of Eudes of Burgundy, with John gaining rights in his father-in-law's inheritance, and the custody of his wife's youngest sisters. In 1294, the count and countess of Burgundy concluded a treaty with Philip the Fair in which it was agreed that their daughter should inherit the county and be married to one of the king's sons; in fact she married the future Philip V.[27]

English kings from the time of the Norman Conquest used their rights as feudal overlord as instruments of power and control, and, in the event of a great fief having no direct heir, exercised the right to control the succession. In the late thirteenth century, Edward I made extensive use of noble marriages and succession to estates in order to strengthen the Crown and enrich members of his family. K. B. McFarlane found that eight families of earls had to accept 'a course of slimming' which left them in a weaker position. Thus the inheritance of Aveline, countess of Aumale, was seized by the Crown after her death in 1274; pressure was brought to bear on Aveline's mother, Isabella de Forz, to surrender her estates to the Crown when she was on her deathbed in 1293; and when Humphrey de Bohun married Edward I's daughter Elizabeth in 1302, his estates were settled jointly on him and his wife, with remainder to the heirs of his body.[28] Control of marriages continued to enrich members of the royal family in the fourteenth century.

Similar policies of control were pursued by Italian rulers, whether they were northern *signori* like the Este of Ferrara, or the Angevins of Naples. The Este made use of fiefs and marriages as a means of reward, intervened in cases of succession, and insisted that licences were required for alienations; the preservation of feudal rights was an essential part of their control of the lordship.[29] The Angevins used strict control over marriages in their designs to extend their rule into Latin Greece, as in the treaty of Viterbo of 1267 when William de Ville-hardouin acknowledged Charles of Anjou as his overlord and surrendered his lands to him, with most of the lands to pass to his daughter Isabelle who was to marry Charles's second son, Philip, and only a small portion of the lands remaining to the Villehardouin heir. Isabelle's life was largely to be controlled by the Angevins. Charles of Anjou took direct control of the lands on William's death in 1278, and it was only in 1289 that Isabelle was granted the title of princess of Achaia in an attempt by Charles to strengthen his hold over the Morea. Isabelle went to Greece with her second husband Florent of Hainault, and ruled the Morea herself for a few years after Florent's death in 1297. In 1306,

27 J. Richard, *Saint Louis* (Paris, 1983), p. 380; J. R. Strayer, *The Reign of Philip the Fair* (Princeton, 1980), pp. 354–5.
28 K. B. McFarlane, 'Had Edward I a "Policy" towards the Earls?', *History*, 1 (1965), pp. 145–59, and reprinted in *The Nobility of Later Medieval England* (Oxford, 1973), pp. 248–67.
29 Dean, *Late Medieval Ferrara*, pp. 77–8, 120–1, 127.

however, the barons of the Morea were released from their allegiance to her, and her third husband, Philip of Savoy, was deposed by Charles II of Naples.[30]

Although royal policies undoubtedly had some influence on patterns of inheritance, it is likely that the main reason for the growing use of primogeniture and entail lay in the Europe-wide concept of the noble family as a dynastic lineage, with a male head, heroic ancestry, coat of arms, and chivalrous reputation. The desire to preserve the lineage was emphasized by the families themselves all over Europe. The importance attached to lineage and ancestry was an essential part of noble living for old and new nobility alike. Possibly it was regarded as especially significant by new members of the nobility who had to establish themselves and their families as true nobles in the eyes of their neighbours and peers. Castile saw the emergence of a new nobility in the fourteenth century as a result of the extinction of old families, warfare, and the policies of Pedro the Cruel and the Trastamare kings; all the lineages creating entails between 1397 and 1474 were members of this new nobility. The head of the lineage exercised moral authority over the family, had a strong and sumptuous town-house, had rights of religious patronage, controlled who was buried in the family tomb, and generally acted as the dynasty's political head.[31]

Elsewhere, the extinction of old families meant that the nobility was constantly renewed, and importance was attached by men and women alike to name, arms, and blood. The property of Matteo Sclafani, count of Aderno in Sicily, was divided between his son-in-law and his grandson in the female line, and both had to take the name and arms of the Sclafani. Aude, lady of Tiran and Bussac in the Bordelais, wanted a stone charnel-house to be built for her bones and for those of her lineage. In some cases, especially where the noblewoman was the last of her family, she laid especial stress on her natal lineage; Eleanor de Bohun in 1399 bequeathed to her son Humphrey a book containing the history of the Knight of the Swan; this was intimately linked to the Bohun family whose badge was the swan.[32] This universal concern with lineage contributed to the concentration of power in the hands of the leading noble families, and was an essential part of their lifestyle.

What effects did the growing emphasis on lineage have on the position of women? At one level, the women could simply be seen as pawns in the marriage market, contributing to the upward or downward mobility of families. The significance of the arranged marriage, with its concerns over land, money, rights, and status, was felt throughout Europe, as was the importance attached to the birth of the heir. Marriages could be arranged to secure peace between feuding families, or alliance, or friendship. Although upward mobility was achieved through royal service in peace and war, marriage made a vital contribution to the

---

[30] *Actes relatifs à la Principauté de Morée 1289–1300*, ed. C. Perrat and J. Longnon (Paris, 1967), pp. 21–9; *History of the Crusades*, ed. Setton, ii, 262–8; Lock, *Franks in the Aegean*, pp. 84–6, 90–7, 102–3, 108.

[31] Gerbet, *Noblesse dans le Royaume de Castille*, pp. 200–201, 206–10, 226.

[32] Bresc, *Un monde Méditerranéen*, ii, 683; Boutruche, *Crise d'une société* p. 274; J.

rise of a family. The Ribera family of Andalusia rose from royal official to top nobility in the course of the fifteenth century, and their brides brought both money and status; the dowry of Beatriz Portocarrero who married Diego Gómez de Ribera (d. 1434) allowed the family to purchase additional lordships, and the marriage of Per Afan II (d. 1455) to Maria de Mendoza, daughter of the marquis of Santillana, took the family into the higher Castilian nobility. In England, the marriages of the Stafford family from the mid-thirteenth century onwards ensured the accumulation of territory and the title of earl of Stafford in 1351 for Ralph Lord Stafford.[33]

Such an interpretation of the arranged marriage would emphasize the importance of the woman's domestic role within the family, and her position as wife, and especially as mother. Yet the evidence suggests in a number of cases that her role was active rather than passive, and that the family provided her with a base from which she could exercise power and influence. The emphasis on patrilineal descent meant that her immediate circle comprised the conjugal family of husband and children, and it was with these that she primarily identified. The range and extent of her activity depended on a wide variety of factors: legal custom and family arrangements defining her role in relation to property, social custom laying down the parameters of acceptable activity, the political circumstances in which she found herself, her relationship with husband and children, and her own personality and ability. Essentially, her economic and political activity depended on the absence of a husband, father, grown-up sons, and other powerful male relatives; in the circumstances of the later Middle Ages many women found themselves in this situation and called on to take political action, as did those who attended the Nikli parliament of 1261.

Many husbands expected that family continuity would be provided by their wives in the event of their deaths; Bernard d'Escoussans ordered that his wife Miramonde should be lady and mistress of all his goods and be supported in his house according to her estate as long as she lived and wished to remain a widow.[34] The practice in England of husbands appointing their wives as executrix of their wills points to the same desire for family continuity. Similar practice is found among patrician families in fifteenth-century Venice, as when Marco Loredan in 1441 made his wife his sole executrix and universal heir.[35] Such duties often had to be assumed unexpectedly and at short notice, and some

Nichols, *A Collection of All the Wills of the Kings and Queens of England* (London, 1780), pp. 181–2.
33 M.-A. Ladero Quesada, 'Aristocratie et régime seigneurial dans l'Andalousie du XV siècle', *Annales E.S.C.*, xxxviii (1983), pp. 1361–2; C. Rawcliffe, *The Staffords, Earls of Stafford and Dukes of Buckingham, 1394–1521* (Cambridge, 1978), pp. 7–11.
34 Boutruche, *Crise d'une société*, p. 286.
35 R. E. Archer and B. E. Ferme, 'Testamentary Procedure with Special Reference to the Executrix', *Medieval Women in Southern England*, Reading Medieval Studies, 15 (1989), pp. 3–34; S. Chojnacki, 'The Power of Love: Wives and Husbands in Late Medieval Venice', *Women and Power in the Middle Ages*, ed. M. Erler and M. Kowaleski (Athens, Ga., 1988), p. 138.

wives found that it took time and effort to discover what had happened to their husbands. Katherine Stafford lost both her husband, Michael de la Pole, earl of Suffolk, and her eldest son in 1415, her husband at the siege of Harfleur and her son at the battle of Agincourt. According to her husband's will, Katherine was appointed one of the executors, and had to arrange for his burial at Wingfield in Suffolk, as well as to hold the family together.[36] Guy de la Trémoille took part in the crusade of Nicopolis of 1396; he was taken prisoner by the Turks, was ransomed, but died of his wounds on the island of Rhodes the following year. His widow, Marie de Sully, sent messengers to try to get news of him, and was informed of his release from prison by the duke of Burgundy.[37]

The mother's main concern after the death of her husband was usually for her children, and it is likely that many women saw their children as their greatest achievement, and saw their own fulfilment as coming through the lives of their children. Evidence from various parts of Europe indicates that the mother's care ranged from providing for the physical needs and education of the child, to ensuring his inheritance, marriage, and adult well-being. When Alessandra Strozzi of Florence was widowed in 1436, she became responsible for safeguarding the family's property and bringing up her children. Although she had affection for her daughters, her interests centred on her two sons. Her daughters were married to men of lower rank in order to keep more property for her sons. She advised her sons on their marriages, and in the mid-1460s was searching in Florence for suitable brides. She wished to ensure the perpetuation of the lineage, and was fully aware of the complex negotiations and bargaining that marriage involved.[38] It is likely that many women regarded their eldest sons in a special light; in 1473, in the will of Amédée de Saluces, *vicomtesse* of Polignac, each of her five sons and six daughters received one hundred écus; all were described as 'beloved' but only the eldest son was described as 'beloved and dearest'.[39]

There were various ways in which a mother could use the power she derived from her conjugal family base; her connections with her natal family and with more distant kin supplemented those with her conjugal family. Agnes, the daughter of William de Valence, made two short-lived marriages to Maurice fitzGerald and Hugh de Balliol, before marrying John d'Avesnes of Hainault in 1277. He died in 1283; they had a family of one daughter and two sons, and Agnes did not marry again after his death. Her activity centred on safeguarding

36 *Testamenta Vetusta*, ed. N. H. Nicolas, 2 vols (London, 1826), i, 189–90; London, British Library, Egerton Roll 8776, gives the household accounts for the family at Wingfield in 1416–17. The tomb of the earl and Katherine can still be seen in Wingfield church, the decoration including the Stafford badge, the knot.
37 Louis de la Trémoille, *Livre de comptes 1395–1406: Guy de la Trémoille et Marie de Sully* (Nantes, 1887), pp. i–ii, no. 32.
38 L. Martines, 'A Way of Looking at Women in Renaissance Florence', *Journal of Medieval and Renaissance Studies*, iv (1974), pp. 19–27; Heers, *Family Clans*, p. 59.
39 A. Jacotin, *Preuves de la Maison de Polignac*, 5 vols (Paris, 1898–1906), ii, 318–20. Each child was described as 'dilectus', and the eldest son as 'dilectus et carissimus'.

her sons' interests in Hainault, and in managing her estates in England and Ireland. Her elder son John died in 1297; in spite of the war situation, Agnes crossed to Flanders to ensure her second son Baldwin's rights to the family estates, and she remained there for the next three years. Unfortunately, Baldwin died shortly before her own death in 1309.[40]

The possibilities for political action were greatest when the mother succeeded in taking over as regent. Marie de Berry was married to Jean I, duke of Bourbon, in 1400. The duke was taken prisoner at the battle of Agincourt, and died in prison in 1434. Marie attempted to negotiate his release and the dauphin provided money for his ransom. However, the duke's acceptance of the treaty of Troyes and of Henry VI in 1429 precluded his return home. Their son was only aged twelve in 1415, and Marie assumed his guardianship and the rule of the duchy in order to try to safeguard its territory. Her husband gave her formal permission to exercise power only in his absence in 1417. Over the years that followed, Marie faced considerable problems arising out of the conflict of Armagnacs and Burgundians. Difficulties also arose over the duchy of Auvergne which her father, John, duke of Berry, in 1386 had declared would revert to the Crown if he died without a male heir, but which Charles VI had agreed at the time of their marriage could pass to Marie and her husband. On her father's death in 1416 Marie occupied the main strongholds of the duchy, but she was only allowed to do homage two years later, and it was not until 1425 that Auvergne was handed over by Charles VII at the time of her son's marriage to Agnes of Burgundy. Marie retired from power in 1427 when her husband gave his son the right to administer the duchy.[41]

The example of Anna of Mecklenburg also points to considerable drive and even ruthlessness on the part of the mother. Anna was the wife of William II of Hesse; their son Philip was aged about five when his father died in 1509. William II's plan of 1506 involved a noble regency in the event of his death; his widow was to retire to her estates. Two years later, Anna persuaded William to appoint her as one of Philip's guardians. Only very slowly after his death did she gain power; William's will was disputed, and the Estates refused to accept her as guardian. However, she secured power in 1514; Philip was declared of age in 1518 and assumed rule two years later.[42]

The mother's concern for and pride in her children shows how she took her identity from her conjugal family, and used the family as her power-base. Many of her religious activities can also be seen within the context of the conjugal family, and such activities were regarded as suitable for women in the later Middle Ages, as the knight of La Tour Landry pointed out to his daughters.[43]

---

40 C. Ó Cléirigh, 'The Absentee Landlady and the Sturdy Robbers: Agnes de Valence', *'The Fragility of her Sex'?*, ed. Meek and Simms, pp. 101–17.

41 A. Leguai, *Les Ducs de Bourbon pendant la crise monarchique du XV siècle* (Paris, 1962), pp. 35–6, 84–130.

42 Carsten, *Princes and Parliaments*, pp. 150–9.

43 *The Book of the Knight of La Tour Landry*, ed. T. Wright (Early English Text Society, o.s., 33, 1868, revised 1906), chapters 2, 20, 90, 101.

The importance of the conjugal family was underlined by the practice of women deciding to be buried next to husband and/or children, in a church often associated with the husband's family. The family church and family tomb were important aspects of the concept of lineage. The Polignac family was buried in the Dominican church at Le Puy in the middle of the choir.[44] This can be compared with the use of the collegiate church of Wingfield by the de la Pole earls of Suffolk, and with the Despenser tombs at Tewkesbury abbey in Gloucestershire. Burial was closely associated with chantry provision which usually named the immediate family as beneficiaries. Armand VII de Polignac asked the Dominicans of Le Puy to celebrate masses for himself, his two wives, and the two children who had died; his first wife, Catherine de Bouzols, asked the friars for masses for herself and her kin, and for her son Armand.[45] Occasionally a wider family circle was envisaged, as when Jeanne de Vienne, lady of Gevry and Pagny, left money to the chapel of the Virgin Mary at Pagny to put into effect the chantries founded by her grandfather, her great-uncle, and her father and mother.[46] A few noblewomen thought in terms of the whole of Christendom; in her statutes for Balliol College, Oxford, Devorguilla de Balliol specified prayers for the soul of her husband John de Balliol, for herself, the souls of their predecessors, and for all the faithful departed.[47]

The conjugal family was therefore of vital importance for the wife's identity and activities in a male-dominated society; however, she was not completely subsumed in her husband's dynasty. If the evidence of tombs, seals, and titles is examined, it is clear that women saw themselves as having a wider identity, and were thinking of their natal family and in some cases of more distant kindred. This is apparent in the description of the tomb of Theobald III, count of Champagne (d. 1201), in the church of St Stephen of Troyes; the tomb itself was destroyed during the French Revolution. The tomb was erected by his widow Blanche of Navarre sometime between 1208 and 1215. Theobald lay on top of the tomb-chest, depicted as pilgrim; he had been expected to lead the fourth crusade. At either end of the tomb stood the figures of the king of England and the king of France. On each side were depicted Theobald's parents, brother, and two sisters, his widow Blanche, and Sancho of Navarre, probably Blanche's brother rather than her father. Also depicted were Theobald's and Blanche's children, and these were the only ones to be picked out in silver-gilt, underlining the importance of continuity of the dynasty.[48] However, the choice of figures shows that the designer and probably Blanche herself were not simply thinking of the patrilineal family.

[44] A. Jacotin, *Preuves de la Maison de Polignac*, 5 vols (Paris, 1898–1906), ii, 1, 318–20.
[45] *Ibid.*, i, 413–14; ii, 4.
[46] Caron, *La Noblesse dans le Duché de Bourgogne*, p. 274.
[47] *The Oxford Deeds of Balliol College*, ed. H. E. Salter, Oxford Historical Society, lxiv (1913), 277–9.
[48] M. Bur, 'L'Image de la parenté chez les comtes de Champagne', *Annales E.S.C.*, xxxviii (1983), 1016–39.

Women's use of seals points to activity and identity independent of their husbands, and the seals themselves indicate that they saw themselves in the context of their own ancestry as well as identifying with their husbands; this was common in the British Isles and in France north of the River Loire. Devorguilla de Balliol depicted herself on her seal as a widow, holding in her right hand her husband's Balliol shield, and in her left the lion-shield of her father's lordship of Galloway; smaller shields provided a reminder of her own connections with the earldom of Chester and the royal house of Scotland. The reverse of the seal gave the place of honour to the lion of Galloway over the Balliol arms. Marie de St Pol, countess of Pembroke, also had a female figure in the centre of her seal; on one side was the shield of her husband Aymer de Valence, and on the other that of her father, Guy de Chastillon, count of St Pol. The seal could also epitomize a woman's claims to power and land; the way in which Galburge de Mévouillon gave herself the title of lady of Serres on her seal in 1259 emphasized her claim to the lordship.[49]

Surnames and titles display a similar desire to advertise birth, marriage, property, and authority. Marie de St Pol continued to use her father's name after her marriage, as did Marie de Berry and Marie de Sully. Hereditary and marital titles were combined, as when Mahaut, heiress to Artois, and wife and widow of Count Otto of Burgundy described herself in the early fourteenth century as 'countess of Artois and palatine Burgundy and lady of Salins'.[50] Anne Stafford, daughter of Thomas of Woodstock, duke of Gloucester, and Eleanor de Bohun, combined ancestral, parental, and marital titles when she styled herself countess of Stafford, Buckingham, Northampton, and Hereford, and lady of Brecon and Holderness. The use of seal and title was designed to impress at the time, but women were also concerned to emphasize their connections to future generations. Anne Stafford was concerned to maintain the Bohun family link with Lanthony priory, and her sons by her third marriage to Sir William Bourchier were received into confraternity there in 1427.[51] The early fourteenth-century windows of the abbey choir at Tewkesbury provided a different kind of family linkage. Eleanor de Clare, married in turn to Hugh Despenser the younger and William de la Zouche, and herself depicted as a small naked figure in the east window, was concerned to display her ancestry; the patrons of the abbey, namely the twelfth-century earls of Gloucester, the Clare earls of the thirteenth and early fourteenth century, and Eleanor's two husbands can still be seen in the south-west and north-west windows.

Family identity for noblewomen was of primary significance, but did not

[49] C. H. Hunter Blair, 'Armorials on English Seals from the Twelfth to the Sixteenth Centuries', *Archaeologia*, lxxxix (1943), 21–2; P. Coss, *The Lady in Medieval England 1000–1500* (Stroud, 1998), pp. 38–47; B. Bedos-Rezak, 'Sceaux seigneuriaux et structures sociales en Dauphiné de 1170 à 1349', *Form and Order in Medieval France: Studies in Social and Quantitative Sigillography* (Aldershot, 1993), pp. 38–9.
[50] *L'industrie drapière en Flandre*, i, 61–2.
[51] London, Public Record Office, SC11/816, m. 1; C115/K2/6682, fol. 180r.

prevent them from having a wider identity as well, mainly with their fellow-nobles, whether these were neighbours, friends, distant kin, or people they met at court. The knightly orders of the late Middle Ages point to the importance of chivalrous networks for men, but these overlapped with social and religious groupings in which both men and women were associated. The evidence of household accounts points to the amount of contact and socializing among the nobility by means of letters, messengers, and hospitality. Mahaut countess of Artois was in touch in this way with many of the nobility of France, and kept up to date with the news of births and deaths; Elizabeth de Burgh, lady of Clare (d. 1360), likewise entertained friends and kin lavishly, and ensured that she was well informed on happenings among the English nobility.[52] Membership of religious confraternities widened a woman's circle; Pierre de Bauffremont and Mary of Burgundy were members of the confraternity of the Virgin Mary at Pouilly, while the gild of Corpus Christi at York and Holy Trinity at Coventry attracted members of the nobility, gentry, and townspeople, both men and women.[53] The extent to which these wider networks overlapped can be seen in the foundation of a chantry in Walden abbey in 1343 by William de Bohun, earl of Northampton. As William was a man who had risen in rank through his service to Edward III, it was fitting that the king should head the list of those to be prayed for; William then listed himself and his wife and their son and heir, his brothers and sisters living and dead, and the parents of himself and his wife; he also included his kinswoman Elizabeth de Burgh with whom he and his wife were in frequent contact, Thomas de Brotherton the earl marshal, Henry Burgh-ersh late bishop of Lincoln, Sir Roger de Clifford, and the souls of all the faithful departed.[54]

With all the emphasis on family and social grouping, was there room for individual identity? Certainly, women had their own preferences in religious and cultural matters, but the evidence of individuality is often ambiguous, and too much can be read into it. Much, for instance has been made of the women Cathars, but it is likely that, for many, family as well as personal factors were at work. The *perfecta*, Esclarmonde de Foix, played a prominent role in the movement, but by putting her in context it can be seen that there were strong family Cathar connections; her brother Count Raymond-Roger of Foix was known to be a protector of heretics, and he appointed Esclarmonde abbess of the *Perfectae* house at Pamiers.[55] Orthodox Catholic women who became vowesses may equally have been influenced by family in their decision, and not just by piety. Why did Philippa Beauchamp become a vowess about three months after her

---

[52] Richard, *Mahaut Comtesse d'Artois*, pp. 62–6, 72; J. C. Ward, *English Noblewomen in the Later Middle Ages* (London, 1992), pp. 77, 105–6.

[53] Caron, *La Noblesse dans le Duché de Bourgogne*, p. 279; *The Register of the Guild of Corpus Christi in the City of York*, ed. R. H. Skaife, Surtees Society, lvii (1871), vi–vii, 63, 69, 86, 89, 97, 121; *The Register of the Guild of Holy Trinity, St Mary, St John the Baptist and St Katherine*, i, ed. M. D. Harris, Dugdale Society, xiii (1935), 28.

[54] London, British Library, Harley MS 3697, fols 258r–259r.

[55] M. D. Lambert, *Medieval Heresy: Popular Movements from Bogomil to Hus* (London,

husband's death?[56] It is likely that many women who adopted a religious life did so for a variety of motives of which family considerations may well have been among the most important.

It is only in a minority of cases that a woman stands out as an individual, largely independent of family. Certain noblewomen had a strong religious vocation, and adopted the religious life before or during marriage, or as widows. Their religious achievement took the place of or superseded their concern with family, as can be seen with St Bridget of Sweden or St Clare of Assisi. On a lesser level, Matilda of Lancaster, the wife of William de Burgh, earl of Ulster, and then of Ralph Ufford, maintained that she always wanted to be a nun, and ended her life at Campsey Ash and at Bruisyard.[57] In the case of older women, it is likely that aspirations could change over time, and other interests besides family developed as they grew older, although this is difficult to trace. Some women may have become more religious as they grew older, or they may have found a comfort and strength in the Church as their children and grandchildren predeceased them. This may explain why Joan de Bohun was recorded as spending much time at Walden abbey in prayer and meditation; she died in 1419, long after her husband, who died in 1373, and her two daughters, and also her brothers, Richard, earl of Arundel, executed in 1397, and Thomas, archbishop of Canterbury, who died in 1414. Cicely duchess of York, mother of Edward IV and Richard III, adopted a religious way of life in her old age.[58]

Possibly, in some cases, childlessness or loss of children contributed to a change of direction, just as it has been found that the interests of childless men could become channelled towards religion and charity. Marie de St Pol, countess of Pembroke, divided her widowhood of over fifty years between England and France, in spite of the Hundred Years War; this division of her time may have led to her being regarded as a foreigner by some members of the nobility on both sides of the Channel, especially in a time of war. She founded Pembroke College at Cambridge in 1348; its contemporary naming as the Hall of Valence Marie sheds further light on her sense of identity. Her will of 1376

1977), pp. 114–16; L. M. Paterson, *The World of the Troubadours: Medieval Occitan Society, c. 1100–c. 1300* (Cambridge, 1993), pp. 249–50; R. Abels and E. Harrison, 'The Participation of Women in Languedocian Catharism', *Medieval Studies*, xli (1979), 227–9.

56 M. C. Erler, 'Three Fifteenth-Century Vowesses', *Medieval London Widows 1300–1500*, ed. C. M. Barron and A. F. Sutton (London, 1994), p. 167; W. Dugdale, *The Baronage of England* (London, 1675), p. 235.

57 *Calendar of Entries in the Papal Registers Relating to Great Britain and Ireland*, 15 vols (London, 1894–1961), *Papal Letters, 1362–1404*, ed. W. H. Bliss and J. A. Twemlow, pp. 37–8; *Petitions to the Pope, 1342–1419*, ed. W. H. Bliss, p. 488.

58 W. Dugdale, *Monasticon Anglicanum*, ed. J. Caley, H. Ellis, and B. Bandinel, 6 vols (London, 1817–30), iv, 134, 140; *Women of the English Nobility and Gentry 1066–1500*, trans. and ed. J. Ward (Manchester, 1995), pp. 217–18; C. A. J. Armstrong, 'The Piety of Cicely, Duchess of York: A Study in Late Medieval Culture', *England, France and Burgundy in the Fifteenth Century* (London, 1983), pp. 135–56.

made no reference to family apart from a bequest to a nephew; she and Aymer de Valence had no children. The codicil to the will contained cash bequests to executors and servants; otherwise, the will was concerned with churches, churchmen, and charity, apart from bequests to the king of England and the king and queen of France; the bequest to the king of France of a sword without a point epitomized her attitude to the war. Apart from Pembroke College, Marie's main interest lay with the Franciscans, and she wanted to be buried in the Franciscan habit in the choir of the Minoresses' church at Denny which she had founded. Her husband had been buried at Westminster, and she provided for gifts to the abbey and for masses for her 'very dear lord' and herself.[59] Marie's will is unusual for its lack of family references, and the concentration on religion may well have resulted from her circumstances.

Looking at noblewomen across Europe in the later Middle Ages, there are both differences and similarities. Women were inevitably affected by different inheritance customs, and in some parts of Europe it was much more likely to find rich propertied women than in others. Yet the similarities of situation grew throughout the period, with the increasing emphasis over much of Europe on primogeniture and male succession by means of the entail. Throughout Europe, the concept of the lineage became more powerful. Noble attitudes towards the arranged marriage and the woman's dowry were virtually universal. With these developments taking place, women could find that they were increasingly limited to the private, domestic sphere, and with fewer landed prospects than many had enjoyed earlier. Yet, in certain circumstances, the conjugal family base enabled the wife or widow to play a political and public role in place of husband or child. The conjugal family unit provided the centre for their lives, and was vital to their identity and activity. At the same time, they never forgot the lineages they belonged to by birth, nor the overall importance of the nobility in society.

[59] H. Jenkinson, 'Mary de Sancto Paulo, Foundress of Pembroke College, Cambridge', *Archaeologia*, lxvi (1915), 409–10, 417–20, 422–4, 432–5.

14

The Western Nobility in the Late Middle Ages: A Survey of the Historiography and Some Prospects for New Research

Martin Aurell

Research on the later medieval nobility is in a healthy state. Everywhere in Europe, new work is being published which adds new clarity to our picture of this social group. The most up-to-date historiography seems to reflect authors' keen awareness of being part of this renewal. Yet with few exceptions, this enthusiasm for the aristocracy is relatively recent and constitutes a kind of defiance of the old prejudices which until recently were attached to the history of élites. The new research coincides with the discovery of a social history based on prosopography, that is, on the biographical study of large numbers of individuals with the aim of situating them in a large-scale network of kinship, group solidarity, and clientship.[1] It is also true that the nobility during the period from the thirteenth to the fifteenth centuries, thanks to the richness of the source materials, constitutes an ideal field of scholarship for anyone interested in applying prosopographical methods. There was at this period a flowering of chronicles and mémoires, witnesses to nobles' subjective consciousness describing their social duties, but also such apparently more objective records as hearth-tax returns, notarial documents, administrative enquiries, and legal case-material. During this same period, moreover, the diffusion of literacy among the aristocracy, and the birth of bureaucratic states, of 'modern' type, vastly increased the quantity of relevant documentation.

Now is the time for syntheses! Philippe Contamine's *La noblesse au royaume de France de Philippe le Bel à Louis XII*, has recently appeared.[2] This fine book, combining large amounts of source material, wide-ranging conclusions, and clarity of presentation, somewhat steals the thunder of the comparable surveys by M.-T. Caron,[3] on royal power and the French nobility, and by M.-C. Gerbet[4] on the Hispanic nobilities. In Britain, Maurice Keen has produced a book of

---

1 The first appearance, in 1980, of the journal *Medieval Prosopography*, published by the University of Michigan, marked a significant moment in this enterprise.
2 Collection 'Moyen Age' (Paris, 1997). This work contains a full and up-to-date bibliography.
3 *Noblesse et pouvoir royal en France (XIIIe–XVIe siècle)* (Paris, 1994).
4 *Les noblesses espagnoles au moyen âge (XIe–XVe siècle)* (Paris, 1994).

similar importance.[5] These works could never have been written, at least on such a large scale, had their authors not been able to build on the foundations (in the strongest sense of that word) laid by many monographs focusing on particular families and regions, tracing the histories of one or more noble lineages in a limited territory. Younger medievalists often pick such themes for their doctoral theses, and research as a whole gains enormously from being sustained by scholarship of a kind that only the most superficial view would label narrow or specialized.

The growth of the State that characterized this period lies at the heart of the problems surrounding the late medieval nobility. For studies of the State tend to use the categories developed by Max Weber (1864–1920) in which the monarchy is credited with a monopoly of violence, and hence the aristocracy appears in a new light. Specifically, this consolidation of State power is alleged to have assured the monarchy of the lion's share of powers that had hitherto been in the hands of territorial lords: the ban, coercion, punishment, and judicial authority. This process provides the backcloth of several new fields of research.

The growth of the State determined both the legal destiny of the nobility in general and the personal status of individual nobles. In 1939, Marc Bloch wrote that the thirteenth century saw a crucial period of change for the aristocracy: from being a nobility of fact, it became a nobility of right.[6] The growing State turned the nobility into an estate. The appearance of the institution of ennoblement by the king – something that in France from Philip IV's reign onwards could be obtained by letters patent issued by the chancery – was a clear indication of these parallel developments. 'Estate' (*status*) is the term which, at least from the twelfth century on, came to denote each juridical category of the social hierarchy. Later, people would use the word 'order' (*ordo*). Economic criteria were not enough in themselves to define each of these strata which divided the social spectrum both vertically and horizontally. In the earliest type of representative assemblies sat bishops, who controlled vast temporal domains, and in some cases a territorial principality, as well as village priests within the relevant limited area. *Mutatis mutandis*, and making allowance for some more complex problems, a similar interpretation could be given to the second estate. Thus the existence of an order was justified not simply by the wealth of its members but by codes of social recognition so subtle that the modern historian, half a millennium later, often finds it hard to pin them down precisely.

The nobility, as order or estate, from this point onwards assumed a juridical reality: it was endowed with specific rights and duties, and with privileges in the strict etymological sense of the phrase *privata lex*. Nobility was less a matter of deportment or life-style than of birth, that is, of blood. Exemption from new taxes, and possession of its own tribunals, were part of this new legal definition of nobility. Equally important in a civilization where appearance and reality

---

5   *Chivalry* (London, 1984).
6   *La société féodale*, 5th edn (Paris, 1968), pp. 445–60.

blurred into each other were the external marks proclaiming to the world that an individual belonged to this order: armorial bearings and aristocratic devices, scarlet stockings or silk robes, were all reserved to the nobility by specific sumptuary laws. Nobles had privileged seats at official ceremonies.

It is worth noting that this appearance of a noble order coincided with the legal establishment of servitude, which became a personal status proper to certain peasant households whose members were hereditarily subject to particular taxes and attached to their lords' demesnes.[7] Alongside this process whereby servitude became more concrete went the rediscovery of Roman law, that most effective of techniques in the construction of the monarchic State. The *adscriptio* of the Justinianic Code, which from the thirteenth century was synonymous with the state of a servile peasant, was the obverse of the equestrian order (*ordo equestris*) which now, in the writings of those who theorized about society, became the nobility.

Historians are still debating the chronology according to which the aristocracy put down juridical roots. Marc Bloch placed this crucial transformation in the early thirteenth century. Philippe Contamine,[8] on the other hand, has pointed out that even late in the thirteenth century this evolution of the aristocracy was still slight in quantitative terms, while Joseph Morsel[9] would incline to put it as late as the fifteenth century. In several studies of great depth and power, Morsel locates the 'sociogenesis' of the nobility around 1450, when the term *nobilitas* was used for the first time to denote the noble group as a whole. The special feature of the region of Germany which is the focus of Morsel's work is that here the birth of nobility occurred independently of any State-construction *manquée* and so escaped any princely control.

Taking refuge behind the alleged geographical diversity of the Middle Ages might seem a justifiable way of evading the debate on late medieval social taxonomy. But in fact the coincidence of the birth of the royal State with that of the noble estate is too striking to be ignored. It was the Mediterranean lands that were the first to experience these developments – lands administered by royal bureaucracies that imitated the governmental methods of Islamic and Byzantine Sicily and the perennially over-staffed Papal States. In these places, Roman Law, erected into an administrative system and a royal ideology at the same time, was widely diffused among the governing and intellectual élites who supplied society with its hierarchical and legal cadres.

The nobility, perceived more than ever before as a group apart, now that it

---

7 P. Freedman, *The Origins of Peasant Servitude in Medieval Catalonia* (Cambridge, 1991).
8 *La noblesse au royaume de France*, p. 329 n. 1.
9 'Une société politique en Franconie à la fin du Moyen Âge: les Thüngen, leurs princes, leurs pairs et leurs hommes (1275–1525)', unpublished thesis, University of Paris-IV, 1993; 'Crise? Quelle crise? Remarques à propos de la prétendue crise de la noblesse allemande à la fin du Moyen Âge', *Sources: Travaux historiques*, xiv (1988), 17–42, a title in which the alert reader should see a learned allusion to *Supertramp*, 'Changements anthroponymiques et sociogenèse de la noblesse en Franconie à la fin du Moyen Age', in *Genèse médiévale de l'anthroponymie moderne*, ed. M. Bourin (Tours, 1995), pp. 89–119.

had become an order acquired a collective identity. The construction of its group-memory is one of the axes on which Georges Bischoff built his brilliant *thèse d'État, Noblesse, pouvoirs et société: les pays antérieurs de l'Autriche (milieu XIVe–milieu XVIe siècle)*.[10] What is true of Alsace, a land of frontiers distant from any State power-centre, is no less true of other western principalities. Now genealogists who were themselves of noble stock traced the histories of their own houses. In the Basque country, Lope García de Salazar (1399–1476) in *El libro de Bienandanzas e Fortunas* gave pride of place to his family's alleged Scandinavian ancestor who had come with a large military following to lend a helping hand to his Visigothic cousins in their struggle against the Arabs: here as in the county of Flanders a few centuries earlier, the story of a founding father sprung from the ranks of Viking adventurers proved to have a long life ahead of it.[11] At the end of the Middle Ages, the genealogical consciousness of noble lineages took concrete form in works of historiography whose authors were themselves often members of those same aristocratic families.

More generally, other origin-myths purport to explain the ancient birth of the nobility and, conversely, of servitude. In Catalonia, the nobility allegedly descended from the twelve companions of Otger Cataló who by force of arms liberated the land from Islam, while the serfs were said to be the distant descendants of those who collaborated with the Arabs. In Hungary, the nobility came from the stock of Attila's warriors, by contrast to the peasantry who, according to the *Tripartitum* of 1514,[12] had been reduced to servitude because of their refusal to answer the call to arms. What was new about this way of imagining the past seems to have lain in the collective definition of aristocratic memory. Just as anyone who has risen in the social scale makes some use of the past to justify that ascent, so the aristocracy found it necessary to construct a mythic genealogical past that attached it to a founding hero. The provost of Paris in the late fourteenth century, for instance, claimed to be born of the ancient lineage of one of Charles Martel's companions-at-arms.[13] At the opposite end of the scale, families of *magnates* evicted from the government of Florence changed their armorial bearings at this very time.[14] We need to recognize these manipulations

---

[10] Defended at the University of Strasbourg in January 1997 and due soon for publication at Strasbourg.

[11] S. Aguirre, *Lope García de Salazar: El primer hitoriador de Bizkaia (1300–1476)* (Bilbao, 1994).

[12] Cited by E. Fügedi, *The Elefánthy Saga* (Budapest, 1996). At the Central European University of Budapest, J. Bak and D. Karbic are conducting a programme of research on the nobility of Central Europe in the late-medieval and early-modern period which has attracted many young scholars. The first round table (18–19 October 1996) enabled the identification of problem areas and avenues of research common to this research.

[13] B. Bove, 'Un cas d'ascension sociale à la fin du XIVe siècle: Audoin Chauveron, prévôt de Paris', *Revue Historique*, ccxcv/1 (1996), 49–82.

[14] C. Klapisch-Zuber, 'Rupture de parenté et changement d'identité chez les magnats flor-

of memory if we are to understand how the nobility increasingly identified itself with a ruling order.

This social preponderance was expressed in other symbolic codes as well. The most conspicuous marks of rank, special clothing and coats of arms, have been mentioned already. Baudouin van den Abeele's recent book[15] shows how the practice of falconry carried a powerful sense of social rank. The *Roman de la Rose* stated without more ado: 'il ont chien et oiseaus/ pour sembler gentis damoiseaux' ('They have a hound and hawks/ to give the impression of being youths of gentle birth'). In frescoes and in manuscript illuminations, the hawk or falcon is often the symbol of nobility and freedom. When a vassal offers a hawk to his lord, that is a gift more prestigious than golden spurs – a gift suitable on occasions of receiving and giving homage between the high-born. Medieval treatises debated the question of whether the glove, or the falcon, should be carried on the right hand or the left: if the right hand was free, it was easier to manage the bird of prey; but if the left hand was occupied, it became hard to mount one's horse. Apparently technical discussions on this subject in fact attest aristocratic fashions and social codes: you could recognize a peasant from the bad posture of his bird. Hunting, games, conduct at table were other areas for the display of aristocratic conduct which was always imitated by those who had recently risen in the social scale. Nevertheless, these codes which created 'distinction', meaning social *savoir-faire* as well as social difference, had to do with social practices, and with fashion. These things were not to be confused with legal norms or rules laid down by government fiat from on high.

The Crown's servants eagerly wanted to integrate the noble order. Françoise Autrand has highlighted the research done by the judges of the Paris parlement on royal ennoblement: these judges constituted a well-defined familial group, a new nobility at the command of the French judicial system.[16] A similar quest for social recognition through entry into the ranks of the nobility can be found among urban élites.[17] Several monographs on urban society describe the strate- gies of family ascent of merchants who invested their commercial capital in land so that they could live off rents and lead a noble lifestyle.[18] In Barcelona, this rush of merchants towards the nobility dates from the fifteenth century, the period when their imitation of noble conduct and their hypergamous matrimo- nial strategies (marriage of a man with a woman from a class higher than his

entins du XIVe siècle', *Annales E.S.C.*, xliii (1988), 1205–40, and M. Pastoureau, 'Strat- égies héraldiques et changements d'armoires chez les magnats florentins du XVe siècle', *ibid.*, pp. 1241–56.

15 *La fauconnerie au Moyen Age: Conaissance, affaitage et médecine des oiseaux de chasse d'après les traités latins* (Paris, 1994).

16 F. Autrand, *Naissance d'un grand corps de l'État: Les gens du parlement de Paris (1345–1454)* (Paris, 1981).

17 Cf. the Acta of the conference held in Rome in May 1996, *Les élites urbains au Moyen Age*, ed. SHMES. (Paris and Rome, 1997); see also T. Dutour, *Une société de l'honneur: Les notables et leur monde à Dijon à la fin du Moyen Age* (Paris, 1997).

18 Cf. for example C. Guilleré, *Girona al segle XIV* (Barcelona, 1993–94).

own) were pushed to frenetic limits. It was at this time that they lost their corporate identity: they abandoned the harbour area and the parish of Santa Maria del Mar to seek parts of the town less clearly linked with their profession. They also became more sedentary, and gave up risk-taking in foreign adventures to live comfortably, instead, on rents. This leaving of old habits, this losing of their taste for enterprise – Fernand Braudel talked of a *trahison de la bourgeoisie* – goes far to explain the crisis undergone on the very eve of the modern age by a great Mediterranean town relegated by the Habsburgs to merely provincial rank.[19] All over the West, the centripetal force of noble values was irresistible. Sooner or later, it drew social climbers into an unprecedented process of aristocratization.[20]

The hierarchical structure, both legal and social, of a whole culture reappeared within the noble group itself, whose various noble houses could not otherwise be subsumed in a homogenous way. This internal taxonomy seems especially pronounced in the Iberian peninsula, where a huge gulf of prestige, wealth, and power separated the high nobility from the lower nobility. At the top of the pyramid, the *ricos hombres* were mighty indeed: in Navarre there were no more than twelve families in this group, and perhaps twenty in Aragon and in Catalonia. They held the key resources in terms of power and land. Lower down, the *infanzones* or *hidalgos* of Castile or the *caballers* of Catalonia were immensely proud of their legal privileges, their tax exemptions, and their military activities – but they remained mere country squires who found it hard to maintain their status. In Navarre, the lesser nobility was split into two subgroups: 'chartered nobles', who could supply documentary proof of their ancient lineages, and 'nobles in clogs', who fought with the infantry.[21] The high aristocracy carefully underlined the vast distance that marked it off from these second-rank nobles: at Catalan representative assemblies, they even tried to divide off these second-rank *caballers* in order to seat them in a fourth estate. The situation of such knights was all the more difficult in that the town corporations forbade them to sit on their councils which were mainly reserved for merchants. In short, the nobility, far from being a monolithic group, was riven by deep social divisions.

These rifts were the deeper at the end of the Middle Ages, because crises enriched the rich and impoverished the poor. In the city of Rome, the baronial houses (*casati baronali*), the Conti, the Colonna, the Orsini, the Annibaldi, and the Savelli, thanks to their ascendance, managed to impose their control over

---

[19] J. Aurell, *Els mercaders catalans al quatre-cents: Mutació de valors i procés d'aristocratització a Barcelona (1370–1470)* (Lleida, 1996).

[20] The process of aristocratization should not be confused with attachment to the values which, like honour – that is to say, the preservation of reputation and renown and increasing social awareness – should not be considered specifically noble, C. Gauvard, *'De Grace especial': Crime, Etat et société en France à la fin du Moyen Age* (Paris, 1991).

[21] B. Leroy, *Le royaume de Navarre à la fin du Moyen Age: Gouvernement et société* (Aldershot, 1990); *eadem, Le royaume de Navarre: Les hommes et le pouvoir (XIIIe–XVe siècle)* (Biarritz, 1996).

still more castles and lordships.[22] They relegated the other urban aristocratic families to second rank.[23] This split into two unequal segments, with the big fish gobbling up the little ones, was not peculiar to Rome where the popes were constructing a state. The process of seigneurialization is likewise well-known in Castile, where it worked to the disadvantage of the royal domain and of the municipal communal authorities. A monograph has just traced the 'rise(?)' of the counts of Ureña – who admittedly started from a high position. By the end of the fifteenth century, royal favour and successful patrimonial tactics made them powerful enough to control and maintain jurisdiction over more than fifty villages across a vast area extending from Old Castile to Andalusia where Osuna, the heart of their lands, was situated.[24] This example is characteristic of the highest layer of the aristocracy, which contrived to come rather well out of the troubles of the fourteenth and fifteenth centuries.[25]

This privileged group was well represented at court, where it participated in the decisions made by the king among his closest entourage. But its presence beside the monarch was also part and parcel of a larger programme through which the ruler aimed to gain the loyalty of the high nobility. From then on, the problem of what we call, in the twentieth century, 'politeness', assumes a key importance for historians. Today, more and more medievalists, and modernists too, focus their research on manners and gestures – things that till recently were considered merely stereotyped or meaningless. Norbert Elias's pathbreaking work has made scholars aware of the full social and political significance of these forms of external conduct which at first seem so second-hand and totally artificial. At the close of the Middle Ages, the State rose again from its ashes, concentrating all powers in itself and reserving a monopoly on coercion. Many lords held on to their exercise of arbitrary violence within their own castellanies. It was therefore necessary that they be taught to control their own aggression, to respect superior jurisdictions, to accept an external discipline: in short, to obey the orders of the king. To achieve this was no minor matter – so deeply rooted in noble mentalities were atavistic modes of conduct, developed in the wordly context of everyday private warfare, and an unlimited taste for independence that rejected any administrative framework which threatened to engulf their autonomous lordships. It is well-known that the simplest way of making these gentlemen sign up to this royal programme of state-building was to bring them to court, where they would learn, by means of etiquette, to show themselves

---

22 S. Carocci, *Dominazioni signorili e lignaggi aristocratici nel Duecento e nel primo Tre-cento* (Rome, 1993).

23 M. Vendittelli, 'Elite citadine: Rome aux XIIe–XIIIe siècles', in *Les élites urbaines* (see above, n. 17), pp. 184–91.

24 F. J. Aguado González, *El ascenso de un linaje castellano en la segunda mitad del siglo XV: los Télllez Girón, condes de Ureña* (Madrid, 1990).

25 Even if it does not enjoy its former prestige, the study of lordship has not been abandoned: *Seigneurs et seigneuries au Moyen Age: Actes du 117e congrès national des Sociétés savantes, Clermont-Ferrand, 1992. Section d'histoire médiévale et de philologie* (Paris, 1993).

docile towards the monarch and to attain self-control.[26] Some historians even speak of a 'domestication' of the nobility: the term can be accepted in its etymological sense, even if its connotations of mastery of the wild lend it a rather unexpected ring.

The education of the women of the high nobility – a topic to which a major conference has recently been devoted[27] – occupies an important place in this project of taming. One only has to think of how much, since the twelfth century, *fin'amors* contributed to teaching young warriors to control their most basic urges, by sublimating these in the idealization of the Lady, attained only after a long wait through which desire was purified. Moderation, a calm and balanced frame of mind, now became the complement of *joy*, that exaltation provoked by the very thought of the beloved woman. The term 'amour courtois', coined by Gaston Paris (1839–1903) to denote these new attitudes, is heavy with meaning in this context. What was true of Love was also true of War which the nobleman could no longer practise without some superior control, nor could he engage in it however he wanted, outside the military structures of the rapidly evolving State. The court was also the place where the nobleman discovered that the constraints of life in society prevented the unfettered exercise of violence and use of weapons, henceforth duly channelled into the royal army. It was the woman who, again, had to give the court its 'tone' and to influence deeply its lifestyle and conduct. The *Roman de Perceforest*, composed between 1315 and 1340, expressed this idea in the plainest fashion: 'If the gentleman who has received the order of chivalry fails to resemble a maid in graces and in virtues, he loses the right to be called knight (*chevalier*), however bold he is.' By means of the history of genres, which described the role and rank of woman in society, increasing courtliness, and the civilizing of conduct, went hand in hand.

Further, in as much as it was the place in which monarchic power was exercised, the court came to seem the centre from which many decisions radiated out through the whole kingdom. Essential, clearly, was the presence of noblemen in the palace centres of power and in the organs of government that linked those to the local level. Long since, Raymond Cazelles's work showed just how hard the aristocracy worked at strengthening monarchy – contrary to earlier received ideas that credited the bourgeoisie with the construction of the modern State.[28] A study of the principality of Savoy in the fourteenth and fifteenth centuries, based on deep theoretical reflection, has just confirmed Cazelles's findings: writing of this Alpine and Piedmontese region, Guido Castelnuovo transcends the outmoded antithesis of officers against gentlemen, between bureaucracy and nobility, to show how deeply rooted were the servants of the State, themselves

---

[26] W. Paravicini, *Die Ritterlich-höfische Kultur des Mittelalters* (Munich, 1994).

[27] *Autour de Marguerite d'Ecosse: Reines, princesses et dames du XVe siècle. Colloque international de Thouars (23–24 mai 1997)*, ed. G. and P. Contamine (Paris, 1999).

[28] *La société politique et la crise de la royauté sous Philippe de Valois* (Paris, 1958); *Société politique, noblesse et couronne sous Jean le Bon et Charles V* (Geneva and Paris, 1982).

often local lords, in the old power structure.[29] As we still see today in developing countries, periods of transition in the establishment of strong governments and administrative frameworks produce networks of clientship grouped around those in whom State power, however frail, is vested. In such a context, the transition from a world of fragmented and segmented power to a State did not come about without certain disadvantages for the nobles, who held a share of commanding authority both at the level of the castle and in the government offices of the royal palace. The songs of the troubadour Bertrand de Lamanon (1210–1270), who was at the same time a local lord and official of the counts of Provence, Raymond Berengar V and Charles I, resonate in a kind of political schizophrenia with the contradictions that such dual roles produced among aristocrats working to consolidate a State which, paradoxically, undermined the seigneurial basis of their own power.[30] The complex reality of service performed for royalty by nobility consists of precisely that.

The relationship between the nobility and war was likewise transformed.[31] Knighthood became definitely Christian in its values,[32] which were borrowed from ancient political ideas based on Augustinianism. In one of the stories in the Arthurian Cycle so familiar to the late medieval nobility, the fairy Viviane explains to Lancelot of the Lake that knighthood was created, as a result of original sin, to defend the weak and poor. Lancelot returns to his warriors to re-establish justice and peace according to this ecclesiastical ideology of power. The clergy took an ever larger part in military ceremonies, and the presence of a bishop became well-nigh essential for a dubbing ritual. Did nobles abandon this ceremony at the close of the Middle Ages? Various indications suggest that they did. Yet there were still families deeply attached to this initiation rite: which allowed war to be conducted while a man preserved his honour. The Bournonvilles, recently examined in Bertrand Schnerb's fine monograph,[33] are a case in point: between 1350 and 1500, seventeen out of the forty-five men known in this family were dubbed, most of them on the battlefield. It is true that these people devoted themselves fervently to the arts of war – and indeed nine of them were killed while fighting. This does not seem to be an isolated example. So we have to conclude, with Philippe Contamine, that 'the nobility preserved its military vocation through all kinds of changes'.[34] To paraphrase the *Grand coutu-*

---

29 *Ufficiali e gentiluomini: La società politica sabauda nel tardo medioevo* (Milan, 1994).

30 M. Aurell, *Le vielle et l'épée: Troubadours et politique en Provence au XIIIe siècle* (Paris, 1989), pp. 203–8.

31 R. W. Kaeuper, *Guerre, justice et ordre public: La France et l'Angleterre à la fin du Moyen Age* (Paris, 1994).

32 J. Flori, *L'idéologie du glaive: Préhistoire de la chevalerie* (Geneva, 1983); *L'essor de la chevalerie (XIe–XIIe siècles)* (Geneva, 1986); *La chevalerie en France au Moyen Âge* (Paris, 1995).

33 *Enguerrand de Bournonville et les siens: Un lignage noble du Boulonnais aux XIVe et XVe siècles* (Paris, 1997).

34 *La noblesse au royaume de France*, p. 329.

mier de Normandie (1235), nobility and knighthood merged with one another.[35]

What seems new at the end of the Middle Ages is a shift from private to public warfare. From this time on, it was the king who benefited from the military superiority conferred by a nobility impregnated with the ideology of combat and whose steady income from rents allowed it to engage in the more or less permanent practice of war. The king, more than ever, summoned nobles to his army. The biographies of Bertrand du Guesclin or Jean le Meingre, nick-named Boucicault, the heroes of the Hundred Years War, insisted on their subordination to the monarch whom they meekly served. These stories contrast with the old epic *chansons* that praised aristocratic revolt against an unworthy king. To make war side by side with the king was another way to domesticate the nobility – to make it more pliable and obedient. In the royal army, each man learned discipline. This notion transformed the old chivalric ideal based on the lineage's family honour and on the exploits of individual knights.

Nevertheless, the disturbances of this period allowed many aristocrats to devote themselves once more to violence wielded outside any military structures. The most recent German historiography is sensitive to the theme of the *Raubritter*, the robber knight. Princes, town governments, and clergy all strove to criminalize this figure: their collective attitudes heaped contempt on the ancient *Fehde*,[36] that is, the personal practice of violence and aristocratic destruction. Far to the south was the kingdom of Navarre: Eloisa Ramírez's work on noble groups and political conflict between 1387 and 1464[37] is based on a data-bank of 1,609 individuals, and analyses the social origins of the struggles of the Agramont party, close to John II and pro-French, and the Beaumonts, supporters of the prince of Viana and pro-English. From this study emerges the thing that gave these conflicts their cutting edge and the rival camps their internal organization, namely, the bonds of kinship and clientage which held different families of the Navarrese aristocracy together. It should be added that the coherence and solidarity of each noble family were not always so strong, and that intra-familial conflicts broke out over disputed inheritance more often than

---

[35] The theoretical problems of the approximation between knighthood and nobility are touched on in the fifteenth-century Castilian treatises examined in Jesús D. Rodríguez Velasco, *El debate sobre la cabellería en el siglo XV: La tratadística caballeresca castellana en su marco europeo* (Salamanca, 1996).

[36] U. Andermann, *Ritterliche Gewalt und bürgerliche Selbstbehauptung: Untersuchungen zur Kriminalisierung und Bekämpfung des spätmittelalterlichen Raubrittertums am Beispiel norddeutscher Hansestädte* (Frankfurt am Main, 1991), and M. Kaufmann, *Fehde und Rechtshilfe: Die Verträge brandenbürgischer Landesfürsten zur Bekämpfung des Raubrittertums im 15. und 16. Jahrhundert* (Pfaffenweiler, 1993). Cf. the reviews and works by J. Morsel, *Bulletin de la Mission Historique Française en Allemagne*, xxvi–xxvii (1993), 168–70, and H. Tugaut, 'La violence nobiliaire en Allemagne (XIVe–XVe siècle)', unpublished Mémoire de maîtrise (University of Rouen, 1992).

[37] *Solaridades nobiliarias y conflictos en Navarra (1387–1464)* (Pamplona, 1990).

is generally realized.[38] The sheer force of physical action remained a widespread way of resolving differences in a milieu where the bearing and use of arms was a right.

The study of structures of kinship lies at the heart of all this work on the nobility. The evolution of these structures was complicated. The strengthening of the State tended, on the one hand, to break up the aristocratic family, while the insecurity provoked by endemic warfare led, on the other hand, to hold the family together. These systolic and diastolic movements would be worth examining in more depth, as would the way in which noble houses branched out very widely, sometimes losing the vital bonds that held them together internally.[39] These divisions brought the segmentation of lands and the splitting of aristocratic lines – and all this, by reducing the power of each family, contributed to the growth of the State. One of the consequences of these partitions was the appearance of new kinds of castles, strongholds that experts on castellology attempt to describe.[40] To compensate for the impoverishment brought by partible inheritance, custom favoured primogeniture and the succession of the eldest son.[41] This occurred everywhere in the West, though to varying extents. Nobles used marriage strategies of hypergamy, that is, they married their sons to newly rich bourgeoises who brought large dowries.[42] All these problems have been examined in more and more depth in the most recent and innovative research.

This rapid survey no doubt leaves untouched many questions raised by recent historiography. I would claim, none the less, that I have pointed to some of the main areas of interest among contemporary medievalists. At the heart of their agendas several themes and problems can be identified: taxonomy and regulation; social codes; gestures and modes of conduct; bonds of clientage and kinship; the increasing theatricality of violence and also its criminalization; regimentation and the making of men into functionaries. The working out of these further lines of scholarly thinking will occupy an entire generation of medievalists in the future.

---

38 Cf. among many others, the example of the family of L. García de Salazar, poisoned, together with his illegitimate daughter, by his relatives, studied by Aguirre, *Lope García de Salazar*.

39 With reference to the five branches of the Hungarian Elefánthy family, Fügedi writes (*Elefánthy Saga*, p. 62), 'They were not connected with each other, yet they formed one and the same kindred.' On the struggles between the different branches of one great family, see F. de Moxó, *La casa de Luna (1276–1348): Factor político y lazos de sangre en la ascensión de un linaje aragonés* (Münster, 1990).

40 *La maison forte au Moyen Age*, ed. M. Bur (Paris, 1986).

41 The importance of the issue of inheritance also shows through in the very strict ritual which pertained to the births of posthumous children among the nobility: N. Coulet, *Affaires d'argent et affaires de famille en Haute Provence au XIVe siècle: Le dossier du procès de Sybille de Cabris contre Matteo Villani et la compagnie des Buonaccorsi (Archivio di Stato di Firenze, Mercanzia, 14143)* (Rome, 1992).

42 M. Aurell, *Une famille de la noblesse provençale au Moyen Age: les Porcelet* (Avignon, 1986), pp. 156–61.

Index

Abbreviations: abp archbishop; bp bishop; dr daughter; kg king

Aachen, coronation at 64
Adam of Bremen 102, 103, 104
Adel 206
adelsstand 206
æþel- 74
æþeling 79
Agnes of Burgundy 257
Agnes, daughter of William de Valence
 256–7
Akova, barony of 248
Albert of Ciepłowoda, the Bearded, knight
 130, 146, 149; nicknamed 'Łyka' 150
Albert, 'knight' 139, 140, 141
Albret, family of 251
Alessandra Strozzi (Florence), widow 256
almugi 210
Altötting 39
Amédée de Saluces, vicomtesse de Polignac,
 will of 256
Amiens 200
amour courtois 270
Angers 112
 abbot of, Guy 59
Anjou
 counts of
  Fulk Richin 102, 106, 111, 112
  Geoffrey 96; memorial plaque
   Frontispiece, 11
  Geoffrey 'Greymantle' 59
  Geoffrey Martel 107, 110
 princely power in 106
Anna of Mecklenburg, wife of William II,
 duke of Hesse 257
Anne Stafford 259; titles of 259
Annibaldi 268
Ansegisel, father of Pippin of Herstal 46
antrustiones 22
Aquitaine 101
aristocracy of blood, of service 19
Armand VII de Polignac 258
ɛrmiger 231
Arnulf of Carinthia 32
Arouca 242

Arques, St-Bertin 60
Arthur 25
Aveline, countess of Aumale 253
Aymer de Valence 259, 262
bad blood 47
Baião 226
Balliol College, Oxford 258
Bamberg 112
Barcelona
 countess of, Almodis 110, 111
 counts of 109–10
  Berenguer Ramon II 111
  Ramon Berenguer I 109, 110, 111
  Ramon Berenguer II 111
  Ramon Berenguer III 109
  Ramon Berenguer IV 103, 109
 parish of Santa Maria del Mar 268
 princely power in 106
barones 123
barons, in Norway 208
battle cries 151
Bavaria, dukes of
 Arnulf 'the Bad' 7, 26–41, *passim*; son
  of, Eberhard 39; title and status of
  40
 Liutpold (?) 31, 32, 34, 36, 39, 40
 Louis I 248
 kingdom of 101
Beatrice of Lorraine 104
Beatriz Portocarrero 255
Bede, *Ecclesiastical History of the English
 People* 3, 72, 92 n. 26
Beowulf 4, 71–2, 79, 84
Berengar, marquis of Gothia 57
Berg 248
Bergen 205, 213, 214, 217
Bernard 'Hairy-Paws' 56
Bernard d'Escoussans 255
Bernard of Septimania 58
Bernard-Ezi II, d'Albret 251
Bertrand de Lamanon 271
Bertrand du Guesclin 272

Printed and bound by CPI Group (UK) Ltd, Croydon, CR0 4YY

09/06/2025

14685716-0004